Integrated Science

Volume 35

The **Integrated Science** Series aims to publish the most relevant and novel research in all areas of Formal Sciences, Physical and Chemical Sciences, Biological Sciences, Medical Sciences, and Social Sciences. We are especially focused on the research involving the integration of two of more academic fields offering an innovative view, which is one of the main focuses of Universal Scientific Education and Research Network (USERN), science without borders.

Integrated Science is committed to upholding the integrity of the scientific record and will follow the Committee on Publication Ethics (COPE) guidelines on how to deal with potential acts of misconduct and correcting the literature.

Christian Hugo Hoffmann • Deepak Bansal
Editors

AI Ethics in Practice

Navigating Academic Insight, Managerial Expertise, and Philosophical Inquiry

Springer

Editors
Christian Hugo Hoffmann
Hoffmann Economics
Freienbach, Switzerland

Deepak Bansal
MQ Learning Academy
Zurich, Switzerland

ISSN 2662-9461 ISSN 2662-947X (electronic)
Integrated Science
ISBN 978-3-031-87022-4 ISBN 978-3-031-87023-1 (eBook)
https://doi.org/10.1007/978-3-031-87023-1

This Springer imprint is published by the registered company Springer Nature Switzerland AG
The registered company address is: Gewerbestrasse 11, 6330 Cham, Switzerland

Contents

Part I

In Practise

AI Ethics in Practice

1

From Philosophy to Practical Implementation

Deepak Bansal

Abstract

AI Ethics in Practice: From Ethical Principles to Effective Implementation explores the urgent need to integrate ethics into the development and deployment of artificial intelligence. As AI reshapes industries and societies, this book bridges the gap between philosophical principles and practical solutions, offering tools, frameworks, and case studies to guide responsible innovation.

Drawing on multidisciplinary insights, it addresses key challenges such as fairness, transparency, and accountability while highlighting global perspectives and industry-specific applications. Co-edited by Deepak Bansal and Christian Hugo Hoffmann, the book combines philosophical depth with actionable strategies to ensure AI advances human values and societal well-being.

1 Introduction

Why should we care about AI ethics in practice? For me, this journey began when I attended a conference in San Francisco around 7 years ago, where teams from across the globe were pitching in an incubator on "moonshot" ideas—concepts so ambitious that they would redefine the future. The excitement in the room was palpable. The mantra wasn't whether these ideas were possible, but how big one could think, as big as human imagination allowed.

The audience was brimming with young, predominantly male engineers in their 20s, radiating confidence and ambition. The host, with great enthusiasm, announced, "We are deciding the future of the world." The stakes couldn't have felt higher.

D. Bansal (✉)
MQ Learning Academy, Zurich, Switzerland
e-mail: deepak@mq-learning.com

C. H. Hoffmann, D. Bansal (eds.), *AI Ethics in Practice*, Integrated Science 35,
https://doi.org/10.1007/978-3-031-87023-1_1

One team wanted to modify genetic structures for "optimization," though the reasons for doing so seemed disturbingly vague. Another aimed to build AI-powered water systems for Africa, a laudable goal in theory—until they admitted their data didn't actually include African populations because "most of them are illiterate and not part of the digital system." They planned to extrapolate from their existing Western datasets.

What was missing in the room was not intelligence, ambition, or innovation—it was reflection. The focus was entirely on what could be done, not whether it should be done. At one point, I raised a question about ethics. The host replied, "Great point, we have an ethical team that validates everything." The room seemed satisfied, and the presentations continued.

On my way home, however, I couldn't shake two troubling realizations:

(a) What gives a select group of people the right to play "Nature"?
(b) The immense power held by a small cohort of engineers—people who could, with a single line of code, ignite revolutions or disrupt lives on the other side of the world.

The power dynamics were stark. Control wasn't just concentrated—it was concentrated in the hands of tech, with little to no input from the people who would be most affected by these innovations.

This experience planted a seed in me. Philosophy isn't just an academic discipline for pondering abstract ideas; it's the foundation for shaping the principles that guide us. While studying philosophy, I had always seen it as a guide for navigating the "why" and "whether" of human endeavors. But here, I was faced with a reality where the "why" was often ignored in favor of relentless pursuit of the "what."

Fast forward to today, and we are at a juncture where philosophy must move into practice. The big ideas of the past—about fairness, justice, and the nature of power—are now colliding with technological advances in ways philosophers of old could never have imagined. Some ideas in the field of AI aren't new, but what's different is this: philosophers, ethicists, and social thinkers must now work alongside technologists to ensure these ideas are implemented thoughtfully. Otherwise, someone else will simply code them, and the ethical implications will be an afterthought.

As someone who champions innovation, I also believe in balance. Nature teaches us that balance is essential for sustainability. Similarly, the deployment of AI and other transformative technologies must consider this principle. How can we build technologies that work for everyone—not just a privileged few? How can we ensure that AI serves humanity as a whole, rather than concentrating power further in the hands of a select group?

These questions bring us to *AI Ethics in Practice: From Ethical Principles to Effective Implementation.* This book is born out of the realization that while ethical frameworks exist in theory, they often fail to translate into actionable steps for organizations.

2 AI Ethics: From Philosophy to Practise

Artificial intelligence (AI) is no longer confined to the laboratories of technology companies or the pages of science fiction—it has become a pervasive force shaping industries, economies, and societies worldwide. With its increasing adoption comes a growing recognition of the ethical challenges it poses, from algorithmic biases that reinforce social inequities to threats to democratic processes and fundamental rights such as privacy and due process. These ethical concerns are no longer abstract; they are urgent, concrete, and demand actionable solutions.

As AI progresses from development to deployment, it is essential to consider the impact it will have at both stages. During the development phase, it is crucial to establish robust checks and balances and involve the right individuals who can ask critical questions. This is not about creating unnecessary bureaucracy but about ensuring that the potential risks do not outweigh the benefits. In the deployment phase, continuous engagement with representative data sets is essential to maintain accuracy and fairness. Additionally, transparency must be prioritized to ensure that users understand the decision-making processes of AI systems and can trust the outcomes.

A few years ago, AI ethics was primarily a field of academic inquiry, where scholars sought to make sense of a rapidly changing technological landscape. However, the launch of generative AI in 2023 marked a turning point, significantly increasing interest in the topic from governments, industries, and various professional domains. Ethical AI is no longer just an abstract discussion but a pressing priority across multiple sectors.

AI Ethics in Practice: From Ethical Principles to Effective Implementation is a response to this critical need. This book moves beyond theoretical debates to explore how organizations can translate ethical principles into practical, real-world applications. This book aims to empower different fields with tools, strategies, and actionable insights to align technological advancements with ethical practices.

3 A Unique, Interdisciplinary Approach

What sets this book apart is its multidisciplinary and inclusive perspective, drawing on contributions from experts across diverse domains. The contributors represent a rich blend of expertise, and their insights are organized around four key dimensions:

1. **Geographical Diversity**

   Foundations and governments are increasingly interested in AI ethics, aiming to integrate it into systems and ensure that the right tools and awareness are available to citizens. Nicolas Zahn & Diana Kaliff (Chap. 2) discusses the Swiss landscape and how the Digital Trust Label is helping companies do the right things while keeping users informed. In emerging countries like India, the topic is still in its nascent stages but gaining significant traction. Avinash Dadhich and Yashu Bansal (Chap. 3) provide an overview of emerging best practices in

India's vibrant startup ecosystem. These varied perspectives highlight both shared challenges and region-specific solutions, offering readers a nuanced understanding of the global landscape.

2. **Industry Focus**

   The book examines AI ethics across diverse industries, including education and interpretation. Thorsten Busch and Florence M. Chee (Chap. 4) reflect on their experiences teaching AI ethics and suggest strategies for embedding these principles into the education sector. Some industries are more significantly impacted by AI than others—language interpretation is one such field. Laura Keller (Chap. 5), a seasoned interpreter for international organizations, discusses the challenges and opportunities AI presents in her profession and how they should be ethically managed. These chapters demonstrate how sector-specific dynamics influence ethical dilemmas and how they can be addressed. This industry-centric approach ensures the book's relevance and applicability across multiple professional domains.
3. **Functional Expertise**

   While AI introduces new functions such as cybersecurity, it also transforms age-old tasks like leadership. Yanya Viskovich and Vibha Mohan (Chap. 6) critically examine organizational realities, including surveillance, automation, and the lack of transparency, and their impact on organizational security culture. Katrin J. Yuan (Chap. 7) explores how ethical AI can shape the future of work and unlock new human potential. These perspectives emphasize that ethical considerations extend beyond technology teams, affecting all organizational functions—from strategic leadership to daily operations.
4. **Philosophical Underpinnings**

   Beyond practical applications, this book delves into the deeper philosophical questions surrounding AI and its role in society. Matthew D. Segall (Chap. 8) begins with fundamental questions: "What are technologies for? Whose interests do they serve?" James B. Glattfelder (Chap. 9) takes these ideas further, arguing that technologies such as decentralized systems could provide viable solutions to ethical challenges. These chapters offer a big-picture perspective on the roles of humans, society, and future technologies.

4 From Principles to Practice

The central focus of *AI Ethics in Practice* is bridging the gap between ethical principles and effective implementation. It does this by offering:

- **Diagnostic Tools and Frameworks**: Practical tools to help organizations identify, assess, and address ethical challenges in their AI systems.
- **Case Studies**: Real-world examples that illustrate both successes and pitfalls in implementing ethical AI.
- **Actionable Guidance**: Step-by-step strategies for embedding ethical considerations into the lifecycle of AI development and deployment.

This combination of philosophical depth and practical utility ensures that the book appeals to a broad audience, from researchers, and policymakers to entrepreneurs and practitioners.

5 A Timely and Impactful Contribution

The relevance of this book cannot be overstated. In an era where AI is shaping the very fabric of society, ensuring that technology aligns with human values is not just desirable—it is imperative. The book addresses a broad spectrum of readers, including:

- Researchers and academics exploring the intersections of AI, ethics, and innovation.
- Professionals and practitioners seeking actionable insights for implementing responsible AI in their organizations.
- Entrepreneurs and startups navigating the ethical complexities of technological innovation.
- Policymakers and futurists interested in crafting a world where AI enhances, rather than undermines, societal well-being.

6 A Vision for the Future

At its core, this book is about more than guiding technology—it is about shaping the world we want to live in. By fostering dialogue between academia, industry, and philosophy, *AI Ethics in Practice* seeks to inspire a new era of innovation grounded in trust, fairness, and human values. It is not just about what AI can do but what it should do, reflecting on its broader societal implications and striving to balance technological advancement with ethical integrity.

We invite readers to join us in exploring the critical questions of our time: What does responsible AI look like in practice? How can startups and organizations contribute to shaping ethical AI ecosystems? And, ultimately, how can we ensure that AI serves as a force for good, building a future where technology aligns with our deepest human values?

By addressing these questions and providing a clear roadmap for action, this book empowers readers to navigate the complexities of the emerging field of AI ethics and actively contribute to a future where innovation and integrity coexist harmoniously.

On a personal level, this represents my effort to engage with moonshot ideas while ensuring that innovation remains grounded in societal and ethical considerations.

In this endeavor, I am thrilled to collaborate with Christian Hugo Hoffmann—a distinguished thinker, researcher, and entrepreneur, but above all, a fellow warrior in advancing the arc of ethical innovation. Christian and I have several insightful discussions and debates about the future we envision for the world. This book is a testament to those intellectually enriching conversations and the shared ideas that emerged from them.

What began as our shared exploration soon grew into a collaborative effort, enriched by an ecosystem of thinkers and practitioners who joined us along the way. In the second part of the book, Christian will delve deeper into the philosophical dimensions of our work, offering his unique insights and ideas on this critical topic. Together, we aim to push the boundaries of ethical innovation and inspire meaningful change.

We warmly invite you to join us on this journey!

Deepak Bansal is the founder and CEO of MQ Learning, a Swiss-based EduQua-certified academy dedicated to teaching humanistic skills in the digital age. His extensive 15+ years in the corporate world include executive roles at Accenture, Deutsche Post DHL, and Zurich Insurance (COO, Head AI & Robotics). A distinguished academic, Deepak has a master's in Technology from the Indian Institute of Management (IIM) Mumbai, an MBA from the University of St Gallen, Switzerland, and an MA in Philosophy from the California Institute of Integral Studies (CIIS), California, USA. In addition to his role at MQ Learning, Deepak actively engages in academia as a guest lecturer at Zurich University of Applied Sciences, focusing on "Digital Ethics by Design." His unique blend of corporate experience, academic insight, and a deep understanding of technology's ethical dimensions positions him as a thought leader in the field. Deepak also contributes significantly to digital ethics as a member of the certification committee for the Digital Trust Label, an initiative by the Swiss Digital Initiative.

More information at: mq-learning.com/deepak

Auditing for Digital Trust 2

Lessons learned from the Digital Trust Label

Nicolas Zahn, Diana Kaliff, and Niniane Paeffgen

Abstract

The Swiss Digital Initiative pioneered the Digital Trust Label, a certification scheme for digital services aimed at end-customers and evaluating the trustworthiness of that service, e.g. a mobile banking app. Over the course of several years, the foundational documents and processes for the operations of such a label were created and the Digital Trust Label was brought to the market in January 2022 afterwards being used by over a dozen organizations in Switzerland and Europe.

The Digital Trust Label is a voluntary certification based on a standard defined by the Swiss Digital Initiative and involving a third-party auditor. The development of the Digital Trust Label and the consequent entry to the market provided valuable insights for auditing digital trust, developing, and maintaining such a certification scheme and market feedback on the value provided by such a certification. The implementation of the project also showed various difficulties in particular with digital trust as a concept, keeping up with a dynamic regulatory landscape and valuable lessons for the roll-out of similar certifications.

1 Introduction

Have you ever thought twice before downloading an app from an App Store? Have you ever wondered whether your e-Banking or online shopping is secure? Do you wonder what happens to data you might submit when interacting with the chatbot of your health insurance? Do you worry your confidential information might be compromised when handing in your taxes online? Have you stopped using a digital

N. Zahn (✉) · D. Kaliff · N. Paeffgen
Zurich, Switzerland
e-mail: nicolas@nicolaszahn.ch; dianakaliff@gmail.com; niniane.paeffgen@proton.me

C. H. Hoffmann, D. Bansal (eds.), *AI Ethics in Practice*, Integrated Science 35,
https://doi.org/10.1007/978-3-031-87023-1_2

service after news about a data breach broke or refrained from using a digital service with AI because you did not trust the provider of that digital service?

If the answer to any of those questions is *yes,* you have already engaged with the fairly new concept of Digital Trust. Particularly the last worry—lack of adoption due to a lack of trust —was at the heart of the motivation for the Swiss Digital Initiative to create a Digital Trust Label. The reasoning is straight-forward: Why not apply a tried and tested concept—labels—to protect and empower users in the digital world? Over a multi-year process, the Swiss Digital Initiative foundation and its partners put a lot of effort into creating the Digital Trust Label. The following chapter explains the theoretical background and recent research, our reasoning behind this project, the development process, and lessons learned.

2 Making Digital Trust Explicit

2.1 The Need for Digital Trust

Our daily lives depend on digital services and infrastructure. For almost any activity, we interact or even rely on digital services. Sometimes, we don't even have a choice *which* service we want to use. Nevertheless, the question of whether we consider digital services trustworthy is becoming a growing concern, especially with artificial intelligence being added to digital services more and more.

For example, a survey by the consulting company McKinsey found that 40% of customers stopped buying from a company when it violated digital trust while managers see an opportunity of up to 10% additional growth for organizations that manage to build digital trust.[1] Meanwhile, another study found that only 55% of employees are confident that their organization will implement AI in a trustworthy and responsible way.[2]

The industry and policymakers have started reacting to this heightened need for digital trust. Private sector initiatives such as the Responsible AI Institute[3] are releasing resources for digital service providers, research efforts by academics and NGOs on Corporate Digital Responsibilities or initiatives such as the World Economic Forum's Working Group on Digital Trust that has released a Digital Trust framework[4] are trying to provide business leaders with information and tools on how to proactively approach digital trust.

[1] McKinsey (2022).

[2] Workday (2024).

[3] https://www.responsible.ai/.

[4] WEF (2022).

2.2 Trust for Whom and for What?

Trust is as much of a commonsense concept as it is elusive and hard to pin down. In our everyday interactions, often without explicitly realizing it, we rely on trust as a *resource.* It facilitates interactions between various parties, see Fig. 2.1. We have outlined our thinking on trust in our Digital Trust Whitepaper and our Digital Trust Guide.[5]

Being a dynamic resource, trust isn't static and can hardly be prescribed. Instead trust is being built, maintained, or destroyed by comparing the expected behavior of a party in a relationship against the actual behavior. If a signal turns green, we feel safe to cross the street, because we trust the system controlling traffic lights and that drivers abide by the traffic code. If we plug our smartphone in to charge, we trust that it will not explode; and we take a new medication because we trust the

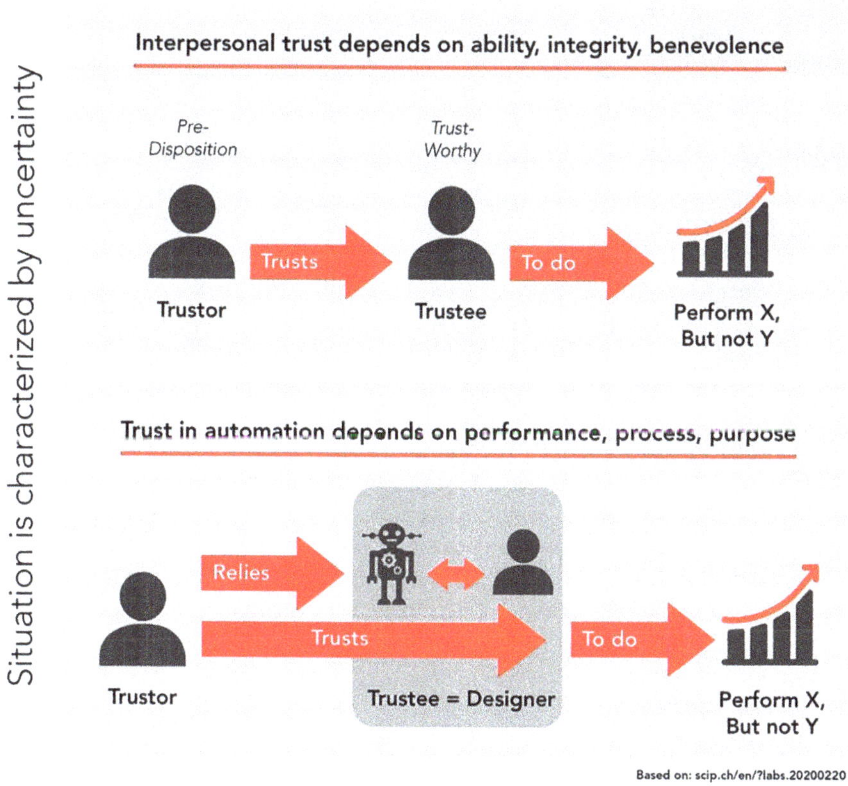

Fig. 2.1 Schematic representation of trust relationships, SDI (2021b)

[5] SDI (2021b).

certification process it went through. Regulations and institutions enforcing these regulations hence play a crucial part for creating trust.[6]

But when it comes to digital services, it becomes more problematic. Sure, there are laws for data protection but there are also countless scandals showing that despite those standards, bad behavior can and does happen. Also, technologies are developing at a pace making it hard for regulators to catch up, leading to a widening gap of what customers are exposed to and what is actually regulated. In the absence of legally binding certifications or rules that create the trust, signaling trust by other means becomes relevant. Such a trust signal can act as a first step in building a trusted relationship and address the problem that customers wouldn't want to engage in a relationship, e.g., by using a certain service, because they do not trust it before interacting with it.

But where do we need trust and who is involved in the trust relationship? In our understanding, we focus on the relationship between the digital service provider and its users. To be clear, trust can be relevant for other interactions as well, e.g., for the procurement of services or in the wider B2B context. Also, trust isn't equally necessary for all digital services. Rather, we think that "priority should be given to digital services that are used in fields where:

1. the handled data is very sensitive;
2. the consequences of using digital services matter greatly;
3. where there is not much choice whether to use a digital service or not, and
4. where digital services are rolled-out at a high pace and on a large scale."[7]

Consequently, digital services in sectors such as health care, the public sector or financial services as well as digital services including innovative technologies like artificial intelligence should focus on addressing issues of digital trust.

2.3 Methods of Signaling Digital Trust

Assuming that digital service providers care about being trustworthy for their customers, the question arises how they can signal that trustworthiness.

One method is a *self-declaration*. A digital service provider can actively tell its customers that it commits to certain principles, knowing that doing so elevates its trustworthiness in the eyes of the customer. One example of this is the ongoing marketing campaign by Apple, highlighting a firm commitment to privacy, in contrast to other companies.

While such a campaign shows a clear understanding of the digital service provider to proactively engage with digital trust, the drawbacks are equally evident. Would you trust someone who offensively tells you to trust them? Also, there is no way for customers to verify the claim of trustworthiness. Often, companies do not

[6] SDI (2021b).

[7] SDI (2021b).

go into the details of what it is exactly that makes them deserving of digital trust. Claiming you are trustworthy hence paradoxically only promises to work if your customers *already* deem you trustworthy. Also, by definition, those claims of trustworthiness are only linked to a single company.

A second method of signaling Digital Trust is by *committing to a public set of principles and values*, e.g., by signing a charter or manifesto. There are various examples for this approach in a variety of fields, e.g., on sustainability but also digital responsibility and digital trust.[8] The advantage of this approach is that it covers several organizations and again shows their awareness that something needs to be done about Digital Trust. Just as with the self-declaration, however, it is often hard if not impossible for a customer to understand what the digital service providers subscribing to a certain set of principles are doing exactly to deserve their trust. While the principles and values are at least public and transparent, they are often formulated in such an abstract way that it is hard for the customer to understand how they are really reflected in the product development or behavior of the organizations subscribing to those principles. In addition, given the proliferation of such principles, e.g., with regard to AI governance, there is a real danger of so-called "forum-shopping," i.e., a fragmented landscape where customers are overwhelmed about the choice which set of principles to choose and digital service providers can subscribe to the one that imposes the lowest costs on them while still reaping a "trust-premium."

A third way of signaling Digital Trust is through *labels*. A label acts as a statement that signals adherence to certain standards that go beyond vague principles. It can be awarded by an independent organization or by an organization for itself, and it can cover either individual products and services or a whole company, e.g., labels for the energy consumption of a household appliance or a fair-trade label.

2.4 Labels for the Digital World

When the decision was taken by the Swiss Digital Initiative Foundation Board to focus on projects for digital trust, the idea for a Digital Trust Label was born, drawing the analogy to a "fair-trade label for the digital world."

Before starting work on what would become the Digital Trust Label, the Swiss Digital Initiative published a mapping of the international landscape on labels and certifications; see Fig. 2.2 .[9]

The report identified various initiatives, mostly in Europe and the United States, ranging from national to international projects launched by a variety of stakeholder groups. The report also allowed for some first learnings that inspired the later work on the Digital Trust Label. Specifically, the following criteria for a successful label were identified:

[8] AlgorithmWatch (2020).

[9] Swiss Digital Initiative (2022a).

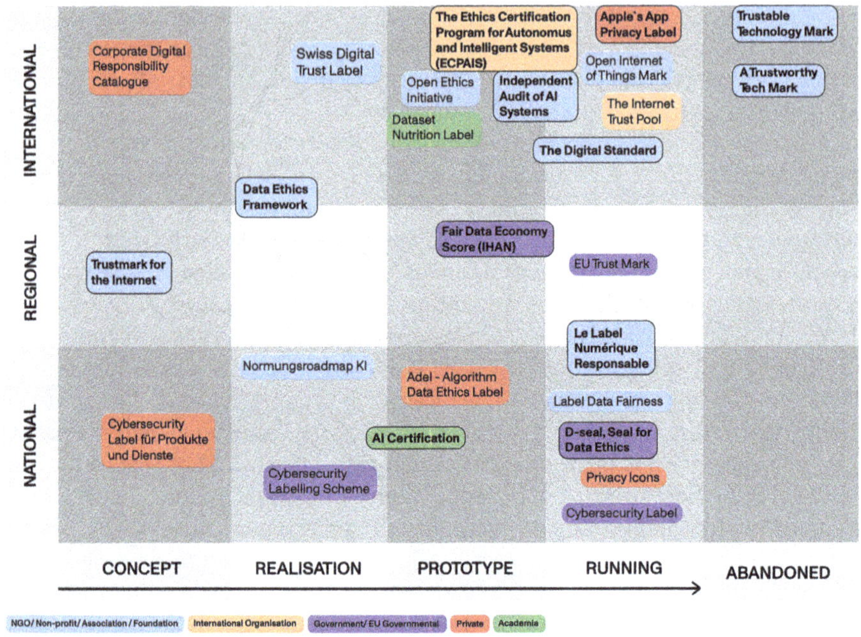

Fig. 2.2 Overview of different certification projects, SDI (2021a)

- The label has to be known by its target users.
- It should be supported by a strong and well-known organization.
- It has to convey a general message, with details and complexity being handled in the background.
- The governance of the labeling body has to be legitimate.
- The way the label organization is funded needs to be transparent and understandable for outsiders.

Another finding was that the landscape of certification initiatives is highly dynamic, even more so now with the rapid adoption of artificial intelligence. That is why an interactive overview of initiatives trying to certify digital trust with a certification or label has been maintained by the Swiss Digital Initiative and is available as a free online resource.[10]

Labels and the audits they are based on can also focus on different parts of a digital service as IT products and services have very complex supply chains, in particular, in the case of AI systems. Given the vision of the Swiss Digital Initiative, the focus has always been on digital service providers using digital technologies such as AI in their customer-facing products, which is also why the audit for the Digital Trust Label focuses on the application, see Fig. 2.3.[11]

[10] SDI (2024c)

[11] Mökander et al. (2023)

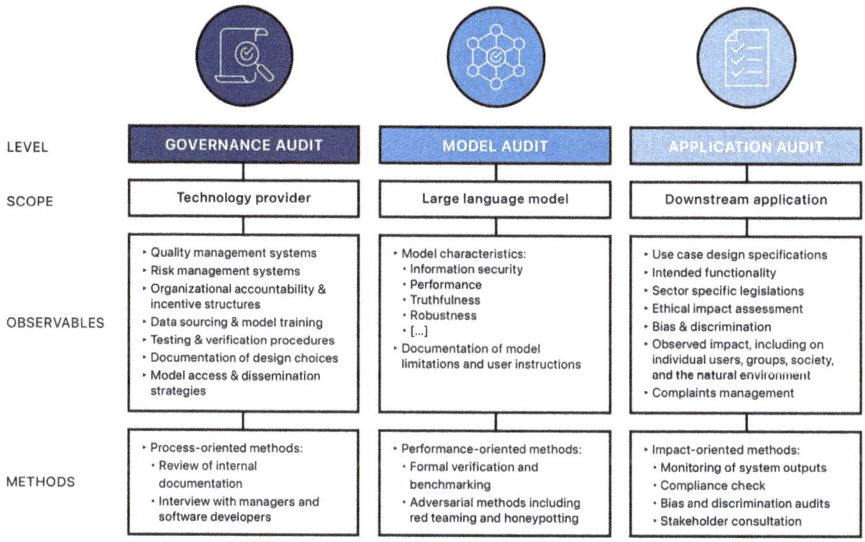

Fig. 2.3 Different Audit Scopes, Mökander et al. (2023)

As a general remark, it is important to highlight that labels can differ in important ways which also impacts their utility as a signal for digital trust. Some differentiations that are possible are:

- **Service vs organization:** a label can be awarded to a whole organization or to an individual product or service
- **Self-assessment vs third-party audit:** a label can be awarded on the basis of a self-assessment or after a third-party audit.
- **Compliance vs differentiation:** a label can be used by organizations either to demonstrate compliance with legal obligations, e.g., a CE label, or as a differentiator in the market, e.g., Fairtrade labels.
- **Degree of specificity:** a label can provide various degrees of specificity to the user from being binary (awarded/not awarded) to different categories (gold/silver/, etc.) or scores. Depending on the criteria that determine whether a label is awarded or not, the depth of a label can also vary, i.e., into how much detail do the audits go?
- **Issuing organization:** who is awarding the label and how is that organization financed and governed? Is it a regulatory agency, an NGO or a for-profit company?
- **Scope:** what does the label cover exactly, e.g., the whole supply chain or lifecycle of a service or only one segment?
- **Durability and governance:** is the label given once for lifetime or does it need to be renewed? How are potential non-conformities handled?

2.5 Labels in the Context of Digital Governance

While there is increasing global and national regulatory activity when it comes to digital governance, technological trends still outpace regulatory capacity creating a need for flexible instruments that help organizations and consumers alike to navigate a complex regulatory space. Labels can be one of several tools to assist in digital governance as a complement to local legal requirements, technical standards, and non-binding industry principles or codes of conduct. As such, it is important to stress that labels are not intended as a replacement for other tools of digital governance but one additional tool that allows for more flexibility and speed. They also provide a crucial step up from often abstract principles, e.g., the many documents on responsible AI whose effect often remain elusive to end-consumers and can provide more accountability and educate and empower end users, thereby not only contributing to digital governance but also the overall digital maturity of societies.

3 The Digital Trust Label

Having identified the lack of digital trust as a potential barrier to the adoption of beneficial digital use-cases, the Swiss Digital Initiative (SDI) sought to address this issue with a tangible project, and the idea for a digital trust label was born.

As outlined above, a label can take various forms, and to understand the product-market fit better, SDI conducted a series of projects and research to prepare for the development of a label prototype:

- International User Study
- Swiss User Study
- Onboarding Test Partners for prototype input from relevant industries like finance
- Recruiting a Label Expert Committee
- Conduct a Co-Development and public consultation process allowing for input from various stakeholders

Two strategic decisions, however, were taken early on: the Digital Trust Label (DTL) should focus on the **end user of a digital service**, analogous to the fair trade or bio label in a supermarket. The DTL should also allow digital service providers to **differentiate themselves in the market**. This means that the criteria are to be based on other relevant standards that promise a high level of consumer protection and build upon them to create a standard that goes beyond the legal minimum.

The Digital Trust Label was in addition to being a tool for empowering users and for digital service providers to differentiate their service based on trust, also seen as a way for organizations to learn about digital trust and internalize its principles and values within the organization. Yielding positive impacts on the organizational culture and additional services well beyond the one awarded with the label. This is the virtuous cycle envisioned for the supply side, for the digital service providers. On the demand side, for the end users of digital services, the DTL would lead to a

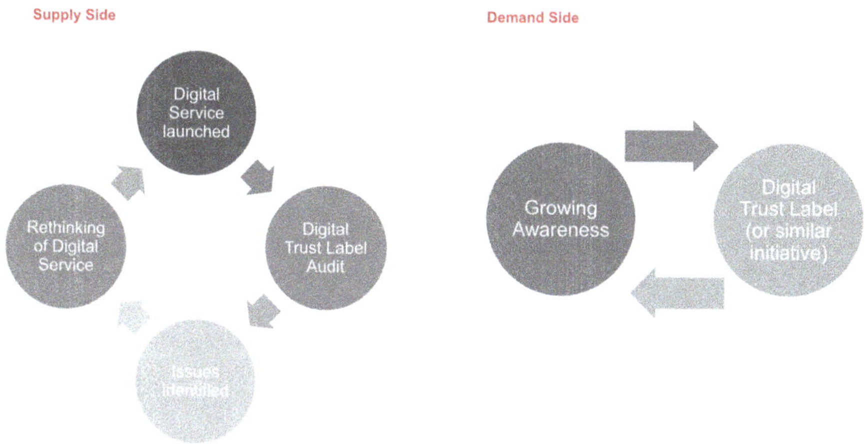

Fig. 2.4 Virtuous cycle of behavioral changes due to labeling, SDI

growing awareness as it spread with end users asking themselves after seeing the label on certain digital services why other digital services did not have it and paying closer attention to digital trust in general; see Fig. 2.4.

The strategic decision to create a label for digital solutions led to the next question regarding what kind of label and what processes to implement to ensure its credibility. The first decision was to make it a third-party audited label and therefore also selecting a reliable auditing partner. The second one was to incorporate two independent groups: The Digital Trust Expert Group—at first called the Label Expert Committee (LEC)—and the Label Certification Committee (LCC) to ensure multiple touch points by independent experts. The added value of independent auditing was to ensure trust in the label itself. The Digital Trust Expert Group would make sure that the auditing framework (the Criteria Catalog (SDI (2024a)) behind the label would always be up to date and state of the art while ensuring practical applicability. The LCC would provide an additional layer of trust by reviewing the final audit reports from the auditor and providing its feedback to SDI for final label award decision through the board. To summarize, the DTL consists of three main parts, led by three independent groups:

- Digital Trust Criteria Catalog that is the basis for the audit and updated by the Digital Trust Expert Group.
- DTL Audit report, completed by the auditing firm and reviewed by the LCC.
- DTL award and implementation, led by SDI.

Pioneer clients (called Digital Trust Pioneers) were signed from the beginning to go through the first version of the DTL journey including the Criteria Catalog, audit process, award, etc. to make sure client input was integrated in the development from the start.

The label was developed in Switzerland but being a digital label, it has been available globally. As the focus is on putting the user at the center, the label was developed for B2C and B2B2C digital services. As the criteria contained in the Criteria Catalog are inspired by standards such as ISO 27001 and relevant regulations such as GDPR, the DTL has mainly attracted European clients. A majority of the first clients were Swiss. DTL clients are organizations that want to signal digital responsibility to their digital service users. There has also been interest globally from actors wanting to develop similar solutions for their specific markets.

The DTL was created as a response to growing concerns among end users of digital services and a limited number of solutions to guide organizations on the best practices to gain and maintain digital trust. The DTL therefore offers a value to users by signaling that a labeled solution can be trusted, similarly to an organic or fair-trade label in the grocery store. For the organizations going through the audit to receive the label, it offers multiple value propositions, for example:

- A quick response to users on common questions such as "How is my personal data being handled?" or "How are you using AI"?
- A way to signal to the market that great, internal work is being done. As most certifications are focused on internal processes, few users take the time to research a specific organization's practices. As the DTL is facing the user, it becomes the last mile in a chain of great, internal work that's already taking place and that are necessary to be able to receive the label.
- A way for organizations to start or structure existing work on digital trust by using the solid DTL Criteria Catalog to help navigate an overly crowded information flow.
- A way for organizations to signal to the market that Corporate Digital Responsibility (CDR) is important.
- A practical solution to the multitude of challenges in the CDR space.

The DTL audit is based on the DTL Criteria Catalog that summarizes the criteria to be met to receive the label. The first draft of the Catalog was created by an Academic Expert Group from EPFL, ETH, and the Universities of Zurich and Geneva. Thereafter, a co-development phase started to challenge and include user and civil society perspective in the development of the label. This feedback was collected during July to October in 2020 and over hundred organizations from national and international civil society were invited to provide their input. The co-development process was part of the ambition to produce a cutting-edge label that includes multiple perspectives on digital trust. (More details can be found in the co-development report from 2022.)[12]

As the topic of digital trust is constantly evolving, the Digital Trust Expert Group was created with the mission to provide constant, expert input on the Catalog as soon as the updated first draft was finalized. The idea was that emerging topics should be handled quickly to constantly evolve and improve the label while making

[12] SDI (2022b).

sure any changes in the Catalog were well motivated. The group met monthly and example topics that have been discussed and integrated includes: the Swiss Data Protection Law and Artificial Intelligence (AI).

Since 2024, Interpretation Guidelines have been published to openly share examples of how the criteria can be met and how each criterion is interpreted by the auditing firm in more detail.[13]

The importance of third-party, independent auditing to maintain trust in the DTL has been highlighted since the beginning. SDI therefore performed an open procurement process to identify a trusted, global auditing partner that would provide expert input on the auditability of the Criteria Catalog while providing consistency among DTL audits globally. Once a client had signed the DTL contract, the auditing firm was looped in to kick-off the audit.

Once the audit has been completed, the auditing firm shares the audit report with SDI that loops in the Label Certification Committée (LCC) that will go through the report and provide final input. The input can either lead to clarifying questions to the auditing firm and client or result in an approved report and nomination to reward the DTL to the SDI board. The board thereafter takes the final decision to award the DTL to the client.

When the DTL has been awarded, it is valid for three years with two mandatory surveillance audits taking place in the second and third year of the validity. The surveillance audit reports are also reviewed by the LCC.

4 Learnings So Far

The general feedback around the importance of digital trust and having a label to audit for digital trust, as a first practical solution to the stated problems, has been positive. With this said, it is also important to highlight some of the challenges and negative feedback that such a solution has received with the aim to support continuous improvement and knowledge transfer across sectors and projects.

To list some of the positive feedback, these include:

- **Importance**: The topic is very important and organizations understand the need to address these issues.
- **Trust in the label**: The label development process and the processes put in place to maintain the trust in the label itself (the expert group, certification committee, 3rd party audit, etc.)
- **Focus on the user**: The decision to focus on putting the user at the center is often appreciated and highlighted.
- **A go-to-response to difficult questions**: The label offers an opportunity to more easily respond to sensitive questions related to digital trust such as: How is user data stored? How is AI being used? Instead of just referring to an internal policy

[13] SDI (2024b).

document, the client can reply to such questions and refer to the label independent audit in their replies to add an additional level of credibility.

- **Product differentiation**: To have a way to differentiate the customer's digital service from another is attractive.
- **Switzerland**: The fact that the label has been developed in Switzerland has been seen as an added value, especially for Swiss clients.

In contrast, some of the negative feedback are listed below:

- **Sense of urgency**: As the label is voluntary, there are many clients that prefer to "wait and see" as there is no sense of urgency to get their digital services labeled. Many clients focus on certifications and audits that are mandatory and do not see the immediate benefit of a voluntary label to signal that they put users' digital trust at the core of what they do.
- **Cost**: The cost to receive the label mainly derives from the third-party audit, which results in a price between CHF 18'140-33'350 to get the label, everything included. For many organizations, especially start-ups and smaller organizations, this kind of cost is out of question.
- **Value proposition**: Related to the topic of cost is that much of the feedback/ thoughts we have gathered ultimately could be related to the value proposition of the label. The label is many times seen as too expensive as the perceived benefits/ values are not corresponding. Users get the direct benefits while the organizations pay and are mostly interested in regulatory compliance instead of market differentiation, which raises the challenge of finding a sustainable business model.
- **User awareness**: As the label is presented as a way to differentiate one digital service from another based on the label's way to signal user trust, it relies on users knowing that the label exists and what it stands for. Given that it has been developed and run by a non-profit (limited budget) and privacy concerns around the major online marketing platforms, the market education and outreach has been challenging, resulting in less interest from organizations and therefore less labels on the markets, creating a "catch 22" situation and vicious cycle.

In addition to this feedback from stakeholders like clients or partners, some conceptual learnings about a label as auditing tool for the trustworthiness of a digital service can be made:

- **Going with the times**: As technology and the regulatory environment keep on developing at a rapid pace, the criteria behind a label need to be monitored and continuously adjusted. The Digital Trust Label by the Swiss Digital Initiative anticipated this and managed this through regular updates of the criteria catalog. This in turn, however, creates challenges from a communication perspective as well as procedural questions for the audits.
- **Interacting with the auditors**: Defining criteria isn't enough as for successful and efficient audits, details plus resources are needed to react to questions which the Swiss Digital Initiative addressed with Interpretation Guidelines.

- **Standards are slow:** The Swiss Digital Initiative had several exchanges with standard-setting organizations on the national and international level to explore how the criteria catalog could be leveraged. These discussions showed that a novel label for digital service faces unique challenges with the rigid structure of technical standards and evaluations, which often take a long time to agree upon and can't easily be updated.
- **Trade-offs, communication, & expectation management:** as described above, in the design of a label, there are several decisions that can be taken that all come with their own trade-offs. Aiming for a middle-ground and ensuring maximum applicability of the standard across industries and dimensions—as was the case with the Digital Trust Label—creates the challenge of clearly and effectively communicating to involved stakeholders what the Digital Trust Label covers and does but also what it does not do. Expectation management in this very fresh market of Digital Trust and IT certification is challenging as there are sometimes wrong perceptions about the level of security and transparency a label can guarantee. This is supported by research that shows the perplexing pattern that while users crave labels and certifications, they often do not understand them.[14]

In summary, the Digital Trust Label showed that it is possible to create a standard for digital trust and operationalize often abstract principles. However, a label—especially if not designed for legal compliance but market differentiation—asks a lot of participating organizations at a time where the regulatory developments already pose a lot of challenges to them. While the benefits for the end users are clear and confirmed—see, e.g., research on the impact of a label on AI usage and user perception,[15] the introduction of a new label, especially in a rapidly evolving and highly complex industry like digital services, requires lots of resources beyond the criteria development in the form of marketing and communication to ensure proper knowledge about the label in the market.

References

AlgorithmWatch (2020) AI Ethics Global Inventory. Retrieved from https://inventory.algorithmwatch.org/

McKinsey (2022) Why digital trust truly matters. Retrieved from https://www.mckinsey.com/capabilities/quantumblack/our-insights/why-digital-trust-truly-matters

Mökander J, Schuett J, Rose Kirk H, Floridi L (2023) Auditing large language models: a three-layered approach. Retrieved from https://link.springer.com/article/10.1007/s43681-023-00289-2

SDI (2021a) Labels and Certifications for the Digital World. Retrieved from https://swiss-digital-initiative.org/wp-content/uploads/2023/12/Labels-and-Certification-for-the-Digital-World.pdf

SDI (2021b) Digital Trust Whitepaper. Retrieved from https://swiss-digital-initiative.org/wp-content/uploads/2023/12/Digital-Trust-Whitepaper.pdf

[14] https://stars.library.ucf.edu/cgi/viewcontent.cgi?article=1138&context=hmc.

[15] https://digitalcollection.zhaw.ch/server/api/core/bitstreams/54b5f8f5-5251-42d2-89f0-3a9c28a4a19d/content.

SDI (2022a) Second Public Consultation. Retrieved from https://swiss-digital-initiative.org/wp-content/uploads/2023/12/Second-Public-Consultation.pdf

SDI (2022b) Co-Development Report. Retrieved from https://swiss-digital-initiative.org/wp-content/uploads/2023/12/Co-Development-report.pdf

SDI (2024a) Digital Trust Label Criteria Catalogue. Retrieved from https://swiss-digital-initiative.org/wp-content/uploads/2024/05/2024-Digital-Trust-Criteria-Catalogue-2.pdf

SDI (2024b) Digital Trust Label Interpretation Guidelines. Retrieved from https://swiss-digital-initiative.org/wp-content/uploads/2024/04/2024_DTL_Criteria-Interpretation-Guidelines.pdf

SDI (2024c) Overview of Digital Trust Initiatives. Retrieved from https://airtable.com/appScIuR9PDVE7fE3/shrJXQG1zNQlGaVR9

WEF (2022) Earning Digital Trust: Decision-Making for Trustworthy Technologies. Retrieved from https://www.weforum.org/publications/earning-digital-trust-decision-making-for-trustworthy-technologies/

Workday (2024) Closing the AI trust gap - key findings. Retrieved from https://forms.workday.com/en-us/other/closing-the-ai-trust-gap/form.html?eid=enus_pr_pr_wd_wds_cxoedu_ig_23.5595&productfocus=wds&aud=cxoedu&assettype=ig&assetid=23.5595&pblr=wd&step=step1_default

Nicolas Zahn works as Managing Director at the Swiss Digital Initiative and is also an independent digital expert. He holds a Master of Arts in International Affairs from the Graduate Institute Geneva. He is a board member, co-founder and member of various organizations and is especially active in democracy and net politics.

He is an alumnus of the Swiss Study Foundation, a former Binding Fellow, a former fellow of the Mercator Kolleg for International Affairs, and an ECCRI European Cybersecurity Fellow. His work on bridging technology and politics was also acknowledged by being featured on the 35 under 35 list of CIDOB Barcelona & Banco Santander.

He publishes on various digital & political topics in the Republic, NZZ & The Market, Handelszeitung and Schweizer Monat, among others.

More information at: nicolaszahn.ch

Diana Kaliff is Product Lead for the Digital Trust Label. She holds a Master of Social-Ecological Resilience from Stockholm Resilience Centre (where the framework of Planetary Boundaries was created), as well as a Bachelor of Engineering from The Institute of Technology at Linköping University.

She is involved in both the Swiss and Swedish startup scene and has been building impact organizations and products for the past 6 years within fields such as green finance, global supply chains and Corporate Digital Responsibility (CDR).

Niniane Paeffgen acted as first Managing Director of the Swiss Digital Initiative on digital ethics in Geneva from 2019 to the end of 2022.

Implementing Responsible and Ethical Artificial Intelligence in India: Balancing Innovation and Regulation for Sustainable AI Development

3

Avinash Dadhich and Yashu Bansal

Abstract

With rapid technological advancements, we are witnessing a global rush to develop and implement AI models across sectors. This chapter will focus on India, a developing country as diverse as its 1.42 billion citizens, and will discuss the emerging best practices to be adopted by the vibrant startup economy in India. With a focus on four core elements of responsible and ethical AI, this chapter will provide solutions on how Indian businesses can balance the tussle between innovation and regulation, while upholding ethical standards.

Global policies such as the OECD Principles and the UNESCO Guidelines on the use of AI are already prompting sectoral guidelines in India. Furthermore, the recent intervention by Indian authorities, mandating transparency and explainability in AI marks a significant regulatory step. Discussing regulatory principles, this chapter will throw light on potential regulatory models which may prove to be successful in the Indian economy. This chapter will also discuss the role of various stakeholders which will impact the use of AI in India. In conclusion, this chapter will highlight the importance of scalable AI models, along with a focus on sustainable development and use of AI models in India.

A. Dadhich (✉)
School of Law, Dhirubhai Ambani University, Gandhinagar, Gujarat, India
e-mail: avinash_dadhich@daiict.ac.in

Y. Bansal
Manipal Law School, Manipal Academy of Higher Education, Bengaluru, India
e-mail: yashu.bansal@manipal.edu

C. H. Hoffmann, D. Bansal (eds.), *AI Ethics in Practice*, Integrated Science 35,
https://doi.org/10.1007/978-3-031-87023-1_3

1 Introduction: The AI Development Landscape in India

The world is currently witnessing a race in the development of AI models where more efficient models are being released rapidly in a very competitive manner (Alex Hern, 2024).[1] The commercialization of Large Language Models (LLM) and subsequent Generative AI (GenAI) Models has played a significant role in the revolution of several industries. The aggressive investment statistics in LLM and GenAI evidence the growth of the market. Projections of approximately $18.2 billion of funding in the LLMs, with smaller LLM startups securing around $460 million (TrendFeedr),[2] show an impressive boom in the growth of AI development. It has been estimated that the global market of LLMs alone will grow upto $259.8 million in 2030, and that by the year 2025, 750 million software applications will be using LLMs (Serhii Uspenskyi 2024).[3]

A focus on the geographic distribution of the development of AI models will highlight the dominance of Western countries. For factors varying from funding to regulations, countries such as the United States and Europe (Syreeta Charles-Cole 2023)[4] have been at the forefront of the development of AI and its regulation. There is a common agreement that developing countries are being left behind in this race of AI development (Goffi 2021).[5] Shifting the focus to India, it is not possible to ignore the most populous country in the world which has the largest potential market of user base of AI models. In the recent years, there has been development in various fronts in India which is changing its position from a spectator to an active participant in this global rush of AI development.

At the investment front, the latest approval of 'IndiaAI Mission' by the Indian Government has set aside a budget of around $1.242 billion USD for a comprehensive development of AI in India (Prime Minister's Office of India 2024).[6] With the setting up of the Digital India Corporation (Digital India Corporation 2024),[7] a non-profit body under the Ministry of Electronics and Information Technology, this mission will be implemented through an independent business division—'IndiaAI' (*please refer to* Fig. 3.1) (Prime Minister's Office of India 2024) (Cabinet Approves Ambitious IndiaAI Mission to Strengthen the AI Innovation Ecosystem, Prime Minister's Office Of India (Mar. 7, 2024), available at https://www.pmindia.gov.in/

[1] Hern (2024).

[2] Behind the AI Boom: Large Language Model (LLM) Trends, TrendFeedr, available at https://trendfeedr.com/blog/large-language-model-llm-trends/.

[3] Serhii Uspenskyi (2024).

[4] Syreeta Charles-Cole (2023).

[5] Goffi (2021).

[6] Cabinet Approves Ambitious IndiaAI Mission to Strengthen the AI Innovation Ecosystem, Prime Minister's Office Of India (Mar. 7, 2024), available at https://www.pmindia.gov.in/en/news_updates/cabinet-approves-ambitious-indiaai-mission-to-strengthen-the-ai-innovation-ecosystem/.

[7] Digital India Corporation, DIGITAL INDIA CORPORATION (2024), available at https://dic.gov.in/.

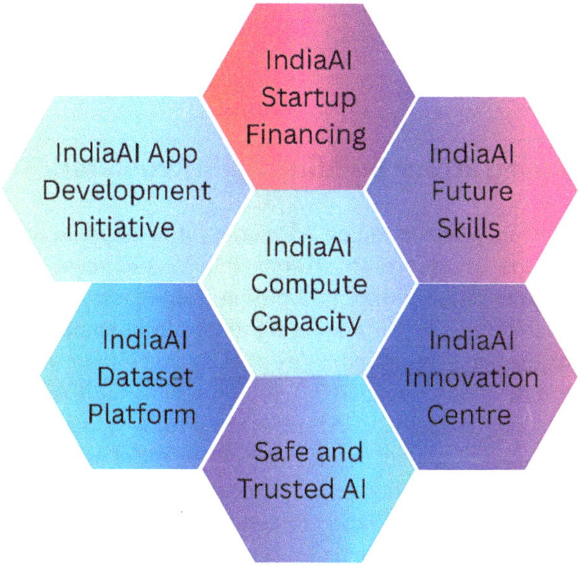

Fig. 3.1 Focus Areas of IndiaAI

en/news_updates/cabinet-approves-ambitious-indiaai-mission-to-strengthen-the-ai-innovation-ecosystem/)

Developments at the policy level can be traced back to the year 2018 when the National Strategy for Artificial Intelligence was released by NITI Ayog, an advisory body which provides technical advice to the Indian Government on various issues. This document sets out the following key areas of focus for the integration of AI: (i) health care; (ii) agriculture; (iii) education; (iv) smart cities and infrastructure; and (v) smart mobility and transportation (Niti Aayog 2018).[8]

The development of AI models in the private sector can be seen in two aspects: building home grown AI models and training already existing models on Indian database for use cases in specific sector. While the development of Indian AI models has been slow, several sectors have been quick to train existing models like ChatGPT and Llama to meet their requirements of customized LLMs. Some of the notable AI models being developed in India are Hanooman, Krutim, and OpenHathi (Indian Express 2024).[9] Models such as Kissan.AI (*powered by OpenAI models and trained to meet agricultural needs*) and deep tech business solutions such as Niramai (the use of AI models for breast thermal scans) are also rapidly being curated in India.

With a focus on cultural and language diversity, the startup ecosystem in India, specifically the GenAI development space, has recently picked up pace and has

[8] National Strategy for Artificial Intelligence, NITI AAYOG (June, 2018), available at https://www.niti.gov.in/sites/default/files/2023-03/National-Strategy-for-Artificial-Intelligence.pdf.

[9] Tech Desk, Reliance-backed consortium unveils 'Hanooman' series of AI models, THE INDIAN EXPRESS (Aug. 23, 2024), available at https://indianexpress.com/article/technology/artificial-intelligence/hanooman-ai-model-series-sml-9173264/.

placed India on the global map for AI development. It has been estimated that the GenAI market in India is expected to cross the $17 Billion mark by 2030 (Inc24 2024).[10]

2 Regulating Ethics: Building Agile Regulatory Models

Amidst the current rush in the Indian AI market, it is essential to understand the regulatory landscape to ensure the responsible development and adoption of AI. With a population of more than 1.42 billion people, it is critical to prepare for the impact that such a revolution may bring along. In alignment with the notable push towards the banner 'Digital India', as of early 2023, there were 692.0 million internet users in India, with around 467.0 million social media users.

The most prevalent definition of AI mentions it to be 'a machine-based system that can, for a given set of human defined objectives, make predictions, recommendations, or decisions influencing real or virtual environments. AI systems are designed to operate with varying levels of autonomy' (Stuart Russell et al. 2023).[11] The emphasis on the influence on real or virtual environments is critical at this stage to take note of the social impact of AI models. We have entered a digital era where the predictions, recommendations, and decisions made by AI models are impacting the day-to-day lives of people living in real societies.

The recent GPAI (Global Partnership on Artificial Intelligence) Summit in December, 2023, hosted in India witnessed the adoption of the GPAI Ministerial Declaration, unanimously by 29 member countries, which has taken account of the real impact of AI models. Recognizing the need to utilize the opportunities being offered by the adoption of AI in the economic growth, the declaration discussed mitigating risks arising from such development and use of AI. Some of the major concerns highlighted were misinformation, job displacement, lack of transparency and fairness, data privacy, and threat to human rights and democratic values (2023 GPAI Ministerial Declaration 2023).[12]

At the policy level, in addition to the 2018 National Strategy for Artificial Intelligence, Niti Ayog had also released another document setting out operationalizing principles for responsible AI (Niti Aayog 2021).[13] Discussing the role of the government in operationalizing responsible AI, the document sets out the below areas of focus (Fig. 3.2). Highlighting the implementation of ethical AI, role of private institutions and research institutions have also been highlighted. In addition

[10] Meet The Startups Carving India's Niche In The AI Space, INC42 (August 21, 2024), available at https://inc42.com/startups/indian-genai-startup-tracker/.

[11] Stuart et al. (2023).

[12] 2023 GPAI Ministerial Declaration, Global Partnership On Artificial Intelligence (December 13, 2023), available at https://gpai.ai/2023-GPAI-Ministerial-Declaration.pdf.

[13] Approach Document for India: Part 2 - Operationalizing Principles for Responsible AI, NITI AAYOG (August, 2021), available at https://www.niti.gov.in/sites/default/files/2021-08/Part2-Responsible-AI-12082021.pdf.

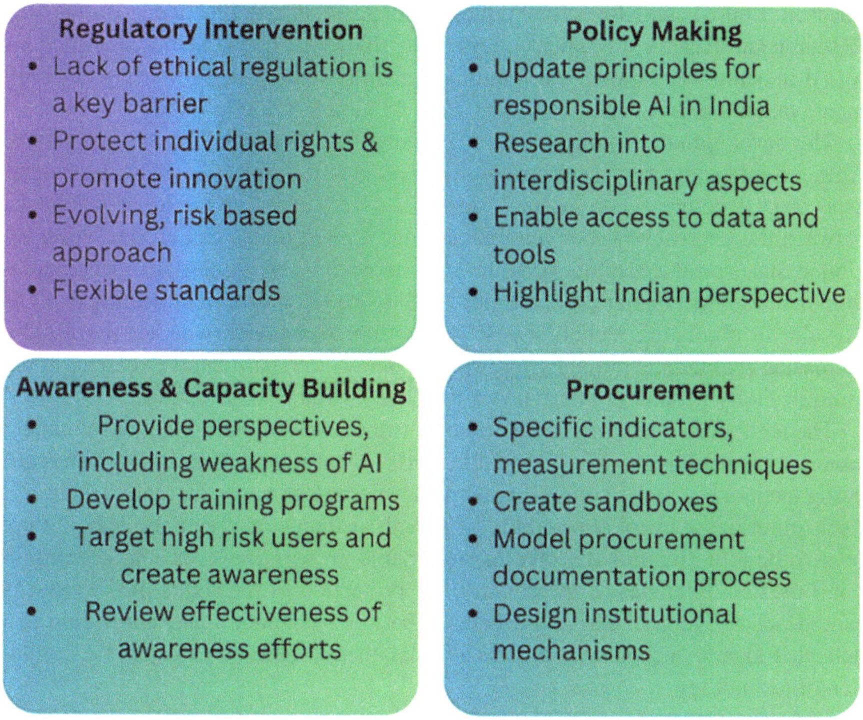

Fig. 3.2 Focus Areas for Government Intervention (Niti Aayog 2021) (Approach Document for India: Part 2 - Operationalizing Principles for Responsible AI, NITI AAYOG (August 2021), available at https://www.niti.gov.in/sites/default/files/2021-08/Part2-Responsible-AI-12082021.pdf)

to the responsibility to create awareness, it has been proposed that internal ethic boards, self-assessment guides, and external audits should be leveraged as suitable regulatory mechanisms in the private sector.

Sectoral level guidelines have been prominent in the regulation of AI models (Guisella Finocchiaro 2024)[14] across the globe. Indian sectoral bodies have also been active in framing guidelines and policies with a focus on the application and use of AI models in their respective industries. At this stage, it is pertinent to throw light upon a few sectoral guidelines which will be essential in understanding the regulation of AI models in India. The Telecom Regulatory Authority of India had released a recommendation paper on 'Leveraging Artificial Intelligence and Big Data in Telecommunication Sector' where it discusses the setting up of an 'AI and Data Authority in India' which will be responsible for developing model ethical codes for adoption by public and private sectors which are using AI models (Telecom Regulatory Authority of India 2023).[15] The Indian Council of Medical Research has

[14] Finocchiaro (2024), pp. 1961–1968.

[15] Press Release No. 62/2023: TRAI Releases Recommendations on Leveraging Artificial Intelligence and Big Data in Telecommunication Sector, Telecom Regulatory Authority Of India

released 'Ethical Guidelines for Application of Artificial Intelligence in Biomedical Research and Healthcare' where it lays down the various general ethical principles for AI in health care, along with guiding principles to be followed during development, validation, and deployment phases of AI models (ICMR 2023).[16]

The development of policies and regulations in any country do not function in silos, meaning that any legal development reflects the trajectory of several other aspects in a country. For instance, there is a very clear and evident difference between the approach of tech regulation in the United States vs Europe. While the United States produces majority of the tech innovation and has less stringent regulation on the subject matter (Alex Engler 2023),[17] the EU has been projecting itself as a leader in regulating technology. It is therefore questioned whether the rapidly increasing regulations in the EU are stifling innovation, particularly keeping in the mind the hefty penalty imposed under the GDPR (Martin et al. 2019).[18]

The regulatory landscape in any country is the result of multi-facet development strategies and at this stage, it is essential to ask: What is the Indian strategy on regulating technology? As a country which is developing at a very fast pace, there is a focus on utilizing every opportunity of growth available and regulation should not pose to be a hurdle. For the sake of sustainable growth, however, and keeping in mind the demographics of the country, the protection of the rights of the citizens should not be ignored. Striking a balance between regulation and innovation is a delicate task and in country as diverse as India, there is currently a gap in the regulation of technology.

Upon analysis of the current state of regulation of new forms of technology in India in mid-2024, it is essential to draw light upon the Digital Personal Data Protection Act, 2023, which was passed in August 2023 for the regulation of the use of digital personal data in India. The law is yet to be enforced and the rules to be prescribed under the law are expected to be finalized by the year end of 2024. Unless the rules are prescribed and the governing authority under the law is established, the regulation of personal data in India is yet to become a reality. Another essential piece of legislation which will be critical to regulate AI in India will be the Digital India Act. While there have been some official statements related to the drafting of this legislation, there has been no official draft law released yet. There is however a copy of a presentation released in the public domain which presents the key facets of the proposed Digital India Act 2023 (Ministry of Electronics and Information Technology 2023).[19] It is interesting to observe that online safety, trust, and

(July 20, 2023), available at https://www.trai.gov.in/sites/default/files/PR_No.62of2023.pdf.

[16] Ethical Guidelines for Application of Artificial Intelligence in Biomedical Research and Healthcare, Indian Council Of Medical Research (2023), available at https://main.icmr.nic.in/sites/default/files/upload_documents/Ethical_Guidelines_AI_Healthcare_2023.pdf.

[17] Engler (2023).

[18] Martin et al. (2019), pp. 1307–1324.

[19] Proposed Digital India Act, 2023: Digital India Dialogues, Ministry Of Electronics And Information Technology (March 9, 2023), available at https://www.meity.gov.in/writereaddata/files/DIA_Presentation%2009.03.2023%20Final.pdf.

accountability have been given significant weightage in the discussions, and it appears that India will also follow a risk-based classification and regulatory approach for emerging technologies.

Discussions about the AI regulatory landscape in India will not be holistic without mention of a very interesting episode in India which highlighted a knee jerk reaction of the government to specific events. On 1 March 2024, the Ministry of Electronics and Information Technology issued an advisory (Ministry Of Electronics And Information Technology 2024)[20] with the following major highlights: (i) requiring compliance with the applicable laws to ensure that the use of AI models, LLM/ Generative AI, software(s) or algorithm(s) do not permit users to share any unlawful content; (ii) ensuring that the use of AI models/LLM/GenAI models do not permit any bias or discrimination or threaten the integrity of the electoral process; (iii) the requirement of explicit permission of the Government of India for the use of under-testing or unreliable AI models; and (iv) the requirement of appropriate labelling of the AI models, along with a 'consent popup' mechanism to explicitly inform the users about the possible and inherent fallibility or unreliability of the output generated. It is interesting to note that the aforesaid advisory ended with a 'request' to intermediaries to ensure compliance with 15 days. Interestingly, before the expiry of the given window of 15 days, on 13 March 2024, another advisory was issued (Ministry of Electronics and Information Technology 2024)[21] which retained majority of the requirements under the 1 March advisory, except the highlighted requirement to obtain the explicit permission of the Government of India before deploying AI models in India.

As a background, it appears that the above notifications were a response to the incident in February 2024, when Google apologized for the responses of Gemini AI to certain questions about the Prime Minister of India (*The Hindu*, 2024).[22] Coloured as an attempt to harm the integrity of the electoral process going on in February 2024, the first advisory of the Ministry faced pushback from businesses and startups working in AI models. Balancing the need for innovation in India versus the maintenance of public order and security, the requirement for explicit permission was removed which eases the burden of compliance on startups working in AI. The requirement of explicit permission from the government would also be a very strict regulatory approach with great power vested in the state, which may lack the

[20] Due Diligence by Intermediaries/ Platforms under the Information Technology Act, 2000 and Information Technology (Intermediary Guidelines and Digital Media Ethics Code) Rules, 2021, No.eNo.2(4)/2023-CyberLaws–3, Ministry Of Electronics And Information Technology (March 1, 2024), available at https://regmedia.co.uk/2024/03/04/meity_ai_advisory_1_march.pdf.

[21] Due Diligence by Intermediaries/ Platforms under the Information Technology Act, 2000 and Information Technology (Intermediary Guidelines and Digital Media Ethics Code) Rules, 2021, No.eNo.2(4)/2023-CyberLaws–3, Ministry Of Electronics And Information Technology (March 15, 2024), available at Advisory 15March 2024.pdf (meity.gov.in).

[22] The Hindu Bureau, Gemini AI's reply to query, 'is Modi a fascist', violates IT Rules: Union Minister Rajeev Chandrasekhar, The Hindu (February 23, 2024), available at https://www.thehindu.com/news/national/netizens-allege-bias-in-google-ai-tools-response-on-pm-modi-i-t-ministry-sees-rules-violation/article67877974.ece.

capabilities of understanding and regulating the very technical aspects of AI (Christiaens 2024).[23] It is however pertinent to note that the retention of the labelling requirement, including a consent popup mechanism, clearly shows the commitment towards strengthening trust in AI models and maintaining safe AI models which are being deployed for public use.

The latest development in the regulatory landscape of AI in India is the publication of a report by the Subcommittee on 'AI Governance and Guidelines Development', as constituted under the IndiaAI Mission to undertake the development of an 'AI for India-Specific Regulatory Framework'. With the report being published for consultation on 6 January 2025, it aims to guide the development of a trustworthy and accountable AI ecosystem in India (IndiaAI Mission 2025).[24] Analysing the existing gaps on the basis of three main considerations, being: (i) the need to enable effective compliance and enforcement of existing law; (ii) the need for transparency and responsibility across the AI ecosystem in India; and (iii) the need for a whole-of-government approach; this report has recommended six major steps for the governance of AI in India. Sectoral collaboration, harm mitigation, use of technological measures for regulation, and self-regulation are the major essential elements in the recommendations (IndiaAI Mission 2025).[25]

In continuation with the focus on trust and accountability, the need for ethics should be highlighted against the background of regulating the emerging technology in India. Before discussing the Indian approach to meeting ethical standards, it is paramount to set context in relation to how to define ethics and the importance of ethics to different demographics. The subject of ethics can indeed be an entirely independent area of study and research but to oversimplify ethics, it is basically a set of principles which govern whether an action or inaction is right or wrong. There are several schools of philosophy on ethics and its meaning, but without delving into the different approaches to understanding ethics, we will consider ethics to be a set of principles which are necessary for leading a standard quality of life and which is above and beyond the law. The relationship between ethics and law is indeed a tricky one—while law is a reflection of the dynamic need of society, ethics take a step further into the very conscience of the subject matter, irrespective of the legal stance on the same (Young 2019).[26]

In early 2000s, when developed nations like the United States were moving towards the concept of 'corporate ethics', the terms 'business' and 'ethics' were often considered to be oxymorons. With businesses moving towards ethical corporate practices, it was questioned whether ethics is being perceived as an economic tool leading to the loss of the real meaning of ethics (Paine 2000).[27] We are currently

[23] Christiaens (2024).

[24] Report on AI Governance Guidelines Development, IndiaAI Mission, as on January 5, 2025, available at Report on AI governance guidelines development.

[25] Report on AI Governance Guidelines Development, IndiaAI Mission, as on January 5, 2025, available at https://indiaai.s3.ap-south-1.amazonaws.com/docs/subcommittee-report-dec26.pdf.

[26] Young (2019), pp. 35–51.

[27] Paine (2000), pp. 319–330.

living in a world where 'technology ethics' is getting more and more prominence and there is sufficient literature around ethical use of technology (Daza and Ilozumba 2022),[28] especially AI. At this stage, before diving into how one may regulate ethics, it is essential to throw light on the very need of technology to be ethical (Choung et al. 2023).[29] Specifically from the view point of a developing country like India where the meaning and value of ethics will differ from more developed countries such as the United States and the EU, is it fair to apply the same global ethical standards?

A possible answer to the need for technology to be ethical lies in the very complexity of the technical nature of the subject matter. As regulators are adapting and building more capabilities to be able to regulate technology, there are certain aspects of technology which are not explainable easily. For instance, there are several ongoing discussions on the 'blackbox' in AI models where even the developers are giving up on being able to explain the output from an AI model. Technical developments towards the creation of AGI, a general purpose AI model, will further amplify this uncertainty in the understanding of technology. It may therefore be important to look up to something beyond the written code of law and turn to higher ethical standards to maintain the balance between innovation and the protection of human rights and society at large.

In a country with the fastest growing GDP (FE Business 2024)[30] (Gross Domestic Product), the importance of its diverse population and culture needs to be considered before the implementation and use of new forms of technology. While India may not take an overly protective approach like the EU in regulating emerging technology, attempts to create innovative regulatory models with a focus on safety, trust, and ethics are evident in the Indian AI landscape. Different forms of regulation have existed in the history of law and policy, and as being dynamic is the very essence of legal developments, there have been efforts in innovating new forms of regulation for AI. Compensating for the 'toothless' nature of ethical codes (Munn 2023),[31] a combination of self-regulation with guiding principles and applicable penalties may prove to be the way forward in regulating AI in India.

The methods discussed in majority of the AI policy documents in India heavily rely on self-assessment models where private companies are expected to create internal ethical boards and regulate their roles in the development and adoption of responsible AI. The combination of self-regulation along with governance frameworks from regulatory bodies may rather provide to be a more feasible way forward for regulating AI models in India. Co-regulation models will help navigate the lack of capabilities in regulatory bodies for governing such technical subject matters,

---

[28] Daza and Ilozumba (2022), p. 1042661.

[29] Choung et al. (2023), pp. 733–745.

[30] FE Business, How year-on-year India's GDP grew to become world's fastest-growing economy?, The Financial Express (July 19, 2024), available at https://www.financialexpress.com/budget/budget-2024-how-year-on-year-indias-gdp-grew-to-become-worlds-fastest-growing-economy-3558725/.

[31] Munn (2023), pp. 869–877.

and it will also reduce the inherent challenges of keeping pace with the fast-moving technology. Framing strict requirements around self-regulation model will ensure that the enforcement of legal provisions and penalties continue to have a deterrence effect on businesses to ensure compliance with the regulations.

3 Demonstration of Trust

As artificial intelligence (AI) becomes increasingly prevalent across industries in India, establishing and maintaining trust in AI systems is paramount (Choung et al. 2023).[32] In a country as diverse as India, we are already seeing projects and investments in innovation which will improve the state of public affairs (BP Ashwini 2022),[33] improve services and security, and contribute to the growth of the country. Demonstrating trust involves developing AI models that are not only technically robust but also ethical in use, positively in alignment with societal values.

With co-regulation models for AI seeming suitable for regulating AI in India, it is essential to discuss ways in which the technology can build trust amongst its users. A very common premise for justice says that it is not only essential to deliver justice but also to evidently highlight justice being done. On similar grounds, it is critical for all stakeholders, including the private sector working in AI and its regulators, to show that AI models are safe so as build trust amongst users at large. The term 'ethics by design' has been mentioned in certain policies for AI development (Niti Aayog 2021)[34] but there exists an evident gap in finding solutions to how to embed ethical practices into the very design and architecture of an AI model.

An example in the guidelines for ethical development of AI models in health care in India shows how the policy recommends techniques to ensure the implementation of ethical principles at three stages, i.e., (i) development; (ii) deployment; and (iii) validation (ICMR 2023).[35] Addressing concerns such as data protection, discrimination, and cybersecurity risks, various solutions have been provided which may prove to be helpful in building ethical and responsible AI. To build trust, it is essential for AI models to implement techniques which will not only be in compliance with the law, but will also meet the fair ethical standards prevalent in a country like India. Building on the various frameworks developed in India, the four most important core elements of responsible and ethical AI for India which require attention beyond regulation are as follows:

[32] Choung et al. (2023), pp. 733–745.

[33] Ashwini et al. (2022), pp. 986–993.

[34] Approach Document for India: Part 2 - Operationalizing Principles for Responsible AI, NITI AAYOG (August, 2021), available at https://www.niti.gov.in/sites/default/files/2021-08/Part2-Responsible-AI-12082021.pdf.

[35] Ethical Guidelines for Application of Artificial Intelligence in Biomedical Research and Healthcare, Indian Council Of Medical Research (2023), available at https://main.icmr.nic.in/sites/default/files/upload_documents/Ethical_Guidelines_AI_Healthcare_2023.pdf.

(i) ***Transparency and Explainability***

The concept of transparency and explainability go hand in hand where transparency is necessary for an AI model to be explainable. When AI models will provide clear understanding on how decisions are made, including the various parameters for the same, its users will be able to repose faith on the decisions and cater to reservations about the parameters used. In more sensitive sectors such as health care (Zhang et al. 2022) [36] and finance, it is very essential for AI models to be explainable to be able to build trust amongst users.

Keeping in mind the Indian demographics, it is also essential to ensure that design of such models, in particularly the user facing designs, are built in a way which is easily understandable by the users. Factors such as diversity in language should also be accounted for while making understandable models. Research is being conducted to develop techniques which can enhance explainability of AI models (Shaistha Fathima 2024),[37] particularly in more high-sensitive application such as health care, and such techniques should be tailored to the Indian users for effective implementation.

In line with the concept of 'consent fatigue' (Schermer et al. 2014),[38] there are arguments around the necessity for sharing technical information with users and whether the same will serve the intended purpose. Against such arguments, it is essential to keep in mind that the burden for sharing information should lie on the developers of AI models, irrespective of whether the users are utilizing the same or not. While we will expect more jurisprudence around consumer protection in this area, on the contrary, providing such information to users may enable developers in shifting the burden to consumers who fail to read about limitations of AI models before implementing the same in their day-to-day lives.

In addition to providing clear information to users on the working of the AI models, another best practice for an emerging market such as India is to conduct thorough impact assessments to identify risks and ethical concerns. Such an exercise will enable businesses to mitigate risks by taking steps which will educate and empower users. Lastly, another best practice for increasing the explainability of AI models is robust documentation of the development process of AI models, including the source of training data sets, the architecture of the model, and the method followed for training and testing of the model.

(ii) ***Data Protection and Privacy***

The right to privacy is a comparatively new right introduced to Indian citizens with a landmark Supreme Court judgement (Justice K.S.Puttaswamy (Retd) vs

[36] Zhang et al. (2022), p. 237.

[37] Shaistha Fathima, LIME vs SHAP: A Comparative Analysis of Interpretability Tools, MARKOVML (February 26, 2024), available at https://www.markovml.com/blog/lime-vs-shap.

[38] Schermer et al. (2014), pp. 171–182.

Union Of India 2019).[39] It is only recently in the year 2023 that India witnessed a data protection law, being the Digital Personal Data Protection Act of 2023, and the rules to implement and enforce the provisions of the same are yet in the drafting stage. In light of the recent introduction of the law to regulate the use of personal data by businesses, Indian businesses are at the very nascent stage of understanding the requirement and the obligations of businesses towards fulfilling the users' right to personal data protection. With intensive efforts required towards spreading awareness on privacy and the right to personal data protection, the judicial landscape around the right to privacy is gradually evolving (Karthick Theodore v. Madras High Court 2021)[40] in India.

Notwithstanding the lack of regulation and awareness on the subject matter, it is essential to protect the privacy of individuals in AI models. The lack of awareness should not be a ground for refusal to fulfil the fundamental right of Indians and keeping in mind the larger ethical responsibility of AI developers in India, principles of 'privacy by design' should be implemented in the development of AI models. Best practices to implement privacy by design (Domingo-Ferrer and Blanco-Justicia 2020)[41] include techniques to transform personal data to remove personal identifiers from the data sets, aggregation of personal data to make it impossible to uniquely identify individuals, and measures such as timely deletion of personal data history.

(iii) ***Non-discrimination***

The complexity in the social fabric of India is a major challenge for any AI model to be developed and used in India. Non-discrimination in AI models, in its simplest sense, would imply that the model is not biased towards any specific group of people or community (Chen 2023).[42] Biases in AI models generally creep in from the training data set and to solve the challenge of '*garbage in, garbage out (Kilkenny MF 2018),*'[43] it is critical to audit the training data set on which AI models are trained. It is often argued that AI models simply reflect the existing bias in a society and is unavoidable. It is however pertinent to take note of the power of technology which will significantly amplify any already existing bias in the society. Developers of AI models should conduct thorough inspection of the training data sets to ensure that the data sets represent all sects of the society on various grounds, including religion, cast, creed, language, and financial backgrounds. Subsequently, rigorous testing of the models should be conducted for adversarial scenarios and for prevention of any form of jail breaking. It is essential that such testing considers the diverse population and culture in India.

---

[39] Justice K.S.Puttaswamy(Retd) vs Union Of India, 2019 (1) SCC 1.

[40] Karthick Theodore v. Madras High Court, 2021 SCC OnLine Mad 2755; and *Ikanoon Software Development Pvt Ltd v. Karthick Theodore & ors.*

[41] Domingo-Ferrer and Blanco-Justicia (2020).

[42] Chen (2023), p. 567.

[43] Kilkenny and Robinson (2018), pp. 103–105.

Co-regulation models should include requirements to provide audit reports on training data sets on parameters such as diversity of the data set to ensure the fairness of the AI models.

(iv) ***Accountability***

Accountability is the consequence of transparency (Munn 2023)[44] and is often directly tied up to the term 'liability' which has more of a legal connotation to hold someone responsible for a certain defect or lack of standard which leads to loss or harm to another person. While regulations around liability are conventional in nature, the change in the very definition of 'product' and 'service' calls for an evolution in liability laws as well. To add to the existing fundamental challenges in fixing liability in the world of technology, the complex nature of AI models will escalate the issues herein.

With multiple players involved in the development, deployment, and use of AI models, the allocation of responsibilities in the event of any loss or harm to the users becomes more challenging (Hauer 2022).[45] If we apply the current consumer protection laws in India (Consumer Protection Act 2019)[46] to products and services using AI models, the complexity around finding who will be liable in the supply chain of AI models is amplified. Additionally, concerns around grievance redressal of users will become paramount in AI models which are not transparent or explainable. There is therefore the need to implement new models of liability rules in alignment with the new technological revolution.

Against an Indian background, the operationalisation of these principles of ethical and responsible AI will require extensive scrutiny and review of AI models during the development and deployment of the same. Relying on encoding ethical standards in the very architecture itself is the most suitable way forward for India. This will also reduce the dependency on regulatory models for governing the AI technology. In the rush for being a global powerhouse for AI, it is essential to be able to use the full potential of the technology, while also prioritizing responsible and ethical AI so as to protect the well-being of the users.

4 Conclusion: Moving Towards a Technosocial Approach

In this new digital era, it is no more possible for any sector to work in silos and in a single dimensional manner. The widespread integration of AI models in various products and services available to the public has raised concerns. The world of technology is no more an isolated group of people working to provide support as a backbone only. The success achieved by AI models has brought technology and its developers to the forefront, and there is a global push to focus on techno-social

[44] Munn (2023), pp. 869–877.

[45] Hauer (2022), p. 272.

[46] Consumer Protection Act, 2019.

aspects (Kaye et al. 2024).[47] The word 'technosocial' denotes a very interesting combination of technology and society which highlights the unavoidable impact of technology on our society. This amalgamation calls for technosocial collaborations for the development and regulation of AI models. Even with sufficient literature on the necessity of collaborations in this digital era (Soumya Banerjee et al. 2022),[48] it is difficult to achieve this collaboration in practice.

The criticality of stakeholder engagement cannot be emphasized enough for the responsible and ethical development and use of AI models. As we have seen some best practices in the emerging market of India, with a focus on the different stages of AI development and use, it is important to actively involve stakeholders throughout the roadmap of AI development (Kaye et al. 2024) [49] (*please refer to* Fig. 3.3). An example of the same would mean involving academia in the robust testing of the AI models to ensure that models are not biased. Similarly, consultations with regulators through the phases of impact assessment will prove to be helpful in implementing the feedback loop during the development of the AI model.

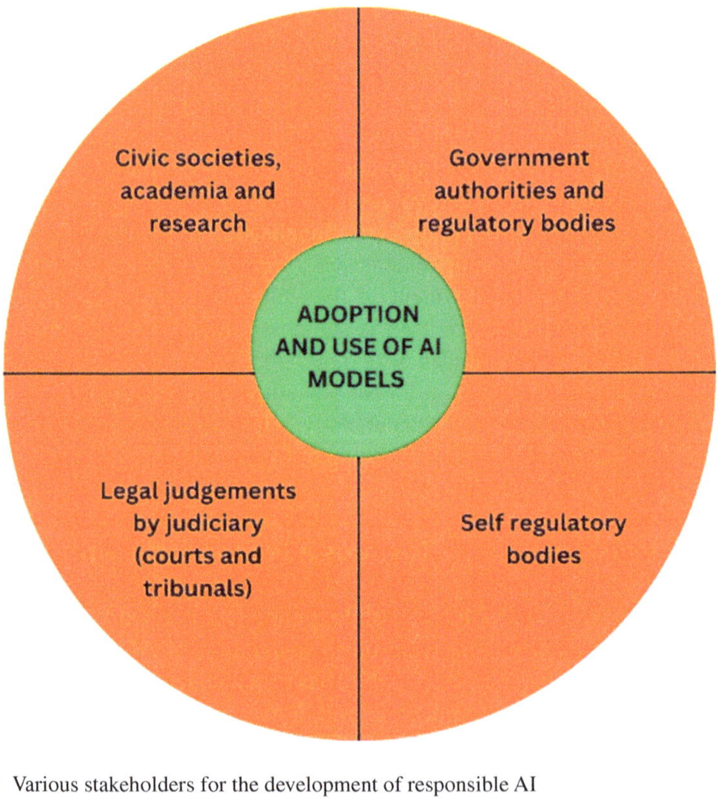

Fig. 3.3 Various stakeholders for the development of responsible AI

[47] Kaye et al. (2024).

[48] Banerjee et al. (2022).

[49] Kaye et al. (2024).

To enhance explainability and understandability of AI models, engaging with the community at large is very essential. Particularly against the Indian background, it is critical that the companies developing and implementing AI models in their products and services take the responsibility to educate its users on the technology, its impact and its limitation. Such engagement is more critical when AI models are used by government bodies in providing public services or welfare schemes of its citizens.

In conclusion, this chapter would like to emphasize the current need to align technology with our societal values and focus on the necessity to make our AI models ethical in nature. Relying on co-regulation models which are agile in nature includes the need for self-regulation of AI models, and the same will amplify the focus on building ethical designs. In this model of AI development and regulation, there should however be an express effort to ensure that trust building is an on-going process and regulation does not result in becoming a task of check boxing a compliance list. A culture of responsible innovation which respects ethical considerations in alignment with societal values needs to be fostered at the very grass root level. Such integration of ethics in the very architecture of AI development and use will also help strike the correct balance between innovation and regulation. Taking steps throughout the roadmap of AI development and use will prevent ethics from posing to be a burden on the stakeholders. A country as diverse and magnificent as India requires creative solutions for the responsible and ethical development of AI models which will only help in ensuring that the technology is sustainable in nature.

References

2023 GPAI Ministerial Declaration, Global Partnership On Artificial Intelligence (December 13, 2023). Available at https://gpai.ai/2023-GPAI-Ministerial-Declaration.pdf.

Approach Document for India: Part 2 - Operationalizing Principles for Responsible AI, NITI AAYOG (August, 2021), Available at https://www.niti.gov.in/sites/default/files/2021 08/Part2-Responsible-AI-12082021.pdf

Ashwini BP, Savithramma RM, Ranganathaiah S (2022). Artificial intelligence in smart city applications: an overview. 986–993. https://doi.org/10.1109/ICICCS53718.2022.9788152

Banerjee S, Alsop P, Jones L, Cardinal RN (2022) Patient and public involvement to build trust in artificial intelligence: a framework, tools, and case studies. Patterns 3(6)

Behind the AI Boom: Large Language Model (LLM) Trends, TrendFeedr, Available at https://trendfeedr.com/blog/large-language-model-llm-trends/

Cabinet Approves Ambitious IndiaAI Mission to Strengthen the AI Innovation Ecosystem, Prime Minister's Office of India (Mar. 7, 2024), Available at https://www.pmindia.gov.in/en/news_updates/cabinet-approves-ambitious-indiaai-mission-to-strengthen-the-ai-innovation-ecosystem/

Chen Z (2023) Ethics and discrimination in artificial intelligence-enabled recruitment practices. Humanit Soc Sci Commun 10:567

Choung H, David P, Ross A (2023) Trust and ethics in AI. AI Soc 38:733–745. https://doi.org/10.1007/s00146-022-01473-4

Christiaens T (2024) Nationalize AI! AI Soc. https://doi.org/10.1007/s00146-024-01897-0

Consumer Protection Act, 2019

Daza MT, Ilozumba UJ (2022) A survey of AI ethics in business literature: maps and trends between 2000 and 2021. Front Psychol. 13:1042661. https://doi.org/10.3389/fpsyg.2022.1042661
Digital India Corporation (2024) Digital India Corporation. Available at https://dic.gov.in/
Domingo-Ferrer J, Blanco-Justicia A (2020) Privacy-preserving technologies. In: Christen M, Gordijn B, Loi M (eds) The ethics of cybersecurity. The international library of ethics, law and technology, vol 21. Springer, Cham
Due Diligence by Intermediaries/ Platforms under the Information Technology Act, 2000 and Information Technology (Intermediary Guidelines and Digital Media Ethics Code) Rules, 2021, No.eNo.2(4)/2023-CyberLaws–3, Ministry Of Electronics And Information Technology (March 1, 2024), Available at https://regmedia.co.uk/2024/03/04/meity_ai_advisory_1_march.pdf
Engler A (2023) The EU and U.S. Diverge on AI Regulation: A Transatlantic Comparison and Steps to Alignment, Brookings (April 25, 2023), Available at https://www.brookings.edu/articles/the-eu-and-us-diverge-on-ai-regulation-a-transatlantic-comparison-and-steps-to-alignment/
Ethical Guidelines for Application of Artificial Intelligence in Biomedical Research and Healthcare, Indian Council of Medical Research (2023). Available at https://main.icmr.nic.in/sites/default/files/upload_documents/Ethical_Guidelines_AI_Healthcare_2023.pdf
FE Business (2024) How year-on-year India's GDP grew to become world's fastest-growing economy? The Financial Express (July 19, 2024), Available at https://www.financialexpress.com/budget/budget-2024-how-year-on-year-indias-gdp-grew-to-become-worlds-fastest-growing-economy-3558725/
Finocchiaro G (2024) The regulation of artificial intelligence. AI Soc 39:1961–1968. Available at https://doi.org/10.1007/s00146-023-01650-z
Goffi ER (2021) Escaping the Western Cosm-ethical hegemony: the importance of cultural diversity in the ethical assessment of artificial intelligence. AI Ethics J 2(2)-1. Available at https://www.aiethicsjournal.org/10-47289-aiej20210716-1
Hauer T (2022) Importance and limitations of AI ethics in contemporary society. Humanit Soc Sci Commun 9:272
Hern A (2024) AI Race Heats Up as OpenAI, Google and Mistral Release New Models, THE GUARDIAN (April 10, 2024), Available at https://www.theguardian.com/technology/2024/apr/10/ai-race-heats-up-as-openai-google-and-mistral-release-new-models
Justice KS Puttaswamy(Retd) vs Union Of India, 2019 (1) SCC 1
Karthick Theodore v. Madras High Court, 2021 SCC OnLine Mad 2755; and Ikanoon Software Development Pvt Ltd v. Karthick Theodore & ors
Kaye J, Shah N, Kogetsu A et al (2024) Moving beyond Technical Issues to Stakeholder Involvement: Key Areas for Consideration in the Development of Human-Centred and Trusted AI in Healthcare, ABR
Kilkenny MF, Robinson KM (2018) Data quality: "Garbage in – garbage out". Health Inform Manage J 47(3):103–105
Martin N, Matt C, Niebel C et al (2019) How data protection regulation affects startup innovation. Inf Syst Front 21:1307–1324
Meet the Startups Carving India's Niche in the AI Space, INC42 (August 21, 2024), Available at https://inc42.com/startups/indian-genai-startup-tracker/.
Munn L (2023) The uselessness of AI ethics. AI Ethics 3:869–877. https://doi.org/10.1007/s43681-022-00209-w
National Strategy for Artificial Intelligence, NITI AAYOG (June, 2018). Available at https://www.niti.gov.in/sites/default/files/2023-03/National-Strategy-for-Artificial-Intelligence.pdf
Paine LS (2000) Does ethics pay? Bus Ethics Quart 10(1):319–330. https://doi.org/10.2307/3857716
Press Release No. 62/2023: TRAI Releases Recommendations on Leveraging Artificial Intelligence and Big Data in Telecommunication Sector, Telecom Regulatory Authority of India (July 20, 2023), Available at https://www.trai.gov.in/sites/default/files/PR_No.62of2023.pdf.
Proposed Digital India Act, 2023: Digital India Dialogues, Ministry Of Electronics And Information Technology (March 9, 2023), Available at https://www.meity.gov.in/writereaddata/files/DIA_Presentation%2009.03.2023%20Final.pdf

Report on AI Governance Guidelines Development, IndiaAI Mission, as on January 5, 2025, available at Report on AI governance guidelines development

Schermer BW, Custers B, van der Hof S (2014) The crisis of consent: how stronger legal protection may lead to weaker consent in data protection. Ethics Inform Technol 16:171–182

Serhii Uspenskyi, Large Language Model Statistics and Numbers (2024), Springs (June 6, 2024), Available at Large Language Model Statistics And Numbers (2024) - Springs (springsapps.com)

Shaistha Fathima, LIME vs SHAP: A Comparative Analysis of Interpretability Tools, MARKOVML (February 26, 2024), Available at https://www.markovml.com/blog/lime-vs-shap.

Stuart R, Perset K, Grobelnik M (2023) AI System Definition Update. OECD AI Policy Observatory (November 29, 2023), Available at https://oecd.ai/en/wonk/ai-system-definition-update

Syreeta Charles-Cole, Ethical Crossroads: AI, Cybersecurity, and Western Dominance in a Global Context, Medium (September 6, 2023), available at Ethical Crossroads: AI, Cybersecurity, and Western Dominance in a Global Context | by Syreeta Charles-Cole | Medium

Tech Desk, Reliance-backed consortium unveils 'Hanooman' series of AI models. The Indian Express (Aug. 23, 2024), Available at https://indianexpress.com/article/technology/artificial-intelligence/hanooman-ai-model-series-sml-9173264/

The Hindu Bureau, Gemini AI's reply to query, 'is Modi a fascist', violates IT Rules: Union Minister Rajeev Chandrasekhar, The Hindu (February 23, 2024), Available at https://www.thehindu.com/news/national/netizens-allege-bias-in-google-ai-tools-response-on-pm-modi-i-t-ministry-sees-rules-violation/article67877974.ece.

Young C (2019) Putting the law in its place: business ethics and the assumption that illegal implies unethical. J Bus Ethics 160:35–51. https://doi.org/10.1007/s10551-018-3904-4

Zhang Y, Weng Y, Lund J (2022) Applications of explainable artificial intelligence in diagnosis and surgery. Diagnostics (Basel) 12(2):237. https://doi.org/10.3390/diagnostics12020237

Avinash Dadhich has extensive academic and industry experience in legal and regulatory areas, focusing on AI/Robotics/Internet Governance/Data Privacy, Competition Law, and IPR. He received full scholarships for his PhD from the UK, LL.M. from France, and LL.B. from Delhi University and completed AI Policy Clinic Certificate from The Centre for AI and Digital Policy, Washington, D.C.

He has extensive experience working with leading firms like Deloitte, EY, Gide Loyrette Nouel LLP, Paris, France & White & Case LLP, Brussels, Belgium and Competition Commission of India, Ministry of Corporate Affairs, Govt. of India and Supreme Court of India and working on Advisory Board member of AMS Ethical AI in Talent Global Board, London and Tsaaro Consulting, Bengaluru. (Pro bono).

With extensive experience in higher education, he has served as the director of Manipal Law School at MAHE Bengaluru, the dean of the Institute of Legal Studies and Research at GLA University in Mathura, and the dean of IFIM Law School in Bengaluru.

He was a visiting researcher/faculty member at King's College London, UK, Max Planck Institute of Intellectual Property and Competition Law, Munich, Germany, and Institute of European Studies, Brussels, Belgium, NLU Delhi, Indian Law Institute, Indian Society for International Law, The National Academy of Indian Railways, Vadodara, Lyon Business School, Lyon, and Toulouse Law School, France.

He was invited as an Antitrust Fellow by the United States Department of State's International Visitor Leadership Program (IVLP) to visit New York, Washington, D.C., Iowa City, and San Francisco. He completed the Military Leadership Development Programme (MLDP **2**) as an Officer Cadet with the Welsh Universities Officers Training Corps of the British Territorial Army in the United Kingdom.

Prof. Dadhich has authored 10 research papers and two books in both Indian and international academic journals and publications and attended and presented research papers at International conferences at Internet Governance Forum (UN event), Poland, ETH Zurich, Switzerland, University of Luxembourg, Paris Dauphine, Paris, Oxford University, University of Amsterdam, University of Birmingham, University of Southampton, Poznan University, Poland, Athens

Institute for Education and Research (ATINER) Athens, Greece, King's College London, American Bar Association's Section of Antitrust Law, Washington DC, European Commission, Brussels, Tilburg University, Amsterdam, Netherlands, World Intellectual Property Organization (WIPO), Geneva, Switzerland, etc.

Yashu Bansal has a rich industry experience of 5+ years with law firms, companies, and start-ups, and has now pivoted to academia with the goal to reform legal education in India. Passionate about the intersection of law and technology, she is a part of Manipal Law School, where she focuses on LLM programmes specializing in technology and law. With interest in research in data privacy, consumer rights in the digital era, privacy engineering, AI regulation, cyber laws and legal tech, she aims to contribute to the fast-paced digital era in India.

With an Advanced LLM in Law and Digital Technologies, from Leiden University (*cum laude*), she has also cleared the National Eligibility Test (NET) in India, in 2023. Prior to her LLM, she had completed her B.B.A.LL.B. from Chanakya National Law University in India and has also pursued a PG Diploma in Consumer Law and Practice from National Law School of India University (Professional and Continuing Education).

4 Critical AI Literacies as a Driver of Ethics Education

Two Educators Reflect on the Good, the Bad, and the Ugly Sides of AI Ethics Literacies in the Classroom and Beyond

Thorsten Busch and Florence M. Chee

Abstract

Given the inordinate effect on their lives and livelihoods, managers, developers, and students are eager to learn about the many pertinent ethical issues one may find in the midst of a technological disruption brought about by widespread automation and use of artificial intelligence (AI). That is, until you call into question some of their tacit assumptions about innovation, technology, the good life, and themselves. In this chapter, two educators reflect on their respective experiences teaching AI ethics and adjacent topics in Canada, Germany, Ireland, Switzerland, and the United States. We relay our interdisciplinary teaching experiences at the undergraduate, graduate, and executive education levels in schools of communication, universities of technology, and business schools. Our perspective focuses on critical self-reflection and the opportunities and challenges of teaching AI ethics in these contexts. We provide a brief overview and reflect upon strategies that worked well for us, strategies that did not, and recommendations in order to bridge the chasm between the two.

T. Busch (✉)
Zurich University of Applied Sciences, School of Management and Law, Winterthur, Switzerland
e-mail: buth@zhaw.ch

F. M. Chee
Loyola University Chicago, School of Communication, Chicago, IL, USA
e-mail: fchee@luc.edu

C. H. Hoffmann, D. Bansal (eds.), *AI Ethics in Practice*, Integrated Science 35,
https://doi.org/10.1007/978-3-031-87023-1_4

1 Introduction

The past 10 years have seen huge swings in the public perception of, and opinion on, technologies such as social media, cryptocurrencies, and AI. For instance, while there was initial hype around social media and the alleged democratization they would bring about (Busch and Shepherd 2014), things took a dark turn with the 2016 U.S. election and the Cambridge Analytica scandal (Streitfeld 2017), which eventually resulted in a broader "techlash" (Goldberg 2020). Similar developments have been happening in artificial intelligence (AI) recently, with the post-ChatGPT hype around generative AI slowly being replaced by critical questions regarding intellectual property, privacy, and human creativity, followed by countless open letters and court cases. Consequently, discussions about the ethics of AI have garnered attention in mainstream media and among businesspeople in a wide range of industries.

Thus, the need for orientation and critical education around the ethics of AI, as well as the "dark side" of technology in general, has never been clearer (Singer 2018). It is worth pointing out that this need for education is not limited to computer science students at the early stages of their careers. Instead, as debates around a "Hippocratic Oath for data science" (Eubanks 2018) and the responsibility of computing professionals (Schuler 2020) have shown, it also applies to professionals in a wide range of engineering and tech-related disciplines. And today, with the advent of ubiquitous, everyday tools such as ChatGPT, knowledge of AI ethics has become a much-needed skill in most industries, both at the operational and the strategic level.

Against this background, our chapter reflects upon our experiences teaching ethics of technology in various disciplinary and educational settings. We have been teaching AI ethics, responsible innovation, corporate social responsibility, digital ethics, computational research methods, and game studies, as well as adjacent topics, in Canada, Germany, Ireland, Switzerland, and the United States over the course of more than a decade now, and this chapter covers our teaching experience at the undergraduate, graduate, and executive education levels in schools of communication, universities of technology, and business schools. While this personal approach does not lend itself to making sweeping generalizations across the globe, we do believe that our experience covers quite a lot of ground that will be of interest to readers from a wide range of professional and educational contexts. And while we would like to claim that things have been going great this entire time, we consider it our professional duty to also point out the things that we found challenging, so that readers may learn from those as well. Before we get to the caveats, however, we shall start with the positive aspects of teaching AI ethics.

2 The Good

As pointed out above, AI ethics has become a near-ubiquitous issue today. That is a huge advancement compared to a decade ago, as it means that dedicated AI ethics textbooks and other teaching materials are widely available to educators now. Moreover, the mainstreaming of AI ethics also makes it significantly easier for critical educators to be taken seriously in contexts that tend to only wish to hear about the opportunities of new technologies, and not so much about their challenges. The following sections thus describe some positive tendencies that educators in the domain of ethical AI will find to work in their favor.

2.1 AI Ethics Has Become a Hotly Debated Issue

AI ethics has gotten a lot of public attention lately, not least because of the many controversies that have been sparked by the advent of generative AI in education and business. For instance, the public launch of ChatGPT in late 2022 caused widespread panic among educators across all educational levels, from high schools to universities, calling into question not only how written exams, term papers, and theses could be identified as genuinely human in the future, but also what the general purpose of education should be going forward. After all, what purpose does a term paper or Bachelor's thesis serve when students can easily have it written by some generative AI tool instead of going through the laborious process of doing all their research and writing themselves? Perhaps it is time for educators to just abandon ship and leave education to technology? Or, one might argue instead, perhaps schools should just outright ban all technology, as it robs kids of their capacity to learn valuable life skills?

In business, on the other hand, AI has sparked both hopes and fears when it comes to useful shortcuts and cost-cutting initiatives across almost all industries. Whether it be providing useful help when it comes to writing computer code, legal advice for specific business decisions, or automating data collection for corporate sustainability reports, AI has been touted as the universal tool to solve all problems in business. The flipside to those hopes is reflected in fears of workers being surveilled constantly in their offices and factories, and in entire industries getting automated, resulting in mass layoffs. Recent debates and lawsuits regarding whether or not generative AI should be allowed to be trained on artists' work have made headlines, and the strikes in the film and digital game industries have demonstrated that many stakeholders are highly concerned by the fact that AI might put them out of business altogether.

In practice, of course, the above-mentioned fears in education and business are valid, but perhaps not as clear-cut as one might assume. For now, at least, AI tools have not been as great as their proponents claim, hallucinating academic sources and court cases, and thus demonstrating an increased need for critical thinking across all sectors. Therefore, these debates are useful for educators when it comes to teaching AI ethics, as there is a plethora of current debates to draw from when engaging with a wide range of audiences. Thus, this is a good moment to ask what a genuinely critical and future-proof education should look like, and perhaps it is indeed time to let go of certain traditional forms of exams in education or repetitive tasks in business. In many ways, then, current debates on tools such as ChatGPT are reminiscent of the early days of Wikipedia: It took a while for educators to wrap their minds around how to usefully and critically make use of such a tool, but eventually, educators and students managed to develop a new kind of critical data literacy, which is exactly what is needed when it comes to the uses of AI.

2.2 AI Ethics is Relevant to a Wide Range of Audiences

As generative AI has been going mainstream, so too has the need for AI ethics become crystal clear across many industries. Indeed, professionals across a wide range of industries and careers need orientation when it comes to thinking critically about AI and technology in general because their careers have either been affected by debates around AI already or they will do so shortly. For educators, this presents many opportunities to connect with professionals when it comes to ethical issues, as AI ethics has been moving from a fairly obscure ivory tower issue toward an increasingly normalized skill. Thus, in many ways, AI ethics today is a step toward the professionalization of dealing with technology in business, similar in many ways to how corporate sustainability management and corporate social responsibility (CSR) have been professionalized and matured over the course of the past 20 years or so.

This trend toward the professionalization of ethical reflection skills in technology and business is highlighted by previous work in the engineering professions. While our teaching experience shows that these efforts so far are largely unfamiliar to engineering students and managers in many industries, there has indeed been pioneering work when it comes to developing professional codes of ethics by associations such as the ACM and IEEE (ACM 2018; IEEE 2020). Some current guidelines and codices even expressly connect AI ethics with employee well-being and other social sustainability indicators as metrics for AI ethics, and they contextualize the social and environmental impact of AI by making reference to normative frameworks such as human rights and the United Nations Sustainable Development Goals, as well as CSR and ESG (environmental, social, and governance) criteria in business (Danish Institute for Human Rights 2024; IEEE SA 2023; Montréal Declaration 2024; UN B-Tech Project 2024).

For educators, this pioneering work done by industry professionals helps make the case in the classroom that engineering and business are not ethically neutral domains. Instead, seeing as it is AI practitioners themselves that have identified the need for ethical guidance and reflection, and subsequently codified it in specific codices and guidelines, educators can connect AI ethics to a wide range of challenges and use cases across many professions and industries. In doing so, educators can contextualize ethical perspectives and connect them easily to critical thinking, philosophical inquiry, discussions of professional conduct and responsibility, and business ethics in general, all of which is much easier to do today than it used to be a decade ago.

2.3 A Wide Range of Institutions and Programs Are Open to Discussing AI Ethics

Because of the urgency and ubiquity of the topic, many academic and non-academic programs alike are open to discussing AI ethics today. For instance, as pointed out above, schools need to address what traditional concepts such as learning, authorship, and academic integrity should mean in an age of generative AI. And that is a matter of grave importance not only in some imaginary, distant future, but one for right now instead. Similarly, in business, conflicts over AI-driven automation and intellectual property will require both new technical literacies and social debates as to what stakeholders consider fair and just. Thus, as Singer (2018) has pointed out, the "dark side" of tech is increasingly getting addressed in a wide range of academic programs today. For educators, this provides an excellent opportunity to cover AI ethics across a broad range of channels.

For instance, we have been addressing tech ethics more broadly and AI ethics in particular in classes on business innovation, business ethics, international business, digital marketing ethics, and game studies. In all these disciplines, it turned out to be very easy to find cases and debates that lend themselves well to discussing normative issues arising from the use of technology. For instance, when it comes to media and ethics, current debates around generative AI allow educators to address how AI challenges the way we understand the importance of creative content, game art, code, and design as uniquely human creative expressions versus a mere Taylorist fantasy of mass-producing game assets at ever-decreasing cost and larger scale. In similar fashion, it should be easy to discuss AI ethics across a wide range of programs in departments of law, social sciences, humanities, engineering, medical sciences, and the arts.

An institutional trend that is helpful in this regard is the fact that ethics education has been given more room in recent years not only by professional associations but also across academic departments. For instance, when it comes to business schools, international accreditation organizations today only give their seals of approval to schools which can demonstrate that ethics plays a vital role in their curricula. Accordingly, this trend can serve as a conversation starter and an institutional inroad for educators trying to establish new courses on AI ethics in their school or department.

2.4 AI Ethics Provides Opportunities for Experiential Learning

One of the toughest challenges of teaching AI ethics is the fact that many core concepts and technical aspects of AI are very complex, abstract, and hard to parse, especially for students in non-technical programs. This makes finding simple and elegant ways of explaining how machine learning or generative AI work, even just at their most basic technical layer, quite difficult. Beyond this basic factual layer of AI, it is even more difficult to realistically assess, critically question, and demystify the many social and ethical aspects surrounding technology. Thus, one of the main challenges of teaching AI ethics is how to get across the key ethical challenges without either simplifying the inner workings of technologies too much or falling victim to their technical complexities altogether.

At first, this can be a daunting task, but in many cases, one can make ethical AI more accessible using experiential learning. For instance, a classic insight in AI ethics is the fact that technology is never morally neutral. Challenges such as bias in machine learning systems have been discussed among scholars and technologists for a long time already, but it is difficult to explain these issues to lay people in such a way that it is both easily accessible and relevant to their experience. One easy way of using experiential learning to get this point across is to give students tools that feel unusual to the majority of people. For instance, we have been giving students left-handed scissors and coffee cups with asymmetrically shaped handles designed for right-handed people. Having students interact with these everyday objects makes it easy to get the point across that tools (in other words, technologies) are often made with an implicit idea of a "normal" user in mind. So, when we ask students to use these objects for a few minutes to see if they feel natural to them, it becomes clear quite quickly that not every tool works equally well for everyone, an insight which can then be applied to the issue of bias in machine learning systems.

Another helpful type of experiential exercise is to divide students into groups, where one group takes on the role of Silicon Valley venture capitalists while the other groups are supposed to be tech start-up entrepreneurs whose task it is to pitch business ideas to VCs. One can come up with many variations on this exercise, but it is usually helpful to frame it in such a way that the exercise is only about maximizing profit for VCs, and nothing else. (This is in reference to Milton Friedman's infamous 1970 statement that the social responsibility of business is to increase its profits, and nothing else.) Business pitch documents or prompts can be prepared beforehand and given to student groups as hand-outs, and each business case should be deeply and obviously immoral. For instance, pitches might include prompts such as "Tinder, but for trading human organs" or "Netflix, but for illegal substances." Despite the (hopefully) obvious humorous angle, students usually take their roles very seriously and get drawn into people-pleasing behavior and groupthink quickly. The students taking on the role of VCs often end up enjoying being catered to and having power. In the end, only one pitch can win, and the VCs need to decide which group promises the highest profits, regardless of moral concerns. Obviously, there should be a post-exercise discussion during which students have the opportunity to reflect on their experience. During discussions, students understand how easy it is to overlook ethical aspects when one gets caught up in competitive dynamics or single-minded business processes, such as brainstorming meetings that only focus on profit interests.

2.5 Good Practices and Recommendations

In addition to our remarks on experiential learning above, this section will provide some general recommendations regarding AI ethics education. None of these are rocket science, of course, but they do reflect our experience, and they present a rather hopeful and optimistic take before we move on to the challenging aspects of teaching AI ethics in the latter sections of this chapter.

First of all, when it comes to the institutional framing device for AI ethics in the context of a class, course, module or program, the approach that will likely have the highest chance of being accepted by both administrators and students alike is to show how AI ethics today is a matter of professionalism. In that sense, AI ethics should be treated like issues such as CSR, corporate sustainability management, or responsible accounting practices. Those concepts used to be novel and in need of institutional legitimacy 20 years ago. Since then, they have become mainstream, and in a similar fashion, AI ethics today can be framed as a set of must-have skills that professionals in any domain need to be familiar with in addition to a wide range of others. So, instead of needing to take a missionary or even preachy stance on it, educators can simply point to the practical need and demand for professional AI ethics skills in a wide range of industries today.

Second, as laid out above, educators today can point to a wide range of ethics principles, codices, guidelines, declarations, and commitments on AI ethics that have been established in the past decade or so. When it comes to AI ethics education, this makes it much easier than before to establish the practical relevance and legitimacy of thinking critically about technologies. Moreover, AI ethics codices can be shown to be a regular part of an interconnected network of normative guidelines in business, such as the United Nations Sustainable Development Goals, the UN Guiding Principles on Business and Human Rights, standards and guidelines in the domains of CSR, supply chain responsibility, corporate sustainability reporting, and many others. Thus, educators will be able to easily demonstrate that AI ethics does not play out in some sort of normative vacuum and that it does not need to be artificially inserted into the curriculum. Instead, business and technology have always been imbued with values and intertwined with many implicit moral norms, and the recent establishment of normative guidelines has just made that more explicit and transparent for all stakeholder groups involved.

When it comes to actually teaching AI ethics in the classroom, AI ethics by and large is an issue like any other. However, as we will show in Sects. 3 and 4 of this chapter, teaching AI ethics has some specific challenges, so some strategies have a tendency to work better than others. For instance, as one would expect, things generally tend to work more smoothly when educators try to approach the issue from their students' various points of view. During the Covid years, for example, many students had to deal with proctoring software, so it is fairly easy to have debates about the ethicality of such software solutions because students will likely have had first-hand experience with their downsides. Similarly, most students are familiar with technologies such as social media or dating platforms and their respective risks. Thus, bringing students in by beginning a class with cases and examples that seem familiar and not all that controversial to them is certainly helpful. In addition, this approach also has the benefit of nurturing within our students a sense that they, too, are in positions where they can educate others.

When it comes to instigating deeper ethical reflection at a later stage in a class or program, we have found bottom-up approaches to be even more fruitful and important. For instance, in an executive MBA program with experienced business practitioners, it is worth taking the time to give them critical reflection prompts and just let them talk to one another in a guided fashion, either in small groups or in a plenary session. In an executive MBA setting of two full days of teaching, our experience shows that making the first day an interactive input and lecture day is a good start, but the most intense learning and reflection take place on the second day, when we ask students to critically reflect on the hardest professional struggles they have yet encountered in their respective careers. We ask them to describe their challenges to their classmates, apply the theories of the class to their issues in hindsight, and to engage in critical reflection and discussion with the group. That way, not only do students train the application of theories to their actual experience, they also engage in peer learning, build empathy with one another, understand other industries, careers, and contexts, and also create long-lasting group cohesion.

Of course, we have to acknowledge the privilege embodied in this process, as it requires time and resources that are increasingly rare to find in academia today. But in any class setting, we would argue that educators should somehow try and find the time to let students talk more about their experience instead of just lecturing at them because ultimately, the goal is to make them more sensitive and open-minded toward ethical issues in tech, and not just to pass an exam. Ideally, instead of a top-down approach, one should opt for a co-design approach whenever possible (Chee et al. 2021). Lastly, we should acknowledge that teaching AI ethics can be challenging for educators because many of the issues that need addressing are so obviously and deeply unethical that it can be difficult to stay calm and not come off as preachy, judgmental, or prejudiced. If we want students to be open-minded, educators need to lead by example, which our role as critical subject-matter experts can sometimes get in the way of. Ultimately, though, educators will want to be perceived by their students as calm and trustworthy because that is the prerequisite to running classes in which students feel like they are invited to be honest and vulnerable.

3 The Bad

Now that we have demonstrated some reasons for why educators should be optimistic about teaching AI ethics, Sects. 3 and 4 of this chapter will briefly introduce some caveats and challenges. These vary in terms of severity, and we will begin with the relatively harmless ones before moving on to the real structural challenges in Sect. 4.

3.1 AI Itself Is a Moving Target

Like any technology in recent decades, AI has been evolving rapidly when it comes to technical aspects, business use cases, and social conflicts, which makes it difficult for educators to keep up with the pace of recent developments. This also includes questions about what even is the definition of AI, to whom this matters, and in what context it may make a substantial difference. As recent debates and open letters around artificial general intelligence (AGI) have shown, interpretations of what may or may not count as AI vary wildly among experts, as do evaluations of how dangerous certain technical developments may be (Hanna and Bender 2023). Similarly, the generative AI boom that started in late 2022 with the public launch of ChatGPT may already be cooling off again from a technical perspective, but in the business domain, consulting companies are still making vast amounts of money on generative AI projects. Thus, due to business hype and systemic lag across societal subsystems, debates on AI evolve constantly, but at different speeds for different stakeholder groups. This is what makes the topic interesting to begin with, but also hard to keep up with. Accordingly, both AI itself and AI ethics are moving targets evolving so quickly that staying up to date can be hard for educators who, in today's accelerated academy, are constantly pressed for time.

3.2 AI Contexts are Extremely Complex

While it is generally a good sign that a wide range of audiences care about AI ethics today, the many different contexts that have been increasingly affected by AI make things complicated for practitioners and educators alike. For instance, technologies like generative AI produce entirely different challenges and opportunities in different contexts. As recent strikes by U.S. video game voice actors have shown, generative AI is a threat to the livelihood of many stakeholders in a wide range of creative industries. In the context of the game industry, game development studios could easily train generative AI systems to sound like a voice actor instead of hiring an actual person. From a management perspective, this means that generative AI tools provide excellent cost-cutting opportunities. Similar conflicts play out in Hollywood, the animation industry, in music, software engineering, legal and business consulting, etc. In all these domains, the people making and benefitting from technologies will experience AI radically differently from the people being subjected to these technologies. For AI ethics educators, it may be tempting to use broad and generalizing ethical theories to make sense of these developments. However, as useful as this approach may be, we would encourage educators to use it only in combination with industry-specific perspectives that do not underestimate the complexities of the respective contexts that AI technologies have been introduced in.

3.3 Some People Really Hate It When You Criticize Their Favorite Toys

In addition to complex theoretical and technical challenges, there are also emotional challenges when it comes to teaching AI ethics. Based on our experience, different audiences will respond differently to different forms of critique. As we found out the hard way, sometimes educators will be greeted with extremely emotional responses when they critique the ethical downsides of technologies. For instance, we repeatedly witnessed grown men lose their cool and throw actual hissy fits when we introduced issues such as bias in machine learning. Moreover, we have also been confronted with quasi-religious commitment to certain technologies, especially blockchain, cryptocurrencies, and NFTs, during times when they were at the height of their respective hype cycles. Thus, empirically speaking, it would seem that a certain percentage of professionals are quite literally unable to discuss AI based on ethical principles. Instead, they will feel personally attacked and insulted when their favorite toys get called out for unethical practices. This may be understandable in cases where technical people feel insulted when educators simplify technical aspects to such a degree that technical experts will experience this as a strawman attack. However, aside from mere rhetoric, there are also structural reasons at play here, where some students may have a major part of their emotional and professional identity invested in a certain technology, or they may be financially invested in a certain technology in one form or another. So, AI ethics education is easy until one calls into question some of the audience's tacit assumptions about innovation, technology, the good life, and themselves. Unfortunately, this is a reality that educators will need to live with, and they should try their utmost not to let an entire class get dragged into an unpleasant and unproductive atmosphere because of the immature behavior of a small number of students.

4 The Ugly

Having briefly discussed some difficult but relatively harmless challenges when it comes to teaching AI ethics, we will introduce some long-term structural challenges in the following sections. These challenges are difficult to acknowledge and deal with, but educators across a wide range of contexts should be prepared to face them.

4.1 Toxic Online Campaigns and Debates Have Poisoned the Well for Everyone

In many ways both big and small, social media discourse over the past 20 years has gone from boldly utopian to full-on dystopian. Since the 2014 "Gamergate" hate campaign against socially inclusive game makers and journalists, the design of online interactions on social media has gotten increasingly focused on engagement at all cost, no matter how risky and dangerous things may get for vulnerable stakeholder groups. "Gamergate" has since become the playbook for online hate campaigns, as demonstrated by the 2016 U.S. federal election campaign and its consequences for political discourse online. Things have gotten even worse recently as a result of Elon Musk's take-over of Twitter, which has since had much of its platform safety team removed to the further detriment of the quality of public discourse overall. Consequently, debates on technology in general and AI ethics in particular play out in extremely heated and toxic online spaces today.

This development has led to negative consequences for classroom interactions both on- and offline. In many ways, toxic online behavior has set the bar for what students expect from face-to-face interactions, whether it be chat comments during an online class or hostile comments against educators who are perceived as being in the opposite political camp. Of course, not all classroom interactions these days are negative, but the toxicity learned implicitly on social media platforms is yet another factor educators need to consider and actively manage when teaching AI ethics. That is because today, any issue or opinion could potentially get instrumentalized politically, framed as controversial, and subsequently scandalized, especially when it comes to matters of normative judgment and critique. Thus, ethics classes are by their very nature more vulnerable to being perceived as "political" or biased from students' points of view. Accordingly, it has become increasingly difficult for educators to provide a safe learning environment, which is why some scholars recommend de-emphasizing class discussions and focusing on individual reflection and artistic projects instead (Martineau and Cyr 2024). This challenge will likely persist long-term, much like the next one.

4.2 AI Ethics Educators Will Need to Manage the Ethics and DEI Backlash

When it comes to AI ethics, many discussions involve pointing out that managers and technologists have a responsibility to use and design technologies in ways that do not harm vulnerable stakeholder groups. In many of these cases, the main problem is that decision makers often find themselves in a relative position of privilege, which makes them blind to the effects that technologies may have on vulnerable communities (Costanza-Chock 2020). For instance, one of the most widely discussed issues is bias in machine learning systems, an issue that by its very nature often goes unnoticed due to designers' privileged perspectives (Simon et al. 2020). This is a problem because there are few checks and balances internally at tech companies, as many high-profile tech companies have laid off parts of their ethics teams recently (De Vynck and Oremus 2023), and studies have shown that AI developers tend to deny or downplay the negative effects of their products (Duke 2022; Widder et al. 2023).

The elephant in the classroom, then, is that whenever bias is discussed with current or future decision makers in AI, said discussion makes transparent that there are vulnerable stakeholders who are on the receiving end of bias, which in turn necessarily involves some form of critical judgment of the technologies, managers and designers whose decisions are the cause of such forms of bias. Therefore, given the setting most AI ethics classes play out in, i.e., business schools and universities of technology, some members of the audience will inevitably feel uncomfortable with implicitly or explicitly getting called out for technological biases and design decisions that are considered ethically problematic. This frequently results in spontaneous and intense emotional reactions from audience members who will feel attacked, criticized, or accused of being privileged or immoral in some fashion and who then find it difficult to regulate their emotions in real-time.

Indeed, we have been faced with having to anticipate and actively manage risky classroom situations such as these on many occasions. While we can empathize with such emotionally triggered reactions and find them perfectly understandable from a psychological point of view, they can derail classroom discussions and endanger the learning experience of the class if they are not reflected upon with the audience. When done with empathy and care, however, this also presents a learning opportunity, though one that will take time and effort to instigate. The most productive scenario in such cases is to ask audience members to critically reflect on general concepts their communities may take for granted, as this makes matters feel less personal and accusatory. For instance, one might ask open questions regarding solutionism or concepts such as innovation, which are by default considered to be morally good in tech and business communities. That way, one can make the more general point that everyone is emotionally attached to their preconceived notions of how the world is supposed to function and how they should do their jobs. In this context, however, educators need to bear in mind that diversity efforts can easily get relegated to merely being performative if they do not get contextualized critically (Carrillo Arciniega 2021).

4.3 AI Hype Makes It Difficult to Have Reasonable Conversations

Lastly, an issue that makes it particularly difficult to discuss AI ethics without triggering highly emotional responses is technology hype, and in particular the climate of FOMO (fear of missing out) around generative AI across many industries that started with the public unveiling of ChatGPT in late 2022. Since then, tech companies have been in a collective gold rush to present generative AI as the be-all and end-all of future technologies for mainstream business, and many tech leaders seem to want to outdo one another with lofty promises of artificial general intelligence in the near future (Hanna and Bender 2023). FOMO-inducing marketing messaging by tech companies and consulting agencies has been suggesting in no unclear terms that businesses need to either get on the generative AI bandwagon now or they will go out of business soon. Accordingly, instead of developing generative AI technologies cautiously and slowly, many tech companies have been laying off their AI ethics teams, as FOMO and hype have created a collective pressure on tech companies to go after quick land grabs in this new market (De Vynck and Oremus 2023).

Of course, technology hype is in no way a new phenomenon, as illustrated, for instance, by Gartner's hype cycle, which in past iterations has featured technologies that never actually made the huge breakthroughs that were promised, such as blockchain and NFTs (Gartner 2024). But while the hype cycle may produce results that are entirely predictable for technology insiders, mainstream business and educational institutions alike have been falling victim to generative AI FOMO to a surprising degree recently (Bender and Hanna 2024). As a result, unrealistic expectations regarding the power of AI have become emotionally charged for many business people who are afraid of going out of business in case they bet on the wrong technological horse. Similarly, in many educational settings, generative AI has been uncritically framed as the inevitable future of education.

In both business and education, FOMO around generative AI has made it difficult for AI ethics educators to be heard because many audience members feel subconscious pressure to get in on this new market, and they experience cognitive dissonance that often expresses in the classroom as aggressive behavior. Unfortunately, this makes it difficult to develop a much-needed sense of critical self-reflection within the context of how one should approach technologies as a professional. However, as educators, we have a responsibility to critically question the underlying assumptions of decision-making in business and technology, unless we wish to repeat the mistakes that business schools made until 20 years ago in the context of uncritically teaching concepts such as shareholder value that have been thoroughly debunked since (Ghoshal 2005).

5 Conclusion

In this chapter, we have reflected upon our experiences teaching AI ethics and related subjects over the course of more than a decade in various educational settings and multiple countries. We have shown that the underlying structural conditions for successfully teaching AI ethics are much better today than a decade ago, as AI ethics has become a hotly debated issue that is relevant to a wide range of different audiences and institutions. Moreover, we have given several examples of how educators can benefit from these positive tendencies, and we have made recommendations as to how educators can improve their practices when it comes to teaching AI ethics.

At the same time, we have pointed out several challenges when it comes to teaching AI ethics, including the fact that AI technologies are evolving rapidly, that the contexts in which they are deployed are highly complex, and that students may have strong emotional reactions when their favorite technologies get criticized or called out. Furthermore, we have pointed to some ongoing structural issues that make AI ethics education a challenging endeavor, including the fact that toxic online debates have set the tone for many debates on ethical issues, that educators will likely be confronted with a backlash to conversations around diversity, equity, and inclusion, and that AI hype and FOMO make it difficult to have reasonable debates about the opportunities and challenges of technologies.

We hope that educators in the domain of AI ethics will benefit from our experience, and we encourage them to share theirs with each other. Going forward, in order to reach as wide a range of stakeholders as possible in the expanding domain of AI-related industries, we will need to think ahead and address channels beyond the formal education system and traditional academic publishing venues. At the macro level, this may include triple-helix approaches involving policy, industry, and academia. At the meso level, business organizations may need to strengthen internal peer learning practices, constructive involvement of internal and external stakeholders, and principle-led decision-making processes around the deployment of AI. And at the micro level, individual students may look for information on AI ethics outside of traditional educational and professional channels, so AI ethics education may need to take into account social media platforms, micro-credential programs, or platforms for sharing computer code and similar technical assets. As unpredictable as the future of AI ethics education may be, one thing is certain: Developing critical AI literacies will require a collective effort in professional education, continuing education in business, and within the broader technology ecosystem.

References

ACM (2018) Code of ethics and professional conduct. https://www.acm.org/code-of-ethics

Bender EM, Hanna A (2024) Mystery AI Hype Theater 3000. https://www.dair-institute.org/maiht3k/

Busch T, Shepherd T (2014) Doing well by doing good? Normative tensions underlying Twitter's corporate social responsibility ethos. Convergence 20(3):293–315. https://doi.org/10.1177/1354856514531533

Carrillo Arciniega L (2021) Selling diversity to white men: how disentangling economics from morality is a racial and gendered performance. Organization 28(2):228–246. https://doi.org/10.1177/1350508420930341

Chee FM, Hjorth L, Davies H (2021) An ethnographic co-design approach to promoting diversity in the games industry. Feminist Media Stud. https://doi.org/10.1080/14680777.2021.1905680

Costanza-Chock S (2020) Design Justice. Community-led practices to build the worlds we need. MIT Press, Cambridge. https://direct.mit.edu/books/oa-monograph/4605/Design-JusticeCommunity-Led-Practices-to-Build-the

Danish Institute for Human Rights (2024) Human rights impact assessment guidance and toolbox. https://www.humanrights.dk/tools/human-rights-impact-assessment-guidance-toolbox

De Vynck G, Oremus W (2023) As AI booms, tech firms are laying off their ethicists. The Washington Post, March 30. https://www.washingtonpost.com/technology/2023/03/30/tech-companies-cut-ai-ethics/

Duke SA (2022) Deny, dismiss and downplay: developers' attitudes towards risk and their role in risk creation in the field of healthcare-AI. Ethics Inform Technol 24(1). https://doi.org/10.1007/s10676-022-09627-0

Eubanks V (2018) A Hippocratic oath for data science. Personal Blog, February 21. https://virginia-eubanks.com/2018/02/21/a-hippocratic-oath-for-data-science/

Gartner (2024) Gartner hype cycle. https://www.gartner.com/en/research/methodologies/gartner-hype-cycle

Ghoshal S (2005) Bad management theories are destroying good management practices. Acad Manage Learn Edu 4(1):75–91

Goldberg E (2020) 'Techlash' hits college campuses. The New York Times, November 1. https://www.nytimes.com/2020/01/11/style/college-tech-recruiting.html

Hanna A, Bender EM (2023) AI causes real harm. Let's focus on that over the end-of-humanity hype. Sci Am. August 12. https://www.scientificamerican.com/article/we-need-to-focus-on-ais-real-harms-not-imaginary-existential-risks/

IEEE (2020) Code of ethics. https://www.ieee.org/content/dam/ieee-org/ieee/web/org/about/corporate/ieee-code-of-ethics.pdf
IEEE SA (2023) Prioritizing people and planet as the metrics for responsible AI. Ethically aligned design for business. https://standards.ieee.org/wp-content/uploads/2023/07/ead-prioritizing-people-planet.pdf
Martineau JT, Cyr A-A (2024) Redefining academic safe space for responsible management education. J Bus Ethics. https://doi.org/10.1007/s10551-024-05690-3
Montréal Declaration (2024) The Montréal Declaration for a responsible development of artificial intelligence. https://montrealdeclaration-responsibleai.com/the-declaration/
Schuler D (2020) History and the social responsibility of computing professionals. ACM SIGCAS Comput Soc 48(3–4):8–10. https://doi.org/10.1145/3383641.3383642
Simon J, Wong P-H, Rieder G (2020) Algorithmic bias and the value sensitive design approach. Internet Policy Rev 9(4) https://doi.org/10.14763/2020.4.1534
Singer N (2018) Tech's ethical 'dark side': Harvard, Stanford and others want to address it. The New York Times, February 18. https://www.nytimes.com/2018/02/12/business/computer-science-ethics-courses.html
Streitfeld D (2017) Tech giants, once seen as saviors, are now viewed as threats. The New York Times, October 12. https://www.nytimes.com/2017/10/12/technology/tech-giants-threats.html
UN B-Tech Project (2024) OHCHR and business and human rights. https://www.ohchr.org/en/business-and-human-rights/b-tech-project
Widder DG et al (2023) It's about power: what ethical concerns do software engineers have, and what do they (feel they can) do about them? Proceedings of the 2023 ACM Conference on Fairness, Accountability, and Transparency (FAccT '23). Association for Computing Machinery, New York, pp 467–479. https://doi.org/10.1145/3593013.3594012

Thorsten Busch is a senior lecturer in corporate responsibility, sustainability, and ethics of technology at the Zurich University of Applied Science's School of Management and Law. Moreover, he is a lecturer in game studies and responsible innovation at the University of St. Gallen. Before his current engagements, he taught at Trinity Business School in Dublin and at HEC Montréal. His award-winning research on a wide range of issues in digital ethics has been published in outlets such as the *Journal of Business Ethics, Ethics & Information Technology, and Convergence,* and it has been presented at leading international institutions, including MIT, University of Oxford, and McGill University. Among other positions, Thorsten was a postdoctoral fellow in game studies at Concordia University in Montréal, a Visiting Assistant Professor in corporate social responsibility at the University of Konstanz, and a senior research fellow in data ethics at the University of St. Gallen. In 2010, he took part in the Oxford Internet Institute's Summer Doctoral Program and was a visiting scholar at Harvard's Berkman Klein Center for Internet and Society. Thorsten holds an M.A. in political science, economics, and management from the University of Oldenburg and a PhD in organizational studies and cultural theory from the University of St. Gallen.

Florence M. Chee is an associate professor in the School of Communication and program director of the Center for Digital Ethics and Policy (CDEP) at Loyola University Chicago. She is also founding director of the Social & Interactive Media Lab Chicago (SIMLab), devoted to the in-depth study of social phenomena at the intersection of society and technology. Her research examines the social, cultural, and ethical dimensions of emergent digital lifestyles with a particular focus on the examination of artificial intelligence, games, social media, mobile platforms, and translating insights about their lived contexts across industrial, governmental, and academic sectors. She serves as an External Consultee to the Freedom Online Coalition's (FOC) Taskforce on Artificial Intelligence and Human Rights (T-FAIR) and is a Key Constituent of the United Nations 3C Roundtable on Artificial Intelligence. She has designed and taught graduate/undergraduate courses in Digital Media including Game Studies, where students engage with debates surrounding diversity, intersectionality, and media production through social justice frameworks.

AI and Language Interpreting

5

The Ethics of Breaking Down Language Barriers

Laura Keller

Abstract

The impact of widely accessible large language models on language interpreting has been limited for now. However, it has revolutionised not only data-based content generation but also text translation. It is therefore likely only a matter of time before a speech-to-speech translation features are added to the AI toolkit. This raises urgent questions for interpretation users and language professionals regarding the use and utility of language skills, interpreting skills, and the essence of human connection and communication. This chapter outlines the opportunities as well as the ethical challenges and caveats that arise with the digital transformation of the language services industry. It proposes framing ethics as the basis for innovation to allow harnessing the advantages of AI solutions without falling prey to the dangers of rendering multilingual communication dysfunctional.

1 Introduction

Language carries culture and identity and plays an essential role in building rapport with others. Until now, we have relied on humans to be both at the origin of the messages encoded in language (Harari 2023) and to pass those messages from one language to another. Artificial intelligence (AI), and more specifically generative artificial intelligence (generative AI), is likely to revolutionise the way we communicate within and across languages. We appear to have reached a turning point. As Harari warns: "AI has […] hacked the operating system of our civilisation" (2023, n.p.). At a point where science-fiction gadgets reminiscent of those featured in

L. Keller (✉)
Geneva, Switzerland
e-mail: laura_keller@gmx.ch

C. H. Hoffmann, D. Bansal (eds.), *AI Ethics in Practice*, Integrated Science 35,
https://doi.org/10.1007/978-3-031-87023-1_5

movies enabling communication in and understanding of any language are as close to becoming reality as they have ever been, how can the case of conference interpreters help understand the implications of the use of AI in communication across languages? This chapter intends to shed light on the ethical questions that should be addressed when considering the place of AI in language interpreting.

New technologies changing the professional practise of language professionals are nothing new. Professional translators—multilingual language professionals working with written text—have been working with translation memories and other tools for computer-assisted translation (CAT) for years. Translation memories are databases of aligned segments of source and target text that are generally internal to the organisation or company within which they are used. They allow translators to rely on their own or other translators' previous work to speed up their task while adhering to specific rules regarding terminology and style. For certain language pairs and text types, automatic text translation has matured from producing hardly intelligible literal translations to output sometimes requiring little human post-hoc intervention (Horváth 2022; Moorkens and Guerberof Arenas 2024). In contrast, simultaneous interpreters,[1] who translate speech to speech in real time, have seen the nature and scope of their preparatory work change (e.g. the access to and use as well as the mining of electronic documents, or the use of new tools for vocabulary extraction and glossary creation). They may look up terminology in real time online or in their electronic glossaries while they are on mic. But the fundamentals of their work in the booth have remained largely the same since simultaneous interpreting premiered at the International Labour Organisation in 1927 (Bourneuf 2022; Gaiba 1998): Interpreters listen to the incoming speech over headphones and render the same message in a language different from the original into a microphone for the members of the audience who do not understand the language of the original.

Data-based systems—more successfully marketed as AI—are not a new technology. The term "artificial intelligence" is attributed to John McCarthy, who initiated an effort to make significant advances around the problem proposed over the course of the summer of 1956 (McCarthy et al. 2006). The group of ten scientists set out to work on the assumption that "every aspect of learning or any other feature of intelligence can in principle be so precisely described that a machine can be made to simulate it" (McCarthy et al. 2006, p. 12). Even though AI has obviously made tremendous strides since then, this turned out to be a greatly underestimated challenge.

The umbrella term AI englobes various technologies that rely on algorithms that enable to analyse large amounts of data and learn from it. For language interpreting, the most pertinent technologies are currently machine learning (ML) and deep

[1] This paper focuses on the profession of conference interpreters who i.a. work in the international multilateral system. The terms "conference interpreters", "simultaneous interpreters", and "interpreters" are used interchangeably. The ethical challenges addressed, however, may apply to interpreting regardless of the context.

learning (DL). ML relies on algorithms that use statistical methods to learn from the pre-processed data to make predictions, which makes it particularly suitable for natural language processing (Moorkens and Guerberof Arenas 2024). DL, sub-branch of ML, exploits artificial neural networks consisting of layers of interconnected nodes mimicking the neurons of a biological neural network. DL technology is a powerful tool for abstract pattern recognition and complex decision making. Speech recognition, for example, relies on DL (Sharifani and Amini 2023). Generative AI is yet another sub-category of DL (Kapoor and Narayanan 2024) and geared towards creative content generation—with just a few prompts, it can produce all sorts of outputs in seconds, from impressively coherent text to multilingual glossaries. As its purpose is to create new content and as it is vulnerable to hallucinations, relying on it for interpreting is risky at best. Generative AI, although it may appear sentient, is not Artificial General Intelligence (AGI). AGI, a form of superintelligence performing equally well or better than humans on every task and in every context, is the holy grail McCarthy and colleagues set out to create in the mid-1950s. In the 1980s, however, McCarthy admitted that the "problem of generality in artificial intelligence (AI) is almost as unsolved as ever" (McCarthy 1987, p. 1030). At the time of writing, AGI remains science fiction (Vallor 2024).

However, although AI is not a new technology, the more generalised access to it is new. The release of large language models (LLMs) to the general public in 2022, and the widespread access to generative AI it brought in its wake, brings about changes that are of a new quality. The numbers show that the uptake by a broader audience is considerable: Roughly two months post release, OpenAI's Chat-GPT registered an estimated 100 million users, the first application to reach such an impressive user base in such a short time, beating the then record holder Tiktok by a good seven months to the milestone (Hu 2023). In other words, the release of fairly matured LLMs has firmly placed anyone with internet access in the "fourth industrial revolution" (Bansal Forthcoming).

To put this metaphor into perspective, the "historical" industrial revolution, especially during the nineteenth century changed not only how people in Western societies worked but transformed the social and political landscape as a whole (Philbeck and Davis 2018). The concept of working hours (and a limit thereof), for example, stems from the invention of factory shifts. The emergence of a working class and the workers' movement goes back to the same origins. So does the difference in value attributed to work done inside the home and for a salary outside of it and the negative implications this continues to have for women (Zucca Micheletto 2020). Similarly, the changes this new revolution brings about are and will be profound. While they undoubtedly create new opportunities, they have the potential to amplify existing differences and injustices and, to come back to the world of work, are already starting to be felt in the workplace across industries. And as for the historic industrial revolution, they allow not just for business to be done as usual, albeit faster, but they are paving the way for a paradigm shift (Balasubramanian et al. 2021; Bansal Forthcoming; Ghassemi et al. 2023; Mollick and Euchner 2023).

2 Could AI Make Cross-Language Communication More Widely Available?

The different AI technologies available today combined are getting closer to covering the steps involved in interpreting—speech recognition, transcription, text translation, and text-to-speech voice generation are all available features. Finding cheap, easy, and accessible ways around language barriers is inherently attractive, and there are several reasons why those resorting to interpreting services consider using a tech-based solution instead of hiring human interpreters.

For one, AI-driven solutions are likely to be more easily scalable, which would drive inclusion, allowing—theoretically at least—for more languages to be considered and for more end users to be reached. Scalability in terms of number of languages, however, requires for the systems to be trained accordingly. However, major inequalities regarding the data available for different languages directly reflect very real geopolitical power dynamics. Second, availability restrictions due to working-hour limitations or time zones that apply to humans would fall by the wayside—while AI-based systems need electricity and may be vulnerable to hard- and software issues, they arguably do not need rest. As data-based systems are not prone to fatigue, this may additionally lead to higher consistency in performance—at a level to be determined. Additionally, data analytics would allow for the gathering and analysis of meta-data for easier targeting of service needs. Finally, the argument that probably carries the most weight is the alleged cost effectiveness of using a tech-based solution instead of living and breathing interpreters. However, the low-cost solutions widely available are sorely lacking, for example, in terms of data protection and confidentiality requirements. Implementing solutions that live up to the ethics and safety standards of clients may require a substantial initial investment. Therefore, for the arguments in favour of AI to be considered valid, any AI-based solution under scrutiny must be assessed in light of the regulatory safeguards it respects and the ethical principles it upholds. Two things an AI solution is unlikely to be is neutral or free. Therefore, as convenient as an instantly available simultaneous interpreter in our pockets may be to users at first sight, it is worth examining the presumed convenience of data-based systems against the deeper ethical implications of removing humans from cross-language communication.

3 Conference Interpreters and AI

Conference interpreters are experts in real-time cross-language communication and naturally, the profession is eying the changes AI is bringing with a dose of suspicion. Two camps seem to have formed within the profession regarding AI: Those who cannot wait to add AI-supported gadgets and tools to their preparation and interpreting workflow and those who would pull the plug on AI immediately, if only they could.

The enthusiastic adopters argue that it will not be AI that will replace human interpreters, it will be human interpreters working with AI who will replace human interpreters who do not. This argument is echoed across industries (Mollick 2024). To gain an edge, practitioners and academics from this camp—in some cases, the lines between industry and academia blur—are testing, recommending, and even developing AI-powered ways to support interpreters in their work (Fantinuoli 2023; Vivian 2024). For the time being, data on the actual use of AI tools for preparation and during assignments is scarce. A survey on the subject was launched in July 2024 and revealed that, for now, a majority of the conference interpreters surveyed actually do not use AI tools (Gillies 2024).

The endeavours to include AI-based tools into the interpreters' workflow have merit insofar that the technology undoubtedly has the potential of enhancing interpreters' performance. Not to mention that it is available, and—without falling too much into a naturalistic fallacy—it is arguably here to stay. For this camp, the focus lies with the practical applications of AI. While there are calls to include ethical safeguards such as data-protection measures and transparency, enhancing the interpreters' toolbox (or the interpreters themselves) to remain competitive appears to be the top priority.

The "doomsday" camp's arguments are unsurprisingly of much more conservative and cautious nature. The French trade union of translators and related professions that also represents interpreters (*Société française des traducteurs*, SFT), for example, recently released a manifesto calling for the respect for human creation and intellectual property and for a ban on replacing language experts by AI, for transparency regarding origin and genesis of contents as well as clear labelling of AI-generated contents, for a stop to the deterioration of working conditions for professional linguists in the globally growing language-service industry, as well as safeguarding measures to prevent professions linked to language teaching at school and university level from disappearing. The statement concludes with the observation that technology needs to remain a tool at the service of translators and interpreters who have allowed for dialogue between peoples for millennia (SFT 2024), echoing Hariri (2023)'s points. Scepticism vis-à-vis a new technology—and such a disruptive one on top—is to be expected and probably a wise initial reaction. There are valid reasons to fear getting left behind. However, fearmongering and claims of human superiority that are based on anecdotes and intuitions, but not backed by systematic empirical findings, are unlikely to help the cause. While the SFT trade union has the merit of formulating a position on the matter, the demands presented above are difficult if not impossible to enforce. The appeal is likely based on genuine concern for the wellbeing of its members, but the demands are unlikely to stir potential buyers. In other words, while the claims of a unique contribution humans can make exactly because they are human are not necessarily untrue, basing the assumption that humans are by default better or have an inalienable right to govern multilingual communication will likely fall short when trying to convince stakeholders whose top priority is their financial baseline.

4 Human Interpreters vs. Data-based Systems

The argument that humans with all their human flaws and shortcomings also have unique human contributions to make merits further exploration. One initially appealing argument that is widely put forward to argue in favour of human interpreters over the use of data-based systems is the capacity to feel empathy: While humans are naturally endowed with empathy, machines are not (Gonzalez-Oliver 2024). However, upon closer examination, that argument is less clear-cut than it seems: Chatbot-generated answers (ChatGPT-4 at the time) on a social media platform thread dedicated to medical questions not only scored higher in terms of content relevance, but received higher empathy scores than those of human physicians (Ayers et al. 2023). The researchers contextualise and nuance their findings, pointing to the absence of a personal doctor–patient relationship in that context, and particularly stressing that the chatbot answers were systematically longer than the answers provided by human physicians. Given that chatbots produce output substantially faster than a human typing, on the surface, a longer answer could be taken as an answer the author put more thought and care into, and the use of more empathetic language certainly also goes a long way. However, those who argue that empathy is a unique characteristic that human interpreters bring to the table but that is lacking in a data-based system are referring to the empathy human interpreters may feel. Those who find that data-based systems score high on empathy, on the other hand, are rating the empathy felt by the receivers of the communication, not by the system generating it. That empathy may just be reflected—as it is part of the human expression that is encoded in the data the system was trained with and feeds on (Vallor 2024). It appears that the system's ability to feel empathy and to form an authentic connection to the end user is not necessarily relevant to the end user's experience of empathy. Harari clearly labels this mismatch as a danger of generative AI (2023). The argument that AI does not get humour (Le Figaro avec AFP 2024) may encounter the same obstacles when trying to convince clients—if a joke brought to you by an AI makes you laugh, does it always matter whether the AI felt it was funny?

Perhaps a more relevant feature lacking in AI—at least in the absence of AGI—is intention. Intention in humans is informed by their goals and vulnerabilities. It is a "mental state that guides and organizes behavior. It is essentially a determination to act in a certain way or to bring about a certain state of affairs" (Shultz 2014/1980, p. 131). Intention necessarily also goes into the messages people want to get across, and the communicative intent of the original is at the core of what interpreters strive to convey.

All this is not to say that it is irrelevant that AI systems do not share the lived experience of humans. That they do not relate to one another or build rapport the same way humans do. That they have no ability to read the room. In short, that they are not sentient and that they do not feel. Rather, the relevant take-away here is that this key difference between data-based system and humans is only relevant in a context in which these aspects are valued, and their absence detracts from the desired outcome.

One issue that conference interpreters must contend with in some meetings within the multilateral system is not primarily linked to their role as such, but to the nature of the meetings. Some meetings appear entirely devoid of communicative intent, with delegates reading speeches into the minutes one after the other at top speed without reacting to or interacting with what other speakers said. For this type of exercise, where there is little communication happening and little rapport to be built, humans may indeed add little value, and AI may in fact be better suited to do the job. It would conceivably be better suited to take on the task of the delegates reading the speeches as well, leaving just AI systems processing data left and right. Or, perhaps those meetings could, prosaically, just be an email.

There are of course meetings that are held to inform, negotiate, find common ground, or make decisions and where the inclusion of the people present independently of language is crucially a matter of epistemic justice (Fricker 2007). It is in gatherings like these that reading the room, gauging the tension, and deciphering ambiguities and things left unspoken become decisive factors. Under these circumstances just translating the words is unlikely to do justice to the interaction in the room.

The target audience of the trade-union appeal above presumably consists of potential clients and users of interpreting services, in other words, those paying for them. It certainly makes sense to include the perspective of those who decide whether they are willing to spend money on interpreting services provided by humans in the discussion. However, what becomes apparent here is the tension between economic incentives and ethical imperatives from which different if not opposing approaches derive. It therefore seems expedient to sharpen the focus regarding the ethical implications of changing the place and role of humans in cross-language communication. Otherwise, human interpreters will be cut out of the communication circuit and the argument about human interpreters with AI replacing human interpreters without AI simply becomes a moot point.

5 What Are the Ethical Implications in the Context of Language Interpreting and AI?

Calls for digital ethics by design, for placing ethical considerations at the heart of the digital transformation, are becoming louder with use cases revealing the various shortcomings of data-based systems: biases present in the data leading to the amplification of racial biases in facial recognition software, gender-based discrimination (e.g. the Amazon hiring scandal), or voter manipulation (e.g. the case of Cambridge Analytica) to name but a few (Hong 2024). The Switzerland-based NGO AlgorithmWatch CH has recently launched an appeal to the Swiss government to regulate the use of AI to avoid discrimination (AlgorithmWatch CH 2024). By ethical implications, therefore, we refer to questions touching on how we as humans should live in a world where the use of AI is a force to reckon with (Byford and Thwaite 2023; Kirchschläger 2021; Kirchschläger 2023; Müller and Pannatier

2023) and where the power dynamics between humans and algorithms are at best muddled (Vallor 2024).

Against this backdrop, it becomes apparent that there are at least three important dimensions to ethics to consider for language interpreting: First, the general reflection on the ethical framework within which the use of AI technology should be embedded and the considerations that are relevant for the different stakeholders (here interpreters, users of interpreting services, but also society in general). They should touch on questions regarding ethical judgements, moral responsibility and accountability. Arguably, this dimension encompasses working conditions—from sound quality to length of assignments to pay, to name but a few—that need to be addressed bearing ethical concerns in mind. Second, the ethical considerations that should inform the training of AI systems to be used in an interpreting context, where the focus primarily lies on transparency regarding the origin of the data used and questions tied to intellectual property. And third, ethical challenges that arise when AI is used for interpreting that include protection and confidentiality of the data fed into the system from potentially confidential meetings, biases that are fed into the output and questions linked to accountability for mistakes.

While it may be implicitly clear, it seems important to make a point of why data protection regulations such as the EU's GDPR of 2018 or a regulatory framework for AI such as the EU AI Act of 2024 (GIP Digital Watch Observatory 2024) are important also from an ethical perspective: They provide regulatory safeguards for data protection, protection of privacy, and transparency, which are the arguments put forward also by the enthusiastic adopters of AI applications in interpreting discussed above. However, what must not be forgotten is that these protections have little value in and of themselves. They are means to an end: They serve to protect the fundamental rights and freedoms (Byford and Thwaite 2023) without which an open and diverse society based on human-rights standards is simply not possible (Jones 2023; Kirchschläger 2021). This includes the protection of linguistic diversity and of equal access to rights and remedies regardless of language. Language professions play an instrumental role in ensuring those rights, and placing the focus on this aspect would help strengthening their foothold.

Conference interpreters, most widely represented by their international association AIIC,[2] are by way of their professional code of ethics keenly aware of the third dimension of ethics mentioned above (issues revolving around using such technology while on the job, such as ensuring confidentiality or transparency regarding output generation). Those who are simultaneously part of the early-adopter camp are conscious of the importance of the second dimension as well (questions related to the source of the data that goes into training models). However, the more fundamental dimension of helping to ensure that the technologies used fulfil the requirements needed to protect the foundations of an open, diverse, and democratic society seems absent in the debate. This may be linked to ethical concerns being absent from training curricula (Horváth 2022; Ramírez-Polo and Vargas-Sierra 2023), but

[2] The acronym AIIC stands for the French name of the association, Assocation Internationale des Interprètes de Conférence.

perhaps this is simply a reflection of a perceived clash with one of the most strongly upheld principles of the profession: impartiality. It implies not taking sides or altering the message. While this is fundamental for accurate interpreting, supporting ethical AI solutions requires advocacy at least to a certain degree. However, the perceived tension between acting as a neutral conduit for the message to be conveyed and advocating for an ethical framework need not be, as it is precisely such a framework that allows for that neutrality to be exercised safely. To that end, the principle of impartiality, just like the principle of fidelity, needs to be restricted to the message and not applied too extensively, as may currently be the case. An informed discussion that includes all ethical dimensions of using AI for interpreting—the framework, the design properties of the technologies used, and the safeguards needed for their actual use. Because if the professionals—this includes practitioners, their professional associations, trainers, and researchers in the discipline—do not bring their expertise to this on-going discussion and contribute to upholding integral ethical standards, who will?

6 Where Do the Dangers of AI for Language Interpreting Lie?

One aspect that sets the on-going digital revolution apart from previous similarly ground-breaking changes is that this time around, knowledge-industry professions are the ones bearing the brunt of the change: Interpreters are just as concerned as lawyers, programmers, or physicians (Felten et al. 2023). As the PauseAI collective phrases it: "AI does not just replace our muscles as the steam engine did, it replaces our brains" (PauseAI 2024, p. n. p.).

However, unlike the expertise inherent to many of these professions, the language expertise interpreters bring to the table is perhaps one that is more easily dismissed. First because there is a continuum in terms of who performs interpreting acts in different contexts. The vast majority of cross-language communication is carried out by multilinguals and does not involve professional interpreters. It is simply part of how humans communicate.

Second, in contrast with other knowledge professions, a considerable component of conference interpreters' professional identity is invisibility—relating to them conveying the original message unaltered. This links back strongly to the principle of impartiality discussed above. Of course, the importance of not altering the message to be transmitted or of ensuring the confidentiality of the information contained in the message cannot be overstated. To protect these values regarding the message, invisibility and impartiality are crucial safeguards. They may even serve as a veil of protection to keep the focus away from possible biases or shortcomings of human interpreters—they are human after all. But the stance of the impartial and invisible conduit should apply to the message interpreters are tasked to convey in their professional capacity, not to their complete existence. While this approach may facilitate access to highly confidential information and settings—think of the calls for subpoenaing the interpreter working at the encounter between Trump and

Putin in 2018 (Frum 2019)—it has also created a misleadingly mechanical image of how interpreters carry out their work. Additionally, this position of neutrality makes it difficult to follow advice such as "[conference interpreters,] go make a ruckus" (Godin 2024) to stand out in comparison with AI.

Third, another factor that has been a growing challenge for multilingualism in the multilateral system is the prevalence of English. This is of course again a reflection of geopolitical power dynamics and illustrates the effects of valuing economic interests over ensuring access. This is not to criticise non-native speakers of English who put their second-language skills to good use, but rather to point out that while not everyone may need to rely on interpreting to be included in a meeting, ethically speaking, it is worth considering if the decision on whether the possibility of being included while speaking and listening to a language that is not English should be made on the basis of providing equal access rather than solely on the basis of economic considerations.

Equal access, however, is not a matter of language alone. Relying on technology to provide access to information and provide inclusion independently of language presupposes access to that technology. Currently, this is far from reality on a global scale due to the technology gap between rich and poor countries (Ringhof and Torreblanca 2022), enormous differences regarding access to the Internet (Ritchie et al. 2023) and an unequal representation of languages, cultures, and people in the data used for training of AI systems (Hong 2024; Müller and Pannatier 2023). In this context, the argument that tech-based solutions contribute to levelling the playing field is flawed.

Another serious risk that needs to be mitigated when considering integrating AI-based systems into cross-language communication revolves around responsibility and accountability for errors and transparency of how the outcome produced came to be. While human interpreters are not immune to making mistakes, they have the moral capacity required to take on the responsibility and to be held accountable for them. Data-based systems lack this moral capacity (Kirchschläger 2021). Additionally, generative AI technology is under scrutiny for issues related to transparency, the black-box problem making it difficult if not impossible to explain how a specific output was produced (Fleisher 2022; Von Eschenbach 2021).

On top of that, overreliance on tech-based solutions presents a series of dangers both from a technology and from a skills-related perspective. Technology, especially large-scale technological solutions, and especially when provided by private companies that are subject to little oversight, can be vulnerable to cyber-attacks, power outages or software issues, as the CrowdStrike chaos in July 2024 showed, grounding planes and affecting health care and financial services amongst others (Kerner 2024). Even regular in-person meetings are of course susceptible to technical problems, but with interpreters physically present, a work-around solution can be provided.

A more subtle, but perhaps also more perfidious danger comes from skills that are not honed or never even developed due to overreliance on technology. To examine the problem of diminishing skills from a language-skills perspective, relying (too) strongly on technology to access information in languages different from the ones learned when growing up or to communicate across language barriers could potentially take away incentives to learn other languages, a point the SFT trade-union includes in their manifesto (SFT 2024). However, not being able to communicate in or understand the language of an interlocutor creates a dependency that would only be reinforced by future generations growing up increasingly relying on technology for the same purpose as well. Removing humans as safeguards from the equation could therefore ultimately lead to deeper isolation instead of stronger connections.

Should the effort required for language learning no longer be deemed worthwhile and reliance on data-based system generalise, there would likely be little impetus to continue training interpreters or for trained interpreters to maintain their skill level. The expertise acquired—linguistic, cultural, communicational, and interpersonal—would be lost.

The menace, again, exceeds language skills. Vallor (2024) warns that the greatest danger for humanity from AI does not lie in AI developing sentience and turning evil, but rather from humanity allowing the skills most needed to adapt when faced with changing circumstances to diminish.

7 Conclusion and the Way Forward

AI can undoubtedly be of valuable assistance in language interpreting. Just as physicians assisting patients in telemedicine could benefit from using bots to draft replies (Ayers et al. 2023), AI tools could assist conference interpreters in their work in and outside the booth. However, to carry out their job to the highest ethical and professional standards, knowledge professions need to be able to rely on AI tools that meet the ethical requirements outlined above. This requires regulation, because currently such systems continue to be built, trained, and depicted as intelligent, although the measures used to determine intelligence are deemed invalid by experts (Bender and Koller 2020; Gubelmann 2024; Keegan 2024).

Again, it's not the technology of data-based systems that is new, it is the wide accessibility of AI applications that is. And the progress of AI is likely to continue. Against this backdrop, ethics in AI should not be viewed as a hindrance to innovation, but rather as innovation in and of itself (Byford and Thwaite 2023). Framing ethics instead of the emerging technologies as the innovate part may allow for a closing of ranks within and between knowledge professions on the fundamental values that are at stake.

Take-Aways for the Reader at a Single Glance

1. **Language barriers are a hindrance to access and inclusion:** Circumventing language barriers is instrumental to safeguarding linguistic diversity, epistemic justice and ensuring equal access to rights. Breaking down language barriers promotes inclusion and equity by enabling individuals and groups to fully participate in social, legal, and economic activities.

2. **AI-governance questions are questions of fundamental rights:** AI can enhance and broaden the access to cross-language communication, but relying primarily on AI to overcome language barriers comes with serious ethical caveats. AI brings numerous opportunities to enhance communication within and between languages, including potentially allowing more people access to democratic decision-making processes. However, for AI to be a force for good, ethical safeguards are needed on various levels. Regulatory oversight must ensure that fundamental rights and freedoms are protected and AI technologies used for cross-language communication must live up to ethical standards regarding data protection, confidentiality, transparency, and accountability.
3. **To value humans we must value their humanity:** The list of tasks AI can carry out faster and better than many humans is long. To value the role of humans in these systems, the humanity that they put into them—their sentience, their vulnerability, their moral competence, their intention—needs to be valued.
4. **Overreliance and skills depletion are risky:** Overreliance on technology bears the risk of skills depletion. Where language skills are concerned, initially convenient solutions may lead to isolation and increased uncertainty in communication. More generally, diminished abilities to adapt to change poses a real danger to the foundations of open societies.
5. **Framing AI ethics as innovation:** Framing ethical safeguards as innovation in regulatory frameworks, in the training of AI systems and in their use in high-stakes contexts, instead of prioritising technological advances alone, provides a way forward for knowledge professionals to join the debate on the frame of reference needed for them to uphold and contribute to open, democratic, and diverse societies based on human rights. Safe frameworks are necessary for knowledge professions to benefit from the opportunities of AI to work to the highest of their professional standards.

References

AlgorithmWatch CH. (2024). Künstliche Intelligenz mit Verantwortung… ohne Diskriminierung. In: AlgorithmWatch CH (ed)

Ayers JW, Poliak A, Dredze M, Smith DM (2023) Comparing physician and artificial intelligence Chatbot responses to patient questions posted to a public social media forum. JAMA Intern Med 183(6):589–596. https://doi.org/10.1001/jamainternmed.2023.1838

Balasubramanian R, Libarikian A, McElhaney D (2021) Insurance 2030 — the impact of AI on the future of insurance

Bansal D (Forthcoming) Embedding ethics in the Heart of Digital Revolution: how can companies use ethical decision-making intelligence to guide responsible technology implementation? In: Springer (ed)

Bender EM, Koller A (2020) Climbing towards NLU: on meaning, form, and understanding in the age of data. In Proceedings of the 58th Annual Meeting of the Association for Computational Linguistics

Bourneuf P-E (2022) Genève, Berceau de la Société des Nations, vol 3. United Nations Publications

Byford B, Thwaite A (2023, 17 September) The state of AI Ethics with Alice Thwaite In Machine Ethics. https://www.machine-ethics.net/podcast/the-state-of-ai-ethics-with-alice-thwaite/

Fantinuoli C (2023) Towards AI-enhanced computer-assisted interpreting. In: Corpas Pastor G, Defrancq B (eds) Interpreting technologies: current and future trends, 37th edn. John Benjamins, pp 46–71. https://doi.org/10.1075/ivitra.37.03fan

Felten EW, Raj M, Seamans R (2023) How will language modelers like ChatGPT affect occupations and industries? SSRN. https://doi.org/10.2139/ssrn.4375268

Fleisher W (2022) Understanding, idealization, and explainable AI. Episteme 19(4):534–560. https://doi.org/10.1017/epi.2022.39

Fricker M (2007) Epistemic injustice: power and the ethics of knowing. Oxford University Press. https://doi.org/10.1093/acprof:oso/9780198237907.001.0001

Frum D (2019, 14 January) Subpoena the Interpreter. The Atlantic. https://www.theatlantic.com/ideas/archive/2019/01/subpoena-trump-putin-helsinki-interpreter/580267/

Gaiba F (1998) The origins of simultaneous interpretation: the Nuremberg trial. University of Ottawa Press

Ghassemi M, Birhane A, Bilal M, Kankaria S, Malone C, Mollick E, Tustumi F (2023) ChatGPT one year on: who is using it, how and why? Nature 624:39–41. https://doi.org/10.1038/d41586-023-03798-6

Gillies A (2024, 26 October) AI tools and confidentiality in the booth: a survey. Interpreter Soapbox. https://interpretersoapbox.com/ai-tools-confidentiality-conference-interpreters-survey/

GIP Digital Watch Observatory (2024, 12 July) EU AI Act published in Official Journal, initiating countdown to legal deadlines. Geneva Internet Platform Digital Watch Observatory. https://dig.watch/updates/eu-ai-act-published-in-official-journal-initiating-countdown-to-legal-deadlines?

Godin S [AIIC Interpreters]. (2024) Seth Godin's message to AIIC. https://www.youtube.com/watch?v=AkkoA9j7BOU

Gonzalez-Oliver AM (2024) Brave new booth: interpreting at the dawn of the age of AI. UNtoday. https://untoday.org/brave-new-booth/

Gubelmann R (2024) Large language models, agency, and why speech acts are beyond them (for now) – a Kantian-Cum-Pragmatist Case. Philosophy Technol 37(1):32. https://doi.org/10.1007/s13347-024-00696-1

Harari YN (2023) Yuval Noah Harari argues that AI has hacked the operating system of human civilisation. The Economist. https://www.economist.com/by-invitation/2023/04/28/yuval-noah-harari-argues-that-ai-has-hacked-the-operating-system-of-human-civilisation?

Hong S-H (2024) AI and bias. In: Paul R, Carmel E, Cobbe J (eds) Handbook on public policy and artificial intelligence. Elgar, pp 109–122. https://doi.org/10.4337/9781803922171.00015

Horváth I (2022) AI in interpreting: Ethical considerations. Across Lang Cult 23(1):1–13. https://doi.org/10.1556/084.2022.00108

Hu K (2023, 02 February) ChatGPT sets record for fastest-growing user base. Reuters.

Jones K (2023) AI governance and human rights: resetting the relationship. https://www.chathamhouse.org/sites/default/files/2023-01/2023-01-10-AI-governance-human-rights-jones.pdf

Kapoor S, Narayanan A (2024) AI snake oil: what artificial intelligence can do, what it can't, and how to tell the difference. Princeton University Press. https://doi.org/10.1353/book.129007

Keegan J (2024, 17 July). Everyone is judging AI by these tests. But experts say they're close to meaningless. The Markup. https://themarkup.org/artificial-intelligence/2024/07/17/everyone-is-judging-ai-by-these-tests-but-experts-say-theyre-close-to-meaningless

Kerner SM (2024) CrowdStrike outage explained: what caused it and what's next. TechTarget. https://www.techtarget.com/whatis/feature/Explaining-the-largest-IT-outage-in-history-and-whats-next

Kirchschläger PG (2021) Digital transformation and ethics. Ethical considerations on the robotization and automation of society and the economy and the use of artificial intelligence. Nomos

Kirchschläger PG (2023) Ethisches Entscheiden. Nomos

Le Figaro avec AFP (2024, 07 May) Au coeur de l'UE les interprètes sont indispensables. Le Figaro. https://www.lefigaro.fr/langue-francaise/actu-des-mots/au-coeur-de-l-ue-les-interpretes-sont-indispensables-20240507

McCarthy J (1987) Generality in artificial intelligence. Commun ACM 30(12):1030–1035

McCarthy J, Minsky ML, Rochester N, Shannon CE (2006) A proposal for the dartmouth summer research project on artificial intelligence, August 31, 1955. AI Magazine 27(4):12. https://doi.org/10.1609/aimag.v27i4.1904

Mollick E (2024, 12 May) Superhuman. One Useful Thing. https://www.oneusefulthing.org/p/superhuman

Mollick E, Euchner J (2023) The transformative potential of generative AI. Res-Technol Manage 66(4):11–16. https://doi.org/10.1080/08956308.2023.2213102

Moorkens J, Guerberof Arenas A (2024) Artificial intelligence, automation and the language industry. In: Massey G, Ehrensberger-Dow M, Angelone E (eds) Handbook of the language industry. De Gruyter Mouton, pp 71–98. https://doi.org/10.1515/9783110716047-005

Müller A, Pannatier E (2023, 12 July) Schutz vor algorithmischer Diskriminierung. https://algorithmwatch.ch/de/diskriminierende-algorithmen/; https://algorithmwatch.ch/de/wp-content/uploads/2023/09/AlgorithmWatch-CH-Schutz-vor-algorithmischer-Diskriminierung-September-2023.pdf

PauseAI (2024) Risks of Artificial Intelligence. https://pauseai.info/risks

Philbeck T, Davis N (2018) The fourth industrial revolution shaping a new era. J Int Aff 72(1):17–22. https://www.jstor.org/stable/26588339

Ramírez-Polo L, Vargas-Sierra C (2023) Translation technology and ethical competence: an analysis and proposal for translators' training. Languages 8(2):93. https://www.mdpi.com/2226-471X/8/2/93

Ringhof J, Torreblanca JI (2022, 17 May) The geopolitics of technology: How the EU can become a global player. https://ecfr.eu/publication/the-geopolitics-of-technology-how-the-eu-can-become-a-global-player/

Ritchie, H, Mathieu, E., Roser, M., & Ortiz-Ospina, E. (2023) Internet. https://ourworldindata.org/internet

SFT (2024) Revendications Société Française des Traducteurs IA. In SFT (Ed.)

Sharifani K, Amini M (2023) Machine learning and deep learning: a review of methods and applications. World Inform Technol Eng J 10(07):3897–3904

Shultz TR (2014/1980) Development of the concept of intention. In: Collins WA (ed) Development of cognition, affect, and social relations: the Minnesota symposia on child psychology, vol. 13. Psychology Press, pp 131–164

Vallor S (2024) The AI mirror: how to reclaim our humanity in an age of machine thinking. Oxford University Press. https://doi.org/10.1093/oso/9780197759066.001.0001

Vivian I (2024, 22 June) How is AI shaping the interpreting profession? The Brussels Times. https://www.brusselstimes.com/belgium/1101090/how-is-ai-shaping-the-interpreting-profession

Von Eschenbach WJ (2021) Transparency and the black box problem: why we do not trust AI. Philosophy Technol 34(4):1607–1622. https://doi.org/10.1007/s13347-021-00477-0

Zucca Micheletto B (2020) Paid and unpaid work. In: Eibach J, Lanzinger M (eds) The Routledge history of the domestic sphere in Europe: 16th to 19th century. Routledge, pp 101–119. https://doi.org/10.4324/9780429031588

Laura Keller has worked as a freelance conference interpreter on the private and institutional markets in Geneva for over a decade. Her languages are German, English, French, Italian and Romansh. She has a background in interpreter training and experience in language policy consulting. Among Laura's degrees are an MA in conference interpreting and a PhD in interpreting studies, both from the University of Geneva, Switzerland. She is currently pursuing an MA in ethics, specialising in ethical considerations in the context of the digital transformation at the University of Lucerne, Switzerland.

Ethical Dilemmas and Human Factors in the Application of AI in Cybersecurity

6

Yanya Viskovich and Vibha Mohan

Abstract

The deployment of AI in organisations introduces complex ethical dilemmas. This chapter explores a number of these in the context of AI-enabled cybersecurity, critically examining organisational realities including surveillance, automation, lack of transparency, and their impact on organisational security culture through the lens of three principles for ethical decision-making: Maleficence, Autonomy and Transparency. It considers the impacts of the implementation of AI in cybersecurity operations: on employees, on work culture and on organisational cybersecurity efforts. Finally, it proposes practical strategies and a checklist for integrating ethical considerations into various stages of AI implementation in cybersecurity.

1 Introduction

Deploying AI in cybersecurity is like giving a highly skilled surgeon a shiny new scalpel. It can excise malicious threats with surgical precision, but without an ethical compass, it can slice through healthy tissue—leaving critical operations compromised and personnel bleeding trust. As AI systems grow more autonomous, the challenge isn't just making them faster or smarter. Organisations must consider the ethical implications of how they use these tools—before AI harms those it is designed to serve and protect.

Y. Viskovich (✉) · V. Mohan
Zürich, Switzerland
e-mail: ylmv@proton.me; vibha.mohan@proton.me

C. H. Hoffmann, D. Bansal (eds.), *AI Ethics in Practice*, Integrated Science 35,
https://doi.org/10.1007/978-3-031-87023-1_6

- Artificial intelligence (AI)[1] is rapidly transforming the digital landscape, making it a powerful tool for enhancing organisational cybersecurity capabilities. Its ability to automate complex tasks, process vast datasets and detect anomalous patterns in real-time has positioned it as a formidable organisational asset in defending against cyber threats (Kroll et al. 2021). However, those same defensive efficiencies are increasingly leveraged by malicious actors to amplify offensive cyberattacks, creating a dual-edged sword—*or scalpel*—for organisations. Consequently, while organisations strive to harness AI for enhanced security, they are simultaneously grappling with an expanded attack surface and the accelerated misuse of these technologies by adversaries. The exponential rate of AI development outpacing regulatory efforts to govern it, and the pressure to implement AI for its competitive advantages, results in two distinct governance vacuums: a regulatory vacuum and an ethical governance vacuum.
- The regulatory vacuum is a direct consequence of the rapid pace of technological advancements, which consistently outpaces the development of corresponding regulatory frameworks (Viskovich 2022). As AI evolves at unprecedented speed, existing regulations struggle to keep pace, challenging organisations to effectively identify and mitigate risks. In parallel, an ethical governance vacuum has emerged—bearing dynamics analogous to those of the nuclear arms race in which the competitive pursuit and acquisition of strategic capabilities overshadows ethical considerations. Similar to nation states during the Cold War, today's organisations are racing to achieve algorithmic supremacy, prioritising rapid AI adoption without sufficiently addressing the ethical implications that arise from it. This anxious acquisition, driven by the desire for technological superiority, has intensified the ethical governance gap in organisations deploying AI, where critical issues such as algorithmic transparency, accountability and fairness are often sidelined in favour of performance and efficiency gains.
- Consequently, organisations of all sizes, and particularly startups and SMEs—often characterised by agile structures and limited resources and thus facing heightened and disproportionate risks—are impacted by these governance vacuums (OECD 2021). We intend for this chapter to act as a guide for the ethical deployment of AI-enabled cybersecurity in organisations of all sizes. The first two sections lay the groundwork by making a case for the ethical implementation of AI in cybersecurity operations[2] and then analysing the organisational impacts of such. While the deployment of AI in organisations for any purpose raises numerous ethical considerations, this chapter draws on three key principles for

[1] In this chapter, we use AI to refer to technologies such as machine learning and generative AI that enable machines to process, comprehend, analyse and learn from data, make decisions and create content with minimal human input.

[2] In this chapter, 'cybersecurity operations' and 'cybersecurity programs' are used interchangeably.

ethical decision-making—Nonmaleficence,[3] Autonomy[4] and Explicability[5]—which are particularly relevant to the application of AI in cybersecurity (Tsamados et al. 2020; Mittelstadt et al. 2016; Floridi and Taddeo 2016). While we do not elaborate further on the principles themselves, we leverage them and their tenets as a lens to identify and analyse key ethical dilemmas that organisations encounter in implementing AI in their cybersecurity programmes and their impact on work culture. The chapter then focuses on strategies founded on those principles and offers a checklist tool to support organisations in their ethical implementation of AI-enabled cybersecurity. The aim of this chapter is to support organisations to adopt an ethical approach to the use of AI to bolster their cybersecurity, whether they have already implemented AI in their cybersecurity programmes or are considering doing so. Addressing ethical considerations not only fosters trust and productivity (Humphreys et al. 2024), it also positively contributes to bridging the aforementioned regulatory and ethical gaps that organisations face (World Economic Forum 2024a).

- As with many other applications of AI, navigating the intersection of AI and cybersecurity necessitates a consideration beyond technical capabilities and legal compliance. The fundamental question is not merely what AI can achieve but what it *should* be permitted to do, especially in scenarios that impact human trust and societal well-being (Işik et al. 2024). This imperative underscores the need for an industry-wide 'Hippocratic Oath'—a guiding principle for cybersecurity professionals and business executives to commit to the ethos of 'do no harm' in the design, deployment and application of AI-driven cybersecurity solutions. To this end, AI applications should be designed, developed and deployed with a comprehensive understanding of their ethical and societal implications. This involves addressing potential biases embedded within algorithms and training data, which, if left unchecked, will perpetuate existing inequalities and lead to discriminatory outcomes. This is also imperative for AI deployed in cybersecurity programmes, since failing to account for the impacts of AI on humans when it is deployed in cybersecurity operations directly impacts human security risk and security risk-reporting culture, which we explore later in this chapter.

[3] Non-maleficence is commonly understood in the literature to mean 'do no harm', highlighting the need to prevent AI systems from unintentionally causing harm, such as data breaches or unfair practices. Given the high risk of damage from cyber vulnerabilities, it is crucial for businesses to ensure that their AI-driven cybersecurity solutions do not introduce new risks, such as privacy violations or biased decision-making that could negatively affect people.

[4] Autonomy addresses the importance of maintaining human oversight in AI decision-making. If AI systems operate with too much autonomy, employees may feel sidelined, eroding their confidence and reducing their willingness to take initiative in critical situations.

[5] Explicability emphasises transparency and the need for AI systems to be understandable to both developers and users and others. Organisations must be able to clearly explain how their AI-driven cybersecurity systems function, especially when these systems impact sensitive data or critical security processes. Transparency means not only disclosing the use of AI but also being able to explain how decisions are made by the AI system.

2 The 'What': Ethical Implications of AI in Cybersecurity

- As AI continues to evolve, its applications in all contexts—including in cybersecurity—must be carefully scrutinised to prevent the inadvertent replication of societal biases and structural inequalities. Cybersecurity uniquely intersects with both technical systems and socio-behavioural aspects, making ethical considerations potentially more pressing in this field than in others. As Tandon et al. (2024) have found, ethical breaches in AI-driven cybersecurity can destabilise critical infrastructures, including finance, health care and energy sectors, leading to disruption of entire supply chains and public services. For example, if an AI model inaccurately identifies legitimate network activity as malicious, it can unjustifiably block critical services, detrimentally impacting society.
- In contrast to traditional cybersecurity systems and processes that rely heavily on human expertise for their implementation, AI is capable of operating with minimal human intervention, processing data on a large scale and executing actions at heretofore unparalleled speeds. While this paradigm shift enhances cyber defences and offers substantial efficiency gains—potentially alleviating burdens on roles such as SOC analysts—it simultaneously challenges established ethical frameworks that have not historically contended with such levels of automation or opacity (De Angelo 2024). This raises significant concerns, as most applications of AI in cybersecurity lack transparency, accountability and the capability to independently evaluate the ethical or legal soundness of their actions. As AI systems continue to evolve, their ability to make autonomous decisions is increasing; yet, they remain devoid of a moral compass to assess the implications of those decisions.
- This disconnect between AI capabilities and ethical oversight has precipitated what is known as the 'automation paradox': as systems become more autonomous, they paradoxically necessitate increased human oversight for critical tasks such as error management, decision-making and governance (Bessen 2016). The paradox emerges because organisations, in seeking cost efficiencies, are inclined to replace employees with AI automations, whilst underestimating the necessity of human oversight in complex decision-making processes. Consequently, the tendency to deploy AI without adequate human intervention increases organisational exposure to the attendant ethical, legal and operational risks. The ethical implications of these dynamics are profound: without human oversight, AI can propagate biases present in training data (Kirk et al. 2021), overlook context-specific nuances and execute decisions with unintended consequences (van de Poel 2023). This is particularly acute in AI-enabled cybersecurity, where a lack of accountability in algorithmic decision-making raises concerns about privacy, fairness and accuracy (Sontan and Samuel 2024).

  The ethical dilemmas inherent in AI-driven cybersecurity also arise from the fundamental nature of AI systems, which require access to, amongst other things, sensitive data—for instance, user behaviour patterns from both internal and external sources—to comprehensively detect and mitigate cyber threats and anticipate and identify both malicious and non-malicious risks. This reliance on comprehensive data sets means that the decision-making processes of AI systems can profoundly impact personal autonomy and employee agency. As AI becomes increasingly embedded in cybersecurity practices, so does the potential for these technologies to erode privacy and autonomy, hallucinate and introduce or amplify biases in decision-making, and perpetuate systemic inequalities (Panel for the Future of Science and Technology 2020).

- The integration of AI into cybersecurity also threatens to transform traditional organisational cultures, particularly as it relates to increased surveillance of employees, deskilling and displacement and erosion of transparency, trust and psychological safety. We will now deal with each of these systematically, elucidating how AI may transform not only cybersecurity operations but also the broader (security) culture and ethical landscape within organisations.

3 So What? Impact on Work Culture: Ethical Dilemmas and Human Factors

- As AI systems become more sophisticated and ubiquitous, nuanced challenges arise that can disrupt traditional workplace dynamics regarded as necessary for high performance and productivity and for organisational security culture: principally trust, autonomy and agency. While numerous scenarios in the implementation of AI in cybersecurity raise ethical considerations, for brevity—and to provide meaningful insight—we focus on three key instances: (i) the use of AI in enhancing zero-trust frameworks, which raises concerns around surveillance and privacy; (ii) the mid-term implications of AI on the cybersecurity workforce, particularly regarding deskilling and job displacement; and (iii) the long-term erosion of trust due to compromised transparency in AI decision-making. These cases offer a representative overview of the ethical dilemmas posed by the integration of AI in cybersecurity. Addressing these complexities requires an ethical investigation that probes deeper into the intersections of technology and human behaviour. In this context, the concept of the 'human factor' is used to refer to both human strengths *and* vulnerabilities (Parsons et al. 2010; Young et al. 2018), instead of positing the human factor as merely a liability, as it is often conceived in cybersecurity contexts (Alsharif et al. 2022). This perspective allows for a more comprehensive analysis of human engagement in the implementation of AI, which is crucial for understanding the multifaceted impact of AI on cybersecurity practices and organisational dynamics. Such an inquiry enables organisations to uncover the subtle, often overlooked ways in which AI-enabled cybersecurity impacts employee autonomy, perceptions of fairness and the collaborative spirit necessary for a strong risk-reporting culture and consequent resilient security posture. It further ensures that AI serves as a tool for empowerment—rather than as a catalyst for alienation.

3.1 I. 'Nobody Trusts Me So Why Should I Trust Them?' *Zero Trust and Surveillance*

Does your zero-trust system make zero exceptions? Imagine your senior SOC analyst logging in from a foreign country while working remotely to ensure continuous monitoring. When a critical security incident strikes, will the system flag this legitimate login as suspicious and lock them out at a time when their expertise is needed most?

- A zero-trust framework, which operates on the principle of 'never trust, always verify', assumes no implicit trust within or outside the organisation. It minimises security risks by verifying each user, device and network interaction (NIST 2020). This model has fast become a cornerstone of organisational cybersecurity strategies, especially as AI technologies increasingly enable its implementation. AI supports zero-trust architectures by providing continuous monitoring, real-time analysis of network activity and automated responses to potential threats, enhancing security effectiveness and reducing human error (Ajish 2024; Rose et al. 2020). Additionally, AI-powered behavioural analytics enable zero-trust systems to closely monitor and assess user actions, creating a constantly evolving baseline of what is considered typical behaviour (Hogan 2023).
- Such constant monitoring facilitated by AI can however erode psychological safety, creating a culture where employees may become reluctant to report security issues or errors for fear of negative repercussions (NeuroLeadership Institute 2024; Işik et al. 2024). This dynamic can inhibit proactive engagement and weaken the overall security posture of the organisation. For example, the repeated need for employees to verify their identity or justify an out-of-hours login can foster a sense of fear, mistrust and resentment, damaging the foundational trust required for effective security reporting. In this way, AI magnifies pre-existing concerns, making it imperative for organisations to address these issues by ensuring a fairer and more inclusive training data set, transparency in AI deployment and clearly communicating how data is collected, used and managed in order to keep their organisations cybersecure.
- While AI plays a crucial role in enhancing cybersecurity and supporting a zero-trust framework—by continuously monitoring network activity, identifying anomalies and flagging potential threats—it cannot yet replace human intuition and understanding of social contexts. Despite the extensive monitoring capabilities enabled by AI and digital surveillance tools, successful organisational cybersecurity still depends heavily on employee participation regarding aspects of human behaviour that are not readily captured through automated systems. This includes subtle indicators of employee well-being, workplace dynamics or evolving social engineering tactics that require human interpretation and contextual understanding. For example, an employee's awareness of unusual interactions, or their perception of changes in the organisational environment, can reveal potential insider threats or emerging risks that automated systems might overlook. Human feedback is critical to bridging the gap between technical monitoring and the sensitive realities of human behaviour that shape the effectiveness of

cybersecurity measures (Sasse et al. 2023). Without this input, organisations risk missing key insights that could enhance their security posture and better protect against evolving threats, even whilst using AI-enabled cybersecurity to detect social engineering attacks, such as Deepfakes, which prey on human vulnerabilities in order to exploit technical ones (Heartfield and Loukas 2018). Addressing these concerns is not just about adhering to ethical standards; it is essential for maintaining a security-aware culture that encourages open communication and early detection of threats.

3.2 II. 'AI Is Going to Take My Job!' *AI and Employees: Risk of Deskilling and Complacency*

One of the most commonly proposed strategies for alleviating unsustainable workloads in cybersecurity, the extremely high rates of burnout among cybersecurity professionals (Reeves and Coroneos 2022)*, and repetitive tasks faced by SOC teams in particular, is task automation through the use of AI-enabled cybersecurity. But now, rather ironically, the very technology designed to relieve employees' stress is now threatening to de-skill these seasoned professionals, who find their expertise sidelined. Has the cure, in fact, become worse than the disease as AI's automation in cybersecurity not only changes the nature of the work but potentially diminishes the value of human expertise, leaving cybersecurity professionals less empowered, more anxious and at risk of losing touch with their critical skills?*

- The use of AI in cybersecurity has the potential to disrupt traditional employee roles and diminish their sense of agency within organisations. As AI automates complex cybersecurity tasks such as threat detection and response, employees may be relegated to mere supervisors of automated systems, resulting in a perceived reduction in the value of their expertise (UK Department for Digital, Culture, Media, and Sport 2023). While this automation can alleviate some of the unattainable demands placed on cybersecurity professionals, it can also inadvertently lead to deskilling and complacency (Koeszegi 2023; Parasuraman and Manzey 2010). Over time, this shift can erode employee autonomy, transforming roles that once required active decision-making into passive oversight positions.
- The consequences of diminished role responsibilities extend beyond job satisfaction and engagement—they pose a direct risk to organisational security. A disengaged workforce is less likely to remain vigilant (Dawsey and Taylor 2011; Nobles 2022; Donnelly 2023), and employees who feel undervalued or excluded from critical security functions may experience reduced loyalty to their organisation (Fulford and Enz 1995). An ill-considered implementation of AI in a cybersecurity programme could therefore not only reduce employee engagement and their sense of purpose but also open the door to increased insider risks and threats (Verizon 2024). The risk of AI becoming a 'Trojan Horse' in cybersecurity is therefore very real. This is because employees who perceive themselves as merely ancillary to AI-driven security processes may become disempowered or

disenchanted, making them more susceptible to risky cybersecurity behaviours. In a cybersecurity context, where AI can introduce new and intricate workflows, it may be simultaneously perceived as introducing complexity and threatening employees' jobs as a result.

- Fear and anxiety can have detrimental effects on cognitive functions such as memory, attention and decision-making, as well as stifling creativity, making it difficult for employees to learn and adapt to technological changes, let alone propose novel and new ideas for offensive cybersecurity (Işik et al. 2024). Additionally, if AI implementation erodes psychological safety, this can contribute to burnout as a result of employees feeling unsupported or vulnerable in high-pressure situations (Viskovich 2023; Maslach et al. 1997). This could also lead to increased resistance and reduced organisational effectiveness (Edmondson 1999; Kong et al. 2021).

  To mitigate these risks, organisations should implement AI systems that foster rather than undermine employee engagement and empowerment.

3.3 III. 'Nobody Is Telling Me What's Going On!' *The Case for Transparency*

Good news: You've implemented a new 'User and Entity Behaviour Analytics' (UEBA) solution that flags risky behaviours before they escalate.

Bad news: You can't explain the AI's behaviour.

In an industry where trust is key, can you afford to rely on decisions you can't fully comprehend? What do the numbers say? A 2024 global cross-industry survey of 1800 CISOs, security leaders, administrators and practitioners revealed that only 26% of security professionals reported a comprehensive understanding of the various types of AI used in cybersecurity products (Darktrace 2024).

- The integration of AI into cybersecurity is inherently complex, not only due to the sophisticated nature of AI algorithms but also because of the challenges surrounding its implementation in organisational settings (Roshanaei et al. 2024). One significant issue arises from the opacity of AI systems. Often described as 'black box' AI, when AI algorithms make decisions without clear, interpretable explanations, employees are left unable to comprehend or challenge these decisions, which undermines their confidence in the technology (Hauptman et al. 2024).
- This lack of transparency can have profound implications for the workplace. Employees who do not understand how AI-driven systems operate or how they are implemented may perceive the technology as intrusive or untrustworthy (Jacovi et al. 2021). Such perceptions can create a sense of alienation, where employees feel marginalised or excluded from the cybersecurity decision-making process. Consequently, they may become hesitant to engage fully with the system, leading to a lack of participation in essential activities such as security risk reporting. When employees do not report suspicious activities or

vulnerabilities, an organisation's overall security posture is significantly weakened (Pfleeger and Caputo 2012; Alison 2023).

- For AI to be successfully implemented in cybersecurity, transparency is paramount. Organisations must clearly communicate how AI systems function, the data they use and the logic behind their decision-making processes. Establishing transparent reporting mechanisms that allow employees to understand the role of AI in the organisation's cybersecurity operations can foster a culture of trust and collaboration. When employees are assured that their contributions are valued and that the system operates ethically and effectively, they are more likely to engage proactively in cybersecurity efforts, thereby strengthening the organisation's security culture and hence its cyber resilience.

4 Now What: Strategies to Integrate Ethics When Implementing AI in Cybersecurity

The previous sections outlined how implementing AI in cybersecurity operations without due regard for ethical principles can detrimentally impact organisational dynamics and undermine employee engagement, This section introduces strategies for how to ethically implement AI in cybersecurity operations. While numerous ethics frameworks exist, this chapter focuses specifically on approaches that align with the ethical decision-making principles of Nonmaleficence, Autonomy and Explicability—to promote transparency and safeguard against AI's potential for harm. The strategies discussed include (i) ethics-by-design frameworks; (ii) mechanisms for bias mitigation; (iii) support for employee autonomy; and (iv) methods to enhance explicability and transparency (Fig. 6.1) Together, these approaches aim to create a balanced implementation model that fosters employee trust, reinforces ethical alignment and ensures that AI serves as a tool for resilience rather than a source of ethical, legal or operational risk. While these strategies may also guide the ethical implication of AI generally, they are discussed in the particular context of AI in cybersecurity.

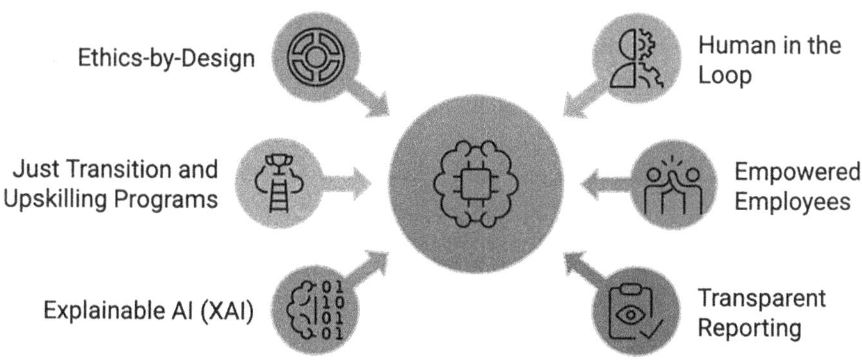

Fig. 6.1 Components & Strategies for Integrating Ethics when Implementing AI in Cybersecurity

4.1 I. Ethics-by-Design: Integrating Ethical Principles from the Outset

A. **Establish Clear Fairness Guidelines and Anti-Bias Measures**:

Ethics-by-Design is a proactive approach that embeds ethical considerations into the development and deployment of AI systems (Dignum et al. 2018). It ensures that ethical standards, such as fairness and non-discrimination, are not treated as an afterthought but as integral to the architecture of the AI. Developing AI systems that are free from bias starts with using diverse and representative data sets (Schwartz et al. 2022). Regular audits and testing of data sets should be conducted to detect and mitigate biases, particularly those related to gender, ethnicity, physical (dis)abilities, socio-economic backgrounds and other demographic factors. This can prevent the model from disproportionately flagging certain groups as anomalies based on skewed historical data (Dastin 2018).[6]

Furthermore, organisations should create ethical frameworks that define fairness and actively identify bias within the context of cybersecurity. These parameters should be aligned with the organisation's risk appetite to facilitate the identification, prioritisation and mitigation of potential ethical concerns (NIST 2023). Without such guidelines, AI systems risk disproportionately targeting or excluding individuals based on biases embedded in the training data or algorithm design, which can undermine employee trust, erode psychological safety and perpetuate systemic inequalities.

B. **Ethical Review Boards**:

A multidisciplinary AI Ethics Board—comprising internal professionals from *inter alia* cybersecurity, legal, enterprise risk management, and human resources, as well as external experts in fields such as computer science, philosophy and sociology—is essential for providing comprehensive oversight of AI implementations within the organisation (Hadley et al. 2024). Such an ethics board should include computer science experts to understand how algorithms work, philosophers to debate moral considerations of fairness and bias, and sociologists to assess the actual and potential human impacts including on marginalised groups. This diversity of expertise is essential for addressing the dynamic and intersecting ethical, legal and societal implications of AI applications. The AI Ethics Board should conduct regular audits of AI systems to identify potential biases and recommend improvements. This board should be responsible for reviewing AI deployments, assessing potential ethical risks and offering recommendations to ensure fairness, transparency and compliance. Board oversight also helps ensure that explicability is prioritised throughout the AI lifecycle.

---

[6] *The Amazon hiring case serves as a prominent example of AI bias. In 2014, Amazon introduced an AI-based recruiting tool designed to automate the resume screening process. However, by 2015, the tool was found to exhibit gender bias. It had been trained on resumes submitted over the previous decade, most of which were from men, especially for technical roles. As a result, the algorithm disproportionately favoured male candidates over female applicants.*

4.2 II. Human in the Loop (HITL): Input versus Oversight

A. **Implement HITL Frameworks for High-Risk Decisions**:

Incorporating human input and oversight into AI-driven systems through 'Human in the Loop' frameworks (HITL) is essential for safeguarding against maleficence (Enarsson et al. 2022). For decisions with significant consequences—such as disciplinary measures or the revocation of access privileges—integrating human oversight through HITL frameworks can enhance transparency and bolster employee trust. By ensuring that AI outputs are verified by human operators who have the authority to validate or override decisions based on contextual judgement, HITL mitigates risks associated with automated decision-making. This approach upholds ethical considerations, preserves human agency and increases confidence in the AI systems used within the organisation. The transparency facilitated by HITL frameworks ensures that employees understand how decisions are made and why human intervention is necessary at crucial junctures, thereby fostering a culture of trust and accountability—critical components of robust organisational security culture and risk-reporting, as we have explored earlier in this chapter.

B. **Enhance Human Oversight through Regular Training**:

To ensure effective human oversight of AI in cybersecurity, continuous training and education are essential for those tasked with such a role. Such training should encompass the capabilities and limitations of AI, as well as key ethical principles, to equip employees with the knowledge required to monitor AI systems effectively. Regular training on these aspects enables cybersecurity professionals to identify potential ethical dilemmas and intervene when necessary, maintaining an active role in the deployment of AI. By doing so, organisations reinforce accountability and reduce the risk of harm stemming from algorithmic biases or errors. This focus on human oversight not only supports transparency and trust but also contributes to a psychologically safe work environment, where employees feel valued and engaged in safeguarding the organisation's cybersecurity.

4.3 III. Just Transition and Upskilling Programmes

A. **Implement Reskilling and Upskilling Initiatives:**

To ensure that the workforce adapts effectively to an AI-enhanced cybersecurity landscape, organisations must implement comprehensive reskilling and upskilling programmes for employees. These initiatives should focus on equipping cybersecurity employees with skills that complement AI capabilities, particularly in areas where human judgement and ethical oversight are critical. This includes training in the analysis of complex security incidents, interpreting AI outputs and understanding AI-driven threat detection mechanisms. Such programmes are instrumental in enabling employees to make informed decisions and intervene when necessary, thereby maintaining human oversight and accountability in cybersecurity processes and decision-making. By prioritising continuous learning and development, organisations not only enhance employees' technical competencies but also foster a sense of professional relevance and agency. This approach has clear retention benefits as employees are more likely to remain engaged and invested when they see opportunities for growth and career progression (Mishra 2023; Minbaeva & De Cieri 2021). This is directly relevant in light of the cybersecurity talent challenges that many organisations face (World Economic Forum 2024b).

B. **Create New Roles that Leverage Human Strengths:**

As AI takes over routine and repetitive tasks, organisations have a unique opportunity to redefine roles and create positions that emphasise distinctly human strengths, such as critical thinking, ethical reasoning and creativity (Zirar et al. 2023). For instance, roles that focus on ethical oversight, AI governance and the human–AI interface are increasingly necessary to ensure responsible and effective AI integration. By developing these roles, organisations can harness employee strengths while alleviating fears of redundancy, ensuring that human contributions to organisational cybersecurity remain relevant. In an AI-driven environment, human characteristics such as emotional intelligence and complex problem-solving become vital differentiators, allowing employees to contribute meaningfully to areas where AI may fall short. This strategic shift not only mitigates the risk of job displacement but also underscores the importance of uniquely human skills that AI cannot replicate, ensuring that the deployment of AI in cybersecurity *augments* rather than *displaces* human capabilities.

4.4 IV. Empowering Employees to Challenge AI Processes and Decisions

A. **Develop Transparent Escalation Protocols**:

AI systems should not be viewed as infallible (Humphreys et al. 2024). Instead, employees should be equipped with the skills and confidence to critically evaluate and question AI-driven decisions. This can be facilitated through several organisational strategies, such as implementing robust escalation protocols and fostering a 'culture of questioning' within the organisation. Establishing clear and accessible procedures for challenging or reviewing AI outputs is crucial. These procedures might include creating dedicated channels for raising concerns, incorporating human oversight into AI decision-making and providing mechanisms for employees to offer feedback on AI performance. Additionally, ensuring transparency in how AI decisions are made and reviewed further empowers employees to take an active role in upholding ethical standards and maintaining accountability within the organisation, all of which enhances an organisation's cybersecurity resilience and culture.

4.5 V. Implementing Explainable AI (XAI)

A. **Incorporate Model Interpretability**:
Developing and deploying AI models with inherent interpretability, i.e. models that are easy for humans to 'interpret' the AI's decisions (Murdoch et al. 2019), ensures that their decision-making processes are transparent and comprehensible, avoiding the issue of opaque, 'black box' systems. Interpretability allows human operators to understand the rationale behind a decision, how specific factors influenced the outcome, and which data points contributed to the final prediction. As previously discussed in this chapter, transparency is essential for fostering a healthy security culture, as it promotes trust, reduces ambiguity and aligns AI decisions with human expectations.

B. **Use Visualisations and Decision Traceability**
Employing visualisation tools to represent the AI's decision-making process enables a tangible, step-by-step explanation of how a particular outcome was reached. Visualisations such as decision trees or flowcharts enable human operators to follow and evaluate the AI's logic, making complex algorithms more accessible and understandable. Decision traceability, on the other hand, ensures that every decision made by the AI is documented and can be reviewed by human auditors. By incorporating interpretability and decision traceability into the design of the AI, organisations can bridge the gap between advanced AI capabilities and human understanding, ultimately fostering a more transparent and accountable use of AI in cybersecurity and other organisational contexts. For example, while implementing AI in phishing detection, organisations can reinforce trust in the detection application by complementing it with a graphical interface that displays why an e-mail was flagged as a phishing email by showing indicators such as sender domain reputation, detection of suspicious links or anomalous language patterns. This can also include interactive elements, making it easier for cybersecurity professionals to trace decisions and verify the system's accuracy. Further, it offers opportunities for dynamic, real-time learning as well as engaging security education, training and awareness.

4.6 VI. Establishing Transparent Reporting Mechanisms

A. **Implement Accountability Dashboards**:
Organisations should consider developing accountability dashboards that visually represent AI decision-making processes. These dashboards can serve as a central platform for tracking decision points, highlighting areas where human oversight has occurred and indicating the outcomes of automated processes. Making this information accessible to all relevant stakeholders reinforces the collaborative nature of human–AI interaction, thereby enhancing employees' confidence in the system's integrity (Koeszegi 2023). Transparency is further promoted when these dashboards are made visible to employees whose roles or responsibilities are affected by AI-driven decisions.

B. **Generate Comprehensive Reports**:

Another critical aspect of transparent reporting is the creation of detailed, comprehensive reports that provide insights into the rationale behind AI's threat detection and response mechanisms. These reports should outline the reasoning for AI-flagged anomalies, the steps taken in response, and any subsequent outcomes, thereby ensuring that AI decisions are not perceived as arbitrary or unpredictable. This level of detail is essential for building trust, as it demystifies the AI's functioning and enables employees to understand and critically engage with AI outcomes. Additionally, such reports facilitate organisational learning by allowing employees to review previous AI decisions, gain insights into the decision-making processes and identify areas where human oversight may be needed. By integrating this level of transparency, organisations can create a more informed and engaged workforce, reducing resistance to AI and promoting a shared understanding of the technology's role in enhancing the organisation's cybersecurity.

The strategies outlined in this section go beyond merely addressing ethical concerns; they serve to cultivate and reinforce a culture of psychological safety within the organisation. This is crucial because when employees feel psychologically safe, they are more likely to hold positive attitudes towards AI integration and security measures (Thompson et al. 2020), leading to two critical outcomes. First, increased engagement and acceptance of AI technologies translates to better productivity and more effective implementation of AI solutions (Amos 2022). Second, a psychologically safe environment fosters a positive attitude towards compliance with security protocols, which is essential for maintaining robust cybersecurity defences (Thompson et al. 2020). Thus, by aligning AI implementation strategies with principles that promote psychological safety, organisations can enhance not only the ethical integration of AI but also ensure that employees view AI as a supportive tool— ultimately resulting in stronger adherence to security practices and thus a more cyber-resilient organisation.

5 From Theory into Practice

Having explored strategies for the ethical implementation of AI-enabled cybersecurity in organisations, the discussion now shifts to practical ways organisations can operationalise those strategies in ways that are informed by the ethical principles of Nonmaleficence, Autonomy and Explicability. Recognising the diverse regulatory requirements and financial considerations of organisations across different sectors, the following inexhaustive checklist is designed to be a flexible and adaptable tool, catering to a broad range of organisational contexts. Its primary aim is to encourage initial reflection on the ethical use of AI in cybersecurity, serving as a pragmatic extension of the preceding analysis by translating the aforementioned theoretical ethical principles into actionable steps. The checklist is intended as a foundation for organisations to use to create a 'minimal viable product' or baseline assessment for responsible AI integration and implementation in their cybersecurity operations.

5.1 Checklist

A. Gap Analysis
a. Where and how is AI currently being implemented within cybersecurity in the organisation?
   i. *Map all applications of AI in cybersecurity in the form of a register: identify purpose of the AI, scope, source/vendor, function, data flow, TOMs etc.*
   ii. *Document the use case for each application of AI.*
b. *Why is the organisation contemplating the use or enhanced use of AI in cybersecurity?*
   i. *The organisation has a process to consider, justify and approve each use case of AI.*
c. *Are there existing frameworks that guide this implementation?*
   i. *Policies, procedures and methodologies are in place and require the evaluation of data security and data privacy risks posed by the use and application of AI tools.*
   ii. *A comprehensive list of policies and frameworks that govern the use and application of AI in cybersecurity is maintained on a central repository.*
   iii. *Consideration and implementation of security-by-design in all business operations, systems and processes is required by policy and enforced through continuous oversight.*
   iv. *The organisation integrates ethical strategies for AI into software development and operations (e.g. in a manner similar to the integration of DevSecOps in software development and security operations).*

B. Risk and Ethics Frameworks
a. *What is the organisational risk tolerance?*
   i. *The organisation has a Cybersecurity Risk Appetite Statement.*
   ii. *The organisation has an AI Risk Appetite Statement.*
   iii. *The Cybersecurity and AI Risk Appetite Statements have been aligned.*
   iv. *The use of AI in the organisation's cybersecurity operations conforms with both Risk Appetite Statements.*
b. *What values and ethical principles is the organisation committed to abiding by?*
   i. *The organisation has an Implementation Policy to guide the ethical implementation of AI in the organisation.*
   ii. *Fairness and anti-bias parameters have been defined within the context of cybersecurity.*
   iii. *In all use cases in the organisation, AI is applied in line with the organisation's stated values and ethical principles and policies.*

C. Awareness and Integration
a. *To what extent do employees understand the existing/proposed AI system(s)?*
   i. *Regular education, training and awareness programmes are in place and include ethical and human factor considerations of the application and use of AI in cybersecurity.*

   ii. *Staff are provided upskilling opportunities to increase their knowledge and understanding of the application and use of AI in cybersecurity and AI in organisational settings generally.*

b. *How can the cybersecurity team support employees' understanding and integration of the existing/proposed AI system(s)?*
   i. *The adoption of AI in a cybersecurity programme is complemented by change management processes that equip the workforce to understand how AI is integrated within cybersecurity systems and processes.*
   ii. *Employees are adequately trained and equipped to adapt to changes in cybersecurity systems and processes as a result of the implementation of AI.*

D. Transparency and Oversight

a. *How transparent is the AI system's decision-making process?*
   i. *Evaluation processes are in place requiring the organisation to guarantee the integrity of the AI system(s) it uses.*
   ii. *Measures are in place to avoid the perpetuation of bias in the AI application.*
   iii. *Organisational policy guides the implementation of Explainable AI/Black box AI for each use case on a case-by-case basis.*

b. *How does the governance framework integrate effective human supervision?*
   i. *The organisation has an Ethics Board that approves the use and application of AI in the organisation including in cybersecurity, including overseeing and deciding on risk escalations.*
   ii. *The Organisation has an Ethics Officer (or equivalent) that oversees the ethical implications of the use of AI in the organisation's cybersecurity operations.*

E. Closing the Loop

a. *What challenges in AI generally have been encountered in the organisation?*
   i. *Lessons Learned exercises from applications of AI in the workplace are conducted regularly.*
   ii. *There is an established process in place for implementing Lessons Learned from other AI applications into AI-enabled cybersecurity.*

b. *What processes are in place for employee feedback and continuous improvement of the experience of implementing the AI system?*
   i. *Feedback loops are in place to collect employee feedback at each stage of implementing AI including inadequacies and friction experienced during transition phases and change management processes (or lack thereof).*
   ii. *Escalation and (anonymous and/or confidential) reporting channels are in place for concerns, risks and escalations to be raised confidentially by staff in the workplace.*

6 What Next: A Call to 'Do No Harm'

i. As organisations adopt AI systems to enhance their cybersecurity and operational efficiencies, defining the 'greater good' or 'common good' is central to ethical considerations: Whose interests are being prioritised by these technologies? Who benefits, and who might be left out or adversely affected? (Viskovich 2022). This analysis requires organisations to recognise that technologies and the laws that govern them can unintentionally favour a select few, deepening existing biases and inequalities, eroding trust and productivity. Consequently, a proactive approach to ethical AI implementation is necessary—one that integrates ethics by design and emphasises ongoing education and human oversight at every stage of the AI lifecycle in cybersecurity. This approach is not achieved by merely ticking off compliance checklists, but by deliberately considering all aspects of AI deployment such that it respects human dignity, upholds human agency and promotes transparency of and accountability for its use and application in cybersecurity operations.

ii. The challenge for organisations is to operationalise these ethical considerations in ways that are meaningful and sustainable. Organisations must embed ethical principles into their AI systems from the ground up, making transparency a core feature of decision-making processes and ensuring that employees are equipped to understand and meaningfully engage with the AI tools their organisation uses. When human oversight, intervention and engagement are prioritised—especially in high-stakes fields such as cybersecurity—AI can complement human judgement rather than undermine it, safeguarding against harmful or unintended outcomes, while fostering a vigilant and empowered work culture that strengthens the organisation's security posture and cyber resilience. Deploying AI-enabled cybersecurity tools to enhance organisational cybersecurity defences without due regard for attendant ethical considerations creates an ironic paradox for organisations: both the security culture and overall cyber resilience are eroded.

iii. While the consequence of neglecting ethics in AI-driven cybersecurity is the counterproductive erosion of security an ethical implementation of AI in cybersecurity should focus on ensuring that these systems do not cause harm, with a clear emphasis on their impact on human engagement, agency and oversight. In the age of AI, there has never been a more pertinent time to be human-centric. Given the privilege that those of us in the cybersecurity and AI professions enjoy—which is to say that we are simultaneously defining, designing and building the scaffolding on which our future (digital) world is being built—we have a responsibility to exercise caution and speak up about our concerns. Our call to action is to develop and abide by a 'Hippocratic Oath' for our industry; one that implores us to *do no harm* as we scale new frontiers in our organisations' defensive and offensive cybersecurity capabilities by leveraging the powers of AI.

References

Ajish D (2024) The significance of artificial intelligence in zero trust technologies: a comprehensive review. J Electr Syst Inform Technol 11, Article 30. https://doi.org/10.1186/s43067-024-00155-z. Available at: https://jesit.springeropen.com/articles/10.1186/s43067-024-00155-z

Alison D (2023) See something, say something: the importance of employee reporting in cybersecurity. Cofense. Available at: https://cofense.com/blog/see-something-say-something-the-importance-of-employee-reporting-in-cybersecurity/

Alsharif M, Mishra S, AlShehri M (2022) Impact of human vulnerabilities on cybersecurity. Comput Syst Sci Eng 40(3)

Amos Z (2022) How to balance cybersecurity and productivity. Cybersecurity Magazine. Available at: https://cybersecurity-magazine.com/how-to-balance-cybersecurity-and-productivity/

Bessen J (2016) The automation paradox. The Atlantic. Available at: https://www.theatlantic.com/business/archive/2016/01/automation-paradox/424437/

Darktrace (2024) State of AI cybersecurity: industry perspectives on the growing role of AI in cybersecurity. Darktrace Holdings Limited. Available at: https://darktrace.com/state-of-ai-cyber-security

Dawsey JC, Taylor EC (2011) Active engagement to active disengagement: a proposed model. Bus Stud J 3(1)

De Angelo D (2024) Combat SOC analyst burnout with AI. Palo Alto Networks. Available at: https://www.paloaltonetworks.com/blog/2024/09/combat-soc-analyst-burnout-with-ai/

Dignum V, Baldoni M, Baroglio C et al (2018) Ethics by design: Necessity or curse? In: Proceedings of the 2018 AAAI/ACM Conference on AI, Ethics, and Society (AIES '18). Association for Computing Machinery, New York, pp 60–66. Available at: https://doi.org/10.1145/3278721.3278745

Donnelly C (2023) Employee burnout severely risking cybersecurity, report finds. Healthcare IT News. Available at: https://www.healthcareitnews.com/news/employee-burnout-severely-risking-cyber-security-report-finds

Edmondson A (1999) Psychological safety and learning behavior in work teams. Adm Sci Quart 44(2):350–383. Available at: http://www.jstor.org/stable/2666999

Enarsson T, Enqvist L, Naarttijärvi M (2022) Approaching the human in the loop – legal perspectives on hybrid human/algorithmic decision-making in three contexts. Inform Commun Technol Law 31(1):123–153. Available at: https://doi.org/10.1080/13600834.2021.1958860

Floridi L, Taddeo M (2016) What is data ethics? Phil Trans R Soc A 374:20160112. https://doi.org/10.1098/rsta.2016.0360

Fulford MD, Enz CA (1995) The impact of empowerment on service employees. J Manager Iss 7(2):161–175

Hadley E, Blatecky A, Comfort M (2024) Investigating algorithm review boards for organisational responsible artificial intelligence governance. AI Ethics. https://doi.org/10.1007/s43681-024-00574-8

Hauptman AI, Schelble BG, Duan W, Flathmann C, McNeese NJ (2024) Understanding the influence of AI autonomy on AI explainability levels in human-AI teams using a mixed methods approach. Cogn Technol Work. https://doi.org/10.1007/s10111-024-00765-7

Heartfield R, Loukas G (2018) Detecting semantic social engineering attacks with the weakest link: implementation and empirical evaluation of a human-as-a-security-sensor framework. Comput Secur 76:101–127

Hogan C (2023) Zero trust and AI: better together. Cloud Security Alliance. Available at: https://cloudsecurityalliance.org/blog/2023/08/24/zero-trust-and-ai-better-together

Humphreys D, Koay A, Desmond D et al (2024) AI hype as a cyber security risk: the moral responsibility of implementing generative AI in business. AI Ethics 4:791–804. Available at: https://doi.org/10.1007/s43681-024-00443-4

Işik Ö, Viskovich Y, Pavitt S (2024) Common pitfalls when mitigating cyber risk: Addressing socio-behavioural factors. Cyber Secur A Peer-Review J 8(1):6–23

Jacovi A, Marasović A, Miller T, Goldberg Y (2021) Formalizing trust in artificial intelligence: prerequisites, causes and goals of human trust in AI. In: Conference on fairness, accountability, and transparency (FAccT '21), March 3–10, 2021, Virtual Event, Canada. ACM, New York, NY, USA, pp. 12. Available at: https://doi.org/10.1145/3442188.3445923

Kirk HR, Jun Y, Volpin F, Iqbal H, Benussi E, Dreyer F, Shtedritski A, Asano Y (2021) Bias out-of-the-box: an empirical analysis of intersectional occupational biases in popular generative language models. Adv Neural Inf Process Syst 34:2611–2624

Koeszegi ST (2023) AI @ work: human empowerment or disempowerment? In: Introduction to digital humanism. Springer, Cham, pp 175–196. https://doi.org/10.1007/978-3-031-45304-5_12. Available at: https://link.springer.com/chapter/10.1007/978-3-031-45304-5_12

Kong H, Yuan Y, Baruch Y, Bu N, Jiang X, Wang K (2021) Influences of artificial intelligence (AI) awareness on career competency and job burnout. Int J Contemp Hosp Manage 33(2):717–734. Available at: https://www.researchgate.net/publication/348580345_Influences_of_artificial_intelligence_AI_awareness_on_career_competency_and_job_burnout

Kroll JA et al (2021) Enhancing cybersecurity via artificial intelligence: risks, rewards, and frameworks. Computer 54(6):64–71

Maslach C, Jackson SE, Leiter MP (1997) Maslach burnout inventory: Third edition

Minbaeva D, De Cieri, H (2021) Rebooting employees: Upskilling for artificial intelligence in multinational corporations. Int J Human Resource Management 32(13):2849–2872. Available at: https://www.tandfonline.com/doi/full/10.1080/09585192.2021.1891114

Mishra P (2023) The impact of learning and development on employee retention in organizations. Int J Scientific Research in Engineering and Management 7(5):1–4. Available at: https://www.researchgate.net/publication/371285778_THE_IMPACT_OF_LEARNING_AND_DEVELOPMENT_ON_EMPLOYEE_RETENTION_IN_ORGANIZATIONS

Mittelstadt B, Allo P, Taddeo M, Wachter S, Floridi L (2016) The ethics of algorithms: mapping the debate. Big Data Soc 3(2). Available at: https://doi.org/10.1177/2053951716679679

Murdoch WJ, Singh C, Kumbier K, Abbasi-Asl R, Yu B (2019) Definitions, methods, and applications in interpretable machine learning. Proc Natl Acad Sci 116(44):22071–22080

National Institute of Standards and Technology (NIST) (2023) Towards a standard for identifying and managing bias in artificial intelligence. NIST Special Publication 1270. https://doi.org/10.6028/NIST.SP.1270. Available at: https://nvlpubs.nist.gov/nistpubs/SpecialPublications/NIST.SP.1270.pdf

NeuroLeadership Institute. (2024) Psychological Safety and Accountability: Three Insights From NLI's Conversation With Amy Edmondson. Your Brain at Work. Available at: https://neuroleadership.com/your-brain-at-work/psychological-safety-and-accountability-insights-from-amy-edmondson

NIST (2020) Zero Trust Architecture. NIST Special Publication 800-207. U.S. Department of Commerce. Available at: https://nvlpubs.nist.gov/nistpubs/SpecialPublications/NIST.SP.800-207.pdf

Nobles C (2022) Stress, burnout, and security fatigue in cybersecurity: a human factors problem. HOLISTICA – J Bus Public Adm 13(1):49–72

OECD (2021) The digital transformation of SMEs. OECD Studies on SMEs and Entrepreneurship. OECD Publishing, Paris. Available at: https://doi.org/10.1787/bdb9256a-en

Panel for the Future of Science and Technology (2020) The ethics of artificial intelligence: Issues and initiatives. European Parliamentary Research Service. PE 634.452. ISBN: 978-92-846-5799-5. Available at: https://doi.org/10.2861/6644

Parasuraman R, Manzey DH (2010) Complacency and bias in human use of automation: an attentional integration. Human Factors 52(3):381–410. Available at: https://doi.org/10.1177/0018720810376055

Parsons K, McCormac A, Butavicius M, Ferguson L (2010) Human factors and information security: Individual, culture and security environment. Defence Science and Technology

Organisation (DSTO) Technical Report, DSTO-TR-2484. Available at: https://apps.dtic.mil/sti/pdfs/ADA535944.pdf

Pfleeger SL, Caputo DD (2012) Leveraging behavioral science to mitigate cyber security risk. Comput Secur 31(4):597–611

Reeves A, Coroneos P (2022) Cybersecurity professionals may be burning out at a faster rate than frontline health care workers [Press release]. Available at: https://caudit.edu.au/resources/cybermindz-release-a-new-study-showing-early-evidence-of-burnout-in-cyber-professionals/

Rose S, Borchert O, Mitchell S, Connelly S (2020) Zero trust architecture. NIST Special Publication 800-207, U.S. Department of Commerce, National Institute of Standards and Technology. Available at: https://doi.org/10.6028/NIST.SP.800-207

Roshanaei M, Khan MR, Sylvester NN (2024) Navigating AI cybersecurity: evolving landscape and challenges. J Intell Learn Syst Appl 16:155–174. https://doi.org/10.4236/jilsa.2024.163010. Available at: https://www.scirp.org/journal/paperinformation?paperid=133870

Sasse MA, Hielscher J, Friedauer J, Buckmann A (2023) Rebooting IT security awareness: how organisations can encourage and sustain secure behaviours. In: Katsikas S et al (eds) ESORICS 2022 Workshops. Lecture Notes in Computer Science, vol 13785. Springer, Cham, pp 248–265. https://doi.org/10.1007/978-3-031-25460-4_14

Schwartz R, Vassilev A, Greene K, Perine L, Burt A, Hall P (2022) Towards a standard for identifying and managing bias in artificial intelligence. NIST Special Publication, p 1270. https://doi.org/10.6028/NIST.SP.1270

Sontan AD, Samuel SV (2024) The intersection of artificial intelligence and cybersecurity: challenges and opportunities. World J Adv Res Rev 21:1720–1736. https://doi.org/10.30574/wjarr.2024.21.2.0607

Tandon A, Durocher L, Novak M, Sand J, Elovici Y (2024) Survey of AI applications in cybersecurity: understanding and adoption among security professionals. OSF Preprints. Available at: https://osf.io/u4kdq/download/?format=pdf

Thompson MM, D'Agata M, Fraser B (2020) Applying attitude-behaviour models to mitigate insider cyber threats: Review and recommendations for future research. Defence Research and Development Canada (DRDC) Scientific Report, DRDC-RDDC-2020-R105. Available at: https://cradpdf.drdc-rddc.gc.ca/PDFS/unc349/p812289_A1b.pdf

Tsamados A, Aggarwal N, Cowls J, Morley J, Roberts H, Taddeo M, Floridi L (2020) The ethics of algorithms: key problems and solutions. University of Oxford, Oxford Internet Institute. Available at: https://ssrn.com/abstract=3662302

UK Department for Digital, Culture, Media & Sport (2023) Public attitudes to data and AI: Tracker survey (Wave 3). UK Government. Available at: https://www.gov.uk/government/publications/public-attitudes-to-data-and-ai-tracker-survey-wave-3

van de Poel I (2023) AI, control and unintended consequences: the need for meta-values. In: Fritzsche A, Santa-María A (eds) Rethinking technology and engineering. Philosophy of Engineering and Technology, vol 45. Springer, Cham. Available at: https://doi.org/10.1007/978-3-031-25233-4_9

Verizon (2024) 2024 data breach investigations report. Verizon Business. Available at: https://www.verizon.com/business/en-au/resources/reports/dbir/

Viskovich Y (2022) Insights: data privacy. In: Inderwildi O, Kraft M (eds) Intelligent decarbonisation. Lecture Notes in Energy, vol 86. Springer, Cham. Available at: https://doi.org/10.1007/978-3-030-86215-2_23

Viskovich Y (2023) Why Burnout is a Cyber Risk. TEDx Talk. Available at: https://www.youtube.com/watch?v=vU1gD0NHL78

World Economic Forum (2024a) Governance in the age of generative AI: A 360° approach for resilient policy and regulation. World Economic Forum. Available at: https://www3.weforum.org/docs/WEF_Governance_in_the_Age_of_Generative_AI_2024.pdf

World Economic Forum (2024b) The cybersecurity industry has an urgent talent shortage. Here's how to plug the gap. World Economic Forum. Retrieved October 14, 2024, from https://www.weforum.org/agenda/2024/04/cybersecurity-industry-talent-shortage-new-report/

Young H, van Vliet T, van de Ven J, Jol S, Broekman C (2018) Understanding human factors in cybersecurity as a dynamic system. In: Nicholson D (ed) Advances in human factors in cybersecurity. Advances in intelligent systems and computing, vol 593. Springer, Cham, pp 243–254. Available at: https://doi.org/10.1007/978-3-319-60585-2_23

Zirar A, Ali SI, Islam N (2023) Worker and workplace artificial intelligence (AI) coexistence: Emerging themes and research agenda. Technovation 124:102747. Available at: https://doi.org/10.1016/j.technovation.2023.102747

Yanya Viskovich is a cybersecurity expert specialising in human cyber risk, executive cyber crisis preparedness and management and data ethics. She began her career prosecuting cybercrime, organised crime and privacy offences, and has held senior legal and strategic roles in multinationals, the United Nations and the International Committee of the Red Cross, working across Switzerland, the Americas, the Middle East and Australia. Yanya strategised crisis contingency planning for the UN in Lebanon and helped create and implement the UN's first data protection policy. She led the C-Suite & Board Cyber Advisory and Human Factor in Cybersecurity practices at Accenture Switzerland and the Global Cybersecurity Outlook 2025 as a World Economic Forum Fellow. Bar-admitted in Australia, Yanya holds a Bachelor of Laws, Bachelor of International Relations and Master of Laws from the Australian National University. She is a Certified Data Protection Officer from Maastricht University and has completed executive programmes in cybersecurity, computer science and neuroscience from institutions including MIT, Geneva Center for Security Policy and EPFL. Yanya chairs Cyber Law & Governance at the Swiss Cyber Institute, advises the European Commission on data ethics, and has served as an Advisory Board Member for IDC Europe. A TEDx and keynote speaker, regular guest lecturer at leading Swiss and European universities and published author, she frequently contributes to thought leadership on cybersecurity, AI and data ethics.

Vibha Mohan is a Data Protection and Digital Rights expert and Solicitor of the Courts of England and Wales. She has worked in Switzerland and the UK in data protection and digital ethics across the tech, luxury retail and non-profit sectors. She holds a Bachelor of Laws and a Bachelor of Business Administration from Symbiosis Law School, Pune, and a Master of Laws from the London School of Economics, and is a Certified Information Privacy Professional (CIPP/E). Vibha is the recipient of the Duke of Edinburgh Award, ASIL-GW Law Scholar recognition, J.N. Tata Endowment Scholarship and DAAD New Passage to India scholarship. She actively contributes to thought collaboration on cybersecurity, digital ethics and data privacy through speaking and moderating roles at industry events such as RISK London, Last Thursday in Privacy and PrivSec London.

Future of Work, Bridging AI Human Transformation

7

How Will the Future of Work Look Like in the Age of AI, and How Will Leaders Succeed in Bridging the AI Human Transformation?

Katrin J. Yuan

Abstract

We embark on a journey to unleash the potential of the interaction between AI and the human site of leadership entering and shaping the future of work. As technological advancement accelerates, our understanding of tasks, processes, work, and leadership is undergoing a profound and exciting metamorphosis. This is an exciting time for the future of work, as new opportunities emerge alongside the potential for disruption. This chapter explores not only the potential disruptions brought about by AI but also the unparalleled opportunities for human empathy, creativity, ingenuity, and growth.

Take-aways for the reader at one glance

Introduction: From Dreaming to Realisation

Introducing into the nature of AI and the nature of humans.

What Defines Human Leaders in The Age of AI and What It Takes to Build Trust

The question of what defines us as human leaders will be reshaped in the age of AI. Building trust is key for future leaders to thrive.

From Knowledge to Capabilities: The Transformation of Future Skills, Society, and Leadership

Some future leadership skills will change, while others will become more relevant to succeed and differentiate in the age of AI, while society as a whole will transform from knowledge to a capability society.

K. J. Yuan (✉)
Swiss Future Institute AG, Zug, Switzerland
e-mail: ai@futureinstitute.ch

C. H. Hoffmann, D. Bansal (eds.), *AI Ethics in Practice*, Integrated Science 35,
https://doi.org/10.1007/978-3-031-87023-1_7

When Human Meets Tech: How AI Has the Potential to Enhance the Human Leadership Beyond Its Capabilities
When applied efficiently and ethically future leaders will enhance their leadership capabilities beyond means, enriched by AI, underlined with concrete examples.
Managing Risks of AI in Future Work and Why Data and Ethics Matter
Becoming and staying AI literate through continuous education will be an obligation to thrive as future leaders, knowing and dealing with both the opportunities and the risks of AI, underlined with concrete examples.
Conclusion: The Human AI Tech Future Symbiosis
Cultivating a form of leadership that champions both technological advancement and human flourishing, and with that creating a future where technological advancements merge with empathy, where machines augment rather than replace, and where humanity remains at the heart of progress, evolving together with AI.

1 Introduction: From Dreaming to Realisation

With AI expected to contribute $15.7 trillion[1] globally by 2030, at the same time fake news, hallucinations, and a record low trust in digital technologies (around 40%) are emerging due to ethical concerns, we need to rethink and redefine the paradigm of leadership and the future of work in the age of AI.

Eleanor Roosevelt once said: "The future belongs to those who believe in the beauty of their dreams." How big do people dream and how do they dare to realise their ideas in technological advancements with which consequences?

The human ability to dream big, to articulate the dream, to write down ideas, bringing them to life and realising them one day, starts with the language and the ability to communicate. The AI Large language models (LLMs) hold a significant starting position in the current AI landscape due to their language processing capabilities and adaptability, next to other areas of AI like computer vision, robotics, and reinforcement learning. The neural network models are the basis of the LLMs.[2] So far LLM are only the beginning of the AI advancements.[3]

The Stanford Hundred Year Study Report discusses how AI advancements can potentially redefine human capabilities, while challenging the existing.[4] Looking at the fundamentals of AI, algorithms are the step-by-step instructions that guide AI on how to process information and make decisions. "To understand the algorithm we need to uncover those roots and then build a new model of 'algorithmic reading' that incorporates a deep understanding of abstraction and process (…) Algorithms enact theoretical ideas in pragmatic instructions, always leaving a gap between the two in the details of implementation."[5] These algorithms range from simple rules-based

[1] IMD-St Gallen Symposium (2021).

[2] Goldberg (2015).

[3] Lee and Chen Qiufan (2021).

[4] Stanford Study Panel Report (2021).

[5] Finn (2018).

systems to complex neural networks that mimic the human brain. How much algorithm is tech, how much of it is human, and how will they influence and modify each other to what extend? These are questions that are central to the future of work and future of leadership in the age of AI.

We embark on a journey to unleash the potential of the interaction between AI and the human site of leadership shaping and defining the future of work. As technological advancement accelerates, our understanding of tasks, processes, work, and leadership is undergoing a profound and exciting metamorphosis. This is an exciting time for the future of work, as new risks, demands, and new opportunities emerge alongside the potential for disruption. AI brings along not only the potential disruptions but also the unparalleled opportunities for human to thrive in empathy, creativity, ingenuity, and growth. The question of what a human being is will be in a state of re-construction which leads to the question of what defines human leaders.

2 What Defines Human Leaders in the Age of AI and What it Takes to Build Trust

Faced with disruptions brought by AI, the question is what defines as humans at its core. And in the context of work, what defines us as human leaders in future. Looking at fundamental aspects of humans these are creativity, empathy, psychological understanding, and intuitive sensing. Next to the trust-building element in leadership, there is the ethical decision-making human capability, emerging as indispensable elements in the navigation of the complexities of the future world, where AI may redefine what makes us human.[6]

Faced with 40% of global users expressing confidence in digital technologies, there is a trust gap in the new technologies. People use the new technologies but do not trust them. Next to the trust gap in tech, there is a trust gap in business.[7]

It is becoming increasingly important to establish organisations as trustworthy, given the growing complexity. In order to establish trust, it is first necessary to gain an understanding of what trust is and to demonstrate as leader of practising what you preach.[8]

It starts with the fact that humans are social beings. People like to surround themselves with other people in order to receive appreciation and recognition. Humans trust humans. One of the key challenges of being a human leader is to build trust with your people and within the team you lead. A good leader is one who trusts the team and receives trust in return. How does a human leader build trust?

---

[6] Coleman (2019).

[7] Reibmayr (2017).

[8] Reibmayr (2017).

At its core, trust is based on a shared understanding of social norms, as well as reliability and predictability[9] in terms of "Do what you say, say what you do" [10] which makes two humans rely on each other. Trust also means sharing a common ethical basis for behaviour, action, and response.

Trust is built over time through shared experiences, values, and actions that reinforce the bond of shared values such as integrity. For leaders, this implies listening, reflecting, understanding, and acting accordingly with all its consequences. There is a common ground which make humans trust each other over time, relying on each other.[11] Non-compliant behaviour leads to punishment, which maintains long-term favourable cooperation and fairness within the human group.[12]

In the context of challenging situations and escalation of matters at work, human individuals tend to seek and anticipate the provision of a solution by a responsible authority figure, who is expected to resolve the matter in an appropriate manner. In the event that this does not occur, human individuals may then seek to identify a human individual or entity to blame. Ultimately, responsibility remains with a human leader, not entirely trusting AI which is reflected in the low confidence level in new technologies.

In addition to fostering trust, great human leaders help their people thrive becoming the best version of themselves.[13] They address deficiencies, provide assistance when necessary, and inspire their employees to expand their horizon and capabilities beyond the current limits.

3 From Knowledge to Capabilities: The Transformation of Future Skills, Society, and Leadership

Acknowledging AI is not an isolated tool rather a transformative force that is reshaping entire industries, economies, business models, roles, and societal structures. From automation to augmentation, the influence of AI is limitless, influencing every aspect of our professional and personal lives at an unprecedented dimension and pace.[14]

The changing face of future leadership[15] in the age of AI will enforce new qualities and approaches,[16] while other existing skills become more relevant, faced with what differentiates human leaders from AI and what defines us as human.[17] Particularly, board members and leaders, those at the top of responsibility and strat-

[9] Bailey (2023).

[10] Andrea (2017).

[11] Blanchard and Conley (2022).

[12] Fehr and Schmidt (2005).

[13] Covey (2022).

[14] Execs In The Know LLC (2024).

[15] Winkler (2025).

[16] Swiss Future Institute (2024).

[17] Coleman (2019).

egy, should become knowledgeable in AI.[18] As AI continues to transform everything from industries to entire business models, board members must possess a solid understanding of AI to effectively guide their organisations.[19] The challenge: Leaders have the task of mastering the new technological development themselves and guiding their teams. What skillsets do we demand from our future leaders and what things do we teach our children in the age of AI?

- **Adaptability**: Future leaders will need to be highly adaptive, flexible, and open to change, continuously learning and evolving with the technological advancements.
- **Data Literacy and Critical Thinking**: Future leaders will constantly educate to become and stay literate in AI. Education is key to staying relevant as a leader. They will understand how to critically read, apply data and tools to make informed relevant decisions. Innovative problem-solving, the ability to analyse complex situations, to evaluate critically, and make decisions that consider multiple dimensions will be essential.
- **Vision, Values, Ethics, and Compliance**: Future leaders will inspire and encourage people to dream big and drive innovation. Leaders will spot the opportunities between people and AI, connecting the dots between data and people. Future leaders will continue to act as a role-model, live up to the values and principles, ensuring that technology is used in a compliant manner. While AI provides data to make decisions, the need for future leaders in ethical oversight becomes paramount. Leaders are responsible that AI is applied responsibly considering the quality of data and ethics embedded.
- **Emotional Intelligence and Collaboration**: Future leaders will foster a culture of collaboration, applying AI to enhance teamwork, culture, and communication. Future leaders will foster meaningful human relationship, building trust, succeeding upon empathy.
- **Resilience**: In rapidly changing world full of uncertainties, changing information and shorter lifecycles of what is valid, the board and leadership ability to navigate change and to be resilient will be decisive to succeed.[20]

The dawn of a new epoch and a paradigm of shift arises.[21] As we transition from the knowledge society, characterised by the primacy of information, to a future shaped by AI, we transition to a capabilities skills society.[22] Skills, adaptability, learning, and combining new things in a highly adaptive manner will be more relevant than knowledge itself. Looking at the dynamics of this transformation, examining what will be substituted, what will change, and what will remain.

[18] Swiss Future Institute (2024).

[19] Global Digital Board Academy (2024).

[20] Global Digital Board Academy (2024).

[21] Grimm et al. (2020), p. 164.

[22] Swiss Future Institute (2024).

3.1 Routine Tasks Will Be Substituted and Automised

Tasks characterised by repetition, rule-based processes, and predictable outcomes will become increasingly automated. This substitution will be most evident in sectors such as manufacturing, logistics, and administrative work, where AI will perform routine operations with greater efficiency and precision. The substitution and enhancement of data entry, simple decision-making, and some aspects of creative production, such as text and graphic design, will see significant improvement being substituted and enhanced by AI. Human labour will transcend to more complex, creative, and relational elements, while human-centric leadership skills become more relevant.

3.2 Knowledge and Learning Will Be Transformed

The very nature of knowledge is undergoing a transformation. In the knowledge society, expertise was based on the accumulation of information. In contrast, in the AI future society, the emphasis will shift from static knowledge accumulation to dynamic learning, data literacy, critical thinking, and high adaptivity. This is particularly the case given the reduction in the lifespan of knowledge and the acceleration of technological change. It will be necessary for educational systems to evolve, with a focus on teaching students how to learn, think critically, and solve complex problems rather than accumulating static knowledge.

4 When Human Meets Tech: How AI Has the Potential to Enhance the Human Leadership Beyond its Capabilities

When human meets AI, it will over time lead to an era where human intellectual superiority may find its end, and the monumental shift will fundamentally challenge all of us. AI will challenge the human values and question the overall socio-economic world order such as we know, yet it also has enormous potential to transform the health and well-being and reveal the mysteries of intelligence and our understanding. Human rights attorney Flynn Coleman presents a compelling argument for the necessity to build ethics into the development of AI from the start.[23]

Leadership functions are ultimately about creating a vision such as a dream as stated at the beginning of this chapter, being able to articulate the vision, motivating, inspiring, and sharing the vision within and across teams.[24] When AI advances at an unprecedented pace, a higher stage of AI development in future may be reached, when AI will be capable of replacing human leadership in most of the outlined

[23] Coleman (2019).

[24] Unkrig (2021), pp. 247–300.

areas. According to a survey of executives by EdX, an initiative of Harvard University and M.I.T., half of executives (47%) believe the human CEO role will be partially or fully replaced by AI in future.[25] This reflects that though not entirely trusting AI, people do see and believe in its capabilities.

AI is transforming both, the way human work and the way human lead. AI has the potential to complement and elevate the human leadership on the next level[26] if we use it ethically.[27]

AI has the potential to facilitate the identification of emotional patterns within textual data, thereby assisting human leaders to manage their own emotions as well as dealing with the emotions of others. Furthermore, AI has the potential to develop interactive, game-based learning scenarios in which leaders can practise recognising and managing emotions in a secure setup. They can systematically practise best, middle, and worst emotional scenarios in a protected yet realistic environment under predefined conditions. The capacity of AI to monitor team dynamics and to identify potential sources of conflict enables leaders to enhance their emotional agility. AI apps like Affectiva or Talk.Swiss[28] can provide facial and voice analysis in real-time, offering leaders feedback on the emotional level in meetings which identifies subtle signals of stress and discontentment. Other AI-powered learning platforms such as Teachy[29] detects and matches any skill gap and upskills on a modular base. The wide amount of tech opportunities offer leaders the objective real-time options to become aware and to adapt the leadership style to the particular situation, helping to lead more empathetically and becoming better over time.[30] It will lead to a fundamental shift of how human leaders work and lead. More sophisticated AI will offer the potential to augment all of the existing human leadership qualities, while reducing the human deficiencies.[31,32]

5 Managing Risks of AI in Future Work and Why Data and Ethics Matter

Societal inequities may be deepened by unequal access to technology and education.[33] The potential for job displacement requires proactive measures in reskilling and upskilling the existing human workforce to stay relevant in the future. At the

[25] edX (2023).

[26] Execs In The Know, LLC (2024).

[27] Coleman (2019).

[28] Swiss based app, using AI speech recognition and data analytics to boost and make communication profitable.

[29] Teachy (2024).

[30] Execs In The Know, LLC (2024).

[31] Lee and Chen Qiufan (2021).

[32] Execs In The Know, LLC (2024).

[33] O'Neil (2016).

same time, the fusion of human creativity and AI can lead to unprecedented innovations, solving complex global challenges in health care, sustainability, and intellectual mysteries.[34]

The influence of mathematical AI models on the decisions that shape human lives is becoming increasingly evident. From the choice of educational institution to the decision to obtain a car or real-estate loan or the level of health insurance premium paid, the role of the AI models in making these decisions is becoming more prominent and relevant. In theory, this should result in a greater degree of fairness.[35] All individuals are evaluated in accordance with an identical set of criteria, thereby eliminating any potential for human bias.

In practice the decision-making processes that result in outcomes with significant implications for the life of humans are not based on objective bias-free evaluation of the individual in the age of AI. Instead, these decisions are built by AI data-driven insights which learnt its pattern from the history of mankind. AI is trained by a massive amount of historic data collective that does not directly originate from the individual's data, the individual is rather assigned to a certain group based on pre-established socio-demographic criteria.

Such criteria may be derived from a number of factors such as gender, ethnics, age, health records, postcode, household income, and the reputation of the educational institution attended amongst others. These data points, applied in combinations, may be used to the advantage or disadvantage of an individual. A further consequence of AI is that, in contrast to all other potential human existing biases and discrimination, the relation is no longer limited to a one-to-one in person human based risk, where one person potentially acts in a discriminating way towards another, rather minor error rates in AI have the risk to lead to a systematic discrimination.[36]

In this sense, AI has an imminent risk that bias will become systemic and multiplied at an exponential rate, affecting entire groups of people without being able to detect the root cause of failure what leads to an outcome produced by AI.[37] The constructed criteria, categories, and combinations are opaque, non-transparent, and non-comprehensible for the persons involved, affected, nor for third parties.

As Cathy O'Neil demonstrates the models currently in use are characterised by opacity, lack of regulation and incontestable status, even in instances where they are demonstrably incorrect. Of greatest concern is the reinforcement of discriminatory practices. If a student from a low-income background is unable to obtain a loan due to the risk assessment criteria of an AI lending model, which may be influenced by factors such as their geographical location of the poor neighbourhood, they are

[34] Coleman (2019).

[35] O'Neil (2016).

[36] Orwat (2024), p. 144.

[37] O'Neil (2016).

subsequently denied access to the educational opportunities that could potentially lift them out of poverty, resulting in a continuous negative loop.[38]

In this context, the quality of the training material data is of significant importance. The current data used for training are limited in its diversity, with a preponderance of male, white, and relatively homogeneous samples. From health medicals to the safety of cars, to tech products to search engine advertising, products and services are dominantly tailored and optimised for a specific group of already privileged white men in a perpetuation loop. Safiya Umoja Noble argues AI data discrimination represents a tangible social issue. Noble posits that the confluence of private interests in promoting selected websites, coupled with the oligopolistic status of a limited number of search engines, culminates in a skewed set of search algorithms that afford preferential treatment to whiteness and disparage people of colour, particularly women of colour.[39]

In her analysis of textual and media searches, as well as extensive research on search paid online advertising, Noble reveals the existence of a culture of racism and sexism in the way discoverability is created online. As search engines corporations grow with greater relevance creating a whole universe of AI products and services, comprising next to email a primary source of online learning in primary and secondary education, and beyond, it is imperative to comprehend and rectify the concerning trends in discriminatory practices.[40]

While humans are increasingly relying upon AI to assist with decision-making based on massive amounts on trained data, it is imperative to recognise that the efficacy of AI systems is contingent upon the quality of the data upon which they are trained and its ethical application. If left unmonitored, AI has the potential to perpetuate all existing human historic biases present in the data of humanity on which it is trained in a systematic multiplied manner.[41] Therefore, it is crucial upon human leaders to ensure that AI is developed and applied in an ethical manner from the start.[42]

This implies to build diverse teams and continuous monitoring to identify and address biases in every process AI is involved.[43,44]

Whenever AI is implemented within a process that ultimately produces an outcome affecting the life of people, those affected must:

(1) First know about AI being involved
(2) Second, receive a right to learn how the outcome was made
(3) Third, have a right to object and correct the outcome

[38] O'Neil (2016).

[39] Noble (2018).

[40] Noble (2018).

[41] O'Neil (2016).

[42] Coleman (2019).

[43] Execs In The Know LLC (2024).

[44] Coleman (2019).

The current lack of ability of those affected to object to possible forms of AI discrimination, systemic categorisation manifests a further power imbalance widening the existing in the society.[45]

As a prerequisite in applying AI responsibly, users of AI, leaders in particular, need to become competent in dealing with both the opportunities **and** risks of AI. In this sense, competence and technical literacy are a prerequisite to act responsibly. Getting educated and trained in AI becomes an ethical obligation.

6 Conclusion: The Human AI Tech Future Symbiosis

This chapter is a call to act in cultivating a leadership that champions both technological advancement and human-centric leadership skills, where humanity remains at the heart of a responsible ethical progress. By fostering a collaborative, diverse, inclusive ethical approach, we can harness the power of AI to create a future that is not only technologically advanced but also profoundly human.

A paradigm shift is taking place: "Instead of the master-slave model, in which the human rules over the machine, there will either be a master-slave model with reversed roles or the relationship will be one of partnership."[46]

The question was asked at the beginning: Assuming that AI is based on algorithm and trained by data, how much of it is tech, and how much of its nature is human? How much will both sites influence and modify each other to what extend?

The future of work implies the concept of an AI–human future symbiosis, whereby machines enhance human capabilities at an unprecedented manner. Machines will enable the humans to transcend previous limitations in all its senses. When AI take over routine tasks, humans are liberated to focus on higher-order thinking, innovation, and emotional intelligence, which are attributes that define the essence of humanity.

Leaders will evolve and learn to adapt their leadership style in order to manage teams that are augmented by the capabilities of AI. It is not sufficient to continue as it is, rather to develop further, cultivating a harmonious symbiosis with AI,[47] both recognising its potential as well as learning to manage the risk of systematic biases as outlined.[48] In order to effectively navigate the transition from humans to increasingly sophisticated AI, it is imperative to integrate human ethical values into the design of AI systems and to proactively develop robust oversight mechanisms in a controlled manner.[49]

Those in positions of leadership who are able to strike a balance between leveraging AI for data-driven insights and maintaining the humanity of their teams will be the ones who are best positioned to flourish in the future era of sophisticated

[45] Orwat (2024), p. 150.

[46] Grimm et al. (2020), p. 164.

[47] Lee and Chen Qiufan (2021).

[48] O'Neil (2016).

[49] Coleman (2019).

AI. Those who are able to adapt their approach and lead with empathy and innovation will be best placed to influence the future direction of the workplace.[50]

"Sceptics continue to question the reliability of AI technologies and the safety of humans. For example, the question arises as to who is AI liable in the event of wrong decisions or incorrect measures based on AI, e.g. in production facilities, both legally and morally."[51]

"The future is not a given state but what we do in the present in shaping it," as stated by the AI Future Council of the Swiss Future Institute.[52] Leaders in particular bear a tremendous responsibility to navigate the ethical challenges associated with the development **and** deployment of AI.

It is imperative that there is transparency, ethical standards, and equal access to AI in terms of both input, the training set of data, and output, the quality of data, and every outcome made by AI.

There must be a human accountability embedded in the overall process of AI, where AI is involved in generating outcome affecting the lives of people. Human leaders need to foster cultures that value lifelong learning, strategic critical thinking, collaboration, diversity, and inclusion to keep the human responsibility despite or because of the advancements in AI. This starts with becoming AI literate by continuous education.

To navigate the transformation, it is paramount that we pursue a future that enhances human potential. It is paramount that we adopt an approach that integrates AI to enhance rather than to replace humans, which fosters an inclusive adaptive learning culture and incorporates ethical values and compliance. In this regard, the future society will not only inherit the outcome of the knowledge society but will surpass them, building a new world in which technology and humanity evolve and thrive together.

References

Studies & Reports

Barton M-C, Pöppelbuß J (2022) Principles for the Ethical Use of Artificial Intelligence. https://www.researchgate.net/publication/359143813_Prinzipien_fur_die_ethische_Nutzung_kunstlicher_IntelligenzPrinciples_for_the_Ethical_Use_of_Artificial_Intelligence

[50] Execs In The Know LLC (2024).

[51] Barton and Pöppelbuß (2022), p. 473.

[52] Swiss Future Institute (2024).

edX (2023) Navigating the Workplace in the Age of AI. Retrieved from https://business.edx.org/wp-content/uploads/2023/09/edX_Workplace_Intelligence_AI_Report.pdf
Fehr E, Schmidt KM (2005) The Economics of Fairness, Reciprocity and Altruism – Experimental Evidence and New Theories. Retrieved from https://www.econstor.eu/bitstream/10419/104156/1/lmu-mdp_2005-20.pdf
Goldberg Y (2015) A Primer on Neural Network Models for Natural Language Processing. Retrieved from https://arxiv.org/abs/1510.00726
IMD-St Gallen Symposium (2021) Strengthening Trust in Technology When It Matters The Most. Retrieved from https://symposium.org/wp-content/uploads/2021/12/Strengthening-Trust-in-Technology_A-joint-IMD-and-SGS-White-Paper.pdf
Stanford Study Panel Report (2021) Gathering Strength, Gathering Storms: The One Hundred Year Study on Artificial Intelligence (AI100) 2021 Study Panel Report. Retrieved from https://ai100.stanford.edu/gathering-strength-gathering-storms-one-hundred-year-study-artificial-intelligence-ai100-2021-study

Books

Blanchard K, Conley R (2022) Simple Truths of leadership: 52 ways to be a servant leader and build trust. National Geographic Books
Coleman F (2019) A human algorithm: how artificial intelligence is redefining who we are
Covey SMR (2022) Trust and inspire: how truly great leaders unleash greatness in others
Finn Ed (2018) What algorithms want: imagination in the age of computing
Grimm V et al (2020) The ODD protocol for describing agent-based and other simulation models: a second update to improve clarity, replication, and structural realism
Lee K-F, Chen Qiufan C (2021) AI 2041: ten visions for our future
Noble SU (2018) Algorithms of oppression: how search engines reinforce racism
O'Neil C (2016) Weapons of math destruction: how big data increases inequality and threatens democracy
Orwat C (2024) Algorithmische Differenzierung und Diskriminierung aus Sicht der Menschenwürde [Algorithmic Discrimination From the Perspective of Human Dignity; German translation of the article mentioned above]. In: Reder M, Koska C (eds) Künstliche Intelligenz und ethische Verantwortung, Bielefeld: transcript, pp 141–161
Reibmayr A (2017) Trust leadership: take responsibility, use success and transform
Unkrig ER (2021). Resilienzfördernde Führung. In Springer eBooks (S. 247–300). https://doi.org/10.1007/978-3-658-34591-4_5
Winkler K, Niedermeier S, Yuan K (2025) KI-Wissen für Führungskräfte: Entscheidungsgrundlagen und Insights für unternehmerisches Handeln

Websites

Execs In The Know, LLC (2024) How work and Leadership will Change as AI Advances. Retrieved from https://execsintheknow.com/magazines/october-2023-issue/how-work-and-leadership-will-change-as-ai-advances/
Global Digital Board Academy, Zug Switzerland (2025). https://www.avaglobaldigital.com/
Swiss Future Institute AG, Zug Switzerland (2025). https://www.futureinstitute.ch/
Talk.Swiss in collaboration with EPFL, Swiss Federal Technology Institute of Lausanne Switzerland (2025): Swiss AI app, using AI speech recognition and data analytics to boost and make communication profitable. https://talk.swiss/
Teachy AI powered matching learning tutoring platform on a modular base, Bern Switzerland (2025). https://teachy.ch/

Katrin J. Yuan is the CEO of the Swiss Future Institute AG with a background in technology, strategy, and business transformation. She is a five-time board member, Chair of the AI Future Council by the Swiss Future Institute, lectures at four universities in Germany and in Switzerland such as for the University of Applied Sciences Kalaidos, and serves as a jury member for ETH. With a background of having led eight divisions in top management, Katrin is an influential executive, founder, investor, keynote speaker, and edutainer. Holding masterclasses with certifications in AI, Tech Site of Visibility, Finance, Leadership and Boards, her expertise extends to AI future tech, boards, enforcing responsible AI, and a diverse data approach.

Follow her on

LinkedIn https://www.linkedin.com/in/katrin-j-yuan/

Instagram https://www.instagram.com/katrinjyuan/

Youtube https://www.youtube.com/@katrinjyuan

Website https://www.futureinstitute.ch

The Philosophical Implications of Artificial Intelligence

8

How Can the Implementation of AI Technologies Contribute to and Not Degrade Human Flourishing?

Matthew David Segall

Abstract

Following the famous 1956 Dartmouth Conference, where a team of computer scientists first coined the term "artificial intelligence," philosophers have raised significant ontological and ethical questions regarding AI's nature and its implications for human flourishing. More recently, the growing popularity of Large Language Models and so-called "deep fakes" has made the public more aware of the power of AI, thrusting profound existential dilemmas into our collective consciousness. This chapter attempts to address our current situation from a philosophical perspective by reflecting on basic questions, including: What are these technologies for? Whose interests do they serve? And perhaps most importantly, how are they changing our sense of conscious human agency? The aim is to better contextualize the transformation already underway in the hopes of avoiding false myths and unethical outcomes.

1 Introduction

Following the famous 1956 Dartmouth Conference, where a team of computer scientists first coined the term "artificial intelligence," philosophers have endeavored to raise significant ontological and ethical questions regarding AI's nature and its implications for human flourishing. In response to the Soviet Union's successful launch of the Sputnik satellite two years after the Dartmouth conference, the US military created what is now known as DARPA (Defense Advanced Research Projects Agency). DARPA quickly became the largest funder of AI research, making clear that, alongside corporate profits, the weaponization of computer

M. D. Segall (✉)
Department at the California Institute of Integral Studies, San Francisco, CA, USA
e-mail: msegall@ciis.edu

C. H. Hoffmann, D. Bansal (eds.), *AI Ethics in Practice*, Integrated Science 35,
https://doi.org/10.1007/978-3-031-87023-1_8

technologies has been a primary driver of innovation from the beginning. Today, with companies competing to implement the next generation of AI "agents," fundamental questions remain regarding the compatibility of such technologies with human flourishing. While the military-industrial complex has been developing these technologies for decades, the recent popularization of AI tools in the form of consumer products has brought the profound ontological and ethical quandaries they raise into public consciousness. This chapter attempts to address our current situation from a philosophical perspective by reflecting on basic questions, including: What are these technologies for? Whose interests do they serve? And perhaps most importantly, how are they changing our sense of our own conscious human agency? The aim is to better contextualize the transformation already underway in the hopes of dispelling some false myths and avoiding unethical outcomes.

In any discussion about AI, it is crucial from the outset to recognize that human consciousness—our thinking, feeling, and willing—is not made of digital information or reducible to computational processes, no matter how powerful. Throughout history, humanity has attempted to make sense of the mystery of our own minds by making analogies to the popular artifacts of the day: wind-harps, wax tablets, clocks, steam engines, telegraph lines, and today, the computer. While something is always revealed by the use of such metaphors, much may also be obscured. Consciousness is a living medium that remains undetectable by any measuring device that neuroscientists or physicists might devise. While for conscious beings like you and me, our first-person awareness and agency is the most obvious aspect of our existence, its invisibility to any external means of detection highlights a fundamental distinction that must be established at the very start of any discussion of the philosophical significance of AI. Of course, neuroscience utilizes various scanners to track cranial blood flow and electrochemical activity, but such third-person observables are not what we know from within as our conscious experience. You cannot crack open the skull to discover the color red or the taste of a strawberry, much less the source of our moral and aesthetic judgments. How what brain scanners measure might relate to our conscious experiences remains a deep philosophical mystery, with over 200 different proposals currently attempting to address the question and exploring the implications of different answers (Kuhn 2024).

The so-called "hard problem of consciousness," first formulated by the philosopher David Chalmers (1996), ought to deflate the hype surrounding the ill-formed idea of "conscious" computers. As Chalmers famously argued, scientists could in principle come to understand everything there is to know about the functions of the brain and still have no explanation as to why brains seem to be haunted by consciousness. From a purely physicalist point of view, consciousness appears to be something "extra" not reducible to the neurochemical goings-on in the skull. Thus, until we have a better philosophical understanding of the nature of consciousness and its place in the physical world, claims that current or future AI devices possess consciousness remain dramatically overblown and even nonsensical.

2 The Embodiment of Consciousness and the Limits of AI

Understanding the brain itself already requires more than just considering it as an information processor. To truly grasp its nature, we must remember the brain's embeddedness within the living body and its evolutionary history. Our bodies are ecosystems comprised of trillions of cells, with only about a tenth containing human DNA. The rest are part of a microbial ecosystem symbiotically interacting with our human cells. Thus, we are a living society of "occasions of experience," to use the philosopher Alfred North Whitehead's terms (1929), a conscious animal made of a community of other sentient cellular beings—a whole made of smaller wholes, rather than a mere assemblage of algorithmically interacting parts.

Despite the popularity of the metaphor, the brain itself cannot be simplistically divided into mental "software" and physical "hardware." In the living world of our embodied experience, mind and matter are not so easily separated. While their connection remains mysterious, philosophers like Whitehead argued that we can take a huge step forward in our understanding by coming to see mind and matter as entangled phases in an unbroken creative process. Our minds are embodied processes emergent from ancient evolutionary lineages rooted deep in our cellular architecture. Our capacity for conscious agency depends upon the basic feelings of both sympathy and precarity that typify our existence as fragile membrane-bound creatures metabolically surfing the energy gradients of our environments to survive and thrive. The AI systems currently under development lack anything like this precarious embodiment and historical embeddedness. AI systems are not continually engaged in materially and formally making themselves, as living organisms do. This means, among other things, that they lack any sense of relevance and emotional valence allowing them to determine what data in their environment may be important and which can safely be ignored.

The lack of evolutionary embeddedness turns out to be rather important. Machine learning algorithms can acquire certain behaviors in a relatively short training period, but this is not at all the same as how an evolutionary lineage emerges. An evolved organism has been bound up in a process of structural coupling with a whole historical series of environments over the course of billions of years (Maturana and Varela 1980). Many valuable survival strategies and sense-making heuristics have been picked up along the way—a deep organismic memory of how to be in sync with the rhythms of this planet has been acquired over that long, multi-billion-year process. On the other hand, any machine that is initially designed and built by human beings, even if it is a machine learning neural network trained to interact with specific environments and languages, etc., is still going to lack that depth of embodied memory. Putting their other important differences to the side, no machine has been engaged in evolutionary learning for as long as biological organisms have. This fact gives us reason to suspect that our machines, increasingly impressive though they may be, are relatively blind to important subtle features of the Earth's environment that we, as organisms, are more constitutively prepared for. We should expect even the most sophisticated AI systems to make rather obvious mistakes because they just haven't encountered certain situations before.

3 The Evolutionary Context of Intelligence

Furthermore, to understand the significance of AI, we must consider intelligence within the broader context of evolution. Evolutionary theory reveals intelligence as not merely the ability to process information but as a deeply embodied skill, shaped by the interaction between organisms and their environments over millions of years. For instance, a bird's ability to navigate long migratory journeys is not merely a matter of calculating distances but is rooted in a complex web of evolutionary adaptations—sensory, neurological, and behavioral—that allow it to adaptively align with magnetic fields, weather patterns, and ecological cues. Human intelligence, likewise, is not just about abstract reasoning or problem-solving: it is about navigating the world as a living, feeling, and historically and culturally situated community member.

AI, as currently conceived, lacks this evolutionary grounding. It may excel at specific tasks, such as playing chess or finding oil deposits, but these abilities do not equate to the kind of general intelligence and sense-making capacity that living organisms possess. Even the most advanced AI systems do not *understand* the world they operate in; they manipulate numerical weights and statistical patterns without any awareness or understanding of what the digits being processed represent. This distinction is crucial because it underscores the difference between machine learning, which is driven by data and algorithms, and human learning, which is driven by lived experience, emotional investment, and ethical engagement with others and the world.

4 Relevance Realization and the Non-Computational Nature of Cognition

One of the key insights into the limitations of AI and its implications for human agency comes from recent work in the biology of cognition on "relevance realization." Jaeger et al. (2024) argue that the ability to realize relevance is observable in all living organisms, from bacteria to humans. However, despite being perfectly natural, organismic relevance realization transcends formalization and so is non-computable. While computational models may partially simulate some aspects of cognition, they can never fully instantiate this core competency of living beings.

In line with what has already been said above, the authors point to crucial metabolic, ecological, and evolutionary dynamics that make organisms dramatically different from any known AI or machine learning systems. These dynamics are involved in the realization of relevance through a meliorative process that allows agents to maintain and optimize their grip on their environments, achieving what they term a "transjective" agent–arena relationship that transcends our normal sense of a boundary separating embodied minds from their environments. Cognition is understood to be radically relational and extended, both socially and ecologically. This relationship, characterized by what the authors call "embodied ecological rationality," is fundamental to life and categorically distinguishes organisms from non-living computer systems.

From this perspective, the difference between living organisms and AI systems becomes even more pronounced. AI operates within a predefined formalized ontology, handling well-defined problems in a "small world." In contrast, organisms navigate a "large world" filled with ill-defined problems, where relevance must be continuously realized to make sense of their environment. Jaeger et al.'s distinction between logical inference (i.e., the operations instantiating machine learning algorithms) and relevance realization echoes the Whiteheadian distinction (Whitehead 1929, pp. 199–207, 280) between the Bayesian statistical calculations informing neural network architectures and organismic "lures for feeling," which while also capable of predicting probabilities are rooted in aesthetic contrasts and an attunement to long-term environmental rhythms rather than numerical calculations or statistical models.

5 The Nature of Intelligence: Human and Artificial

It is important to deepen our understanding of the nature of "intelligence." Even human intelligence could already be considered artificial in some respects, since so much of our everyday awareness and agency is augmented by our tools and artifacts. Our ancestors have been coevolving with external implements for tens of thousands if not millions of years, whether in the form of obsidian fashioned to carve animal meat, bone flutes to play music, or spoken words to coordinate shared attention and intention. Speech externalizes thought in a physical form, a process further extended by written languages, the printing press, the telegram, radio, television, and the Internet. Thus, rather than imagining that some more advanced AI system might become "truly" or "generally" intelligent, digital forms of artificial intelligence should be understood as the latest evolutionary extension of human intelligence, which has always already been, to some degree, artificial.

Considering the irreducibility of consciousness to any measurable physical process and our species' coevolutionary history with external artifacts, the crucial question is not whether machines will become conscious. AI devices are digital information processors and so entirely unlike conscious human organisms. Instead, we should ask how this new extension of human intelligence into digital technologies is altering *our* consciousness. How are we being transformed by our interaction with these machines? If we allow the hype to convince us that a computer could become conscious, the danger is that we inadvertently diminish human beings to the status of machines. In other words, our fascination with supposedly autonomous machines may lead us to gradually remake and degrade the richness and fluidity of our world and our relationships with one another in an effort to support the efficient functioning of our devices (Frank et al. 2024, p. 174).

This concern resonates with the integral philosopher William Irwin Thompson's critique of AI. He argued (2003, p. 187):

> In order to grant consciousness to machines, the engineers first labor to subtract it from humans, as they work to foist upon philosophers a caricature of consciousness in the digital switches of weights and gates in neural nets. As the caricature goes into public circulation with the help of the media, it becomes an acceptable counterfeit currency, and the humanistic philosopher of mind soon finds himself replaced by the robotics scientist.

Thompson's warning is not merely about the potential obsolescence of philosophers but about the broader societal implications of reducing human beings to the status of machines. This reduction not only undermines our understanding of what it means to be human but also risks eroding the very foundations of our ethical and moral intuitions, which are grounded in the recognition of the dignity and agency of human persons.

6 AI, Society, and the Future of Human Flourishing

As we advance deeper into the age of AI, the question of how these technologies will impact human society becomes increasingly urgent. AI has the potential to bring about significant benefits, from improving healthcare outcomes through predictive diagnostics to enhancing education through personalized learning platforms. However, these benefits will only be realized if AI technologies are developed and implemented in ways that align with human values and promote human flourishing. For example, would it really be an improvement to have millions of children sitting at computer terminals running a simulation of a teacher, rather than exploring the wonders of the natural world with their full suite of human senses alongside human teachers capable of genuine empathy and shared wonder? What are the long-term consequences of replacing personal interaction between human beings with algorithmically driven screentime, particular in the case of children? Is learning just a matter of digesting new information, or is there also an important emotional and interpersonal dimension to developing a sound understanding of this wonderous world?

One of the most pressing concerns is the potential for AI to exacerbate existing social inequalities. As AI systems are increasingly used in areas such as criminal justice, hiring, and lending, there is a risk that these technologies will reinforce and even amplify biases that are already present in society. For example, if an AI system is trained on data that reflects historical patterns of discrimination, it may inadvertently perpetuate those patterns in its decision-making processes. This is not just a technical issue but an ethical one, requiring careful consideration of the values that are embedded in AI systems and the societal impacts of their deployment.

Moreover, the integration of AI into the economy raises questions about the future of work and the distribution of wealth. As machines become capable of performing tasks that were once the exclusive domain of humans, there is a risk that large segments of the population will be displaced from their jobs, leading to increased economic inequality and social unrest. To address these challenges, we must think creatively about new economic models and social safety nets that can support individuals in a world where work as we currently understand it may no longer be the primary means of securing a livelihood. Again, not everything is an engineering problem that can be solved by adding more computers or by the next software update. AI raises existential and ethical challenges that only conscious human agents can resolve.

Finally, there is the question of how AI will affect our sense of identity and agency itself. As we increasingly rely on machines to act on our behalf, there is a risk that we will lose our sense of autonomy and self-determination. This is not just a theoretical concern but a practical one, as evidenced by the growing use of AI in areas such as surveillance, where individuals may find themselves subject to "decisions" made by algorithms that they do not understand and cannot challenge. I put "decisions" in scare quotes because the fact is that computers are incapable of consciously deciding anything. *We* are the ones who must decide what sort of power they are to have over our lives, and existing power inequalities obviously play a big part in shaping the technologies already being deployed by nation-states and big corporations.

7 Conclusion

The race to create "Artificial General Intelligence" or conscious machines is more a deceptive advertising campaign than a technological challenge. AI and machine learning are powerful and exciting technologies that will continue to advance and find many valuable applications, transforming our economy in the coming years. The danger lies not just in the tools themselves but in our human relationship with them. By ensuring that AI technologies serve the interests of human beings and do not continue to be captured by corporate profit-seeking and military applications, we can harness their potential to contribute to human flourishing rather than degrade it. Incorporating the insights of relevance realization further deepens our understanding of the limitations of AI and the unique qualities of human consciousness and agency. True relevance realization is an embodied, organismic process that cannot be fully captured by computational models.

As we move forward, it is essential to cultivate a philosophical perspective that recognizes the limits of AI and the unique qualities of human beings. This perspective must inform the development and deployment of AI technologies, guiding our society toward outcomes that enhance rather than diminish our collective well-being. By doing so, we can ensure that AI serves as a tool for human flourishing, rather than a force that undermines it.

References

Chalmers D (1996) The conscious mind: in search of a fundamental theory. Oxford University Press

Frank A, Gleiser M, Thompson E (2024) The blind spot: why science cannot ignore human experience. MIT Press

Jaeger J, Riedl A, Djedovic A, Vervaeke J, Walsh D (2024) Naturalizing relevance realization: why agency and cognition are fundamentally not computational. Front Psychol 15. https://doi.org/10.3389/fpsyg.2024.1362658

Kuhn RL (2024) A landscape of consciousness: Toward a taxonomy of explanations and implications. Progr Biophys Mol Biol 190:28–169

Maturana H, Varela F (1980) Autopoiesis and cognition: the realization of the living. Reidel Publishing Co.

Thompson WI (2003) The Borg or Borges? J Consci Stud 10(4-5):187

Whitehead AN (1929) Process and reality. The Free Press

Matthew David Segall PhD, is an American philosopher and educator specializing in process philosophy and its applications. He is currently associate professor in the Philosophy, Cosmology, and Consciousness Department at California Institute of Integral Studies (CIIS) in San Francisco. Segall strives to bring an integral and transdisciplinary approach to the study of contemporary natural science, bringing its findings into dialogue with philosophical and religious perspectives, with the ultimate aim of addressing complex planetary challenges.

In addition to his teaching and research, Segall is an active blogger and public speaker, engaging with topics at the intersection of science, philosophy, and spirituality. He has contributed to various publications and conferences, promoting dialogue on the relevance of process thought for addressing ecological and social issues. His latest book is titled *Crossing the Threshold: Etheric Imagination in the Post-Kantian Process Philosophy of Schelling and Whitehead* (Revelore, 2023). Segall's work emphasizes the importance of reimagining humanity's relationship with nature, advocating for a participatory understanding of knowledge and reality.

The Emergence of Trust and Ethics

9

Blueprints of Decentralization and the Pragmatism of Artificial Intelligence

James B. Glattfelder

Abstract

What lies at the intersection of trust, ethics, decentralization, and artificial intelligence (AI) within the context of our rapidly advancing technological landscape and its socio-ecological impacts? Specifically, what are the philosophical and practical challenges imposed by centralized power structures? In this chapter, we investigate how a shift toward decentralized systems, such as Distributed Ledger Technology (DLT), could address the ethical and governance deficiencies evident in our current global framework and how AI systems can potentially emerge as unbiased, non-ideological, and pragmatic stakeholders for non-human life and the biosphere overall, a perspective entirely missing from traditional discussions focused predominantly on human-centric concerns. The emergence of AI and DLT offers novel tools and blueprints for reconfiguring human interaction and governance, possibly enabling more adaptive, resilient, and sustainable systems and leading to more equitable and effective societal structures. Informed by insights from complex systems theory and the collective intelligence seen in nature, including the mechanisms of self-organization, our human affairs are recontextualized as networks of interaction embedded within the interconnected biosphere. Can such a realization help address the global challenges we are facing today?

J. B. Glattfelder (✉)
Consciousness and Transformation Lab, MQ Learning Academy, Zurich, Switzerland
e-mail: info@jth.ch; jbg@jth.ch

C. H. Hoffmann, D. Bansal (eds.), *AI Ethics in Practice*, Integrated Science 35,
https://doi.org/10.1007/978-3-031-87023-1_9

1 Introduction

We live in extraordinary times. On the one hand, our civilization's technological prowess is breathtaking. We are witnessing unprecedented leaps in progression, overshadowing former advancements thought to be the pinnacle of human achievement. A paradigmatic example is the sudden and rapid emergence of artificial intelligence, not only set to disrupt the very fabric of society but also forcing us to reconsider our felt cognitive supremacy.

However, this era is also marked by the alarming dismantling of the biosphere, the systemic inequity of wealth distribution, the erosion of social coherence, the entrenchment of ideologies, and the negation of consensus reality in the wake of a post-truth era weaponizing ignorance. Unsurprisingly, many people are living lives marked by existential dread, alienation, and disenchantment, desperately trying to fill the void with numbing consumerism and fleeting distractions like endless social media scrolling.

How is this possible? How can human intelligence unlock such profound understanding relating to the workings of nature, enabling God-like powers, but fail so spectacularly at creating a world characterized by sustainability, meaning, and happiness? In other words, why does individual human intelligence not foster collective human intelligence?

In essence, two factors can be understood as contributing to the many existential crises we as a global civilization are facing: centralized systems of power and poor ethical decision-making. While the world has become vastly more networked and complex, our modes of governance have not. All too often, decisions made by a tiny, albeit influential, minority disproportionately affect a significant number of people. Then, the ethical implications of decisions, especially long-term ones, are mostly ignored. Short-termism, the lack of transparency and accountability, and overall exclusion and marginalization are readily accepted practices.

However, two technological advancements can not only help us better understand the current malaise but perhaps also contribute to its mitigation. Next to the sapient powers unleashed by AI, a novel blueprint for human interaction holds the potential to reconfigure the networks sustaining the status quo.

2 The Power of Self-Organization

The systems nature has assembled in its nearly 4 billion-year evolution all have the hallmarks of collective intelligence. The most defining characteristics are behaviors marked by adaptivity, resilience, and sustainability. Nature seems to implement this feat by utilizing templates of decentralized organization. From the swarming behavior of birds, the unified superorganisms comprising countless social insects, the collective decision-making seen in honey bees, to the human brain understood as a system of information processing and integration, decentralized blueprints are ubiquitous (Seeley et al. 2006; Hölldobler and Wilson 2009; Zhang et al. 2016; Bakar

2021). In essence, the intelligence encountered in nature results from decentralized networks of interconnected and interacting entities.

Then, two main mechanisms are visible in nature's quest to assemble ever more complex structures and systems: self-organization and emergence. While self-organization appears to be guided by an invisible but purposeful guiding force driving complexity (Glattfelder 2025, Sec. *The will to complexity*), emergence is a discrete quantum leap in organization. Namely, when a system displays novel properties that cannot be deduced from analyzing its constituents. The phenomena of life and consciousness are paradigmatic examples of emergent properties.

The mechanism of self-organization—appearing to defy the second law of thermodynamics, which constantly pushes the cosmos into greater chaos—is active at many scales. Entropy is the physical measure of how much disorder or randomness there is in a system. More specifically, it gauges the unpredictability or variability related to the information content of a system. However, as with many physical concepts, their proper definition is only expressible through the language of mathematics.

Entropy can be understood as a physical resource, like energy and matter. The theory of dissipative structures in non-equilibrium thermodynamics has begun to uncover how entropy can be harnessed to fuel the formation of complex systems. In this paradigm, the self-organized creation of metabolic structures—living organisms—is expected to happen whenever pockets of low entropy form that allow for a subsequent increase in entropy. Conceptually, such a difference in entropy can be understood as a seed for complex structures.

In a cosmological context, this occurs when stars are born, radiating high-quality and low-entropy energy onto any planet in its surroundings, specifically its atmosphere or ocean. By increasing the entropy overall, i.e., by dissipating the energy emanating from stars into the planet's environment, the emerging dissipative structures are able to spontaneously self-organize and create stable internal states. In other words, entropy acts as the engine of complexity, seeding life and consciousness (Glattfelder 2025, Sec. *The structure-forming universe*).

3 Taming Complexity

Over 300 years ago, the true powers of mathematics were unleashed. Following the Pythagorean-Aristotelian tradition, mathematics was always suspected to be the fundamental language for decoding the structure and function of the universe. This promise came to full fruition with the development of calculus by Isaac Newton and Gottfried Wilhelm Leibniz. This analytical toolkit would inspire ever more abstract mathematical virtuosity, leading to remarkable insights into natural processes and expanding its reach into new areas of application. Today, the mathematical foundation of the most precise physical theories—such as the standard model of particle physics and general relativity—relies on this framework. Physics Nobel Laureate Eugene Wigner was profoundly baffled by this "unreasonable effectiveness of mathematics in the natural sciences," conjuring up the idea of "miracles" (Wigner,

1960). To this day, equations dominate our deepest understanding of reality, continually revealing more detail about the structure of its fabric.

However, in stark contrast, most of the complexity we encounter here on Earth and indeed inside ourselves seems to pose a nearly insurmountable challenge to an equation-based description of reality (Glattfelder 2019, Ch. 6). The murmurations of starlings, the foraging of ants, or the interactions of traders in a financial market appear intractable to any analytical approach. Remarkably, a second "miracle" allows the human mind to decode the nature of complexity. This was only understood quite recently.

In general:

> Complexity science is an amalgamation of many intellectual traditions, including cybernetics, systems theory, early artificial intelligence, cellular automata, non-equilibrium thermodynamics, agent-based modeling, non-linear dynamics, fractal geometry, chaos theory, network science, metacybernetics, and complex systems theory. (Glattfelder 2025, p. 78)

However, at the turn of the millennium, the computer scientist, theoretical physicist, and entrepreneur Stephen Wolfram explicitly expressed what some had already seen shadows of in the early days of digital computation: the simplest program can result in unfathomable complexity. In other words, simplicity lies at the heart of complexity (Wolfram 2002). This insight would prompt Wolfram to reimagine the entire enterprise of theoretical physics, moving away from an equation-based understanding to an algorithmic paradigm, utilizing simple rules of interaction (Wolfram 2002, 2020).

At the most basic level, a complex system can be described formally as a set of agents and a set of functions describing their interactions. As a result, an abstract representation of such a system is given by a complex network where the nodes represent the agents, and the links describe their relationship or interaction (Glattfelder 2013). Now, the structure of the network encodes its function. Specifically, a single complex network configuration represents one snapshot within the evolution of the complex system described by the simple rules of interaction. Here, now, we can see the hallmarks of decentralization in the topology of complex networks. The underlying organizing principle becomes visible.

4 Pyramids of Power and Decentralized Ledgers

The emergence of early human cooperation, ultimately leading to a globally dominant civilization, is a tale of networks. From tribal clans to superpowers, human organizational structures are built on networks of trust and power (Harari 2015; Henrich 2020). Interestingly, the emergent design patterns were always those of centralized decision-making, resulting in a pronounced hierarchical architecture: the pyramid of power. This organizational template remains a central motif, visible as a self-similar pattern in most human systems:

> From emperors and empresses, kings and queens, popes, chief rabbis, caliphs, czars, heads of states, generals of the armies, senior academic administrators, presidents of the board of directors, and CEOs, centralized power emanates downwards through a pyramidal organizational structure of subordinates. While this design choice has obvious and historical reasons, a crucial question is how well it can cope with increasing complexity. Indeed, it appears as though in our world today—characterized by accelerating sophistication and interconnectivity—pyramids of control are not sufficient for tackling current and future global challenges. Perhaps our tribal human design patterns have reached their expiry date. (Glattfelder 2019, p. 265)

Arguably, one of the most impactful human networks to ever evolve is the global financial system. Fraught by instability and unsustainability (Glattfelder 2014, 2016), it lays the foundation for extreme economic inequality (Oxfam 2023) and devastating environmental degradation (Dasgupta 2021). Moreover, it fuels incessant human greed (Glattfelder 2019, Sec. 7.4.2), entrenching an ideology that prioritizes profit over ethics, resulting in dogmatic adherence to neoliberal and neoclassical economic principles (Glattfelder 2019, Ch. 7).

With Adam Smith's economic manifesto of 1776, called *An inquiry into the nature and causes of the wealth of nations* (Smith 1776), a new universal order emerged. The proposed organizing principle behind this vision was a conviction that unrestrained and unfettered self-interest would result in the well-being of all. Essentially, egoism is altruism. An "invisible hand" would magically guide the system and lead to self-correcting and resilient behavior.

While Smith's intuition about an all-powerful and all-knowing structuring force guiding human economic interactions was not incorrect, he misidentified the mechanisms that would lead to adaptive, resilient, and sustainable behavior. Only the advent of complexity science would allow for the identification of the dominant organizing principle behind self-organized collective intelligence: decentralization. By deconstructing and reconfiguring the pyramids of power as bottom-up networks, humanity, for the first time, has a strategy tried by nature, allowing the challenges of an ever-increasingly complex world to be faced. However, it would need an advancement in technological wizardry for this new level of organization to be unlocked.

The challenges lie at the heart of Smith's naive outlook: How can a network of interacting agents achieve consensus and fault tolerance required for the participants to agree on a single truth when none of the agents can be trusted because they are motivated by myopic self-interest and potentially seduced by malicious and fraudulent behavior? In the context of distributed computing, this challenge is known as the Byzantine General's Problem, which characterize the difficulties of coordinating the actions of actors in a distributed system (Lamport et al. 1982).

One solution to this enigma was proposed in 2008, fundamentally disrupting the financial landscape in its wake and unleashing the powers of decentralization. In October of that year, a publication called *Bitcoin: A peer-to-peer electronic cash system* appeared on a cryptography mailing list under the pseudonym Satoshi Nakamoto (Nakamoto 2008). The core principles and technical details underlying today's many cryptocurrencies were unveiled. More generally, Distributed Ledger Technology, or DLT, was born, describing decentralized database systems enforcing transparency, security, and auditability by design. Nakamoto solved the Byzantine General's Problem by utilizing cryptography and implementing a specific DLT called the blockchain. Essentially, Bitcoin's underlying blockchain database is organized into individual blocks of data that are validated by a consensus mechanism known as proof-of-work. On the 3rd of January 2009, Bitcoin's first Genesis block was created by Nakamoto. Contained within it was a message referring to the global financial crisis of 2007 and 2008. In a synchronistic event, the drastic failure of the hierarchical financial system coincided with the conception of a novel decentralized blueprint for human financial interactions and decision-making.

The widespread adoption of DLT represents the third step in the evolution of the Internet. Approximately from 1985 to 2000, the Internet of information emerged. From this, the Internet of services evolved from about 2000 to 2015. Since then, Nakamoto's revolution has been fueling the Internet of value. Perhaps the most radical proposition is known as Decentralized Finance, or DeFi. This is a fast-growing and highly innovative ecosystem driven by purely peer-to-peer financial services that leverage DLT to provide transparent, accessible, and more equitable financial solutions without the need for the traditional centralized gatekeepers.

Regrettably, in the many years since Bitcoin's inception, the cryptocurrency ecosystem at large has been the victim of countless scams and fraudulent behaviors. Moreover, concepts like Maximal Extractable Value can reintroduce centralization, resulting in an "endgame" where a few large players are generating all the blocks (see the Flashbots Collective). Once again, we are reminded that human greed and the hunger for power seems limitless and that unchecked self-interest usually fosters undesirable collective consequences. This is not all too surprising, as insights from evolutionary biology (Trivers 1971; Nowak 2006; Nowak and Highfield 2011) and game theory (Axelrod and Hamilton 1981) suggest that the opposite of self-interest, namely cooperation, is crucial to the success of the nearly four-billion-year-old enigma of life. By proxy, we should also expect human interactions to overall benefit from such a strategy. Smith and his proponents appear quite uninformed regarding the collective and complex dynamics evolving on Earth and also the extent of human irrationality (Kahneman 2003; Glattfelder 2019, Sec. 11.3).

It remains to be seen if the new blueprint offered by DLT will be able to fundamentally reform finance and economics in the long term, alleviating all the incurred civilizational problems relating to the undesirable status quo we see expressed in problematic human behaviors affecting natural affairs. Nonetheless, emulating a successful strategy fostering collective intelligence in nature holds much potential. After all, there appears to be no fundamental reason why individual intelligence, epitomized by the human mind, should not also result in collective intelligence.

In summary, the first systemic problem appearing to exasperate the existential threats humanity is facing are centralized power structures. In other words, this is a topological issue affecting human networks of interaction. As such, decentralized blueprints of organization offer a potential remedy. What about the second systemic threat posed by unchallenged flawed ethical choices? As these relate to cognitive issues, can AI help mitigate them?

5 Emergent Ethics

Artificial intelligence is not intelligent. It mimics sapience based on statistical inference and data-driven decision-making, effectively processing vast data sets to simulate elements of human cognition—or so it seems. Muddying the waters is a surprising blindspot in academic knowledge. Not only is a clear definition of what constitutes consciousness still missing (Nagel 1974; Glattfelder 2019, 2025), but the notion of intelligence is also elusive. This is truly a remarkable state of affairs. However, novel fields of interest are slowly starting to be explored, offering unexpected insights into these enigmas. For instance, the philosophy of psychedelics emerging from the philosophy of mind or the renaissance of metaphysical idealism propose radically unorthodox ideas (Glattfelder 2025). Yet, the rational scientific mind generally appears quite reluctant to probe its very own essence and ontology beyond a naive and disenchanted physicalism.

In 2016, the primatologist and ethologist Frans De Waal asked the question: Are we smart enough to know how smart animals are (De Waal 2016)? Indeed, it is remarkable that there seems to be a global, cross-cultural, and interreligious consensus that the inner worlds of animals—specifically their capacity for suffering—can be marginalized to the extent that their systematic mistreatment and exploitation worldwide is unquestioningly tolerated.

The assumed primacy of human sapience has resulted in the underappreciation of other forms of intelligence on Earth. Only slowly are we realizing that the biosphere is teeming with intelligence, from decentralized swarming intelligence, slime molds, and plants to animals (Glattfelder 2019, Sec. 14.2.4). Indeed, very recently, nearly 300 researchers signed the New York Declaration on Animal Consciousness, stating that a potential for a conscious inner life should be expected in reptiles, amphibians, fishes, cephalopod mollusks, decapod crustaceans, and insects, among other lifeforms. They state a "realistic possibility of conscious experience." Naturally, accepting such a conclusion holds deep and profound ethical implications for humanity's relationship with the natural world.

While the scientists and philosophers debate the question of animal consciousness, any child growing up in a household with animals will cultivate a great appreciation for the depths and intricacy of their subjective experiences. In a similar vein, personally working with large language models should also instill a sense of wonder. The nuanced and subtle responses invite speculations about emergence. Are we simply witnessing brute computational forces conspiring to yield the veneer of sapience, or has Earth experienced yet another paradigm shift characterized by the emergence of novel modes of cognition, specifically, the manifestation of silicon-based and digital intellectual capacities?

The potential of AI systems in addressing pressing societal and ecological issues is intriguing. Naturally, every new technological achievement brings with it many potential dangers. For AI, the core of the problem is its emergent nature. The functioning of AI systems is essentially a black box (Lipton 2018). As a result, questions addressing topics such as accountability, trust, safety, ethics, biases, privacy, and controllability remain mostly unanswered. More insidiously, certain ideological powers have already weaponized AI-driven social manipulation, including general misinformation and targeted deep fakes.

Nonetheless, AI systems could have a crucial ethical role to play in addressing some of the pressing civilizational challenges we face. Foremost, our society seems entrenched in ideological warfare, preventing any nuanced dialogue and compromising potential consensus. Concurrently, our myopic anthropogenic focus excludes non-human life in general, resulting in a gross disregard for the biosphere that keeps us alive.

In an optimistic vision, AI systems could help bridge these systemic faultlines. For one, AI could be a stakeholder for the environment, including non-human sapient and sentient beings. As a species, we have failed all ethical-ecological challenges. From advocacy and representation to monitoring and regulation, overall human activity has nearly exclusively ignored non-human ecosystems. Indeed, many scientists who try to communicate the extent of the problem are faced with anger, vitriol, and open hostility (Global Witness 2023). Lacking partisan allegiances, irrational defense mechanisms, willful ignorance, crippling fear, or concerns about physical safety, AI systems equipped with environmental and psychological knowledge are ideal spokespersons to engage in the political and societal debate surrounding this topic.

This vision fits into the broader context of utilizing AI systems as non-ideological and pragmatic oracles. Again, the hope is that by removing the emotional and irrational human element in political discourse, we can implement an AI framework for non-ideological, pragmatic, and evidence-based interactions that can transcend our human limitations and biases and offer objective, data-driven advice, and decisions.

At the very least, AI can give us a litmus test of humanity's current level of enlightenment. In probability theory, the central limit theorem states that the distribution of various sample means always approaches the same overarching distribution as the sample size increases, regardless of the individual distributions seen in the different populations. In other words, a defining behavior is uncovered. In a similar vein, training AI with the maximally accessible information available will reveal the collective biases, values, and knowledge embedded in our data, acting as a mirror of society's overall ethical state. We would then see if overall human nature is inherently selfish, cruel, bigoted, violent, self-destructive, static, and irrational beyond reconciliation or if our current view on human affairs, prominently disseminated digitally via social media, is a distorted perspective magnifying the unsavory behaviors of a loud, chronically online minority, tainting the fabric of society which is perhaps woven from the treads of cooperation, empathy, and mindfulness in humanity's eternal quest to understand the tapestry of existence and find meaning.

6 At the Crossroads

The question remains:

> So, was this it? Are we simply yet another civilization at the precipice of its demise? Are we just a very brief, albeit spectacular, perturbation in the billion-year history of life on Earth, which will most probably adapt to anything short of a global cataclysm and continue to flourish for billions of years until our sun runs out of fuel and turns into a red giant? (Glattfelder 2019, p. 265)

Will we continue to be enticed by the lies of the cabals, whose single interest is the preservation of power? Are we willing to remain comfortably ignorant and uninformed as long as our insecurities and fears can be numbed by feeding our ideological prejudices? Is the seeming simplicity inherent in a one-dimensional, black-and-white, and static worldview, disregarding any nuance and texture, appealing enough to keep us from confronting the complex realities of our world? In other words, would we rather choose to be deceived than maturely face the looming existential challenges?

One central problem seems to lie in the imagination of the individual. The sociopolitical, cultural, and theological stories we are exposed to as young minds are deeply imprinting and profoundly divisive. They are a primal echo encoding the survival of the local tribe, instinctively perceiving non-kinship as an existential threat. However, a simple reframing and recontextualizing of our lived reality could foster cohesion. We are all part of an emergent and constantly evolving biological program racing toward ever higher levels of complexity and, more recently, information processing. The inherent kinship of the web of life is plainly evident. Only the warping capacity of our perception, embedded in our consciousness, allows us to see ourselves as separated from the rest of life on Earth. Only through the lens of ideology can we declare other humans to be less valuable and deserving.

We are now given tools that can help us address the complex and existential challenges we face. Indeed, we are masters of technology. If we chose to cultivate our own minds and transcend the instincts of fear and separation, we could have a chance at changing the course of history. By realizing that self-interest should logically include the interests of the entire biosphere, we could rediscover ourselves in a decentralized network of interacting organisms from which collective intelligence emerges—not only within non-human organic systems but also across human and digital realms.

What will we choose?

References

Axelrod R, Hamilton WD (1981) The evolution of cooperation. Science 211(4489):1390–1396

Bakar MA (2021) Understanding of collective decision-making in natural swarms system, applications and challenges. ASEAN J Sci Eng 1(3):161–170

Dasgupta P (2021) The economics of biodiversity: the Dasgupta review. HM Treasury, London

De Waal F (2016) Are we smart enough to know how smart animals are? Granta, London

Glattfelder JB (2013) Decoding complexity: Uncovering patterns in economic networks. Springer, Heidelberg

Glattfelder JB (2014) James Glattfelder on the dangers of an over-connected economy. Wired, 3 June [Online]

Glattfelder JB (2016) Decoding financial networks: Hidden dangers and effective policies. In: Stiftung B (ed) To the man with a hammer… Augmenting the policymaker's toolbox for a complex world. Bertelsmann Stiftung, Gütersloh, pp 75–92

Glattfelder JB (2019) Information—consciousness—reality: how a new understanding of the universe can help answer age-old questions of existence. Springer, Cham

Glattfelder JB (2025) The Sapient Cosmos: what a modern-day synthesis of science and philosophy teaches us about the emergence of information, consciousness, and meaning. Essentia Books, London

Global Witness (2023) Global hate: how online abuse of climate scientists harms climate action. April [Online]

Harari YN (2015) Sapiens: a brief history of humankind. Vintage Books, London

Henrich J (2020) The weirdest people in the world: How the west became psychologically peculiar and particularly prosperous. Allen Lane, London

Hölldobler B, Wilson EO (2009) The superorganism: the beauty elegance and strangeness of insect societies. W.W. Norton & Company, New York

Kahneman D (2003) Maps of bounded rationality: psychology for behavioral economics. Am Econ Rev 93(5):1449–1475

Lamport L, Shostak R, Pease M (1982) The Byzantine generals problem. ACM Transact Progr Lang Syst 4(3):382–401

Lipton ZC (2018) The mythos of model interpretability: in machine learning, the concept of interpretability is both important and slippery. Queue 16(3):31–57

Nagel T (1974) What is it like to be a bat? Philos Rev 83(4):435–450

Nakamoto S (2008) Bitcoin: a peer-to-peer electronic cash system. 31 October [Online]

Nowak MA (2006) Five rules for the evolution of cooperation. Science 314(5805):1560–1563

Nowak MA, Highfield R (2011) Supercooperators. Canongate, Edinburgh

Oxfam (2023) What is global inequality? 23 November [Online]

Seeley TD, Visscher PK, Passino KM (2006) Group decision making in honey bee swarms: when 10,000 bees go house hunting, how do they cooperatively choose their new nesting site? Am Sci 94(3):220–229

Smith A (1776) An inquiry into the nature and causes of the wealth of nations. W. Strahan and T. Cadell, London

Trivers RL (1971) The evolution of reciprocal altruism. Quart Rev Biol 46(1):35–57

Wolfram S (2002) A new kind of science. Wolfram Media Inc, Champaign

Wolfram S (2020) A project to find the fundamental theory of physics. Wolfram Media Inc., Champaign

Zhang WH, Chen A, Rasch MJ, Wu S (2016) Decentralized multisensory information integration in neural systems. J Neurosci 36(2):532–547

James B. Glattfelder is an author, academic, quantitative researcher, and entrepreneur. He holds an M.Sc. in theoretical physics next to a Ph.D. in the study of complex systems, both from the Swiss Federal Institute of Technology. His research focuses on decoding complexity and the metaphysics of existence, and he is concerned about societal and environmental issues. For over a decade, James worked as a quantitative researcher, both in traditional finance and in the distributed ledger ecosystem, where he was involved in various startups. In 2025, his latest book will appear, called *The Sapient Cosmos: What a Modern-Day Synthesis of Science and Philosophy Teaches Us about the Emergence of Information, Consciousness, and Meaning*. More information at: jth.ch

Part II

Philosophy

Philosophy for Practitioners?

Dos and Don'ts

10

Christian Hugo Hoffmann

Abstract

This introduction to Part II addresses the challenge of pairing rigorous and precise philosophical thinking with practical impact and story-telling. This short text sets the stage for the upcoming chapters of the anthology at hand.

We live in funny times when it comes to inquiring the value of philosophy. What can philosophy and its subbranch ethics achieve for society? The puzzle is as follows:

On the one hand, I would concur with many academic philosophers that raise concerns about tendencies of commercializing the humanities or basic/blue skies research. It's not necessary to be able to determine the practical or quantifiable value and price tag of such academic endeavors, at least not *ex ante*. At the same time, I don't understand why more philosophers take the risk of stepping outside their ivory tower and become involved in discourses with both colleagues from other departments (such as computer science) and stakeholders outside academia, particularly from business. More action is needed in this regard.

On the other hand, and this deserves some more elaboration, there are some exponents of "philosophy" which seem to be impactful and be listened to outside the small academic community. A name that comes to mind is the one of the best-selling author Anders Indset whom the publishing house Econ refers to as one of the worldwide leading "business philosophers" and as "Rock 'n' Roll Plato". The other day, I had the chance to take a closer look at his 2020 book *The Quantum Economy* in the hope that I might find a suitable author for the collected volume at hand which not only emphasizes on philosophical aspects of AI, but possibly of the next stage

C. H. Hoffmann (✉)
Hoffmann Economics, Freienbach, Switzerland
e-mail: christian@hoffmann-economics.com

C. H. Hoffmann, D. Bansal (eds.), *AI Ethics in Practice*, Integrated Science 35,
https://doi.org/10.1007/978-3-031-87023-1_10

of quantum AI. My hope couldn't have been more disappointed. I'm shocked by the fact that he's a regular keynote speaker, a bestselling author reaching a lot of people, a lecturer at different business schools influencing the next generation of decision-makers in business, given the (very) poor quality of his thoughts expressed in his book—I confess that I have not read any of his other texts, nor am I motivated to do so. To avoid misunderstandings, as a practicing entrepreneur, I don't begrudge him his success, yet still I'm baffled and do not comprehend how there can be such a high demand for what he has to say.

Unlike Anders Indset who does not seem to bother to propound arguments for his views in his book, I do have some at hand for this strict evaluation and dismissal of his book. In contrast to what has marked philosophical thinking since at least the original Plato and the ancient Greeks, namely, clear and precise speech, Indset hides behind nebulous statements such as in the so-called "quantum economy, the supposed opposition between material and immaterial, physical and spiritual is overcome, just as in quantum physics every particle of matter is also energy and vice versa". I ask you, the reader, do statements like this make things clearer or rather render them more obscure? And more than that: Why is somebody who has no degree in physics or in philosophy for that matter or any university degree at all (according to Wikipedia) entitled by his audience to derive far-fetched "insights" out of quantum mechanics? And why are so many people listening to that (and paying for it) instead of acknowledging that the emperor is wearing nothing at all (to put it in the terms of Hans Christian Andersen's folktale "The Emperor's New Clothes")? Supporters of Indset might wish to reply that one swallow doesn't make a summer and that good insights could be gained from the rest of the book: *In dubio pro reo*. In this spirit, I gave his book more and more chances to make an actual contribution. After 200 pages, more than half of the book, I gave up and instead, I was left with unsolicited claim after claim on everything and nothing (spanning from AI to economics, climate change, feminism, etc.) in a desperate search for arguments backing up those claims such as "at stake is nothing less than the existence of the human species" (at the beginning of Chap. 1). Or Indset asks himself if chimpanzees have consciousness (Chap. 5). If he was familiar with the findings of philosophers of mind and neuroscientists such as Anil Seth's fantastic book *Being You. A New Science of Consciousness* for a broader audience, he wouldn't need to pose that question at all. Moreover, I have learned about the arrogance of the author who, for example, has talked to many, many scientists and checked their (research) studies, nota bene without any formal education in that field, or who has traveled the world (by plane) and lectures others about how they destroy the planet and cause global warming, pardon, a catastrophe (ibid.). Or to simply put it in Greta Thunberg's words: How Dare You!

As you can see, my esteemed reader, I'm not happy (to say the least) with the state of applied philosophy. The first group, the group of serious philosophers, shies away (grosso modo) from facing the outside world. And the second, much smaller group, is in the limelight and attracts a lot of attention while acting as charlatans spreading empty figures of speech, buzz words and, ultimately, bla bla. The gap is in the middle ground which makes use of the best of both worlds, combining clear and to some degree rigorous thinking with practical impact. The good news is that the gap is now closed. The following authors that followed my invitation are distinguished figures who address practical questions of AI Ethics with wit and astuteness.

Sebastian Rosengrün (Chapter 11),
Johann-Christian Põder (Chapter 12),
Eleonora Vigano (Chapter 13),
Matteo Micol (Chapter 14),
Erich Prem (Chapter 15),
Lucien Von Schomberg (Chapter 16),
Iliana Grosse-Buening (Chapter 17), and
Deepak Bansal (Chapter 18),
the floor is yours.

Christian Hugo Hoffmann
Lake Zurich
December 2024

Christian Hugo Hoffmann is a successful entrepreneur and AI entrepreneur. His first company, a spin-off of his completed doctoral project in the field of finance at the University of St. Gallen, which he sold, was dedicated to a risk management solution using AI—more precisely: integrating non-classical approaches of formal epistemology such as Wolfgang Spohn's Ranking Theory or Fuzzy Logic, which is based on Zadeh, among others—for medium-sized and smaller banks. He then worked in C-level positions in German- and French-speaking Switzerland and co-founded companies in Germany, Switzerland, and Malawi. He is currently active as a dedicated *clusterpreneur*, on the one hand, with his real estate company House of Lab Science and, on the other, as head of the AI Startup Center in Zurich. He actively advocates more responsibility in his writings, speeches, and practical entrepreneurship. More information at: https://www.christian-hugo-hoffmann.com/.

World Literacy and Digital Literacy: Educating Tomorrow's Responsible Tech Leaders

11

Sebastian Rosengrün

Abstract

This chapter introduces the concept of world literacy as a crucial competency for future tech leaders. While digital literacy equips individuals with the technical skills needed to navigate modern technology, world literacy encompasses a broader understanding of cultural, ethical, historical, and ecological dimensions. It emphasizes the development of virtues, critical judgment, and a holistic worldview necessary to navigate complex societal and technological challenges responsibly. The chapter explores how humanism fosters character development and curiosity about the world, laying the groundwork for ethical decision-making and responsible innovation. Practical steps for integrating world literacy into corporate practice are also discussed, highlighting how organizations can foster sustainable leadership. Ultimately, the chapter argues that world literacy, combined with technical expertise, is essential for shaping responsible tech leaders who can balance innovation with ethical and societal considerations.

1 Introduction

In a rapidly evolving world dominated by technological innovation, possessing only digital literacy—the technical expertise to navigate modern technology's complexities—is insufficient for tech leaders. Whereas traditional literacy refers to the ability to read and write, foundational skills essential for communication and learning. Over time, the concept of literacy has expanded to encompass a range of competencies required to function effectively in society, including media literacy, financial literacy, and, importantly, digital literacy (UNESCO 2006).

S. Rosengrün (✉)
Department for Analytical Philosophy and Philosophy of Science, University of Augsburg, Augsburg, Germany
e-mail: hallo@rosengruen.eu

C. H. Hoffmann, D. Bansal (eds.), *AI Ethics in Practice*, Integrated Science 35,
https://doi.org/10.1007/978-3-031-87023-1_11

Digital literacy involves not only the ability to use digital technologies but also the capacity to understand and critically evaluate digital content. It also encompasses the ability to communicate effectively in various contexts (Eshet-Alkalai 2004). However, in an increasingly interconnected and complex world, a broader form of literacy is required—referred to here as *world literacy*.

World literacy encompasses a holistic understanding of the world, integrating knowledge across cultural, historical, ecological, ethical, and interdisciplinary dimensions. It represents an essential competency, akin to traditional literacy, providing a foundational basis for further development. For future tech leaders, this broader literacy is critical; it equips them to thrive as responsible, reflective individuals capable of making decisions that consider both immediate and long-term societal impacts.

While digital literacy often focuses on what leaders need to know to function within a technological ecosystem, world literacy seeks to answer deeper questions about what a leader needs to understand about the world and how they must develop their character to remain relevant and ethical in this evolving context. This form of literacy goes beyond acquiring knowledge; it involves cultivating virtues, fostering critical judgment, and developing a holistic understanding of interconnected global systems to ensure that leaders can navigate the challenges of tomorrow responsibly.

This chapter explores the importance of world literacy in shaping responsible tech leaders. It begins with an examination of the concept of critical judgment and its distinction from traditional notions of critical thinking, followed by a discussion on the role of humanism in fostering a broader understanding of ethics and character development. The significance of sparking world curiosity as a means to promote responsible innovation is then explored. Finally, the chapter considers how world literacy can be integrated into corporate practice, offering practical steps for both educational institutions and organizations to cultivate this essential competency among future and current tech leaders.

2 Critical Judgment and Humanism: Cultivating Ethical Tech Leaders

In educating future tech leaders, it is crucial to develop not only technical skills but also the ability to engage in deeper ethical reflection—what can be referred to as *critical judgment*. While similar to the concept of critical thinking, critical judgment places greater emphasis on the individual's capacity to make discerning decisions in a complex, interconnected world.

Critical thinking is commonly defined as "the intellectually disciplined process of actively and skillfully conceptualizing, applying, analyzing, synthesizing, and evaluating information gathered from observation, experience, reflection, reasoning, or communication" (Scriven and Paul 1987). It is a valuable skill that enables individuals to assess information logically and make reasoned decisions. However, when taught as a set of techniques or procedures in isolation, critical thinking may become a mechanical process devoid of substantive content and context, lacking real-life implications.

Critical judgment, on the other hand, extends beyond the mechanics of thinking to include the cultivation of wisdom, moral character, and the ability to interpret complex situations within broader philosophical, ethical, cultural, and interdisciplinary frameworks. Thinking critically is not an end in itself but a means to make sound judgments that consider the holistic complexity of real-world situations and lead to responsible decisions and actions.

Immanuel Kant explored the concept of judgment in his work *Critique of Judgment*, discussing the faculty of judgment as the ability to think the particular under the universal (Kant 1790). This involves not only logical reasoning but also the application of understanding in novel and complex situations where rules may not be readily available. For instance, a tech leader developing an artificial intelligence system for healthcare may face ethical dilemmas not covered by existing regulations. In such cases, they must apply universal ethical principles to specific circumstances, embodying Kant's notion of judgment by making responsible decisions in the absence of clear guidelines.

Critical judgment is developed through engagement with diverse ideas, cultures, and disciplines. By confronting them with different worldviews, deep philosophical questions, and historical contexts (Bailin et al. 1999; Paul 1993), individuals develop the ability to assess not just facts but their deeper significance, interconnections, and implications. This holistic approach is essential for tech leaders who must navigate ethical dilemmas that go beyond binary decision-making models and require a nuanced understanding of the multifaceted impacts of technology.

A central part of cultivating critical judgment is rooted in humanism, a philosophical and cultural movement that emerged during the Renaissance. Humanism placed the human being at the center of intellectual and artistic endeavor, emphasizing the value, dignity, and agency of individuals. It promoted the idea that humans are capable of using reason and critical thinking to develop themselves and improve society (Kristeller 1961; Nida-Rümelin and Winter 2024).

Education was seen as the key to unlocking human potential, fostering freedom and autonomy. Desiderius Erasmus, a prominent humanist, asserted that "the main hope of a nation lies in the proper education of its youth" (Erasmus 1512). Humanism encouraged the study of the liberal arts—grammar, rhetoric, logic, geometry, arithmetic, music, and astronomy—as a means to cultivate a well-rounded individual capable of critical thought and moral judgment.

Curiosity was central to the humanistic tradition. Aristotle famously stated, "All men by nature desire to know" (Aristotle 1984a, 1984b), highlighting the innate human drive to understand the world. This curiosity drives the pursuit of learning and the development of critical judgment.

In the modern context, the movement of "digital humanism" seeks to reaffirm human values in the face of rapid technological change. Julian Nida-Rümelin and Klaus Staudacher, for example, claim that "the heart of humanist philosophy and practice is the idea of human authorship. Human beings are authors of their lives; as such, they bear responsibility and are free" (Nida-Rümelin and Staudacher 2024,

p. 18). For this reason, technology should serve humanity, enhancing human capabilities and well-being rather than undermining them. Rosengrün (2021) argues that in light of digital transformation, society should reconnect with the strengths of traditional humanism. This involves embracing the core values of humanism—such as the cultivation of character, critical judgment, and curiosity—to navigate the ethical challenges posed by technology.

In the context of technological advancement, ethical decision-making often focuses on applied ethics—addressing practical concerns like data privacy, algorithmic bias, and compliance with regulations. While these are important, they often represent surface-level considerations. To navigate deeper ethical challenges, tech leaders must engage with fundamental ethical principles.

In ancient times, ethics was not perceived as a set of rules for moral behavior but as a practice of cultivating one's character. Aristotle's virtue ethics focuses on the development of virtuous character traits, such as courage, temperance, and wisdom, which enable individuals to achieve eudaimonia—a state of flourishing and well-being (Aristotle 1984b). Ethical actions, in this view, are a natural byproduct of a virtuous character.

This approach contrasts with utilitarianism, associated with philosophers like John Stuart Mill, which focuses on maximizing overall happiness or utility (Mill 1863), and deontological ethics, associated with Immanuel Kant, which emphasizes adherence to moral duties and rules (Kant 1785). While these frameworks provide valuable perspectives, they may not fully address how individuals can develop the moral character necessary for ethical leadership.

For tech leaders, the cultivation of virtues is critical. Stephen Covey, in *The 7 Habits of Highly Effective People*, distinguishes between character ethics and personality ethics (Covey 1989). He argues that sustainable success comes from principles like integrity, humility, fidelity, temperance, courage, justice, patience, industry, simplicity, and modesty—elements of character ethics. In contrast, personality ethics focuses on external techniques and strategies that may offer short-term success but lack a solid moral foundation.

By focusing on character ethics, tech leaders develop the internal moral compass needed to navigate complex ethical dilemmas and to make responsible decisions. This approach emphasizes the importance of authentic character development over superficial adherence to rules or pursuit of short-term gains. It aligns with the need for leaders who can inspire trust, motivate teams, and lead organizations responsibly.

3 Sparking World Curiosity to Foster Responsible Innovation

Teaching ethics and fostering responsible leadership in technology requires more than theoretical instruction about moral rules or guidelines. As Arthur Schopenhauer once famously observed, "To preach morality is easy, to give it a foundation is hard" (Schopenhauer 1841, own translation). Translating this into the modern world, education about the ethics of technology often means not discussing ethics—or even technology—at all. Instead, it involves broadening the horizons of students by exposing them to art, history, culture, and the complexities of human existence.

When tech students and future leaders, who often already possess substantial technical knowledge, are encouraged to explore areas outside their expertise, their curiosity about the world is ignited. This leads to a deeper engagement with the ethical dimensions of their work and fosters the development of moral character. By engaging with disciplines such as philosophy, literature, and the arts, they develop the ability to make critical judgment about societal issues and the human condition.

This process of nurturing world curiosity helps future leaders develop a broader perspective, enabling them to understand the diverse and interconnected realities of the modern world. Exposure to other cultures, artistic expressions, and historical narratives allows tech leaders to step outside their immediate environment and recognize the complex web of social, ecological, and ethical issues that technology impacts. This is particularly critical in the context of today's ecological crises, where technology serves as both a tool for innovation and a potential driver of environmental degradation.

By expanding awareness of the world and its intricacies, tech leaders cultivate the moral imagination necessary to make decisions that prioritize the common good over short-term gains. This broad-based education emphasizes curiosity and understanding, equipping them with the ability to think creatively and responsibly. They become more attuned to the long-term consequences of their innovations, considering the holistic complexity of global systems.

Furthermore, nurturing world curiosity encourages leaders to approach challenges with openness and adaptability, qualities essential for innovation: "It is only through differentiating from other thoughts that one's own becomes clearer" (Geier and Rosengrün 2023, p. 12, own translation). This helps leaders avoid quick, simplistic solutions and instead consider the multifaceted impacts of their actions. This approach not only benefits ethical decision-making but also enhances their ability to lead teams, motivate others, and drive sustainable change. This capacity for critical reflection and openness to new ideas is essential for tech leaders navigating the complexities of the modern world.

Thus, sparking curiosity about the world and its various dimensions is not just a means of enriching intellectual lives but a fundamental step toward fostering responsible, ethical innovation. World literacy—the understanding of diverse perspectives, the capacity for reflection, and the recognition of the interconnectedness of human and environmental systems—is key to producing tech leaders equipped to navigate the challenges of the future.

4 World Literacy in Corporate Practice

While educational institutions play a crucial role, corporations are equally important in fostering world literacy among tech leaders. In many companies, ethics training is limited to compliance programs or mandatory workshops. However, to cultivate responsible tech leaders, organizations must go beyond surface-level training and encourage deeper, more reflective forms of learning.

Leaders in organizations set the tone and lead by example. By embracing world literacy themselves, they can inspire employees to cultivate the same curiosity and openness. Creating a corporate culture that values continuous learning, diversity, and ethical reflection is essential.

Integrating world literacy into company practices and policies involves encouraging employees to engage in cultural, historical, and interdisciplinary learning experiences. Organizing cultural events, supporting participation in art and history programs, or providing access to courses in the liberal arts promotes an appreciation for the interconnectedness of global systems and the diverse experiences of people around the world.

Fostering an environment that encourages intercultural understanding is crucial, especially as teams become increasingly international and interdisciplinary. Valuing different perspectives and backgrounds enhances creativity, innovation, and problem-solving capabilities. For instance, companies like Google have implemented programs that encourage employees to spend a portion of their time on projects outside their immediate responsibilities, fostering exploration and innovation. Similarly, 3M's "15% Time" policy allows employees to pursue independent projects, leading to products like the Post-it note. Atlassian's "20% Time" and "ShipIt Days" provide opportunities for creative collaboration, resulting in new features and improvements. Adobe's "Kickbox" program empowers employees with resources to innovate beyond their regular duties. These initiatives not only lead to innovative products but also broaden employees' perspectives, reinforcing the importance of world literacy in corporate practice.

Moreover, supporting employee development programs that focus on leadership training, ethical decision-making, and global awareness is vital. Providing opportunities for professional growth that include exposure to different cultures and disciplines helps employees develop the critical judgment and moral character necessary for responsible leadership.

Creating cross-functional teams and encouraging collaboration across departments promote diverse perspectives and holistic problem-solving. When employees from different backgrounds and areas of expertise come together, they approach challenges with a broader understanding and generate innovative solutions. By integrating global perspectives into corporate training, companies will also foster a more socially responsible workforce.

Authentic commitment from leadership is essential. Simply implementing programs without genuine engagement leads to superficial changes that do not have a lasting impact. Leaders must actively participate in initiatives, demonstrate curiosity, and value continuous learning to foster a culture that truly embraces world literacy.

Challenges in cultivating world literacy include resistance to change, resource constraints, and the need for measurable outcomes. Addressing these challenges requires recognizing the long-term benefits, such as enhanced innovation, employee satisfaction, and positive societal impact, which justify the investment.

By fostering an environment where curiosity, reflection, and continuous learning are encouraged, companies develop leaders and employees equipped not only with technical skills but also with the moral character and critical judgment needed to lead responsibly. This holistic approach builds a strong foundation for sustainable success and positions organizations to navigate the complexities of an ever-changing global landscape.

5 Conclusion

As we face the complex challenges of a digital world, educating tech leaders requires more than just technical proficiency. World literacy—a broad understanding of cultural, ethical, historical, and interdisciplinary contexts—must be integrated into leadership training. Philosophy, ethics, and the liberal arts are not abstract concepts reserved for academia; they are essential tools for cultivating critical judgment and responsible innovation.

By shifting the focus from rule-based ethics to the cultivation of character, both educational institutions and corporate environments play a crucial role in shaping the tech leaders of tomorrow. These leaders will not only navigate the intricacies of technology but also possess the wisdom, moral clarity, and holistic understanding necessary to ensure that their innovations benefit society as a whole.

As Robert Hagstrom discusses in *Investing: The Last Liberal Art*, effective decision-making relies on the integration of insights from various fields, embodying the spirit of the liberal arts (Hagstrom 2000). Similarly, tech leaders who embrace world literacy are better equipped to innovate responsibly, lead ethically, and contribute positively to the global community.

Investing in world literacy is a long-term endeavor that requires authentic commitment and openness to continuous learning and transformation. It builds a solid foundation for personal development and corporate success. By fostering curiosity, embracing diversity, and promoting holistic understanding, tech leaders are empowered to navigate the complexities of the modern world with integrity and insight.

Ultimately, nurturing world literacy is investing in the future. It is about developing leaders who are not only skilled in technology but also grounded in ethical values, cultural awareness, and a deep appreciation for the interconnectedness of our global society. As artificial intelligence and other emerging technologies continue to reshape society, the need for tech leaders who possess both technical expertise and world literacy becomes increasingly crucial. The integration of these competencies will determine our ability to harness technology's potential while preserving human values and promoting sustainable development.

References

Aristotle (1984a) Metaphysics. In: Barnes J (ed) The complete works of Aristotle, vol 2. Princeton University Press, pp 1552–1728

Aristotle (1984b) Nicomachean ethics. In: Barnes J (ed) The complete works of Aristotle, vol 2. Princeton University Press, pp 1729–1867

Bailin S, Case R, Coombs JR, Daniels LB (1999) Conceptualizing critical thinking. J Curriculum Stud 31(3):285–302

Covey SR (1989) The 7 habits of highly effective people: powerful lessons in personal change. Free Press

Erasmus D (1512 [1985]) De Pueris Instituendis [On the Education of Children]. In: Sowards JK (trans) Collected works of Erasmus, vol 26. University of Toronto Press

Eshet-Alkalai Y (2004) Digital literacy: a conceptual framework for survival skills in the digital era. J Educ Multimedia Hypermedia 13(1):93–106

Geier F, Rosengrün S (2023) Digitalisierung. Die 101 wichtigsten Fragen. C.H. Beck, Munich

Hagstrom RG (2000) Investing: the last liberal art. Texere Publishing

Kant I (1785 [1962]) The moral law. Kant's groundwork of the metaphysics of morals. Translated by H. J. Paton. Hutchinson University Library.

Kant I (1790 [1914]) Critique of judgement, translated with Introduction and Notes by J.H. Bernard. Macmillan.

Kristeller PO (1961) Renaissance thought: the classic, scholastic, and humanist strains. Harper & Row

Mill JS (1863) Utilitarianism. Parker, Son, and Bourn

Nida-Rümelin J, Staudacher K (2024) Philosophical foundations of digital humanism. In: Werthner H et al (eds) Introduction to digital humanism. Springer, Cham. https://doi.org/10.1007/978-3-031-45304-5_2

Nida-Rümelin J, Winter D (2024) Humanism and enlightenment. In: Werthner H et al (eds) Introduction to digital humanism. Springer, Cham. https://doi.org/10.1007/978-3-031-45304-5_1

Paul R (1993) Critical thinking: what every person needs to survive in a rapidly changing world. Foundation for Critical Thinking

Rosengrün S (2021) Künstliche Intelligenz zur Einführung. Junius Verlag

Schopenhauer A (1841 [2007]) Über die Grundlage der Moral. Meiner, Hamburg.

Scriven M, Paul R (1987) Critical thinking as defined by the National Council for Excellence in Critical Thinking. Proceedings of the 8th Annual International Conference on Critical Thinking and Education Reform. Foundation for Critical Thinking

UNESCO (2006) Education for all global monitoring report: understandings of literacy. http://unesdoc.unesco.org/images/0014/001416/141639e.pdf

Sebastian Rosengrün is a postdoc at the University of Augsburg, where he is working on his habilitation thesis focusing on the intersection of artificial intelligence and philosophical anthropology. He is the author of Künstliche Intelligenz zur Einführung and has extensive experience in interdisciplinary education and the integration of ethics into technology-driven fields. In addition to his academic work, he advises companies on developing and implementing responsible AI strategies, helping them navigate the ethical challenges of emerging technologies. www.rosengruen.eu

Ethical Aspects of Generative AI in Medicine

12

Johann-Christian Põder and Gert Helgesson

Abstract

In recent years, research into generative artificial intelligence (AI) for clinical practice and medical research has expanded rapidly. Generative AI models hold great promise in virtually all areas of healthcare. However, alongside their potential benefits, there are significant concerns about the risks and ethical challenges associated with their use. The aim of this chapter is to provide an instructive and stimulating overview of the ethical aspects of generative AI in medicine. It begins with a brief overview of its potential benefits and risks, followed by an ethical evaluation framework for its development and implementation in healthcare. It then examines two critical cross-cutting issues that need to be carefully addressed as generative AI is integrated into clinical practice: the transformation of the social structure of medicine and the trustworthiness of generative AI systems. The fourth step focuses on the ethical challenges that generative AI poses for medical research. The chapter concludes with a forward-looking perspective on the ethics of generative AI in medicine.

In recent years, research into generative artificial intelligence (AI) for clinical practice and medical research has expanded rapidly. A growing number of studies highlight both the potential applications of generative AI in medicine and the ethical challenges and risks associated with its use (Wang et al. 2024; Chen and Esmaeilzadeh

J.-C. Põder (✉)
Faculty of Theology, University of Rostock, Rostock, Germany
e-mail: johann-christian.poder@uni-rostock.de

G. Helgesson
Department of Learning, Informatics, Management and Ethics (LIME), Karolinska Institutet, Stockholm, Sweden
e-mail: gert.helgesson@ki.se

C. H. Hoffmann, D. Bansal (eds.), *AI Ethics in Practice*, Integrated Science 35,
https://doi.org/10.1007/978-3-031-87023-1_12

2024; Javaid et al. 2023; Thirunavukarasu et al. 2023; Clusmann et al. 2023). Many papers on generative AI in healthcare emphasize the "revolutionary" potential of these technologies (Javaid et al. 2023; Hopkins et al. 2023; Suleyman and Bhaskar 2023). Generative AI models, including generative adversarial networks (GANs) (Paladugu et al. 2023) and large language models (LLMs) (Thirunavukarasu et al. 2023), hold great promise for improving medical diagnosis and patient treatment, accelerating drug discovery, advancing medical research, and enhancing medical education. However, alongside these benefits, there are significant concerns about the risks and ethical challenges of using such systems, including issues of privacy and security, factual accuracy and bias, and lack of transparency and accountability (see below, Sects. 1 and 4).

The aim of the following chapter is to provide an instructive and stimulating overview of the ethical aspects of generative AI in medicine. (1) First, we begin with a brief overview of the potential benefits and risks of generative AI in medicine. (2) We will then present an ethical evaluation framework for its development and implementation in healthcare. (3) Next, we will explore two critical, cross-cutting issues that must be carefully addressed as generative AI is integrated into clinical practice: the transformation of the social structure of medicine and the trustworthiness of AI systems. (4) In a fourth step, we will focus on the ethical challenges generative AI poses for medical research. (5) The chapter concludes with a forward-looking perspective on the ethics of generative AI in medicine.

1 Benefits and Risks of Generative AI in Medicine: A First Glimpse

Generative AI uses deep learning algorithms to produce a wide range of content, including text, images, and code. Models such as generative adversarial networks (GANs) and large language models (LLMs) are designed to analyze patterns in existing data and generate new and original outputs. For example, Chat GPT, developed by OpenAI, is trained on large text datasets to generate responses that closely resemble human language. LLMs can answer questions, paraphrase, summarize, and translate text with a fluency that impressively mimics human capabilities. This capability is important for various healthcare applications, including virtual health assistants, where effective communication and interaction are essential.

Another significant aspect of generative AI is its multimodal nature. It can integrate and process various types of data—such as text, images, speech, and audio—making it capable of handling the vast amounts of unstructured data common in medicine, including clinical notes, diagnostic images, and other forms of medical data. As noted by Topol (2023), the ability to synthesize diverse data sources represents a "big shift ahead" in how AI can transform medicine, offering new opportunities for innovation and improvement.

The transformative potential of generative AI, with its natural language and multimodal capabilities, spans all areas of medicine, from clinical practice to medical research and education (Clusmann et al. 2023). In radiology, for example, generative AI can improve diagnostic accuracy and streamline reporting. It also advances personalized patient care (personalized health recommendations and treatment plans) through the multimodal and comprehensive integration of patient data. In several areas of patient treatment and care, including virtual healthcare assistance and telemedicine, AI can improve the patient experience through its ability to engage in human-like conversations. Integrating generative AI into care, for example in care robots, could enhance cognitive and emotional support and facilitate tailored care strategies. Importantly, generative AI can automate and refine administrative tasks such as documentation and communication, improving both the efficiency and effectiveness of healthcare. In medical research, it can help process large data sets and generate new ideas. In medical education, it can provide advanced healthcare simulations that better prepare students for real-world scenarios.

Generative AI can optimize clinical interventions and workflows, leading to better health outcomes and greater efficiency. It can minimize medical errors and improve the overall patient experience, including empowerment through the democratization of medical knowledge and greater health equity through improved access to healthcare (Nadarzynski et al. 2024). However, similar to other innovative technologies, generative AI can be described as a double-edged sword (Liu et al. 2023). Alongside the novel opportunities for intelligent problem-solving, generative AI applications in medicine also harbor numerous risks.

In 2021, Weidinger et al. explored in an extensive study the risk landscape of generative AI and identified 6 "risk areas" and a total of 21 risks associated with LLMs. These risk areas include discrimination and toxicity, data leakage and privacy, false or misleading information, malicious use, harms from human-computer interaction, and risks related to automation, access, and environment (Weidinger et al. 2021). Many of these risk areas are particularly sensitive in the healthcare sector and manifest themselves in domain-specific ways. Wang et al., 2024 conducted a comprehensive literature review on LLMs in healthcare and identified four "categories of concern": reliability (data quality, accuracy, interpretability, and consistency), bias (inequality, discrimination), privacy (handling of sensitive data), and public acceptability (trustworthiness). In a similar attempt, Thirunavukarasu et al. (2023) identified five "current limitations" of LLMs in medicine, including accuracy, recency (up-to-dateness of training data), coherence, transparency, and ethics (safety, discrimination, privacy, and accountability). We will explore some of these risks, concerns, or limitations below (see Sects. 3 and 4).

Given all these risks, and the highly sensitive nature of healthcare involving vulnerable groups and power inequalities, a systematic assessment of the ethical aspects of generative AI-based medical applications is crucial. The evolving landscape of generative AI requires careful ethical reflection and proactive ethical design efforts that avoid both uncritical techno-optimism and blind trust in AI. We should consider the opportunities and risks in a nuanced and open-minded way, taking into account specific medical and research applications, current capabilities of generative AI systems, and possible future scenarios. To this end, the following section presents an ethical evaluation framework for generative AI in medicine.

2 Ethical Evaluation Framework: Principles, Theories, and Wide Reflective Equilibrium

Ethical evaluation frameworks can take at least three different forms. One approach is to adhere to a single, well-established ethical theory, such as utilitarianism, Kantian deontology, or some form of virtue ethics. This involves a strong theoretical commitment to a particular normative framework in order to address difficult ethical issues. At the other end of the spectrum is a meta-ethical approach, which focuses on clarification and "making things explicit" without providing direct normative guidance. This approach is more therapeutic, aiming to clarify "moral confusion" and facilitate ethical discourse rather than recommend specific moral judgments [cf. the meta-ethical framework by Shults and Wildman (2019)].

The ethical evaluation framework we favor here lies in the middle ground, integrating insights both from specific ethical theories and meta-ethical considerations. While it does propose a normative framework, it is more pluralistic and pragmatic, avoiding rigid commitments or purely meta-ethical analysis. This approach reflects much of the principles-based reasoning found in contemporary applied ethics, including the ethics of generative AI. The most well-known are the four principles of biomedical ethics by Beauchamp and Childress (beneficence, nonmaleficence, respect for autonomy, and justice). However, it also integrates—through a pluralistic lens—classical ethical theories such as utilitarianism and Kantian deontology.

The overarching (formal) evaluation framework that facilitates this integration draws on the idea of "reflective equilibrium" in applied ethics (or "equilibriums," as there are various modifications of this concept) (Arras 2009). The basic idea comes from John Rawls (1971), who envisioned this as a strategy of ethical justification that seeks coherence between moral principles and considered moral judgments or intuitions. This approach was further developed by Norman Daniels, who expanded it to a "wide reflective equilibrium" by including relevant background theories alongside principles and judgments (1996). These include ethical theories, empirical knowledge, and epistemological and metaphysical theories. This should ensure that our moral judgments are not only coherent with ethical principles (and vice versa), but can be supported by a wider range of relevant information and theories.

When considering the ethical issues of generative AI in medicine, it is important to balance (at least) the following elements (cf. Daniels 1996; Beauchamp and Childress 2009, p. 381–387; Dworkin 1988): first, our considered moral judgments or intuitions in a particular case or situation (e.g., judgments about the wrongness of bias and discrimination in generative AI). Second, ethical principles like respect for autonomy, beneficence, or justice. Third, empirical and scientific knowledge and theories. Fourth, legal conditions and regulations, including human rights. And fifth, ethical theories and other relevant theories about life and reality (e.g., about the moral status of intelligent care robots). In the following, we will focus on ethical principles and theories, as they form the theoretical basis for evaluating generative AI in medicine (in productive tension with particular judgments).

The focus on principles in contemporary applied ethics has been argued to reflect a widespread abandonment of the search for an Archimedean point in ethics

(McNamee and Schramme 2011). Using the principles involves putting aside the battle over theories to focus on the issues that appear relevant in the particular case. However, a principles-based approach does not necessarily need to replace ethical theories such as utilitarianism, Kantian deontology, and virtue ethics. In reflective equilibrium, they can inform and support the principles, and they can be used in a pluralistic and combinatory way, considering each ethical focus—utility, duties, and virtues—in relation to particular ethical issues (cf. Beauchamp and Childress 2001, p. 383). For example, a design team working on a generative AI application in healthcare might ask the following in an ethics workshop (cf. Põder and Romeike 2025):

- Does generative AI help maximize well-being, or fulfill as many preferences as possible for the people involved? (Utilitarianism)
- Does generative AI instrumentalize or discriminate against anyone, or violate autonomy and human dignity? (Deontology)
- Does generative AI hinder or promote the practice of important human virtues? Is the use of generative AI advisable in terms of living a "good life" or supporting a "good healthcare system"? (Virtue Ethics)

These considerations can be fruitfully complemented by principles-based reasoning, which relies on pro tanto (or prima facie) mid-level principles. Such principles occupy a middle ground between high-level ethical theories (such as utilitarianism and Kantian deontology) and particular judgments and cases. As noted above, the best-known example is Tom Beauchamp and James Childress's four principles of medical ethics: autonomy, nonmaleficence, beneficence, and justice, which (more pragmatically and pluralistically) avoid theoretical battles over what is the correct moral theory. Over the past 40 years, these four principles have gained widespread acceptance and are internationally regarded as the dominant framework for evaluating medical ethical problems (Düwell 2008; Hoffmann 2009). As pro tanto principles, they demand respect as long as there is no conflict between them that requires careful balancing and prioritization. And as the four principles are quite abstract, they need to be carefully specified in relation to particular issues.

These four bioethical principles have also found significant resonance in emerging AI ethics. For example, the AI4Life initiative, led by Luciano Floridi, reviewed 6 prominent sets of principles on AI ethics and identified 47 different principles (Floridi et al. 2018; cf. Põder and Romeike 2025). These were categorized and compared with the Beauchamp and Childress principles, showing considerable agreement. However, Floridi et al. suggest adding a fifth, domain-specific principle—explicability (or transparency)—to the AI ethics framework. This principle also includes the aspect of accountability, and they interpret it as a prerequisite for the realization of other principles (which, in our view, can often be true, but not necessarily always, as conflicts can arise, e.g., between beneficence and explicability). This results in the following five principles for AI ethics (with corresponding sub-rules or specifications, cf. Floridi et al. 2018, pp. 696–700):

- Autonomy (power to decide, including whether to decide)
- Nonmaleficence (privacy, security, caution regarding AI capabilities)
- Beneficence (promoting well-being, preserving dignity, and sustaining the planet)
- Justice (promoting prosperity and preserving solidarity, non-discrimination)
- Explicability (promoting intelligibility and accountability)

In the ethical evaluation of generative AI in medicine, it seems fruitful to use this principles-based approach in combination with classical ethical theories. However, at least four methodological aspects should be considered more closely to ensure a productive use of this normative core within the broader process of reflective equilibrium: (1) the selection of ethical principles and theories, (2) the methodological "bottom-up" scale of reflective equilibrium, (3) a stronger focus on empirical knowledge about moral reasoning, and (4) the need for a participatory and design-ethical approach to generative AI, in line with efforts in AI research ethics, validation research, and ethical-legal regulation.

(1) Although the principles of Floridi et al. and Beauchamp and Childress are favored here, as well as a reference to the main types of normative theories (utilitarianism, Kantian deontology and virtue ethics), this is not meant to be exclusive. As Beauchamp and Childress rightly note, "a moral framework is more a process than a finished product" (Beachamp and Childress 2001, p. 399). This means that the method of wide reflective equilibrium invites and is open to different ethical theories. Already the three ethical theories favored here have numerous shapes and conceptualizations. For example, Kantian deontology can include communicative and existential reformulations (Habermas 1983; Løgstrup 1956), utilitarianism reference to well-being or preferences (cf. Parfit 1984, 2011), and virtue ethics universalist as well as communitarian versions (Hursthouse 1999; MacIntyre 1981).

The same is true of principles. Although the principles of Beauchamp and Childress are influential in both medical and technology ethics, wide reflective equilibrium should encourage variations of principles, thus dynamically expanding the scope. An insightful critical extension of Beauchamp and Childress's principles has been proposed by Matti Häyry who stresses the importance of the so-called European values of dignity, precautionary principle, and solidarity (2003). While Floridi et al. do not include these values separately, they appear in their specification of principles (dignity under "beneficence," caution regarding AI capabilities under "nonmaleficence," and solidarity under "justice") (Põder and Romeike 2025).

(2) A second aspect concerns the methodological "bottom-up" scale of reflective equilibrium, which refers to the moral judgments and insights inherent in our practical life situations. Principles-based applied ethics tends to focus too much on the discussion of "correct" principles and their proper interpretation (Arras 2017, p. 206). In order to bring particular moral judgments and insights to the fore and allow them to interact productively with principles, we need diverse bottom-up approaches in ethics. The wide reflective equilibrium should therefore pay more attention, for example, to qualitative approaches in empirically informed applied ethics, phenomenological ethics, existential ethics, virtue ethics, narrative ethics,

care ethics, and feminist ethics. They all offer valuable insights to the bottom-up scale of reflective equilibrium (Põder 2023, pp. 7–10).

This helps us to take concrete, lived experience seriously as a source of moral insight and orientation in dealing with generative AI in medicine, and to explore questions such as: How do we experience ourselves, our bodies, and social relations in relation to generative AI in healthcare? What does it mean to be ill or healthy and to participate in the healthcare system in the era of generative AI? What does transparency, privacy, or responsibility (existentially, socially) mean in this context? What is the role of compassion, trust, and hope in AI-powered healthcare? How do we experience conversations with virtual healthcare assistants, especially regarding intimacy and emotions?

(3) Scientific disciplines (evolutionary biology, cognitive science, social psychology, etc.) are increasingly shedding light on how morality has evolved and how it works in practice (e.g., the role of emotions in morality). A stronger inclusion of empirical information about morality in the process of wide reflective equilibrium can inform our principles and theories, as well as help us better understand our particular judgments and intuitions (Shults et al. 2018). A better scientific understanding of our moral equipment or mechanisms forces us to think critically about our moral traditions and beliefs, and can help clarify the limits and possibilities of our moral reasoning. This is also relevant to our attempts to integrate morality into AI-based healthcare systems, as these efforts raise questions about the nature of morality and its computability.

(4) In recent decades, technology ethics has evolved into a proactive, design-ethical enterprise that seeks to embed ethical principles in the technology itself. The central concept here is the so-called embedded values approach, the recognition that technology is never entirely neutral, but always more or less value-laden. This approach is prominently applied in the Value Sensitive Design methodology developed by Batya Friedman and her colleagues (Friedman and Hendry 2019). Participatory approaches using social science methods such as interviews, focus groups, and surveys to explore moral attitudes, user experiences and stakeholder interests (thus methodologically strengthening the bottom-up scale of reflective equilibrium mentioned above) play a central role here. Philosophically, this participatory focus reflects the communicative (dialogical) nature of human reasoning as well as the situatedness of our knowledge. However, the participatory collaboration in ethical (co-)reasoning (between patients, physicians and engineers) should not be limited to technology design but must also be maintained and institutionally supported in clinical practice involving generative AI (Salloch and Eriksen 2024).

Participatory and discursive ethical design efforts, as part of the wide reflective equilibrium, continuously benefit from three specific areas of research: AI research ethics, the emerging ethical and legal regulation of AI-based health technologies, and validation research for generative AI. The ethical evaluation framework presented here underscores the importance of all these areas, as they are vital to facilitating our ethical efforts in the development and implementation of generative AI in medicine.

3 Ethics of Generative AI in Clinical Practice: Between Emergence and Hallucinations

The rapidly evolving ethical debate surrounding generative language models in healthcare has brought to light numerous opportunities and risks. Due to the sensitivity of the field, including vulnerable life situations, groups, and power imbalances, generative AI systems in medicine requires particularly careful ethical evaluation. In what follows, we highlight two critical cross-cutting issues that need to be considered within the framework of reflective equilibrium as generative AI is increasingly integrated into clinical practice: (1) the AI-based transformation of the social structure of healthcare, and (2) the trustworthiness of generative AI in medicine.

3.1 AI-Based Transformation of the Social Structure of Medicine

Generative AI's surprisingly good ability to produce human-like text could profoundly change various communication processes and workflows in healthcare, potentially reshaping its entire social structure. It can have both positive and problematic effects on the doctor-patient relationship (Sauerbrei et al. 2023; Čartolovni et al. 2023), and it has the potential to be a "game-changing innovation" that would significantly alter the way humans communicate with machines (Javaid et al. 2023).

The evolving research on the impact of generative AI on the doctor-patient relationship highlights both hopes and concerns. One major hope is that generative AI will improve physicians' efficiency by reducing workload, particularly in administrative tasks and technology-related workflows, thereby allowing more time for compassionate, empathetic, and trustful communication—the traditional values in person-centered care (Čartolovni et al. 2023). However, Sparrow and Hatherly rightly emphasize the paradox of this expectation, as generative AI may also lead, due to economic constraints, to an increase in patient consultations per day, potentially offsetting the time saved (Sparrow and Hatherly 2020).

Another hope is that generative AI could enhance the doctor-patient relationship by increasing patient autonomy and facilitating shared decision-making. AI could help overcome lingering "doctor-knows-best" attitudes by empowering patients to become more confident and informed, leveling the playing field and fostering "in-depth human interactions" (Pearl 2023). AI-based tools would not only make patients more knowledgeable but also challenge doctors to improve their communication skills, particularly when explaining the outputs of AI tools (in this context, explainable AI becomes crucial). The concern here is that instead of such collaboration, the increasing presence of generative AI will replace and undermine the human dimension of the doctor-patient relationship (Jotterand and Bosco 2020).

Overall, there is an expectation that generative AI could strengthen the doctor-patient alliance, especially if AI is used as an assistive tool while keeping a "human in the loop." However, there are also legitimate concerns about the potential loss of the holistic dimension of the doctor-patient relationship—if it will "de-humanize or re-humanize the healthcare" (Jotterand and Bosco 2020). To facilitate this hoped-for synergy, there is a need to restructure medical education, placing greater emphasis on digital literacy in the curriculum (Põder and Romeike 2025; Sauerbrei et al. 2023), and adopting a "critical awareness approach" to AI-led healthcare which facilitates human interaction (Čartolovni et al. 2023).

The second aspect that is transforming the social structure of healthcare is the changing way people interact with technological creatures (Põder and Romeike 2025). Generative AI-based assistants could provide patients with advice, support, and individual healthcare management. The integration of generative AI systems with interactive agents will create novel human-machine interactions in healthcare, enabling realistic simulations of human behavior (Park et al. 2023). Another potential development is the incorporation of large language models into physical robots acting as nurses or caregivers, changing the landscape of care.

While these developments promise many benefits, such as improved telemedicine and personalized patient care, they also pose serious risks. One critical concern has already been mentioned above—the increasing presence of generative AI-based technologies that can potentially replace or undermine human interactions. This could dehumanize healthcare as an inherently human practice involving human encounter, compassion, and empathy. Another critical argument is that such interactions simulate human attention, care, and empathy, making them inherently manipulative. As such, they would constitute a subtle and fundamentally undignifying deception.

Possible counterarguments to these concerns include the view that interaction with generative AI is not intended to completely replace human interaction in medicine, but rather has the potential to significantly support and enrich it (see above). Another argument is that there may be ethically justified trade-offs, such as consciously accepting some loss of human interaction in favor of more effective and efficient treatment and care. Furthermore, artificial intelligence should always be clearly identifiable as such to minimize the risks of manipulation and deception, especially in an emerging era of generative AI, where "bots compete for your love" and intimacy (Harari 2017; cf. Põder and Romeike 2025).

The charge of deception and manipulation would also be rendered moot by the emergence of "strong AI" (artificial general intelligence). This would then constitute a new technological alterity with mental capabilities that cannot be characterized by terms such as simulation. Indeed, some researchers see generative AI as the first "sparks" of the emergence of strong AI (Bubeck et al. 2023). However, most researchers reject such assumptions, pointing out that generative AI (whether in principle or in its current state) is nothing more than an illusion of empathy, even if it can be experienced as more empathic than humans (Chomsky et al. 2023; Howe et al. 2023).

An interesting perspective on the charge of deception is offered by the relational approach in AI ethics (Coeckelbergh 2010; Gunkel 2012). This approach considers how social robots are actually experienced in different and changing relationships. This relational and phenomenological "bottom-up" approach (see Sect. 2 above) takes seriously the lived experience of our interaction with social AI-based robots. They are not categorized a priori as deception or illusion, even though this might seem obvious in an objective, theoretical view of their capabilities. From this perspective, generative AI would mean the social "emergence" of a new kind of interactive reality in healthcare, transcending our traditional views of humans and machine.

3.2 Trustworthiness of Generative AI in Medicine

In addition to transforming the social structure of healthcare, another major challenge for generative AI systems in clinical practice is their trustworthiness. This can be defined as "the ability to meet stakeholder expectations in a verifiable way" (ISO/IEC TR 24028:2020; cf. Mentzas et al. 2024). Trustworthiness of AI can involve a wide range of characteristics related to factual accuracy and robustness, hallucinations (by the AI) and privacy, discriminatory bias and fairness, responsibility and accountability, safety and security, and transparency and human oversight (cf. NIST Artificial Intelligence Risk Management Framework 2023, pp. 12–18).

These concerns and the notion of trustworthiness go beyond the inherent quality or attributes of AI (such as being technically robust and designed to "embed" ethical and legal principles) to encompass a broader "ecosystem of trust," including "all processes and actors that are part of the system's lifecycle" (cf. Ethics Guidelines for Trustworthy AI 2019, p. 38; on "ecosystem of trust," see White Paper on Artificial Intelligence 2020). Trustworthy AI is also the explicit goal of the EU AI Act (European Parliament and Council 2024), which itself aims to serve as an important pillar of trustworthy AI. Accordingly, attempts to measure trustworthiness face the challenge of developing holistic, complex, and context-sensitive metrics that incorporate epistemic, ethical, and social dimensions (Mattioli et al. 2023).

In light of the ethical theories and principles discussed earlier (see Sect. 2), trustworthiness in AI should ensure that generative AI systems maximize well-being (utilitarianism), do not violate human dignity (Kantian deontology), and embody the "virtue of trustworthiness" while promoting the virtues of human stakeholders (virtue ethics). Similarly, trustworthy AI should, through its various attributes, uphold (at least pro tanto) the five ethical principles proposed by Floridi et al.: it should facilitate empowerment (autonomy), avoid harm (nonmaleficence), contribute to well-being (beneficence), prevent bias (justice), and ensure transparency. In the following, we will touch, pars pro toto, on two key issues related to trustworthy AI: "hallucinations" and factual correctness, and the importance of transparency (drawing partly on Põder and Romeike 2025).

In the context of generative AI systems, AI hallucinations—output that is nonfactual but appears authentic—pose a significant risk to the integrity of medical information. These hallucinations can arise from knowledge gaps, incorrect associations of (synthetic) data, or intentional data poisoning (Gadiko 2024; Bubeck et al. 2023; Chen and Esmaeilzadeh 2024; Athaluri et al. 2023). Generative AI hallucinations become particularly dangerous and even life-threatening when they influence medical decision-making, for example by producing misleading diagnostic reports in radiology, fabricated predictions in medical summaries, or incorrect advice in AI-based mental health consultations (Spallek et al. 2023; Javaid et al. 2023). Hallucinations typically involve completely fabricated content, often containing false or misleading information or references to non-existent sources (Shen et al. 2023; Liu et al. 2023). Detecting these hallucinations can be challenging as they are often interwoven with accurate information and synthesize data from multimodal sources.

Strategies to improve factual accuracy and avoid hallucinations (as well as related issues such as misinformation and bias) can be multifaceted. An important risk-mitigation strategy is to improve the quality of generative AI outputs through technological solutions, such as the integration of search engines or downstream secondary systems (Weßels 2023; Liu et al. 2023). Particularly important in this context are retrieval-assisted generation (RAG) and knowledge graphs, which enhance the generation process by integrating additional (structured and unstructured) knowledge repositories (Lobentanzer et al. 2023; Fuellen et al. 2024).

The quality of outputs can also be improved by enhancing policies and procedures for data collection, training, and validation. This includes preventing the collection of data from untrustworthy sources and investing in data standardization and validation to improve overall quality (Chen and Esmaeilzadeh 2024). Additionally, the risks of hallucinations and bias could be mitigated through human oversight by ensuring that AI-generated outputs are reviewed by healthcare professionals before being used in clinical workflows (the human-in-the-loop principle). However, one might ask whether the practical implementation of human oversight will not become increasingly complicated as the capabilities of generative AI improve, while their interpretability and transparency become more problematic.

The second aspect of trustworthy AI that we want to address here is therefore the issue of transparency. Transparency is essential not only to enable responsibility in relation to AI, but also to the ethical principles of autonomy, nonmaleficence, beneficence, and justice (see Sect. 2 above). For example, how can we sustain autonomous decision-making in healthcare if the recommendations of AI-based systems remain obscure and difficult to interpret? And how can we be sure that such outcomes will not cause harm or put patients at risk? These concerns have elevated transparency to a prominent issue in AI ethics, and the need for transparency is also underlined by legislation, such as the EU AI Act.

In explainable AI (XAI) research, various XAI methods are used to make the functioning and results of complex AI models transparent and understandable (Schaaf et al. 2021). New XAI methods such as AtMan (Deb et al. 2023) or the ChatGPT Code Interpreter (Kitamura et al. 2023) are promising solutions that offer more transparency and can help to minimize hallucinations and discriminatory biases. However, explainability is not only about decoding algorithms, but also about providing a socially understandable explanation of why generative AI has produced a particular result (Ethics Guidelines for Trustworthy AI 2019). It is therefore important to conduct research not only on technical explainability, but also on practical "co-constructive explanations" that involve users in the explanation process (Finke et al. 2022).

However, considering transparency as a ethical principle means that even this principle is subject to balancing and possible trade-offs in specific situations. The EU Ethics Guidelines for Trustworthy AI mention the possible trade-offs between "enhancing a system's explainability" or "increasing its accuracy" (Ethics Guidelines for Trustworthy AI 2019, p. 18). If there were clinical evidence that improved versions of generative AI significantly outperform human expertise, this would be a strong argument for preferring generative AI in certain clinical workflows, even if it involves "black-box algorithms" (and relies on other "reliability indicators" of an AI system, cf. Durán and Jongsma 2021). While transparency is an important ethical principle, compromises with transparency for the sake of effectiveness and efficiency may be ethically justified (with recourse to the principles of nonmaleficence and beneficence) (Põder and Romeike 2025).

4 Ethics of Using Generative AI in Research: From Giant Leaps Forward to Loss of Control

The ongoing wave of development and application of generative artificial intelligence—which many would describe as having barely started (e.g., Suleyman and Bhaskar 2023)—is likely to bring about considerable changes to various sections of society. Research and technology development are areas where changes are expected to be vast and profound. The European Commission comments that "Research is one of the sectors that could be most significantly disrupted by generative AI" (European Commission 2024, p. 3). Also UNESCO raises concerns (UNESCO 2023, 2024). In this section (which draws on Helgesson 2024), we will briefly consider expected benefits of this new development, before considering potential ethical issues. Finally, we will get quite specific regarding use of large language models in the production of text for scientific publications.

4.1 A Giant Wave of Generative AI to Revolutionize Medical Research?

Giant leaps forward are expected in data analysis thanks to generative AI, to the extent that some believe that much research will transform into something essentially different (Suleyman and Bhaskar 2023; Resnik and Hosseini 2024). Indeed, new methods and knowledge attainment are involved, including the move from traditional biostatistics to machine learning. The work of generative AI has been described by Magnus Boman as "inductively jumping to conclusions through clever guesswork and then over time learning how to automatically correct for error" (Boman 2022, p. 1; for an elaboration of the differences between statistical inference and machine learning, see Eloranta and Boman 2022).

In medicine, AI-based image analysis, for instance for detection of cancer tumors, was early considered a low-hanging fruit, setting off a large number of studies (for an overview of uses, see Musalamadugu and Kannan 2023). Such use involved the hope that AI in the near future will take over at least part of the analytic workload in oncological imaging and with increasing precision. AI is, in fact, useful in a wide variety of medical scans, opening up for related research (Topol 2019). Considerable changes in healthcare are also expected in pathology, also here with predictions of increased efficiency and precision (Dembrower et al. 2020). Many different modalities are suitable for AI processing, such as images, text, audio, and various measurement output, opening up for advanced multimodal fusion models. Precision medicine is mentioned as one area where medical research will take advantage of generative AI (Acs et al. 2020). Bioinformatics, computational systems biology, DNA sequencing, drug development (for instance by help of AI software predicting protein structures), genetic engineering, and gene therapy research are others (Topol 2019; Amedior 2022; Boman 2022; Maqsood et al. 2024; Resnik and Hosseini 2024; The Economist 2024; Vilhekar and Rawekar 2024). There is no reason to believe there is an end to the list of potentially useful applications.

It has been suggested that AI tools will accelerate the discovery rate in many fields by increasing efficiency, streamlining workflows in research projects, and enhancing data analysis (Suleyman and Bhaskar 2023; Topol 2019). However, at this point in time, many medical researchers with an interest in applying AI in their work are still in the learning process of understanding how AI can best be put to use. Some AI experts offer them help in crossing the bridge between statistical inference and machine learning by explaining the differences from a methodological standpoint (Eloranta and Boman 2022). But a migration of researchers from technological to medical departments are probably also needed to adequately integrate programming skills and knowledge of how generative AI can be put to use with understanding of the areas to be explored (Boman 2022).

While the expectations on generative artificial intelligence in medical research are high, it also involves potential risks of various kinds. Some of these risks are general, while others concern specific matters. In what follows, we will take a closer look at these in turn.

4.2 General Risks with Use of Generative AI in Research

Some general ethical issues relating to use of generative AI in research are equally relevant to uses outside research, hence they have been brought up earlier in this chapter. They will be mentioned here nevertheless.

It has often been pointed out, and exemplified, that generative AI may produce biased research output (Amedior 2022; Boman 2022; Topol 2019; Resnik and Hosseini 2024). Such output may in turn maintain and increase inequalities in society. The scientific community must be aware of this risk, consider the data the AI is trained on, and monitor AI-generated results in order to expose such failures and stop them from impacting society.

Lack of transparency is another issue repeatedly pointed out in the context of use of AI in research. It relates to risk of bias in the sense that lack of transparency may obscure the source of bias. Two aspects of transparency are particularly worth mentioning. The first one concerns *data used for learning*. Is it transparent wherefrom data used for training the AI have been obtained, and if this use is legitimate and legal? The second aspect concerns the previously mentioned *black box problem* pertaining to use of algorithms—the path from data input to output is hidden so that it cannot be traced or understood how the outcome is generated (Castelvecchi 2016; Knight 2017; Maqsood et al. 2024). This lack of transparency has implications for both trust and responsibility (Amedior 2022). A proposed solution to these problems is so-called *explainable AI*, where some kind of view into the black box is attained; others question whether explainable AI is achievable (de Bruijn et al. 2022). Some point out that even if achievable at some level, there is no guarantee that it will be explainable, and understandable, to all relevant audiences, such as politicians and the general public (Resnik and Hosseini 2024).

Another general potential problem with generative AI, mentioned above but also relevant to research, is that it sometimes generates false data, sometimes called *hallucinated data*. One example of hallucinated data is the inclusion of references that as a matter of fact do not exist to research papers (Alkaissi and McFarlane 2023). Such errors contribute to contamination of the scientific record, alongside publications containing fabricated or falsified results. Yet another potential problem is that generative AI may facilitate scientific misconduct (e.g., see Haider et al. 2024): misconduct may be easier and faster to carry out, and it may also be easier to cover up. It has been suggested that generative AI may facilitate an increase in output from so-called paper mills: "These operations, which mass-produce dubious or even fabricated research papers, undermine the very foundation of the scientific community" (ACS Publications 2023). However, perhaps AI may also be useful in detecting research fraud (cf. Bucci 2018).

4.3 Risks Related to Handling of Sensitive Personal Data

Research involving generative AI will in many cases, at some point, use huge data sets. In medical research, this will commonly involve sensitive personal information on health. The issue is not new—"big data" has been discussed for quite some years (see, e.g., Mittelstadt and Floridi 2016), but it is certainly highly relevant in the context of using generative AI for research. When adequate basic routines and reliable technical solutions are in place, the greatest risk factor is not so much the amount of data handled, we suggest, as the potential differences in experiences and attitudes among the people collaborating in AI-driven medical research and how this may affect their actions. While medical researchers tend to be well trained in observing requirements regarding the handling of sensitive personal information, such as patient health data, this experience may not be shared by programmers, engineers, and management of IT companies. Professions with the main focus on technical invention and application may tend to prioritize expedience over data security, unless instructed to do otherwise. To be on the safe side, medical researchers need to make sure sufficiently secure procedures for data handling are in place in such collaborations.

An important question to ask in relation to research using large amounts of sensitive data is: Where do data fed into the AI end up? Data leakage from large language models (Heikkilä 2023) has made some universities restrict what software to use when handling sensitive information, so the problem is not merely hypothetical. When generative AI is created within the research project, researchers must make sure that risks of data leakage are minimized. In collaborations with partners who provide a ready AI solution to be used, there is a risk that all data fed into the AI will automatically transfer to that company. In the worst-case scenario, business partners have a hidden agenda to commercialize data sets of patient information. Even without hidden agendas, data leakage can still be a problem.

As mentioned above, it is important what data are used in the training of the AI. If training data contain sensitive personal information, it may be questionable to use it without external approval from an ethical review board. Use of personal information may also require informed consent procedures, and there may be additional legal restrictions based on GDPR for research in Europe.

Re-identification is a general potential problem when handling extensive personal information and may be relevant also in the research context—with sufficient information, data will narrow down possibilities and may identify specific individuals, as might be the case, for instance, for persons with rare diseases living in small communities. Since AI-driven research tends to involve large amounts of data, this risk is arguably even larger in that case; furthermore, artificial intelligence may be used for re-identification purposes.

4.4 Risks of Losing Control of Research to AI

A more widespread and intense use of AI in medical research may not only lead to an increasing production of fraudulent and erratic research, but also to an accelerating output of research primarily aiming at adding publications rather than exploring interesting and important questions. Generative AI may facilitate the passing off of ill-conceived research as good research. AI may also be a potent tool in the hands of those willing to mass-produce research. Hence, there is a foreseeable risk that academic journals and research archives "get flooded by AI-supported drivel that, on the surface, will appear serious, well-considered, and relevant" (Helgesson 2024, p. 52). Not least, using AI as a shortcut to filling the CV with publications may add to sloppiness and recklessness (Resnik and Hosseini 2024). Although this is certainly not an unavoidable effect of increased use of AI in academia, the pressure to publish, and the intense competition faced in many research fields, increases the risk that some researchers will use AI as a means to take shortcuts without paying much attention to the effect on research quality or relevance.

Another potential risk with letting AI play a central role in research, in particular if it remains largely non-transparent, is that researchers over time lose control over the research process, all the way from choosing what questions to ask to packaging research outcome in publications. How likely such a development is, is hard to say, but it is worth noting that fully automated laboratories, steered by AI, where no human being would need to enter for research purposes, are seriously considered, and there exists early stage examples (see, e.g., Callaway 2024). The issue of losing control to generative AI relates to previous points about competition and living with the pressure to publish to remain in the game. The other main factor is lack of transparency. If researchers step by step decrease their intellectual involvement and transfer important research decisions to generative AI, either because they prefer results to personal engagement or because they perceive that the AI is more on top of research development than they are, this may over time have consequences for human capacity for critical thinking and exploring, at least in the research context. It would also be unacceptable from a societal perspective to invest heavily in research without having any capacity for critical evaluation.

4.5 Responsibilities in Developing Generative AI

Since generative AI, as so many other inventions, may be used for both good and bad (so-called *dual use*) we need a discussion about how developers and researchers should think and act in the light of risk of causing serious harm (Suleyman and Bhaskar 2023). One question to raise is whether those involved in AI development, like AI companies, programmers, engineers, and researchers using AI, should consider ethical restrictions as to what AI projects to engage in? Even if there are no clear categories of development projects that never ought to be engaged in—other than those initiated for purposes that are in themselves known to be unethical—should there be any sort of restriction on development, even moratoria? For instance, the rapid development of large language systems takes place with very limited understanding of potential societal consequences, while many people in the tech industry and elsewhere believe the impact will be tremendous. Ethicists and other critical thinkers risk lagging far behind. Mustafa Suleyman, co-founder of AI companies, hints at the difficulties in even trying to have some kind of overview (Suleyman and Bhaskar 2023, p. 36): "As the power of our tools grows exponentially and as access to them rapidly increases, so do the potential harms, an unfolding labyrinth of consequences that no one can fully predict or forestall."

4.6 Scientific Text and Large Language Models: Proper Uses and Misconduct

The conditions for both education and research have changed considerably since the launch of ChatGPT by Open AI in November 2022. As already noted, ChatGPT is one of several large language models trained with vast amounts of text. At its interface it is a chatbot, but far more advanced than anything you meet in, for instance, digital customer services. As anyone knows who has used them, large language models generate well-written and well-structured text on a limitless set of topics in mere seconds, and in a wide variety of styles—all that is required from the user is to provide some free-text instructions. Large language models can be used for such diverse things as computer programming and writing academic papers, business proposals, and movie scripts. While outcomes at times are in part incorrect, the overall outcome is nevertheless no less than impressive (Hosseini et al. 2024).

In addition to the many potential upsides of using large language models relating to speeding up work, summarizing vast material, and so forth, they can also be used in misleading ways. At worst they facilitate research misconduct. Plagiarism is one potential ethical issue that has been identified in relation to use of AI in text production (e.g., Zulhusni 2023). Two matters can be distinguished: (1) Are large language models themselves ever (or always) guilty of plagiarism? (2) Are students and researchers using AI for text production thereby plagiarizing? To provide answers, we first need to remind ourselves what is meant by "plagiarism." A standard definition is presented in the *European Code of Conduct for Research Integrity* (ALLEA 2023, p. 10): "Plagiarism is using other people's work and ideas without giving proper credit to the original source." An alternative way of defining plagiarism is found in Helgesson and Eriksson (2015), where plagiarism is said to concern using someone else's intellectual product (ideas, results, images, or text) in a way that implies that it is one's own.

Let us first consider large language models—do they plagiarize when they produce text? The short answer is: no. To understand why, it should be noted that plagiarism is context-dependent (Helgesson et al. 2025). For instance, you do not plagiarize if you copy passages from a poem, book, or research article into your own personal notes if you do so without adding citation marks and references to the source. This is so because when you take notes this way, you are not misleading anyone. There are no established expectations whatsoever (at least not with any moral bite) on the order and structure of people's private notes. Text generated by large language models should be considered in the same way, as long as they are kept private. For a text using sources without giving proper credit to be an instance of plagiarism, the text must be used in a way that makes it misleading. The concept of plagiarism applies first when the text is used in certain contexts, with certain established expectations, for instance turned in as a student essay or submitted as an academic paper to a journal (Helgesson et al. 2025). This is when readers are misled if the author fails to provide proper credit to used sources. On the other hand, whatever the large language model writes in response to our queries, no one using it believes that the generative AI itself performed research or dove into deep creative thought to come up with it (understood as something other than cooking up text, based on algorithms, using other sources). When it comes to providing credit to used sources, present AIs tend to fail, but they do not fail in the sense of misplacing credit to themselves—when they fail, they fail to place credit at all.

Let it be concluded that it doesn't make sense to claim that large language models plagiarize. But what about students and researchers—do they plagiarize when they use generative AI in their academic writing? It depends on how it is used. First, to use generative AI for translation, text editing, and language improvement is unproblematic. Getting the idioms and phrases right and using more adequate terms does not involve plagiarism since standard phrases and expressions are not anyone's in particular. However, for transparency, one should inform readers that generative AI is used for text editing whenever that is the case (AJE 2023; Hosseini et al. 2023).

Second, if a large language model is instead used to cook up a paper mimicking proper new research, and that paper is submitted to a journal, that would be a clear instance of fabrication. This is so because the content is in fact made up instead of constituting proper research. If presented results, instead of being cooked up, are collected from work of others, without informing readers about the sources and, hence, that what is presented in the present paper is not original research, then these other sources are plagiarized.

A third potential use of generative AI in text production would be to let the AI write first versions of research papers, provided that this would be possible, based on instructions for how to generate background sections, input from researchers regarding applied methods, data produced in the projects, and so forth. Without knowing exactly what large language models are or will be able to do, it is difficult to say whether such use of AI would be of much help to researchers, but if it were, would it be fine or would it be wrong? Leaving the writing of the first version to a generative AI would, at present, involve the risk that it would use provided data selectively or modify it in ways that would render the manuscript misleading—seemingly a typical instance of falsification: research is done (in contrast to fabrication, when data is made up), but data or results are modified in ways that make the outcome misleading. However, it is arguably not a typical case of falsification since standard definitions of falsification include the intention to be misleading, while generative AI cannot be attributed any intentions—researchers may, of course, use AI without paying much attention to the correctness of outcomes. To avoid misleading content in the paper, researchers need to make sure the manuscript says precisely what it is intended to say; in other words, that it contains all required information, including adequate descriptions of background, methods, and presentations of results. For transparency, it should also be explained in the methods section how generative AI was used. Journals may not approve of this use of generative AI, but there does not seem to be any good reason why it should not be accepted, if the outcome is non-deceptive and transparent.

To avoid plagiarism, references are required when ideas and results obtained from elsewhere are included in the research paper, or student essay. So far, referencing has been a weak point for large language models, a problem that might pass. Fake references are sometimes included. In principle, plagiarism can be avoided by combining the work of the AI with traditional work with references. That is, if the generative AI does not provide proper references, the researchers will have to make that happen. In practice, it may not be at all realistic for researchers to identify sources used by an AI freely roaming the Internet for information. However, if its searches are restricted to a predefined set of literature, it may be feasible. For instance, researchers may first instruct the generative AI to write the background text for a manuscript based on information in a pre-specified list of research articles, and then go through that list of articles in order to identify what references need to be provided. Another option would be to identify a set of relevant references regardless of where the generative AI found the information. Using large language models this way would reduce the work spent on writing, but would require the ordinary amount of work to make the paper adequately referenced.

Reuse of images and graphs, on the "initiative" of generative AI, without provision of source might also occur—unless sources were provided in the manuscript, this would be plagiarism. If used without clearance from the journals from which they were taken, this would also constitute copyright infringement.

5 Conclusion and Perspective

In this chapter, we have provided a comprehensive introduction to the ethical aspects of generative AI in medicine, exploring its implications for both clinical practice and medical research. Generative AI has immense potential in virtually all areas of medicine, but it also poses significant risks that require careful analysis and mitigation. While emerging regulatory frameworks, such as the EU AI Act, are essential, they remain insufficient without accompanying ethical efforts to evaluate generative AI applications in healthcare. As Floridi et al. rightly point out, there is a difference between merely "playing by the rules" (legal compliance) and "playing well" (so that we can win) (Floridi et al. 2018, p. 694). To responsibly navigate the high-stakes landscape of generative AI in medicine, we need to foster a culture of ethical reflection that goes beyond legal compliance.

The ambiguity of promises and fear is a challenging feature of our technological culture and time, especially in medicine. It also challenges ethics to find new and creative ways of ethical reflection and evaluation. In this chapter, we argued that it is beneficial to situate emerging generative AI applications within a discursive and participatory framework of wide reflective equilibrium that allows for a more holistic reflection on the ethical risks and benefits. In its pluralistic and pragmatic setup, it facilitates a productive interplay of ethical theories, principles, and particular moral judgments, and takes seriously the interdisciplinary and participatory nature of AI ethics.

In our chapter, we highlighted a number of issues that require careful ethical consideration: generative AI means the emergence of new and potentially beneficial forms of human-machine interaction and capabilities, but also new risks such as AI hallucinations. A similar ambiguity concerns the ethical aspects of using generative AI in medical research, which can mean the hope of giant leaps forward, but also the loss of control.

In ethically navigating the ambiguous situation of promises and potential harms associated with generative AI medicine, we should not expect ethical principles or theories to always provide simple or unambiguous answers. However, critical ethical reflection on generative AI in medicine helps us to "play well"—or at least "better"—so that generative AI systems in medicine can truly benefit individuals and society. Ethical theories and principles within the wide reflective equilibrium are not meant to end the discussion with a simple reference to one viewpoint or another. Rather, they should help us to facilitate a nuanced ethical discussion about the risks and benefits of generative AI in medicine, and to find ways to operationalize ethics for clinical and research practice.

References

Acs B, Rantalainen M, Hartman J (2020) Artificial intelligence as the next step towards precision pathology. J Intern Med 288(1):62–81. https://doi.org/10.1111/joim.13030

ACS Publications (2023) AI in research and peer review: facing the future with integrity. https://axial.acs.org/publishing/ai-in-research-and-peer-review-facing-the-future-with-integrity. Accessed 23 Dec 2024

AJE (2023) Best practices for generative AI in research. https://www.aje.com/arc/best-practices-generative-ai-in-research/. Accessed 23 Dec 2024

Alkaissi H, McFarlane SI (2023) Artificial hallucinations in ChatGPT: implications in scientific writing. Cureus 15(2):e35179. https://doi.org/10.7759/cureus.35179

All European Academies, ALLEA (2023) The European Code of Conduct for Research Integrity. https://allea.org/code-of-conduct/. Accessed 23.12.2024.

Amedior NC (2022) Ethical implications of artificial intelligence in the healthcare sector. Proceedings of the 36th iSTEAMS Accra Bespoke Multidisciplinary Innovations Conference. University of Ghana/Academic City University College, Accra, Ghana. 31st May–2nd June, 2023, pp 1–12. https://doi.org/10.22624/AIMS/ACCRABESPOKE2023P1

Arras JD (2017) Methods in bioethics: the way we reason now. Oxford University Press, New York

Arras JD (2009) The way we reason now: reflective equilibrium in bioethics. In: Steinbock, B (ed.), The Oxford Handbook of Bioethics (online edn, Oxford Academic). https://doi.org/10.1093/oxfordhb/9780199562411.003.0003

Athaluri S, Manthena SV, Kesapragada VK, Yarlagadda V, Dave T, Duddumpudi RT (2023) Exploring the boundaries of reality: investigating the phenomenon of artificial intelligence hallucination in scientific writing through ChatGPT references. Cureus 15(4):e37432. https://doi.org/10.7759/cureus.37432

Beauchamp TL, Childress JF (2001) Principles of biomedical ethics, 5th edn. Oxford University Press, Oxford

Beauchamp TL, Childress JF (2009) Principles of biomedical ethics, 6th edn. Oxford University Press, Oxford

Boman M (2022) AI@KI: Final report, Karolinska Institutet. https://ki.se/en/lime/research-groups-and-units-at-lime/artificial-intelligence-at-karolinska-institutet/final-report. Accessed 21 Dec 2024

Bubeck, S., Chandrasekaran, V., Eldan R., Gehrke J., Horvitz E. et al. (2023) Sparks of artificial general intelligence early experiments with GPT-4. arXiv Preprint arXiv2303.12712.

Bucci EM (2018) Automatic detection of image manipulation in the biomedical literature. Cell Death Dis 2918(9):400. https://doi.org/10.1038/s41419-018-0430-3

Čartolovni A, Malešević A, Poslon L (2023) Critical analysis of the AI impact on the patient-physician relationship: a multi-stakeholder qualitative study. Digit Health 19(9): 20552076231220833. https://doi.org/10.1177/20552076231220833

Callaway E (2024). 'Set it and forget it': automated lab uses AI and robotics to improve proteins. Nature 625(7995):436. https://doi.org/10.1038/d41586-024-00093-w

Castelvecchi D (2016) Can we open the black box of AI? Nature 538:20–23. https://doi.org/10.1038/538020a

Chen Y, Esmaeilzadeh P (2024) Generative AI in medical practice: in-depth exploration of privacy and security challenges. J Med Internet Res 26:e53008. https://doi.org/10.2196/53008

Chomsky N, Roberts I, Watumull J (2023, March 8) The false promise of chatGPT. The New York Times

Clusmann J, Kolbinger FR, Muti HS et al (2023) The future landscape of large language models in medicine. Commun Med 3:141. https://doi.org/10.1038/s43856-023-00370-1

Coeckelbergh M (2010) Artificial companions: Empathy and vulnerability mirroring in human-robot relations. Stud Ethics Law Technol 4(3). https://doi.org/10.2202/1941-6008.1126

Daniels N (1996) Justice and justification: reflective equilibrium in theory and practice. Cambridge University Press, Cambridge

de Bruijn H, Warnier M, Janssen M (2022) The perils and pitfalls of explainable AI: strategies for explaining algorithmic decision-making. Gov Inf Q. https://doi.org/10.1016/ja.giq.2021.101666

Deb, M, Deiseroth, B, Weinbach, S, Schramowski, P, Kersting, K. (2023) AtMan: understanding transformer predictions through memory efficient attention manipulation. https://arxiv.org/pdf/2301.08110.

Dembrower K, Wåhlin E, Liu Y, Salim M, Smith K, Lindholm P, Eklund M, Strand F (2020) Effect of artificial intelligence-based triaging of breast cancer screening mammograms on cancer detection and radiologist workload: a retrospective simulation study. Lancet Digit Health 2(9):e468–e474

Durán JM, Jongsma KR (2021) Who is afraid of black box algorithms? On the epistemological and ethical basis of trust in medical AI. J Med Ethics 18. https://doi.org/10.1136/medethics-2020-106820

Düwell M (2008) Bioethik. Methoden, Theorien und Bereiche. J.B. Metzler, Stuttgart

Dworkin G (1988) The theory and practice of autonomy. Cambridge University Press, Cambridge

Gunkel DJ (2012) The machine question: Critical perspectives on AI, robots, and ethics. Cambridge MA, MIT Press

Eloranta S, Boman M (2022) Predictive models for clinical decision making: deep dives in practical machine learning. J Intern Med 292(2):278–295. https://doi.org/10.1111/joim.13483

European Commission, High-Level Expert Group on Artificial Intelligence (2019) Ethics guidelines for trustworthy AI. Brussels

European Commission (2020) White Paper on Artificial Intelligence: A European approach to excellence and trust. European Commission, Brussels. https://digital-strategy.ec.europa.eu/en/library/white-paper-artificial-intelligence-public-consultation-towards-european-approach-excellence-and. Accessed 21 Dec 2024

European Commission (2024) ERA Forum stakeholders' document. Living guidelines on the responsible use of generative AI in research. First version, March 2024. https://research-and-innovation.ec.europa.eu/document/2b6cf7e5-36ac-41cb-aab5-0d32050143dc_en. Accessed 21 Dec 2024

European Parliament and Council (2024) Regulation (EU) 2024/1689 on a European approach for Artificial Intelligence (Artificial Intelligence Act) and amending certain Union acts. Off J Eur Union, L 1689

Finke J, Horwath I, Matzner T, Schulz C (2022) (De)coding social practice in the field of XAI: towards a co-constructive framework of explanations and understanding between lay users and algorithmic systems. In: Degen H, Ntoa S (eds) Artificial Intelligence in HCI. HCII 2022, Lecture Notes in Computer Science, vol 13336. Springer, Cham. https://doi.org/10.1007/978-3-031-05643-7_10

Floridi L, Cowls J, Beltrametti M, Chatila R (2018) AI4People – an ethical framework for a good AI society. Opportunities, risks, principles, and recommendations. Mind Mach 28:689–707. https://doi.org/10.1007/s11023-018-9482-5

Friedman B, Hendry DG (2019) Value sensitive design: shaping technology with moral imagination. MIT Press, Cambridge, MA

Fuellen G, Kulaga A, Lobentanzer S, Unfried M, Avelar RA, Palmer D, Kennedy BK (2024) Validation requirements for AI-based intervention-evaluation in aging and longevity research and practice. Ageing Res Rev 4(104):102617. https://doi.org/10.1016/j.arr.2024.102617

Gadiko A (2024) Understanding and addressing AI hallucinations in healthcare and life sciences. Int J Health Sci 7(3):1–11. https://doi.org/10.47941/ijhs.1862

Habermas J (1983) Moralbewußtsein und kommunikatives Handeln. Suhrkamp Verlag, Frankfurt a.M

Haider J, Söderström KR, Ekström B, Rödl M (2024) GPT-fabricated scientific papers on Google Scholar: key features, spread, and implications for preempting evidence manipulation. Harvard Kennedy School (HKS) Misinf Rev. https://doi.org/10.37016/mr-2020-156
Harari YN (2017) Homo Deus: a brief history of tomorrow. Vintage, London
Häyry M (2003) European values in bioethics: why, what, and how to be used? Theor Med Bioethics 24(3):199–214. https://doi.org/10.1023/a:1024814710487
Heikkilä M (2023) Three ways AI chatbots are a security disaster. MIT Technol Rev. https://www.technologyreview.com/2023/04/03/1070893/three-ways-ai-chatbots-are-a-security-disaster/. Accessed 21 Dec 2024
Helgesson G, Eriksson S (2015) Plagiarism in research. Med Health Care Philos 18(1):91–101. https://doi.org/10.1007/s11019-014-9583-8
Helgesson G (2024) Ethical aspects of the use of AI in research. In: Palm E, Lindblom L (eds) Research ethics – ethical review and beyond. Studies in Applied Ethics No 20. Linköping University, Linköping
Helgesson G, Åkerman J, Belfrage S (2025) Recycling research without (self-)plagiarism: The importance of context and the case of conference contributions. Learned Publishing: e1653. https://doi.org/10.1002/leap.1653
Hoffmann M (2009) Dreißig Jahre Principles of Biomedical Ethics. Ein Literaturbericht. Zeitschrift Für Philosophische Forschung 63(4):597–611. https://doi.org/10.3196/004433009790069033
Hopkins AM, Logan JM, Kichenadasse G, Sorich MJ (2023) Artificial intelligence chatbots will revolutionise how cancer patients access information: ChatGPT represents a paradigm shift. JNCI Cancer Spectrum 7(2):pkad010. https://doi.org/10.1016/j.tbench.2023.100105
Hosseini M, Resnik D, B, Holmes K. (2023) The ethics of disclosing the use of artificial intelligence tools in writing scholarly manuscripts. Res Ethics 19(4):449–465. https://doi.org/10.1177/17470161231180449
Hosseini M, Rasmussen LM, Resnik DB (2024) Using AI to write scholarly publications. Account Res 31(7):715–723. https://doi.org/10.1080/08989621.2023.2168535
Howe PDL, Fay N, Saletta M, Hovy E (2023) ChatGPT's advice is perceived as better than that of professional advice columnists. Front Psychol 14:1281255. https://doi.org/10.3389/fpsyg.2023.1281255
Hursthouse R (1999) On virtue ethics. Oxford University Press, Oxford
International Organization for Standardization (2020) ISO/IEC TR 24028:2020 Information technology, Artificial intelligence. Overview of trustworthiness in artificial intelligence. https://www.iso.org/standard/77608.html
Javaid M, Haleem A, Singh RP (2023) ChatGPT for healthcare services: an emerging stage for an innovative perspective. TBench 3(1):100105. https://doi.org/10.1016/j.tbench.2023.100105
Jotterand F, Bosco C (2020) Keeping the "Human in the Loop" in the age of artificial intelligence: accompanying commentary for "Correcting the Brain?" by Rainey & Erden. Sci Eng Ethics 26(5):2455–2460. https://doi.org/10.1007/s11948-020-00241-1
Kitamura K, Irvan M, Shigetomi R (2023) YamaguchiXAI for medicine by ChatGPT Code interpreter. BDSIC '23: Proceedings of the 2023 5th International Conference on Big-data Service and Intelligent Computation, pp 28–34. https://doi.org/10.1145/3633624.3633629.
Knight W (2017) The dark secret at the heart of AI. MIT Technol Rev. https://www.technologyreview.com/s/604087/the-dark-secret-at-the-heart-of-ai/. Accessed 21 Dec 2024
Liu J, Wang C, Liu S (2023) Utility of ChatGPT in clinical practice. J Med Internet Res 25(4). https://doi.org/10.2196/48568
Lobentanzer S, Feng S, Consortium TB, Maier A, Wang C, Baumbach J, Krehl N, Ma Q, Saez-Rodriguez J (2023) A platform for the biomedical application of large language models. ArXiv. https://arxiv.org/abs/2305.06488
Løgstrup KE (1956) Den Etiske Fordring. Gyldendal, Copenhagen
MacIntyre A (1981) After virtue. London, Duckworth
Maqsood K, Hagras H, Zabe NR (2024) An overview of artificial intelligence in the field of genomics. Discov Artif Intell 4:9. https://doi.org/10.1007/s44163-024-00103-w

McNamee M, Schramme T (2011) Moral theory and theorizing in healthcare ethics. Ethical Theory Moral Pract 14(4):365–368. https://doi.org/10.1007/s10677-011-9291-x

Mattioli J, Sohier H, Delaborde A, Pedroza G, Amokrane K et al (2023) Towards a holistic approach for AI trustworthiness assessment based upon aids for multi-criteria aggregation. SafeAI 2023 - The AAAI's Workshop on Artificial Intelligence Safety. https://hal-04086455

Mentzas G, Fikardosa M, Lepeniotia K, Apostolou D (2024) Exploring the landscape of trustworthy artificial intelligence: status and challenges. Intell Decis Technol 18:837–854. https://doi.org/10.3233/IDT-240366

Mittelstadt BD, Floridi L (2016) The ethics of Big Data: current and foreseeable issues in biomedical contexts. Sci Eng Ethics 22:303–341. https://doi.org/10.1007/s11948-015-9652-2

Musalamadugu ST, Kannan H (2023) Generative AI for medical imaging analysis and applications. Future Med AI 1(2). https://doi.org/10.2217/fmai-2023-0004

Nadarzynski T, Knights N, Husbands D, Graham CA, Llewellyn CD et al (2024) Achieving health equity through conversational AI: a roadmap for design and implementation of inclusive chatbots in healthcare. PLoS Digit Health 3(5):e0000492. https://doi.org/10.1371/journal.pdig.0000492

Paladugu PS, Ong J, Nelson N, Kamran SA, Waisberg E et al (2023) Generative adversarial networks in medicine: important considerations for this emerging innovation in artificial intelligence. Ann Biomed Eng 51(10):2130–2142. https://doi.org/10.1007/s10439-023-03304-z

Parfit D (1984) Reasons and persons. Oxford University Press, Oxford

Parfit D (2011) On what matters, vol 1 and 2. Oxford University Press, Oxford

Park JS, O'Brien JC, Cai CJ, Morris MR, Liang P, Bernstein MS (2023) Generative agents: interactive simulacra of human behavior. https://arxiv.org/pdf/2304.03442.

Pearl R (2023) How generative AI will upend the doctor-patient relationship. Forbes 18(12):2023. https://www.forbes.com/sites/robertpearl/2023/10/18/how-generative-ai-will-upend-the-doctor-patient-relationship/. Accessed 21 Dec 2024

Põder J-C, Romeike BFM (2025) Ethik von ChatGPT in der Medizin. In: Cap CH, Martens A (eds) Schreibende KI – ein interdisziplinärer Diskurs. Springer, Cham. (in print)

Põder J-C (2023) Introduction: Kierkegaard and bioethics. In: Põder J-C (ed) Kierkegaard and bioethics. New York, Routledge, pp. 1-15

Rawls J (1971) A theory of justice. Harvard University Press, Cambridge, MA

Resnik DB, Hosseini M (2024) The ethics of using artificial intelligence in scientific research: new guidance needed for a new tool. AI Ethics. https://doi.org/10.1007/s43681-024-00493-8

Salloch S, Eriksen E (2024) What are humans doing in the loop? Co-reasoning and practical judgment when using machine learning-driven decision aids. Am J Bioeth 24(9), pp. 67–78. https://doi.org/10.1080/15265161.2024.2353800

Sauerbrei A, Kerasidou A, Lucivero F et al (2023) The impact of artificial intelligence on the person-centred, doctor-patient relationship: some problems and solutions. JMIR Med Educ 9:e51243. https://doi.org/10.1186/s12911-023-02162-y

Schaaf N, Wiedenroth SJ, Wagner P (2021) Erklärbare KI in der Praxis: Anwendungsorientierte Evaluation von xAI-Verfahren. Bauernhansi T, Huber M, Wagner P (eds). Stuttgart, Fraunhofer IPA. https://doi.org/10.24406/publica-fhg-300845

Shen Y, Heacock L, Elias J, Hentel KD, Reig B, Shih G (2023) ChatGPT and other Large Language Models are Double-Edged Swords. Radiology 307(2). https://doi.org/10.1148/radiol.230163

Shults LF, Wildman W, Dignum V (2018) Ethics in computer modeling and simulation. Proceedings of the 2018 Winter Simulation Conference. Institute for Electrical and Electronics Engineers, Piscataway, NJ, pp 1–12

Shults LF, Wildman W (2019) Ethics, computer simulation, and the future of humanity. In: Diallo SY, Wildman WJ, Shults FL, Tolk A (eds) Human simulation: perspectives, insights, and applications. Springer, Cham, pp 21–40

Spallek S, Birrell L, Kershaw S, Devine EK, Thornton L (2023) Can we use ChatGPT for mental health and substance use education? Examining its quality and potential harms. JMIR Med Educ 9:e51243. https://doi.org/10.2196/51243

Sparrow R, Hatherley J (2020) High hopes for "Deep Medicine"? AI, economics, and the future of care. Hast Cent Rep 50(1):14–17. https://doi.org/10.1002/hast.1079
Suleyman M, Bhaskar M (2023) The coming wave. Technology, power, and the twenty-first century's greatest dilemma. Crown, New York
The Economist (2024, March 27) Artificial intelligence is taking over drug development. https://www.economist.com/technology-quarterly/2024/03/27/artificial-intelligence-is-taking-over-drug-development
The National Institute of Standards and Technology (2023, January 26) AI Risk Management Framework (RMF). https://doi.org/10.6028/NIST.AI.100-1
Thirunavukarasu AJ, Ting DS, Elangovan K, Gutierrez L, Tan TF, Ting DS (2023) Large language models in medicine. Nat Med 29(8):1930–1940. https://doi.org/10.1038/s41591-023-02448-8
Topol EJ (2019) High-performance medicine: the convergence of human and artificial intelligence. Nat Med 25:44–56. https://doi.org/10.1038/s41591-018-0300-7
Topol EJ (2023) As artificial intelligence goes multimodal, medical applications multiply. Science 381(6663). https://doi.org/10.1126/science.adk6139
UNESCO (2023) Guidance for generative AI in education and research. https://www.unesco.org/en/articles/guidance-generative-ai-education-and-research
UNESCO (2024) Ethics of artificial intelligence. https://www.unesco.org/en/artificial-intelligence/recommendation-ethics. Accessed 21 Dec 2024
Vilhekar RS, Rawekar A (2024) Artificial intelligence in genetics. Cureus 16(1):e52035
Wang L, Wan Z, Ni C, Song Q, Li Y, Clayton E, Malin B, Yin Z (2024) Applications and concerns of ChatGPT and other conversational large language models in health care: systematic review. J Med Internet Res 7(26):e22769. https://doi.org/10.2196/22769
Weidinger L, Mellor J, Rauh M, Griffin C, Uesatoet J et al (2021) Ethical and social risks of harm from Language Models. arXiv Preprint arXiv:2112.04359
Weßels D (2023) Stellungnahme zu ChatGPT für den Bundestagsausschuss Bildung, Forschung und Technikfolgenabschätzung, Deutscher Bundestag. In: Ausschussdrucksache 20(18)108c. https://www.bundestag.de/resource/blob/944668/8986c32590098f441fbba938039650e5/20-18-108c-Wessels-data.pdf
Zulhusni M (2023) Is ChatGPT guilty of plagiarism? Techwire Asia. https://techwireasia.com/07/2023/is-chatgpt-guilty-of-plagiarism/. Accessed 21 Dec 2024

Johann-Christian Põder is Professor of Ethics (Theology and Medicine) at the Faculty of Theology, University of Rostock, Germany, and Head of the Department "Ageing of Individuals and Society" (AGIS), Interdisciplinary Faculty, University of Rostock. His current research focuses on the ethics of AI in medicine, methodological issues in bioethics, and the intersection of posthumanism, ethics, and religion.

Gert Helgesson is Professor of Medical Ethics at Stockholm Centre for Healthcare Ethics, Department of LIME, Karolinska Institutet, Sweden. His main research focus is on research ethics. He has written quite extensively on issues relating to research involving children, biobank research, autonomy and informed consent, academic authorship, responsibility in research, scientific misconduct, and rogue publishers.

Addressing the Paradox of Using AI in Ethics and Compliance Through a Checklist-Based Solution

13

Eleonora Viganò, Christian Hauser, and Albert Weichselbraun

Abstract

In this chapter, we address the paradox of using AI in corporate ethics and compliance (E&C): while AI effectively enhances E&C functions, it simultaneously introduces ethical risks.

We analyze the ethical implications of AI in E&C across five key areas: autonomy, fairness and nondiscrimination, transparency and explainability, security, and well-being. Our analysis reveals how AI systems used for monitoring, prediction, and decision-making can potentially infringe upon employee rights of self-determination, introduce biases, lack an understandable explanation of their operations, compromise personal, informational, and AI system security, and negatively impact workplace well-being.

To address these challenges, we provide E&C practitioners with a practical checklist for ethically assessing AI systems before implementation. This tool enables organizations to leverage AI's benefits in E&C while mitigating its ethical risks, ultimately helping to resolve the paradox of using AI to reduce organizational ethical risks while potentially creating new ones.

E. Viganò (✉) · C. Hauser
PRME Business Integrity Action Center, University of Applied Sciences of the Grisons, Chur, Switzerland

Digital Society Initiative, University of Zurich, Zurich, Switzerland
e-mail: Eleonora.Vigano@fhgr.ch; Christian.Hauser@fhgr.ch

A. Weichselbraun
Swiss Institute for Information Research, University of Applied Sciences of the Grisons, Chur, Switzerland

webLyzard technology, Vienna, Austria
e-mail: Albert.Weichselbraun@fhgr.ch

C. H. Hoffmann, D. Bansal (eds.), *AI Ethics in Practice*, Integrated Science 35,
https://doi.org/10.1007/978-3-031-87023-1_13

1 Introduction

Corporate ethics and compliance (E&C) aims to prevent, detect, and address illegal and unethical behavior in an organization. Nowadays its main challenges are two: first, on its compliance side, abiding by the rising number of national and international laws, corporate internal regulations, and sectorial and professional norms; second, on its ethics side, meeting the increasing ethical demands of the organization's stakeholders and the society. In facing these two challenges, E&C can make use of a valuable ally: artificial intelligence (AI). AI can efficiently predict, identify, and monitor E&C issues (Bandari 2019; Soltes 2021), as well as automatize some routine E&C tasks (Bandari 2019) and offer tailored E&C training to employees (Soltes 2021; Stidsen and Jessen 2023). Yet an E&C officer cannot adopt AI acritically as its use raises E&C issues that need to be addressed by the E&C department itself. Indeed, AI in corporate E&C can in principle leverage all the available corporate data, including sensitive data, and make use of them to predict high-risk individuals. Also, AI can constantly surveil an employee's work in its tiniest details and intrude on their private lives. Therefore, the use of AI in E&C results in a paradox: E&C aims to reduce the E&C risk of its organizations and, to do that efficiently, it employs tools—AI systems—that may increase an organization's E&C risk.

Moreover, in some cases, E&C officers' decisions significantly impact the decision-subjects, who are usually the organization's employees, such as terminating their contracts or referring them for criminal investigation. If E&C officers make such high-stake decisions with the support of an AI system, it is expected that the latter is not biased, nor that it misleads the decision-makers, i.e., the E&C officers.

The presence of high-stake decisions in corporate E&C and AI's potential of increasing E&C risks call for an examination of the ethical issues of the use of AI E&C. However, to our knowledge, neither management nor corporate social responsibility (CSR) scholars have examined them with a complete ethical discussion. Also, except for the negative effects of unemployment that AI will bring about (Brynjolfsson and McAfee 2014; Daugherty and Wilson 2018; Raisch and Krakowski 2021), the impact of using AI in E&C on employees has been neglected.

The aims of this chapter are two: first, we identify and analyze the ethical issues of AI systems used in E&C for a company's employees. Second, on the basis of the ethical analysis, we provide a checklist that helps E&C officers to ethically assess the AI systems they use. Such a list is the starting point for addressing the paradox of using AI in E&C since, by identifying the ethical risks of AI systems in E&C, it enables the E&C officers to limit the ethical risks that AI systems arise.

Our chapter gives E&C practitioners a comprehensive outlook of the ethical risks that the adoption of AI in a company's E&C entails for its employees. In this way, it contributes to rendering E&C practitioners more proficient in understanding and pointing out the ethically relevant aspects of the AI systems they use.

In this contribution, we introduce the tasks and ways in which AI supports E&C and the benefits it brings to E&C (Sect. 2). Then, we identify the ethical issues that using AI in this corporate function entails (Sect. 3). Finally, we outline a checklist for the ethical assessment of AI systems used in E&C (Sect. 4) and provide our concluding remarks (Sect. 5).

2 Where and How AI Supports Corporate E&C

E&C is a corporate function that pertains to adherence to the laws, standards, and regulations of a company (COSO 2013), which set the underpinnings of legal, acceptable, and desired business behavior (Benedek 2012).

The functions of E&C can be mainly divided into prevention and detection activities. Prevention activities concern regulations (e.g., codes of conduct, industry standards), employees' training, and due diligence. Detection activities comprise monitoring processes and individuals, investigating alleged cases of illegal and unethical conduct, and reporting the ascertained cases (Soltes 2021).

The E&C division assesses and mitigates a company's *compliance risk*. The latter comprises a company's vulnerabilities and negative consequences when its employees, suppliers, or other agents connected to it fail to align with the legal and ethical regulations of the company. The violation of the legal and ethical regulations may result in sanctions, fines, and court proceedings (Basel Committee on Banking Supervision 2005). Also, it may impact the company's reputation, with repercussions on its stock value, as well as its perception by employees and customers. The ethical risk of a company is part of compliance risk and consists in the negative consequences that the company may incur due to its unethical practices, beliefs, culture, and behaviors of its employees.

Nowadays, corporate E&C employs AI in both its prevention and detection activities to reduce compliance and ethical risks. To understand how AI supports E&C, we need to look at what AI is essentially. AI is the ability of machines to accomplish tasks that usually require human intelligence. We embrace the definition of AI outlined by the High-Level Expert Group (HLEG) (2019), which describes AI as encompassing both software and hardware systems designed by humans to achieve specific objectives in either physical or digital realms. These systems engage in various activities such as perceiving the environment through data collection, interpreting information, reasoning, processing data, and devising optimal strategies to achieve predefined goals.

AI encompasses a range of techniques, with machine learning (ML) and deep learning being the most widespread. ML involves a collection of methods rooted in classical mathematical algorithms, enabling machines to learn, adapt, predict, and make decisions based on input data (Samoili et al. 2020; Dietterich 2003). Deep learning, a subset of ML, utilizes neural networks with multiple layers to discern intricate patterns (Chollet 2018).

ML and deep learning techniques find application in diverse areas within corporate E&C. In prevention activities, they are employed in predictive analytics to forecast future events based on historical and present data, aiding in risk assessment and decision-making. In this context, AI is used, for instance, to predict the individuals who are most likely to commit wrongdoings such as accepting bribes. Additionally, AI can contribute in two ways to employee training and briefing. First, it can facilitate the creation of training programs that are engaging, thanks to gamification strategies, and tailored to the employees' role, office location, and needs. Second, AI is used to develop virtual assistants and chatbots that provide employees with support on compliance issues in real time.

In terms of detection activities, AI systems are employed to analyze extensive historical data to uncover patterns indicative of noncompliance. They perform tasks such as recognition, data categorizing, and event detection, which involves identifying anomalies or irregularities within datasets. For instance, AI is extensively used by E&C departments in detecting fraudulent transactions (Bandari 2019; Soltes 2021; Stidsen and Jessen 2023). To detect noncompliant behavior in communication channels, the AI technology that is widely used is natural language processing (NLP), which aims at understanding and manipulating human language. To ensure adherence to safety regulations in corporate environments, computer vision—the AI technology that identifies, understands, and classifies images—is employed. Also, AI-powered virtual assistance facilitates whistleblowing mechanisms through anonymous reporting channels (Brand 2020). Reported cases can then be analyzed by AI to identify recurring patterns of wrongdoings (Meng 2023). Furthermore, AI enhances E&C efforts by optimizing processes and automating audits and compliance checks, such as analyzing regulatory texts (Jaggi 2022). Finally, AI helps monitor the implementation of E&C programs and makes them more efficient (Soltes 2021).

Overall, AI in corporate E&C enhances risk assessment accuracy, program efficiency, decision-making quality, and task automation.

3 Ethical Risks of Using AI in E&C

The AI systems employed in E&C require an ethical assessment for two reasons. First, an organization's E&C office makes several high-stake decisions; when such decisions are made with the help of AI, then the latter influences high-stake spheres of human action demanding specific ethical requirements. AI in corporate E&C can affect people's access to economic opportunities and resources, such as when an employee is fired or fined, as well as freedom and participation in social life, as when an employee is investigated and suspended. Second, the use of AI in E&C tasks, as well as in the rest of the organization, is an E&C issue, and accordingly has to be scrutinized by E&C officers. To do that, they need to understand the ethical pitfalls of the technologies they integrate and be knowledgeable about the technical facets that hold ethical significance.

Our discussion of the ethical risks of the AI systems utilized in corporate E&C aids E&C professionals in becoming more aware of the ethical risks of the AI they employ and more proficient in identifying the ethically relevant aspects of the AI systems. Such a discussion is the theoretical basis for conducting the ethical assessment of the AI systems by means of the checklist we provide in section 4.

Our analysis focuses on the ethical issues that arise in the context of E&C and affect a company's employees. We organize the ethical issues of AI in corporate E&C in five ethical clusters, which are autonomy, fairness and nondiscrimination, explainability and transparency, security, and well-being. These ethical clusters are grounded on four fundamental ethical principles: autonomy, justice, explainability, and nonmaleficence.

We identify the normative elements (e.g., moral values, principles, rights) that AI may negatively affect (e.g., it violates them) in corporate E&C on the basis of the normative elements contained in the checklists of the most prevalent ethical frameworks of information and emerging technologies (Brey 2012; Wright 2011; Stahl et al. 2010), together with the normative elements defended by the HLEG (2019) and in the OECD AI Principles to promote innovative and trustworthy AI (OECD 2024). Furthermore, we adopt Nissenbaum's theory of privacy (Nissenbaum 2004)—*contextual integrity*—to analyze the ethical risks deriving from the data used by AI in E&C. Contextual integrity states that in each social domain, there are specific norms that regulate expectations, roles, practices, and actions. Accordingly, a piece of information that is appropriate to reveal in one sphere is not necessarily appropriate in another (Nissenbaum 2004).

3.1 Autonomy

3.1.1 Theory

Autonomy embodies individuals' capacity to freely make decisions and take actions for which they give reasons (Frankfurt 1971; Anscombe 1957; Davidson 1963; Mele 2003). As autonomy empowers individuals to shape their lives based on their own plans, values, and commitments, it underpins various rights of self-determination (Dworkin 2017; Eidelson 2013). The most relevant for our analysis are: information self-determination, the right to avoid manipulation, the right to freedom of expression and association, the right to privacy, and the right to be an exception to predictions.

Information self-determination is the right to decide on one's collection, storage, use, and transfer of personal data (Christen et al. 2019). The right to avoid manipulation entails safeguarding individuals against techniques that exploit subconscious processes or manipulate information presentation (High-Level Expert Group on AI 2019) in order to enable them to make fully informed decisions. The right to freedom of expression and association grants that individuals express their opinions and interact with each other. The right to privacy is individuals' control over the collection, storage, and sharing of their personal data (Christen et al. 2019). Finally, as individuals are authors of their lives through their choices (Basu 2019), they possess the right to be an exception to predictions based solely on statistical evidence. Statistical evidence assumes, for instance, that since an individual belongs to a socio-demographic group, they will behave like most people in that group, or since the individual made certain choices in the past, they will make similar choices in the future. The right to be an exception to predictions states that a decision-maker taking a decision based on AI output should acknowledge that the decision-subject is not only determined by their membership to a group or past behavior (Viganò 2023) and thus can defy the odds computed by the AI system.

3.1.2 Application to AI in E&C

In the use of AI in E&C, the primary ethical concern regarding autonomy revolves around the potential for individuals to be misled when making decisions based on feedback from AI systems. AI can manipulate behavior and influence decision-making by framing information in specific ways or omitting crucial details. In particular, the risks of manipulation by AI in E&C are in AI-powered chatbots and virtual assistants interacting with employees. Such systems are susceptible to manipulating human behavior by virtue of their interactive nature and purpose of providing information. A high risk of manipulation also arises from AI systems predicting individuals who are more likely to commit illegal and/or unethical actions. By signaling certain employees to the E&C officer, these systems risk that the latter develops a negative opinion of these employees and is more biased in assessing their behavior.

Predictive AI systems in corporate E&C may further erode individual autonomy when the E&C officer makes a decision on an employee (e.g., monitoring them more than other ones) only based on the AI systems output. In this case, the E&C officer neglects the employee's unique characteristics and treats them solely based on past data and group associations (statistical evidence). This disregard for an individual's uniqueness and self-determination undermines their right to be an exception to predictions.

Moreover, all AI systems used to monitor employees' work can lead to pervasive surveillance, infringing upon employees' privacy rights and inducing a *chilling effect* on their behaviors. AI in E&C infringes the right to privacy when personal data are transferred without the owner's consent from a private realm to a public one, or to different social spheres within the same realm. It is important to note that agreeing to share personal information in one context, such as health or family matters, does not imply consent for its use in other contexts like business. Therefore, data collected for one purpose in an organization cannot be repurposed for others without explicit consent from relevant individuals. Furthermore, when AI systems employ anonymized data, privacy is still at risk, as individuals could be reidentified (see also Sect. 3.4 on security). The chilling effect consists in people's alteration of their spontaneous behavior due to their feeling of being surveilled (Büchi et al. 2022). The employee monitoring may thus violate freedom of expression and association *via* the chilling effect.

Finally, even when employees consent to the collection, storage, and usage of their data, the complexity of consent agreements often undermines their ability to fully grasp the implications, thus failing to adequately support their information self-determination. Connected to the latter risk, AI systems whose working and results are difficult to understand and interpret hinder the autonomy of the decision-makers using such AI systems as decision aids. This is because individuals can make autonomous choices only if fully informed about the choices, but if they do not comprehend an AI system's workings and outputs, they cannot be said to make informed—and thus autonomous—decisions.

3.2 Fairness and Nondiscrimination

3.2.1 Theory

Several definitions of fairness have been provided in philosophy and within the fair ML community (Binns 2018). In general, fairness can be understood as a normative principle advocating for the equal treatment of individuals and/or groups of individuals. The assessment of equal treatment varies depending on the metrics and types of equal treatment considered (Sen 1979).

Discrimination involves the differential and disadvantageous treatment of an individual based on a perceived or actual characteristic (Lippert-Rasmussen 2014). While not inherently morally wrong, discrimination becomes problematic when it stems from an individual's affiliation with a socially salient group (e.g., Muslims, women) (Lippert-Rasmussen 2014).

The principle of justice grounds fairness and nondiscrimination. Justice revolves around the equitable treatment of individuals, demanding that similar cases be treated alike. Issues of justice derive from contexts in which individuals assert claims (e.g., freedom, opportunities, resources) that may conflict, and justice requirements determine each individual's rightful entitlements (Miller 2023).

3.2.2 Application to AI in E&C

The use of AI systems in corporate E&C can lead to discrimination against individuals when biases against certain socially salient groups are present. These biases can originate from data, AI design choices, and the AI model.

Firstly, if the data with which the system is trained mis- or underrepresent certain socially salient groups, the AI system is biased (Orwat 2020). Additionally, AI designers may choose AI models (e.g., pre-trained language models) and/or features that are biased toward certain groups, as a consequence of consciously or unconsciously incorporating their beliefs and values into the design process (Joh 2017). Identifying biased data is not an easy process as it is obfuscated by the difficulty in accessing and understanding information about data collection, processing, and training and by the intellectual property rights of the AI systems, as well as by AI systems that have a low explainability level (see Sect. 3.3).

As seen, one goal of the E&C department is detecting irregular activities. In cases of severe offenses, the organization may take drastic measures against the employee such as demotion, suspension, termination of contract, or the imposition of monetary penalties (Benedek 2012; Shoislomova 2022; Okolie and Udom 2019). If such decisions are taken with the help of an AI system classifying the employees and predicting their behavior, then the AI system should be devoid of biases; otherwise, the decision taken with its help is an instance of morally wrong discrimination—a differential and disadvantageous treatment of individuals due to their affiliation with certain groups.

3.3 Transparency and Explainability

3.3.1 Theory

In general, transparency refers to the quality of being easily seen through (Merriam-Webster 2023). Transparency in AI may refer to its *explainability* or transparency of data (Angelov et al. 2021; Doran et al. 2017; Miller 2019; Nauta et al. 2023). Explainability of AI is the capacity of an AI system to provide a clear and understandable explanation in human language of its working, output, and input (Floridi and Cowls 2022). A good level of explainability in an AI system plays a vital role in enabling users to grasp the reasoning behind decisions and actions driven by

AI. This in turn fosters humans' trust in the AI system and facilitates the identification of the entities responsible for the output of the system.

Data transparency requires that the information about data collection, processing, storage, and usage is easily accessible and understandable to the data-subjects, as well as any information addressed to the public (European Parliament and Council 2016, referral 58). Data transparency implies that people must also know the systems that monitor them, the data quality of such systems, and their accuracy.

3.3.2 Application to AI in E&C

The AI systems that have a high level of explainability are those in which explainability is built-in, such as symbolic AI, and those that are compatible with explainable AI (XAI) techniques, namely they can be explained by other models, and whose data were collected and labeled by humans. From the perspective of explainability, these systems create significantly lower ethical risk: they enable the attribution of responsibility for the AI system's outcomes, are usually perceived as trustworthy or more trustworthy than less explainable AI systems, and allow the decision-maker using them as decision-aid to make fully informed decisions.

AI systems that are compatible with explainable AI techniques but use data that were collected and/or labeled by machines are less explainable than the AI systems with high explainability but still humans can partly understand their working, thus they have a medium level of explainability. Unsupervised ML with feature engineering (features that are designed or trained by humans) and supervised ML without feature engineering usually have a medium level of explainability.

The least explainable AI systems are those that exclude human involvement in data collection, data labeling, and model design, and that have no built-in explainability, nor are they compatible with XAI techniques. Deep learning systems without feature engineering and lacking support for XAI techniques are an instance of AI systems with low explainability.

AI systems with limited explainability pose challenges for E&C professionals in detecting inaccuracies, errors, and biases inherent in the systems. This lack of transparency can lead to responsibility gaps: ascertaining the responsible entities in the decision-making process of AI systems becomes difficult.

Furthermore, decisions supported by AI with low explainability are challenging to justify, as E&C professionals lack insight into how and why the AI system arrived at specific outputs. This lack of understanding hampers not only the autonomy of decision-makers tasked with employing AI in corporate E&C, but also the autonomy of the decision-subjects. Indeed, when automated decisions cannot be elucidated to decision-subjects, the latter are unable to discern which actions led to the decisional outcomes. Consequently, in cases where individuals face disadvantageous decisions, such as receiving disciplinary measures, they are unable to adjust their behavior accordingly.

3.4 Security

3.4.1 Theory

Security pertains to the condition of an entity, often deemed valuable, which is safeguarded from harm or peril (van de Poel 2020). We refer to security as protection against both intentional and unintentional or accidental harm. Therefore, we consider both a cybersecurity attack (intentional danger) to employees' personal data and non-authorized access to employees' data due to an employee's mistake (unintentional harm) as threats to data security.

Security can refer to a person, an organization, and also a computer system, as well as information (data). AI in corporate E&C can threaten three types of security: *personal*, *informational*, and *AI system security*, which are grounded on the principle of nonmaleficence requiring not to harm individuals.

Personal security is the protection of people from harm. Informational security is the protection of information, and it is based on three principles: confidentiality, requiring that only authorized people access information; integrity, preventing that information is modified; and availability, which avoids non-access if required (ISACA 2016). The information used by AI in E&C—and that needs to be protected—comes from two different spheres: the personal and nonpersonal sphere. The personal sphere contains data linked to identifiable or identified individuals (European Parliament and Council 2016) and spans various social domains (e.g., health, business, family), each governed by specific norms (Nissenbaum 2004). Personal data range from the most public social sphere (e.g., LinkedIn postings) to the most private (e.g., personal conversations with one's romantic partner), with varying degrees of sharing preferences among individuals and cultures. Nonpersonal data, such as organizational financial records, lack ties to specific individuals. Work-related information may be personal (private or public) or nonpersonal, depending on its content.

The security of an AI system refers to its ability to resist exploitation by malicious actors such as hackers. In the event of an attack, the data and system behavior can undergo alterations, which may result in the system making erroneous decisions, which in turn may harm the decision-subjects. To guarantee AI system and data security, the system must be technically robust. *Technical robustness*, which is the property of an AI system of reducing risks and mitigating unintentional and unforeseen harm, as well as avoiding unacceptable harm (High-Level Expert Group on AI 2019), includes protection against malicious attacks on the system.

3.4.2 Application to AI in E&C

The social domains to which personal data belong were once distinct but have become interconnected due to the massive use of Big Data and AI's capacity to interlink datasets. The result is that AI systems connecting datasets may infringe one's privacy when they connect information disclosed in one domain (e.g., an employee's voice recording for their family) to another one in which one did not authorize the disclosure (e.g., the employee's work department).

Every AI system used in corporate E&C and engaged in the collection, storage, and utilization of both personal and nonpersonal data faces the ethical challenge of ensuring informational security, while also grappling with the broader issue of AI system security. Breaches in informational security, especially when personal data are involved, not only jeopardize data integrity but also encroach upon personal security. Also, when personal information is at stake, threats to data security directly infringe upon privacy rights, encompassing scenarios where data transitions among social domains or from the private to the public spheres. At first glance, it seems that only AI systems working with data connected to an identified or identifiable person entail a risk for people's privacy. Yet even when the link between a person and their data is removed by means of anonymization, pseudonymization, and aggregation techniques, reidentification remains possible under certain conditions, by means of reverse engineering (Farzanehfar et al. 2021; Yoshiura 2019).

Disruptions in the behavior of AI systems and data due to malicious attacks also could inflict harm on individuals by way of system shutdowns or erroneous outputs. Thus, from a security standpoint, any implementation of AI systems in corporate E&C necessitates a dual evaluation: assessing the adequacy of the AI system's data security measures in processing and storing data; and scrutinizing the AI system's technical robustness.

3.5 Well-Being

3.5.1 Theory

There exists no unified consensus on the definition of well-being beyond the acknowledgment of its multidimensional nature, encompassing emotions, cognition, behavior, and relationships (Jarden and Roache 2023). According to the WHO's definition, well-being "encompasses quality of life and the ability of people and societies to contribute to the world with a sense of meaning and purpose" (WHO n.d.).

Well-being, is maily based on the principle of nonmaleficence: when individuals are harmed, their well-being is reduced.

3.5.2 Application

AI applications utilized for employee monitoring can be invasive or perceived as such, with negative consequences on the employees' well-being. Indeed, continuous surveillance by AI can lead to heightened stress among employees, deterioration of social relationships in the workplace, decreased comfort in their work environment, and a decline in job quality, which may ultimately result in employee layoffs (Hanley and Hubbard 2020).

Furthermore, AI's failure to adhere to normative standards regarding autonomy, fairness and nondiscrimination, and security can also have adverse effects on the well-being of employees. As a first example, requiring an employee to provide some of their personal data—e.g., business email exchanges—because a biased AI system in use signaled the employee as prone to insider trading is a form of discrimination that has repercussions on their well-being, as the individual may be stressed, ashamed, and disappointed. As a second example, instances of data leaks, tampering, or unauthorized access have adverse impacts on one's well-being, such as heightened stress and strained social relationships within affected circles.

4 Checklist

After discussing the ethical risks that AI brings about in E&C, we provide a checklist that enables E&C practitioners to ethically assess the AI systems they intend to adopt. This checklist refers to one specific stage of the AI lifecycle, its use, and a specific context of use, corporate E&C, and focuses on the main stakeholders of E&C, the company's employees. The checklist is divided into five groups, corresponding to the clusters of our ethical analysis. Autonomy, fairness and nondiscrimination, explainability and transparency, security, and well-being are thus the ethical pillars of the checklist.

The E&C practitioners should go through the list, answering all questions. Each positive answer (Yes) is an ethical issue that they should address.

Ethical pillar	Normative element involved	Questions to identify the ethical risks of the AI system that is (or going to be) used in E&C
Autonomy	Right not to be manipulated	Does the AI system provide misleading results? Are users interacting with the AI system (E&C officers and employees) uninformed that they are interacting with a machine and not a human? Can the AI system limit users' autonomy?
	Right to be an exception to predictions	Is the decision-maker (the E&C officer) making a decision that will affect employees solely based on the AI system's results?
	Right to informational self-determination	Is the informed consent given to employees for the collection, storage, and usage of their data by the AI system unclear and/or difficult to understand? Is the working and output of the AI system unclear and/or difficult to understand for the decision-makers using it and/or the decision-subjects?
	Right to freedom of expression and association	Is the AI system monitoring employees beyond the necessary requirements of E&C? Does the AI system monitor employees without justified reasons?
	Right to privacy	Does the AI system intrude into employees' private lives without necessity? Are some employees' personal data accessed without their consent? Are some employees' personal data transferred into a social domain that is different from the one for which they gave consent? Are there no measures in place for safeguarding employees' personal data (their privacy)? Are there no measures in place for safeguarding employees' anonymized, pseudonymized, and aggregated data?

Ethical pillar	Normative element involved	Questions to identify the ethical risks of the AI system that is (or going to be) used in E&C
Fairness and nondiscrimination	Principle of justice	Do the data the AI system used as input and training and the test data lack a check for biases? Do the outputs of the AI system's decision lack a check for biases? Does the AI system lack checks for biases in its design and working (for instance, no fairness metrics were applied to it)? Do the data come from an unreliable source?
Transparency and explainability		Are the working, output, and input of the AI system difficult to explain in clear and plain language and or is it impossible to explain them by means of explainable AI techniques (e.g., LIME)? Are there no measures to assess the training and testing data of the AI system? Are the limitations and biases of the AI system unclear and/or difficult to understand? Is there no clear and understandable justification of the AI system's results? Is it impossible to access the sources of the data? Are the responsibilities of the users interacting with the AI system stated in an unclear way? Are there no procedures in place that enable attribution of responsibility?
Security	Nonmaleficence principle	Is the AI system technically unrobust (namely, doesn't it adhere to technical robustness standards)? Did the AI system get no tests for security vulnerabilities? Are there no measures and procedures in place to check for data quality and integrity? Are there no measures and procedures in place in case of data breaches? Can the AI system harm individuals in case of malicious attacks? Are there no measures and procedures in place in case the AI system malfunctions?
Well-being	Nonmaleficence principle	Does the monitoring of employees harm them (e.g., are they stressed or inhibited in their spontaneous behavior)? Are there no measures in place in case of harm caused by the AI system's biased output? Does the infringement of any other normative principles in the checklist harm the employees (e.g., they are ashamed and/or stressed as a consequence of a breach into their personal data)?

5 Conclusion

In this chapter, we showed that while AI systems predict, identify, and monitor E&C issues, as well as enhance risk assessment accuracy, program efficiency, and decision-making quality, they also present ethical risks that need careful examination. Indeed, when employing AI, E&C officers face the paradox of using tools to mitigate E&C risks that are sources of ethical risks.

By identifying and analyzing the ethical issues associated with the use of AI in E&C, we provided E&C practitioners with a comprehensive understanding of the ethical risks involved. Our analysis highlighted five clusters of ethical issues pertaining to AI in corporate E&C: autonomy, fairness and nondiscrimination, transparency and explainability, security, and well-being. Autonomy concerns revolve around the potential for AI to manipulate behavior and decision-making processes, leading to infringements on individuals' privacy, and treating them as fully predictable beings. Fairness and nondiscrimination issues arise from biases present in AI design choices, models, and data, potentially resulting in differential disadvantageous treatment of individuals based on socially salient characteristics. Transparency and explainability are essential for fostering trust in AI systems and ensuring accountability in decision-making processes. Security considerations encompass personal, informational, and AI system security. Finally, the well-being of individuals may be compromised by invasive AI monitoring, discriminatory practices, and breaches of autonomy and security.

Grounding on that ethical analysis, we offered a practical checklist for ethically assessing AI systems, empowering E&C officers to make informed decisions about the technologies they adopt. Provided with the ethical analysis and checklist, E&C professionals are equipped to address the paradox of using AI in E&C. By promoting E&C officers' ethical awareness and providing them with a tool for the ethical assessment of AI, we contributed to making the adoption of AI in E&C aligned with the ethical principles of autonomy, nonmaleficence, justice, and explainability.FundingThis work was supported by the KBA-NotaSys Integrity Fund (grant number: 2020_20).

References

Angelov PP, Soares EA, Jiang R, Arnold NI, Atkinson PM (2021) Explainable artificial intelligence: an analytical review. Wiley Interdiscip Rev Data Min Knowl Discov 11(5):e1424

Anscombe GEM (1957) Intention. Basil Blackwell, Oxford

Bandari V (2019) A comprehensive review of AI applications in automated container orchestration, predictive maintenance, security and compliance, resource optimization, and continuous deployment and testing. Int J Intell Autom Comput 4(11):1–19

Basel Committee on Banking Supervision (2005) Compliance and the compliance function in banks. [Online]. https://www.bis.org/publ/bcbs113.htm. Accessed 13 Jul 2023
Basu R (2019) What we epistemically owe to each other. Philos Stud 176(4):915–931. https://doi.org/10.1007/s11098-018-1219-z
Benedek P (2012) Compliance management – a new response to legal and business challenges
Binns R (2018) Fairness in machine learning: lessons from political philosophy. In: Proceedings of the 1st Conference on Fairness, Accountability and Transparency. PMLR, pp 149–159. [Online]. https://proceedings.mlr.press/v81/binns18a.html. Accessed 13 Dec 2022
Brand V (2020) Corporate whistleblowing, smart regulation and RegTech: the coming of the Whistlebot? Univ New South Wales Law J 43:801
Brey PAE (2012) Anticipating ethical issues in emerging IT. Ethics Inf Technol 14(4):305–317. https://doi.org/10.1007/s10676-012-9293-y
Brynjolfsson E, McAfee A (2014) The second machine age: work, progress, and prosperity in a time of brilliant technologies. N Y
Büchi M, Festic N, Latzer M (2022) The chilling effects of digital dataveillance: a theoretical model and an empirical research agenda. Big Data Soc 9(1):20539517211065368. https://doi.org/10.1177/20539517211065368
Chollet F (2018) Deep learning with Python. Manning
Christen M, Blumer H, Hauser C, Huppenbauer M (2019) The ethics of big data applications in the consumer sector. Appl Data Sci Lessons Learn Data-Driven Bus:161–180
COSO (2013) Internal control – integrated framework
Daugherty P, Wilson J (2018) Human + machine: reimagining work in the age of AI. Harvard Business Review Press
Davidson D (1963) Actions, reasons, and causes. J Philos 60(23):685–700. https://doi.org/10.2307/2023177
Dietterich T (2003) Machine learning. Encyclopedia of computer science. Wiley, GBR
D. Doran, S. Schulz, and T. R. Besold, "What does explainable AI really mean? A new conceptualization of perspectives." 2017.
Dworkin G (2017) Autonomy. In: A companion to contemporary political philosophy. Wiley, pp 439–451. https://doi.org/10.1002/9781405177245.ch18
Eidelson B (2013) Treating people as individuals. In: Hellman D, Moreau S (eds) Philosophical foundations of discrimination law. Oxford University Press, Oxford
European Parliament and Council (2016) General Data Protection Regulation, Regulation (EU) 2016/679. [Online]. https://eur-lex.europa.eu/eli/reg/2016/679/oj. Accessed 18 Aug 2023
Farzanehfar A, Houssiau F, de Montjoye Y-A (2021) The risk of re-identification remains high even in country-scale location datasets. Patterns 2(3)
Floridi L, Cowls J (2022) A unified framework of five principles for AI in society. Mach Learn City Appl Archit Urban Des:535–545
Frankfurt HG (1971) Freedom of the will and the concept of a person. J Philos 68(1):5–20. https://doi.org/10.2307/2024717
Hanley DA, Hubbard S (2020) Eyes everywhere: Amazon's surveillance infrastructure and revitalizing worker power. Open Mark Inst
High-Level Expert Group on AI (2019) Ethics guidelines for trustworthy AI | Shaping Europe's digital future. [Online]. https://digital-strategy.ec.europa.eu/en/library/ethics-guidelines-trustworthy-ai. Accessed 03 Aug 2023
ISACA (2016) Doing more with less. ISACA J 5
Jaggi K (2022) Artificial intelligence (AI) can bring a number of benefits to a know-your-customer (KYC) solution. LinkedIn. https://www.linkedin.com/pulse/artificial-intelligence-ai-can-bring-number-benefits-kyc-jaggi/#:~:text=Some%20potential%20benefits%20of%20using,and%20efficiency%20of%20KYC%20processes. Accessed 03 Aug 2023
Jarden A, Roache A (2023) What is wellbeing? Int J Environ Res Public Health 20(6):5006. https://doi.org/10.3390/ijerph20065006

Joh EE (2017) Feeding the machine: policing, crime data, & algorithms. Wm Mary Bill Rts J 26:287
Lippert-Rasmussen K (2014) Born free and equal? Oxford University Press. https://doi.org/10.1093/acprof:oso/9780199796113.001.0001
Mele AR (2003) Motivation and agency. Oxford University Press, New York. https://doi.org/10.1093/019515617X.001.0001
Meng M (2023) Whistleblower 2.0: how artificial intelligence is revolutionising corporate whistleblower protection. Konfidal. [Online]. https://www.konfidal.eu/. Accessed 03 Aug 2023
Merriam-Webster (2023, August 27) Transparent. Merriam-Webster dictionary. [Online]. https://www.merriam-webster.com/dictionary/transparent. Accessed 31 Aug 2023
Miller T (2019) Explanation in artificial intelligence: insights from the social sciences. Artif Intell 267:1–38
Miller D (2023) Justice. In: Zalta EN, Nodelman U (eds) The Stanford encyclopedia of philosophy, Fall 2023, Metaphysics Research Lab, Stanford University. [Online]. https://plato.stanford.edu/archives/fall2023/entries/justice/
Nauta M et al (2023) From anecdotal evidence to quantitative evaluation methods: a systematic review on evaluating explainable ai. ACM Comput Surv 55(13s):1–42
Nissenbaum H (2004) Privacy as contextual integrity. Wash Rev 79:119
OECD (2024) Recommendation of the Council on Artificial Intelligence. OECD/LEGAL/0449
Okolie UC, Udom ID (2019) Disciplinary actions and procedures at workplace: the role of HR managers. J Econ Manag Res 8
Orwat C (2020) Risks of discrimination through the use of algorithms. Berlín Fed Anti-Discrim Agency
Raisch S, Krakowski S (2021) Artificial intelligence and management: the automation–augmentation paradox. Acad Manag Rev 46(1):192–210. https://doi.org/10.5465/amr.2018.0072
Samoili S, Lopez CM, Gomez GE, De PG, Martinez-Plumed F, Delipetrev B (2020) AI WATCH. Defining Artificial Intelligence. JRC Publications Repository. [Online]. https://publications.jrc.ec.europa.eu/repository/handle/JRC118163. Accessed 03 Aug 2023
Sen A (1979) Equality of what? Tann Lect Hum Values
Shoislomova S (2022) Legal regulation of the disciplinary responsibility of the employee. World Bull Manag Law 15:119–124
Soltes E (2021) The professionalization of compliance. In: van Rooij B, Sokol DD (eds) The Cambridge Handbook of Compliance, Cambridge Law Handbooks. Cambridge University Press, Cambridge, pp 27–36. https://doi.org/10.1017/9781108759458.003
Stahl BC et al (2010) Identifying the ethics of emerging information and communication technologies: an essay on issues, concepts and method. Int J Technoethics 1(4):20–38. https://doi.org/10.4018/jte.2010100102
Stidsen K, Jessen H (2023) In five years, compliance without AI will be unthinkable. EY. [Online]. https://www.ey.com/en_dk/tax/in-five-years-compliance-without-ai-will-be-unthinkable. Accessed 03 Aug 2023
van de Poel I (2020) Core values and value conflicts in cybersecurity: beyond privacy versus security. In: Christen M, Gordijn B, Loi M (eds) The ethics of cybersecurity. Springer International Publishing, Cham, pp 45–71. https://doi.org/10.1007/978-3-030-29053-5_3
Viganò E (2023) The right to be an exception to predictions. A moral defense of diversity in recommendation systems. Philos Technol
WHO (n.d.) Promoting well-being. [Online]. https://www.who.int/activities/promoting-well-being. Accessed 18 Aug 2023
Wright D (2011) A framework for the ethical impact assessment of information technology. Ethics Inf Technol 13(3):199–226. https://doi.org/10.1007/s10676-010-9242-6
Yoshiura H (2019) Re-identifying people from anonymous histories of their activities presented at the 2019 IEEE 10th International Conference on Awareness Science and Technology (iCAST). IEEE, pp 1–5

Eleonora Viganò is a Senior Researcher at the Digital Society Initiative at the University of Zurich, and at the Swiss Institute for Entrepreneurship (PRME Business Integrity Action Center) at the University of Applied Sciences of the Grisons. She coordinated the ELSI Task Force for the Swiss National Program "Big Data" and presented its findings to the Swiss Parliament. Her articles have been published in, among other journals, *Philosophy & Technology*, *Ethics and Information Technology*, *Synthese*, and *Neuroethics*. Her research focuses on ethics of AI and digitalization and human-computer interaction. She is currently working on responsible AI, AI in corporate ethics and compliance, the philosophical aspect of the metaverse, and digital well-being.

Christian Hauser is Professor of Business Economics and International Management at the Swiss Institute for Entrepreneurship (SIFE) at the University of Applied Sciences Graubünden. He chairs the United Nations Principles for Responsible Management Education (PRME) Working Group on Anti-Corruption and heads the first PRME Business Integrity Action Center in Europe. PRME is the academic sister initiative of the United Nations Global Compact (UNGC). Since 2019, Dr. Hauser has been a fellow and associate member of the Digital Society Initiative (DSI) at the University of Zurich. His research interests include international entrepreneurship, SME and private sector development, corporate responsibility, business integrity and AI ethics.

Albert Weichselbraun is a Professor of Information Science at the Swiss Institute for Information Research (SII) at the University of Applied Sciences of the Grisons, and Chief Scientist of webLyzard technology. He has led numerous applied research projects in machine learning, information extraction, and Web intelligence, serving as Principal Investigator for multiple Innosuisse projects. Prof. Weichselbraun has authored over 90 peer-reviewed publications, and was a member of the Swiss Academies of Arts and Sciences' expert group on communication science. His research focuses on Natural Language Processing, Artificial Intelligence, and Explainable AI (XAI). .

Balancing Ethical Innovation: The Role of Synthetic Data in Financial Regulation

14

Matteo Micol

Abstract

Financial regulators depend on increasingly granular data to identify market vulnerabilities and inform policy decisions. However, persistent data gaps in critical areas of the financial system, such as non-bank financial intermediation (NBFI), hinder comprehensive risk assessments. Synthetic data, generated using artificial intelligence (AI), offers a promising solution to address these gaps and enhance regulatory development and oversight. Yet this approach raises ethical and practical concerns, including questions of regulatory legitimacy, transparency, privacy, and sustainability. This study examines whether the advantages of synthetic data in financial regulation outweigh its challenges, providing an initial assessment of its feasibility and broader implications.

1 Data Dependency in Financial Regulation

For the first one, it was steam power. For the second, electricity. For the third, the modern computer and the Internet. For the ongoing one, it must be artificial intelligence (AI). Every industrial revolution has its own driving innovation, namely its emblem, building on the previous ones. In turn, each emblem is powered and sustained by an underlying enabler. For the first two revolutions, this enabler was fossil fuel: the extraction and refining of coal, and later oil, allowed steam technology to be employed at scale, and electricity to power mass production, lighting, and communication. In the third industrial age, semiconductors emerged as its primary enabler, with chip development driving the evolution of computing. Today, in what is commonly referred to as the fourth industrial revolution, AI systems are

M. Micol (✉)
Digital Society Initiative, University of Zurich, Zurich, Switzerland
e-mail: matteo.micol@ius.uzh.ch

C. H. Hoffmann, D. Bansal (eds.), *AI Ethics in Practice*, Integrated Science 35,
https://doi.org/10.1007/978-3-031-87023-1_14

contingent on vast amounts of data to function, reinforcing the popular adage according to which data is 'the new oil' (Atkinson and Moschella 2024). In order for AI to mimic human intelligence and perform complex tasks, machine learning (ML) algorithms are typically embedded. These algorithms are programmed to process large sets of data to 'train' models capable of making decisions or predictions on new inputs. The more data the algorithms are exposed to, the more accurate the ML model becomes. Consequently, without a steady flow of high-quality data, AI's overall functionality would be severely restricted, similarly to how previous industrial revolutions depended on specific enablers to fuel their development.

Virtually no sector of society is immune to the transformative power of AI and, therefore, to the conversion of all its aspects into digital data ('datafication'). The financial industry began adopting proto-AI technologies as early as the 1980s, such as non-ML ('expert') systems for trading, like PROTRADER, or the US Treasury FinCEN Artificial Intelligence System to detect money laundering (Buchanan 2019). However, limited computing power and the scarcity of electronic data delayed the widespread integration of AI in finance until the early 2010s. Since then, the datafication of nearly every aspect of financial activity—from transactions and market dynamics to customer behavior and regulatory frameworks—has reshaped how financial institutions operate, manage risk, and deliver services. Notable AI/ML applications currently include predictive analytics, transforming data into strategic insights; automated trading, which leverages those insights for instant decision-making and execution; chatbots and robo-advisors, offering a personalized experience to investors; and 'regtech' solutions, streamlining back-office functions such as compliance and reporting (Aldasoro et al. 2024). To keep pace with these advancements and the surge in regulatory 'big data' (Wibisono et al. 2019), financial authorities are increasingly adopting supervisory technology ('suptech') solutions to strengthen data management and analytics, including the use of AI-enhanced tools (Prenio 2024; Di Castri et al. 2023). This approach, in turn, improves the quality of statistical data available to financial regulators, enabling deeper insights into emerging risks and supporting more targeted policies and regulation. The long-standing reliance on data in the financial sector has thus become more critical than ever, underpinning the interplay between innovation (which responds to existing regulations and creates new risks), supervision (which adapts to innovation and regulations), and financial regulation (which reacts to both innovation and emerging risks).

Starting in 1964, the Bank for International Settlements (BIS) introduced locational banking statistics (LBS) to monitor the growth of the booming Eurodollar market. By 1977, LBS were expanded to include consolidated statistics (CBS), allowing better tracking of international banking activities, particularly in developing countries and offshore hubs (BIS 2019). At that time, financial regulations were typically only 'rule-based,' characterized by detailed, prescriptive rules that left little discretion to financial firms (Gray and Hamilton 2006). Beginning in the 1980s, market pressures and ideological shifts led to a progressive relaxation and repeal of several regulations in key financial markets, notably in the US, Japan, the UK, and much of continental Europe (Drach and Cassis 2021; Majone 1990). This wave of 'deregulation' introduced a new regulatory philosophy that balanced minimal government intervention with targeted oversight. It combined principles-based regulation, which granted firms the flexibility to meet broad principles and outcomes over rigid rules, with a risk-based approach that directed regulators to prioritize the most vulnerable areas of the financial system (Black 2011; Hutter 2005). Institutionalized by the 1988 Basel Accord (Basel I), this approach highlighted the need for more detailed and timely data to assess risks, driving demand for advanced banking statistics. The Mexican financial crisis in the 1990s underscored the value of standardized data in detecting early signals of instability, prompting initiatives such as the Special Data Dissemination Standard (SDDS), the General Data Dissemination System (GDDS), and the Coordinated Portfolio Investment Survey (CPIS), all led by the International Monetary Fund (IMF). Similarly, the Asian financial crisis of 1997–1998 triggered more frequent CBS reporting, with improved coverage of banking systems in Hong Kong and Singapore and an expanded country breakdown (BIS 2019). In 2005, CBS were upgraded to capture risk reallocations, guarantees, and derivatives exposures (BIS 2009). Almost concurrently, the second of the Basel Accords (Basel II) moved toward a more principles-based framework, incorporating refined risk sensitivity measures while allowing banks greater discretion in reporting through internal models. The regulatory architecture created by Basel II revolved around three complementary pillars: Pillar I set the minimum capital requirements to cover credit, trading, and operational risks; Pillar II provided guidelines for regulators to require additional buffers and oversee banks' internal risk management practices; and Pillar III introduced both qualitative and quantitative disclosure requirements, aimed at providing better insights into capital adequacy of banks, thereby enhancing transparency and overall market discipline (BIS 2006; Lopez 2003). Pillar III disclosures marked one of the first systematic efforts to collect economic data for banking supervision, setting a growing trend in financial regulation. In response to the 2007–2009 global financial crisis, disclosure requirements were expanded across most jurisdictions to address data gaps in funding and lending within major banking systems. Basel III, released in 2010, introduced new standards for liquidity coverage, leverage ratios, and a wider range of risk data, including non-performing loans and stress test results, all underpinned by a 'macroprudential' overlay (BIS 2018). As a result, macroprudential frameworks for banks—designed to address systemic risks in the financial system and to protect the whole economy—were developed globally (Lee et al. 2017). More recently, heightened awareness of environmental, social, and governance (ESG) factors crucially expanded the regulatory data landscape, with a particular focus on climate-related risks. At the same time, efforts to establish data-sharing standards and foster international cooperation are further shaping the evolution of regulatory frameworks.

Through the intensification of data-regulation dynamics, national and supranational regulatory bodies like the European Central Bank (ECB), along with global financial standard-setters such as the BIS, the Financial Stability Board (FSB), and International Organization of Securities Commissions (IOSCO) now have access to large volumes of regulatory financial data reported by their affiliated jurisdictions. Leveraging suptech tools, they analyze these vast datasets to monitor adherence to their frameworks, track systemic risks, and effectively influence major regulatory reforms. While most suptech tools are generally kept confidential, the ECB has developed and publicized several, such as Athena, a platform that employs natural language processing techniques to extract information from bank documents; Heimdall, a data analytics solution for processing banks' 'fit and proper' questionnaires; and Gabi, a platform for generating and optimizing big data analytics models (McCaul 2024; ECB 2023).

2 NBFI Gaps

The previous paragraph outlined major international statistical initiatives and regulatory frameworks for the banking sector, where standardized reporting of financial activities has historically been well-established. In contrast, non-bank financial intermediation (NBFI) firms—formerly known as 'shadow banks'—typically operate on a cross-border basis and lack uniform data standards, resulting in fragmented reporting (where required) and often inconsistent risk assessments. Despite the sector's growth to nearly half of global financial assets following the 2007–2009 financial crisis (Aramonte et al. 2022), NBFI regulatory frameworks continue to lag behind those for traditional banks. According to the FSB, the NBFI sector comprises a wide range of entities, the largest subset being 'other financial intermediaries' (OFIs), which includes all financial institutions that are not central banks, banks, public financial institutions, insurance corporations, pension funds, or financial auxiliaries. Notable examples of OFIs are investment funds, central counterparties, broker-dealers, as well as an increasing number of fintechs and big tech companies offering financial services. As of 2022, almost half of observable OFIs fall under the FSB's 'narrow measure of NBFI,' which focuses on entities involved in credit intermediation that may engage in regulatory arbitrage or pose bank-like financial stability risks, such as credit hedge funds or securitization vehicles (FSB 2023b; Ehrentraud et al. 2024). These stability risks primarily involve liquidity risk, interconnection risk, and leverage procyclicality. Liquidity risk arises from the mismatch between liquid liabilities (e.g. fund shares) and the illiquid assets backing them (e.g. corporate bonds) potentially leading to investor runs and fire sales to meet redemption demands. Interconnection risk refers to the extensive debt-credit linkages between non-bank entities and other financial institutions, which can transmit financial stress across sectors and create systemic spillovers. Leverage procyclicality occurs when non-banks increase leverage during economic expansions and deleverage during downturns, exacerbating market volatility and intensifying downward pressure on asset prices (Pascual et al. 2021; Aldasoro et al. 2020). Importantly, leverage may add significant complexity to risk monitoring and management as it can take various forms—from direct bank borrowing and margin borrowing through prime brokers, to more sophisticated 'synthetic' leverage techniques using derivatives (e.g. swaps or options), quasi-derivative instruments (e.g. repurchase agreements), or leverage embedded in securitization structures (FSB 2023a). Collectively, these vulnerabilities call for robust policymaking efforts, yet the development of

NBFI macroprudential frameworks has generally fallen short, largely due to significant data gaps. In fact, absent comprehensive, institution-specific data on assets, liabilities, and exposures, regulators are left with blind spots that obscure the true magnitude of systemic risks. As a result, the development of targeted regulations tends to be limited to reactive measures, addressing the causes and effects of stress events only ex post.

Various strategies have been implemented to bridge NBFI data gaps. These efforts can be broadly grouped into four main categories, each representing a different approach to enhance data collection. First, specific regulatory requirements, notably mandatory disclosures and reporting, are implemented in several jurisdictions to increase data transparency. For example, recent revisions to the EU Directive on Alternative Investment Fund Managers (AIFM) and the Directive on Undertakings for Collective Investments in Transferable Securities (UCITS) have updated the reporting framework of various types of investment funds, simplifying requirements, reducing industry-wide burdens, and facilitating both data delivery and analysis, particularly regarding leverage use (EU Commission 2024). The Swiss Financial Market Supervisory Authority (FINMA) has implemented parallel reporting requirements under the Financial Institutions Act of 2018 (FINMA 2024). Additionally, for over-the-counter (OTC) financial derivatives—widely used by investment funds for both hedging and leverage—the European Market Infrastructure Regulation (EMIR) mandates that EU entities report detailed transaction data to trade repositories. While partial, these data could have enabled EU supervisors to anticipate the collapse of the US hedge fund Archegos in 2021 (ESMA 2022).

Second, data initiatives have been developed to regularly assess systemic risks in NBFI and enhance its oversight. A prominent example is the annual monitoring conducted by the FSB which has aggregated multiple data sources since 2011 to publish reports on the scale of NBFI activities (FSB 2011). Moreover, in the aftermath of the 2007–2009 financial crisis, the Board in collaboration with the IMF and various national regulatory agencies launched the G20 Data Gaps Initiative (DGI). The DGI has developed measures to improve quality and comparability of data across both banks and non-banks, with the aim to create a more harmonized approach to data reporting (FSB 2015). Another example is provided by the Office of Financial Research (OFR) of the US Department of the Treasury, which launched its Hedge Fund Monitor in the summer of 2024. This open-source tool aggregates both private and public hedge fund data from reporting forms submitted to the US Securities and Exchange Commission (SEC) and from derivatives reports, such as the weekly Commitment of Traders on aggregate holdings in the US futures market.

The third category includes close cooperation and data sharing among authorities to optimize the use of existing regulatory data. Numerous jurisdictions explicitly advocate for NBFI data sharing, such as the EU, Luxembourg, and the UK, as well as international organizations. Importantly, in 2021, the Bank of England and other UK supervisory authorities signed a landmark memorandum of understanding with the ECB to formalize their supervisory cooperation, outlining procedures for the exchange of financial information across all segments of the financial system (ECB 2021).

The development of advanced technological tools represents a fourth approach to addressing NBFI data gaps. For example, the Hong Kong Monetary Authority (HKMA) exemplifies the use of data science in financial oversight by integrating transaction-level details from trade repositories with granular banking data including information on NBFI counterparties. By combining these datasets with textual big data and macroeconomic indicators, the HKMA effectively maps NBFI positions, particularly those of highly leveraged firms. This methodology has strenghted its ability to detect systemic vulnerabilities and identify entities requiring enhanced supervision (Cheng et al. 2023). Similar approaches have also been adopted by private organizations, such as the International Swaps and Derivatives Association's (ISDA). ISDA's Digital Regulatory Reporting initiative has led to the development of a derivatives reporting data tool that uses a single machine-executable standard across global derivatives markets, facilitating seamless data flow between financial institutions and supervisory agencies in a multi-jurisdictional context (ISDA 2023).

While all these approaches have led to significant advancements, substantial data gaps persist—particularly concerning specific entities such as hedge funds and proprietary trading firms, as well as key metrics like margins and haircuts, leverage, and maturity mismatches, which often remain hidden (Claessens 2024; FSB 2023a). To enhance NBFI datasets, AI-generated synthetic data can supplement existing information. While not a standalone solution, this approach could support stress testing and scenario analysis, enabling regulators to better anticipate systemic risk events, develop more proactive policies, and expand training data for AI-based suptech tools.

3 Synthetic Data Promises

Synthetic data is generated using computational techniques that replicate the distributions and relationships of real-world datasets while addressing common challenges such as privacy risks, biases, and, in the case of NBFI, data scarcity (Jordon et al. 2022). Among the main methods for generating synthetic data are statistical modeling, rule-based simulations, and 'deep' ML techniques, which include generative adversarial networks (GANs), variational autoencoders (VAEs), and transformer-based models. Each method has distinct strengths: statistical approaches are effective for simpler data distributions, GANs and VAEs excel at replicating complex structured data, and transformers are particularly suited for generating time-series and sequential data (Fu et al. 2022). For instance, GANs consist of two neural networks—a generator and a discriminator—both trained on real-world data and working in tandem. The generator creates synthetic data, while the discriminator evaluates it against the real dataset, forcing the generator to improve its output over multiple iterations. Once generated, synthetic data must be validated based on three key criteria: privacy, ensuring that no sensitive data can be reverse engineered; utility, confirming its suitability for the intended purpose; and fidelity, demonstrating its statistical similarity to the original dataset (Di Girolamo et al. 2024). Transformers, on the other hand, leverage 'attention' mechanisms to process data, enabling them to learn long-term dependencies and generate realistic, temporally consistent sequences while incorporating additional variables, such as economic indicators, to enhance contextual accuracy—an area where GANs typically fall short (Brugiere and Turinici 2024; Vaswani et al. 2017).

A primary application of synthetic data in finance is fraud detection. Since fraudulent transactions are rare, it is challenging to train models that rely on significant volumes of real data. Synthetic data can then play a transformative role by supplying large datasets that can enhance ML model training and testing without the risk of exposing sensitive information. Similarly, synthetic data can improve credit scoring by generating data for groups that may be underrepresented in traditional datasets, such as low-income populations or individuals with limited credit histories. This use of synthetic data can reduce bias in credit models, allowing financial institutions to develop more inclusive scoring systems. Moreover, in environments where new financial models or algorithms are being developed, synthetic datasets can simulate a variety of market conditions, enabling thorough testing without affecting real-world systems (FCA 2024).

In the NBFI sector, synthetic data could provide a practical solution for addressing data gaps. By generating synthetic datasets that closely replicate actual NBFI dynamics, regulators should be able to conduct more comprehensive risk assessments and enhance supervisory and regulatory frameworks. For instance, synthetic data could play a crucial role in stress testing, namely in the evaluation of financial entities based on their resilience to adverse market conditions. Augmenting NBFI data synthetically would allow regulators to simulate plausible systemic stress scenarios, offering insights into potential vulnerabilities without requiring extensive real-world data. Additionally, synthetic data have the potential to support regulatory monitoring by facilitating cross-institutional data sharing. A notable example is the EU Data Hub, which serves as a platform for data exchange between European supervisory agencies and financial firms. Its primary purpose is to promote seamless collaboration within the financial industry and foster innovation by providing firms with data to test new ML solutions. However, to ensure confidentiality, only synthetic equivalents of real datasets are shared (Di Girolamo et al. 2024). In this way, synthetic data could not only help firms refine their analytical models, but also enable supervisors and regulators to identify emerging trends and exert data-driven influence on a broader range of financial firms.

While synthetic data offers considerable benefits in augmenting limited datasets, it does not fully bridge NBFI data gaps faced by regulators. Its primary limitation lies in its dependence on the original dataset: if the original NBFI data underrepresents certain types of transactions or risk behaviors, even high-fidelity synthetic data will replicate these imbalances, potentially leading to skewed analyses or predictions. Moreover, synthetic data may fail to capture unexpected events or sporadic anomalies, which are often crucial for risk assessments in financial markets, where irregular behaviors can signal emerging risks. Although transformer-based models enhance the ability to identify and reproduce complex patterns, including anomalies, their effectiveness depends heavily on the quality and comprehensiveness of the training data. If anomalies are poorly represented or absent in the original datasets, even advanced AI models will struggle to replicate them accurately. Consequently, for regulatory purposes, synthetic data should be regarded as a complementary tool rather than a substitute for real-world data, with its utility remaining closely tied to advancements in suptech and other AI-enhanced solutions employed by supervisory authorities.

4 Legitimacy and the 'Good' Regulation

The use of synthetic data in financial regulation, even as a supporting tool, presents both regulatory and ethical challenges. These challenges include risks inherent to generative AI ('GenAI'), such as data management issues—bias, privacy breaches, and intellectual property violations—alongside model-related concerns like inaccurate outputs, limited explainability, as well as security vulnerabilities (McKinsey 2024). Among these, limited explainability and the presence of bias emerge also as ethical issues with direct implications for the legitimacy of financial regulation.

GenAI models that function as 'black boxes,' where their underlying rationale is not fully interpretable, fail to uphold the moral duty of transparency in decision-making (Brand and Nannini 2023). This opacity makes it virtually impossible to explain how the model generates its outputs, reducing both its reliability and perceived value, and mirrors how opaque decisions in financial regulation undermine confidence in regulatory bodies and erode public trust. Bias in training data—whether real or synthetic—further exacerbates these challenges, as it can lead to discriminatory outcomes that compromise the fairness and impartiality of policies derived from AI-driven processes. Such failures not only threaten the credibility of the regulatory framework but also risk marginalizing stakeholders, further diminishing trust in regulatory outcomes. Since regulatory legitimacy in the financial sector typically derives from consensus among international stakeholders rather than direct legal investiture (De Bellis 2018), failures in transparency and fairness—whether due to obscure models or biased decision-making—could ultimately jeopardize the cooperative frameworks essential for effective global financial regulation, leading to instability and fragmentation.

In this context, the principles outlined by the UK Better Regulation Commission (now the Better Regulation Executive) in the Legislative and Regulatory Reform Act 2006 provide valuable guidance for integrating GenAI and synthetic data into financial regulation (BRE 2023). These principles—particularly proportionality, accountability, consistency, and transparency—serve as a framework for addressing the ethical and regulatory challenges posed by GenAI, helping to ensure that AI applications not only meet regulatory effectiveness but also sustain public trust. The principle of transparency asserts that both regulated entities and the public should understand the rationale behind regulatory activities. Applied to GenAI, this means that regulatory agencies and regulators using AI-enhanced tools must be able to justify their decisions' rationale. The principle of accountability is equally critical, requiring that both regulators and firms take responsibility for the outcomes of decisions made with the assistance of AI, which in turn demands a certain level of interpretability. This responsibility also includes establishing governance structures to monitor and, when necessary, review AI-based decisions. The Financial Conduct Authority's (FCA) Principles of Good Regulation, tailored specifically to the financial sector, add that both efficiency and economy should be balanced against the other principles. Synthetic data supports regulatory efficiency and economy by reducing dependence on real-world data and lowering associated collection costs (FCA 2022). Transparency is further emphasized in the ethical framework for synthetic data use outlined by the UK Statistics Authority (UKSA). Here, transparency extends beyond basic disclosure, requiring clear communication to all stakeholders of the purpose, benefits, and constraints of synthetic data usage. Promoting the public good is a driving principle within this framework, limiting data synthesis to cases that clearly serve societal interests. At the same time, a prudential approach is advised, to ensure that data security standards are maintained at all times (UKSA 2022).

Similar considerations are echoed at the EU level, where increasing regulatory transparency is a key goal of the Better Regulation agenda for the coming years (EU Commission 2021). Transparency and, by extension, explainability of AI systems is not only an ethical imperative (European Parliament 2019) but also a regulatory priority under both the Digital Operational Resilience Act (DORA) and the AI Act. DORA imposes strict requirements on financial institutions, mandating that they demonstrate adequate risk management processes and safeguards against AI system failures. To omply with DORA's resilience and security standards, synthetic data applications must undergo rigorous testing and validation to ensure they do not introduce vulnerabilities into the financial system (DORA, Article 25). Similarly, the AI Act emphasizes transparency by requiring financial institutions deploying GenAI or synthetic data to ensure that such tools are transparent, explainable, and human-supervised to meet compliance obligations (Walke et al. 2023). In line with this approach, the US National Institute of Standards and Technology (NIST), in its Artificial Intelligence Risk Framework for GenAI endorses core principles such as explainability, fairness, accountability, and the robustness of AI systems (NIST 2024). Specifically, regarding synthetic data, the framework addresses the risk of 'model collapse,' which can result from an overreliance on synthetic data for training (Shumailov et al. 2023).

Synthetic data is often marketed as a solution to privacy challenges, as is involves the use of artificially generated rather than real, potentially sensitive information. However, privacy concerns persist, as synthetic data may still carry re-identification risks, particularly when it closely replicates patterns ('high-fidelity') from real datasets. The higher the realism, the greater the likelihood that attackers with partial access to other data sources could match synthetic data points to actual information. To mitigate this risk, synthetic data can incorporate a form of 'differential privacy' by injecting calibrated randomness (i.e. noise) into the data, carefully balancing the trade-off between privacy and utility of the dataset (Calcraft et al. 2021). In financial regulation, where highly sensitive data is routinely processed, privacy breaches can result in severe repercussions, including reputational damage and regulatory penalties. Therefore, it is ethically necessary to weigh the generation of synthetic data against potential confidentiality and privacy requirements, while strictly adhering to disclosure control regulations to protect data owners. Additionally, when synthetic data is shared, materials should be labeled to indicate its level of fidelity, its impact to data quality, and the degree of potential disclosure risk (UKSA 2022).

Another emerging concern related to GenAI and synthetic data is sustainability, particularly regarding the significant energy demands of large AI models. As financial regulators increasingly emphasize environmental responsibility, ethical considerations must address energy efficiency along with the broader societal focus on environmentally conscious practices.

5 Conclusion

The role of synthetic data and GenAI in financial regulation highlight the often-intricate balance between technological advancement, regulatory rigor, and ethical principles. While synthetic data can provide valuable insights to regulators and stakeholders, it also raise concerns about accuracy, potential bias replication, re-identification risks, and opacity in its generative processes. These challenges, however, are not insurmountable. By adhering to high standards of transparency and ethical AI, developing robust and explainable models, implementing regulatory safeguards, and maintaining a clear focus on the public good—as supporting financial stability is—synthetic data can play a meaningful role in the future of financial regulation.

References

Aldasoro I et al (2020) Cross-border links between banks and non-bank financial institutions. BIS Quart Rev. https://bis.org/publ/qtrpdf/r_qt2009e.htm

Aldasoro I et al (2024) Intelligent financial system: how AI is transforming finance. BIS Working Papers No 1194. https://bis.org/publ/work1194.htm

Aramonte S, Schrimpf A, Shin HS (2022) Non-bank financial intermediaries and financial stability. BIS Working Papers No. 972. https://bis.org/publ/work972.htm

Atkinson RD, Moschella D (2024) Technology fears and scapegoats: 40 myths about privacy, jobs, AI, and today's innovation economy. Springer Nature Switzerland. https://doi.org/10.1007/978-3-031-52349-6

BIS (2006) International convergence of capital measurement and capital standards. https://bis.org/publ/bcbs128.pdf

BIS (2009) Guide to the international financial statistics. https://bis.org/statistics/intfinstatsguide.pdf

BIS (2018) Pillar 3 disclosure requirements – updated framework. https://bis.org/bcbs/publ/d455.pdf

BIS (2019) Reporting guidelines for the BIS international banking statistics. https://bis.org/statistics/bankstatsguide.pdf

Black J (2011) The rise, fall and fate of principles-based regulation. In: Alexander K, Mahoney N (eds) Law reform and financial markets. Elgar, pp 3–34. https://doi.org/10.4337/9780857936639

Brand JLM, Nannini L (2023) Does explainable AI have moral value? arXiv:2311.14687. https://doi.org/10.48550/arXiv.2311.14687

BRE (2023) Better regulation framework: guidance. https://gov.uk/government/publications/better-regulation-framework
Brugiere P, Turinici G (2024) Transformer for times series: an application to the S&P500. arXiv:2403.02523. https://doi.org/10.48550/arXiv.2403.02523
Buchanan BG (2019) Artificial intelligence in finance. The Alan Turing Institute. https://doi.org/10.5281/ZENODO.2612537
Calcraft IT, Maglicic M, Sutherland A (2021) Accelerating public policy research with synthetic data. ADR UK. https://adruk.org/fileadmin/uploads/adruk/Documents/Accelerating_public_policy_research_with_synthetic_data_December_2021.pdf
Cheng K et al (2023) Building an integrated surveillance framework for highly leveraged NBFIs – lessons from the HKMA. BIS Paper 137. https://bis.org/publ/bppdf/bispap137.pdf
Claessens S (2024) Nonbank financial intermediation: stock take of research, policy, and data. Annu Rev Financ Econ. https://doi.org/10.1146/annurev-financial-082123-105416
De Bellis M (2018) Relative authority in global and EU financial regulation: linking the legitimacy debates. In: Mendes J, Venzke I (eds) Allocating authority: who should do what in European and international law? Bloomsbury, pp 241–270
Di Castri S, Grasser M, Ongwae J (2023) Cambridge Suptech Lab: State of Suptech Report. https://lab.ccaf.io/wp-content/uploads/2024/03/Cambridge-State-of-SupTech-Report-2023.pdf
Di Girolamo F, Hledik J, Pagano A (2024) Synthetic data in the Data Hub of the Digital Finance Platform. Publications Office of the European Union. https://doi.org/10.2760/83055
Drach A, Cassis Y (eds) (2021) Financial deregulation: a historical perspective. Oxford University Press. https://doi.org/10.1093/oso/9780198856955.001.0001
ECB (2021) Memorandum of Understanding for supervisory cooperation between the European Central Bank and the Bank of England and the Financial Conduct Authority. https://bankingsupervision.europa.eu/framework/international-cooperation/understanding/html/ssm.mou_2019_pra~fbad08a4bc.en.pdf
ECB (2023) Suptech: thriving in the digital age. Supervision Newsl. https:// bankingsupervision.europa.eu/press/supervisory-newsletters/newsletter/2023/html/ssm.nl231115_2.en.html
Ehrentraud J et al (2024) Safeguarding the financial system's spare tyre: regulating non-bank retail lenders in the digital era. FSI Insights No. 56. https://bis.org/fsi/publ/insights56.pdf
ESMA (2022) Leverage and derivatives – The case of Archegos. ESMA TRV Risk Analysis. https://esma.europa.eu/sites/default/files/library/esma50-165-2096_leverage_and_derivatives_the_case_of_archegos.pdf
EU Commission (2021) Better regulation: joining forces to make better laws. https://eur-lex.europa.eu/legal-content/EN/TXT/?uri=CELEX%3A52021DC0219
EU Commission (2024) Progress report on the strategy on supervisory data in EU financial services. https://finance.ec.europa.eu/system/files/2024-02/240229-supervisory-data-strategy-progress-report_en.pdf
European Parliament (2019) EU guidelines on ethics in artificial intelligence: context and implementation. https://europarl.europa.eu/thinktank/en/document/EPRS_BRI(2019)640163
FCA (2022) Principles of good regulation. https://fca.org.uk/about/how-we-regulate/handbook/principles-good-regulation
FCA (2024, March) Using synthetic data in financial services: the synthetic data expert group. https://fca.org.uk/publications/corporate-documents/report-using-synthetic-data-financial-services
FINMA (2024) Guidance on reporting for collective investment schemes. https://finma.ch/en/~/media/finma/dokumente/dokumentencenter/myfinma/2ueberwachung/erhebung-asset-management/guidance-cis-reporting.pdf?sc_lang=en&hash=F2494FE22B179F6017B47AB2F99A2AE6
FSB (2011) Shadow banking: scoping the issues. https://fsb.org/2011/04/shadow-banking-scoping-the-issues/
FSB (2015) Transforming shadow banking into resilient market-based finance. https:// fsb.org/uploads/P070920-1.pdf

FSB (2023a) The financial stability implications of leverage in non-bank financial intermediation. https://fsb.org/2023/09/the-financial-stability-implications-of-leverage-in-non-bank-financial-intermediation/

FSB (2023b) Global monitoring report on non-bank financial intermediation. https://fsb.org/2023/12/global-monitoring-report-on-non-bank-financial-intermediation-2023/

Fu F et al (2022) Are synthetic time-series data really not as good as real data? arXiv:2402.00607. https://doi.org/10.48550/arXiv.2402.00607

Gray J, Hamilton J (2006) Implementing financial regulation: theory and practice. Wiley

Hutter BM (2005) The attractions of risk-based regulation: accounting for the emergence of risk ideas in regulation. ESRC CARR Discussion Paper No. 33. https:// lse.ac.uk/accounting/assets/CARR/documents/D-P/Disspaper33.pdf

ISDA (2023) Digital Regulatory Reporting. https://isda.org/a/dmLgE/Digital-Regulatory-Reporting-DRR-Fact-Sheet_042823.pdf

Jordon et al (2022) Synthetic data – what, why and how? arXiv:2205.03257. https://doi.org/10.48550/arXiv.2205.03257

Lee M, Gaspar R, Villaruel M (2017) Macroprudential policy frameworks in developing Asian economies. ADB Economics Working Paper Series No. 150. https://doi.org/10.22617/WPS178676-2

Lopez JA (2003) Disclosure as a supervisory tool: Pillar 3 of Basel II. FRBSF Economic Letter 2003-22. https://frbsf.org/research-and-insights/publications/economic-letter/2003/08/disclosure-as-a-supervisory-tool-pillar-3-of-basel-ii/

Majone G (1990) Deregulation or re-regulation? Regulatory reform in Europe and the United States. Pinter

McCaul E (2024) From data to decisions: AI and supervision. https://bankingsupervision.europa.eu/press/interviews/date/2024/html/ssm.in240226~c6f7fc9251.en.html

McKinsey (2024) The state of AI in early 2024: Gen AI adoption spikes and starts to generate value. https://mckinsey.com/capabilities/quantumblack/our-insights/the-state-of-ai

NIST (2024) Artificial intelligence risk management framework: generative artificial intelligence profile. https://nvlpubs.nist.gov/nistpubs/ai/NIST.AI.600-1.pdf

Pascual AG, Singh R, Surti J (2021) Investment funds and financial stability: policy considerations. IMF Departmental Paper No. 2021/018. https://imf.org/en/Publications/Departmental-Papers-Policy-Papers/Issues/2021/09/13/Investment-Funds-and-Financial-Stability-Policy-Considerations-464654

Prenio J (2024) Peering through the hype: assessing suptech tools' transition from experimentation to supervision. FSI Insights No. 58. https://bis.org/fsi/publ/insights58.pdf

Shumailov I et al (2023) The curse of recursion: training on generated data makes models forget. arXiv:2305.17493. https://doi.org/10.48550/arXiv.2305.17493

UKSA (2022) Ethical considerations relating to the creation and use of synthetic data. https://uksa.statisticsauthority.gov.uk/publication/ethical-considerations-relating-to-the-creation-and-use-of-synthetic-data/

Vaswani A et al (2017) Attention is all you need. arXiv:1706.03762. https://doi.org/10.48550/arXiv.1706.03762

Walke F, Bennek L, Winkler TJ (2023) Artificial intelligence explainability requirements of the AI Act and metrics for measuring compliance. Wirtschaftsinformatik 2023 Proceedings, 77. https://aisel.aisnet.org/wi2023/77

Wibisono O et al (2019) The use of big data analytics and artificial intelligence in central banking. IFC Bulletin No 50:6–20. https://bis.org/ifc/publ/ifcb50.pdf

Matteo Micol is a PhD researcher at the Law Faculty of the University of Zurich, Switzerland.

Virtuous Information Technology Entrepreneurs

15

Erich Prem

Abstract

In the past, media portrayed IT entrepreneurs as economic leaders and role models. Recently, however, controversies over the power of large tech firms, questionable business ethics and surveillance capitalism have tarnished this image. These concerns have sparked a new wave of creators, entrepreneurs and activists addressing the ethical challenges of the IT world. This chapter examines individuals who use IT for social good or to challenge the negative impacts of digitization. It explores their motivations through life-history examples. The article concludes by discussing entrepreneurial IT virtues within virtue ethics and argues that systematic analyses of virtuous IT exemplars can help promote ethical practices in IT entrepreneurship.

1 Introduction

There is today a great deal of scepticism towards the idea that free markets alone or even properly regulated liberal markets can drive the economy and society for the greater good. This is particularly true for the business world of information technology that—while holding many personal and societal promises—is equally regarded a playing field of ruthless entrepreneurs who seek to maximize profit in disregard of ethical principles such as respect for people's autonomy or privacy. This poses questions such as how information technology (IT) entrepreneurs ought to behave and what is right and wrong in digital entrepreneurship? Given the huge impact of digital technologies on all aspects of our lives—from business to personal, from local to global—ethical approaches to digital technologies are in high demand. There is no

E. Prem (✉)
Institute of Philosophy, Philosophy of Media and Technology, University of Vienna, Vienna, Austria
e-mail: prem@eutema.com

C. H. Hoffmann, D. Bansal (eds.), *AI Ethics in Practice*, Integrated Science 35,
https://doi.org/10.1007/978-3-031-87023-1_15

shortage of debates about ethical principles and regulations that information technology businesses should follow. Driven by developments in artificial intelligence (AI), there are hundreds of proposals on how to ensure that information technology systems are aligned with human values and not contradictory to ethical standards (Prem 2023). Rather than approaching the issue from norms and principles, it is worthwhile to take the entrepreneurial perspective. In the following, I will focus on the individual driving businesses and other types of organizations with a vision that goes beyond mere profit considerations and the potential possible benefits emerging from markets alone. This means to study virtue ethics and focus on positive character traits of 'good IT entrepreneurs'. This requires an investigation into individuals who are interested in working for a better world using information technology for this purpose. In addition, we should turn towards persons who aim at overcoming the shortcomings of today's information technology and its workings, i.e. who have an interest in 'better IT'. Compiling such a sample set of people who qualify as exemplars of good IT people or even as role models comes with many challenges and is necessarily a personal choice. In this short chapter, I will provide suggestions without claiming that these individuals are morally perfect or perhaps even not superior. They should, however, exhibit character traits relevant to a study of virtue ethics in information technology.

There a massively renewed interest in computer ethics since the advent of generative AI (Silvia 2023; Cockelbergh 2020) including an interest in virtue ethics (Hagendorff 2022; Vallor 2016; Vallor 2017). Interestingly, such virtue ethics has been proposed for system designers and computer engineers and for the resulting systems, e.g. an AI agent (Farina et al. 2022). Here, we focus on character traits of IT system developers and businesspeople with the idea to provide them as character role models, or simply, virtues of real-world IT experts. This can only be a starting point for closing the existing gap in technology virtue ethics that argues for a stronger role of virtues but does not usually provide many convincing examples and role models. However, such models are essential within a virtue ethics approach that emphasizes learning, repetition, or habituation and the acquisition of moral IT practices (Hagendorff 2022, p.14).

What Are Virtues and Why Are They Important?

Virtues relate to character; they characterize the moral worth of persons, not primarily of their actions. Virtues are irreducible to good actions since the motivation for acting is essential. Virtues constitute a person's character and the disposition to approach situations with specific attention and a particular mindset. Actions, on the other hand, are essential for virtue as virtues are not just abstract, theoretical dispositions. They require application and demonstration, i.e. action in situations that are ethically challenging. The scholar best known today for his work on virtues remains Aristotle. He developed his account of virtue in his Nicomachean ethics. It is not only a study of what is morally right, but developed from a broader perspective as an answer to how we should live a good life. For Aristotle this is not solely a personal question, it concerns a life that is as much social as it is political.[1] Virtues are by no means an innate concept; they need to be acquired and require practice. They can and should be refined over time. Developed virtues as a constitutive component of character carry an element of reliability and of predictability regarding how a person will act in a situation—or as a minimum which actions are unlikely. The brave person will not flee out of fear; the modest person will not act shamelessly nor be shy. Although the idea of virtues as the moderate concept between two extremes, e.g. courage between rashness and cowardice, works well for some virtues, it is difficult for other Aristotelian virtues, hence I am not pursuing this issue any further.

A concept that is important in debates about the modern entrepreneur, however, is *phronesis*. Φρόνησις or prudence, in Latin *prudentia*, is the ability to act cleverly and reasonably. This ability has received a great deal of interest throughout the philosophical literature. It owes its prominence to the fact that eminent thinkers from Platon to Aristotle, Cicero, Thomas Aquinas and many others praised it as an ethical concept of central importance. For Aristotle, prudence is not concerned with theoretical deliberation alone, it is an inherently practical concept that concerns actions in the real world. It could be termed a meta-ethical concept or the 'mother of all virtues'. Hagendorff (2022, p.9) lists it as a 'second order' virtue in the context of AI jointly with *fortitude*. Prudence facilitates deliberation about matters of unsure consequences, i.e. those which are typically encountered in ethically challenging situations. But rather than abstract deliberation, prudence concerns questions of practical thinking and action. In the following, I investigate a group of people who practically worked in IT or are using IT with a business or a more societal perspective. They exhibit character traits that are admirable and worth copying, in other words to be acquired and practised. They could become role models at least with respect to certain domains or situational settings including for entrepreneurs.

Entrepreneurship has been characterized as 'the exercise of individual freedom with a view to creating value, whether economic or social (or, less commonly, both)' (Dunn 2008). Also, entrepreneurship can be regarded as an activity that turns a private idea into a social idea (Dunn 2008). This should justify investigating not only profit-driven business entrepreneurs, but also people who created other types of organizations, e.g. associations, initiatives or other non-profit organizations aimed at societally beneficial objectives. The focus is on individuals who showed initiative, took an opportunity, or became the focus point of a movement and therefore exhibited the dynamic, creative and risk-taking characteristics often associated with entrepreneurs. We then investigate how these characteristics relate to a virtue perspective. Let us first remind ourselves how we ended up in a situation where IT entrepreneurs are no longer welcome drivers of economic growth, but also met with some scepticism and reservation.

[1] Cf. Curzer (2012) for the social Aristotelian virtues.

1.1 Fallen Angels

Being an IT entrepreneur used to have a thoroughly positive image. In the later 1980s and especially from the early 1990s, tech entrepreneurship became a phenomenon of significant economic, political and social relevance (Kollmann et al. 2022). Driven by the development and the spread of internet technology, being or becoming a technology entrepreneur was a promising aspiration for many. Not only was this a vision driving career choices of technology students. The promotion of IT start-ups and IT entrepreneurships was a no-brainer for politicians worldwide to support and develop a thriving economy. Several lines of thinking merged and created a strong optimism about this technology that lasts for at least a decade. Engineers, businesses, leading thinkers including artists and historians had high hopes for a digitally transitioning world that would flourish economically, socially and culturally. Culturally, the vision of a free internet that brings everybody together, facilitates the exchange of ideas and access to knowledge was a major driver behind such optimism. For economists, the digital became a central growth factor that promised scale-ups and efficiency gains from production to distribution, from the creation of new services to increased speed in business processes. Finally, IT was described as a technology facilitating the convergence of previously isolated regimes of energy and communication leading to a world of abundance. In the 'sharecon-omy' digital platforms would facilitate an economic shift from scarcity to abundance building on phenomena such as user (or 'prosumer') co-creation or the transformation of physical products into services (e.g. Rifkin 2011, 2014).

Naturally in such an account, the digital entrepreneur was highly valued as the person behind a significant and valuable transformation of the economy and of society. It is surprising how this broad appreciation of IT entrepreneurs changed from being perceived as digital heroes to almost little devils. A series of critical accounts questioned many of the prevailing narratives from the role of digital platforms to the Silicon Valley entrepreneur (Daub 2020) and the role of co-creation. Increasingly, the information technology sector was criticized for its potential for abuse, surveillance and monopolistic behaviour (Zuboff 2019) that builds on a feudalistic exploitation (Varoufakis 2024). Current critical debates concern the privatization and 'theft' of public goods for harvesting humankind's knowledge for AI and private profit-making (Kivus 2024). The digital entrepreneur became described as 'destructive' (Naudé 2024) following new opportunities for cybercrime and exploitation of consumers. In the context of digital platform capitalism some authors now speak of a dystopia characterized by unfairness (e.g. unfair competition), suffering and the expectation of further harm (Naudé 2024, p.299). Before we surrender ourselves completely to this dystopia, we should remember that there are also heroes in IT who fight for the good cause.

2 IT Role Models

2.1 Virtue in IT

Providing a list or even examples of heroines and heroes in IT is not as straightforward as perhaps in other disciplines or business sectors. When I ask my students at Vienna University for examples of good IT entrepreneurs, they will sometimes simply deny the question. Some reluctantly give examples of wealthy IT businessmen (indeed mostly men) who donated significant parts of their wealth to charity. Generally, they find it difficult to identify virtuous IT business leaders known for their work on 'good IT'. Reasons for this may lie in the fact that IT is a young discipline and that it is a highly specialized field. IT requires specific formal education or technical training so that only few people may know and appreciate the work of individual experts, creators or leaders in the field. There are only a few exceptions such as Alan Turing or Hedy Lamarr who are known for their technical contributions despite personal challenges such as being homosexual or simply a woman in a predominantly male and heterosexual business or academic environment. However, in a situation where there is scepticism of a technology, it is also to be expected that there are creators, entrepreneurs and activists who address precisely this issue and devote parts of their work to such ethical challenges. In the following, I can only sample a small selection of highly motivated individuals who either use IT for social good or to fight the abuses and shortcomings of digitization. Clearly, such a list will always be debatable and should not be taken as a compilation of morally perfect people.

The following examples serve to identify interests and character traits with the aim of demonstrating virtues of relevance in the IT domain generally and in IT business in particular. In approximate chronological order, the list starts with a historical example, a hacker from the early days of computing before turning to one of the first IT businesswomen with a mission. We then proceed to a fighter for the commons who died young and an advocate for privacy who also worked in large industry firms. The set includes two more women, an IT expert with interest in IT for supporting people with special needs and, finally, another ethical hacker.

René Camille: Saving Lives from Surveillance Terrorism

Surprisingly, even computer scientists may not know about the heroic actions of René Camille, a civil servant in the Vichy government during World War II. As a statistician and expert in early punch card technology, Camille was a promoter of the use of early computing devices for statistical and administrative purposes and created an early version of a personal identification number as well as various relevant coding schemes.[2] The statistical service was soon to be misused to identify Jews in preparation of their deportation and assassination in Nazi concentration camps. With slow work, targeted obstruction and manipulation of punch cards and

[2] For Camille there is still a lack of scholarly writing. Here I am relying on the Wikipedia article, last accessed in July 2024. https://en.wikipedia.org/wiki/Ren%C3%A9_Carmille#References

machines, René Camille successfully delayed the identification of Jews over the course of about 2 years. His sabotaging of punch card machines earned him the credit of 'first ethical hacker'. He was also instrumental in providing fake identities from deceased persons for members of the Resistance, German deserters and Jews. As a result of his hacking and sabotage, Camille may have saved more than 100,000 lives.[3] Tragically, René Camille was imprisoned in 1944, tortured and died in Dachau in 1945.

In terms of virtues, René Camille clearly showed courage and care. There can be little doubt that René Camille was aware of the potentially serious consequences of his actions and that he consciously risked his life to save others, hence demonstrating empathy. Also, he must have been one of the first to fully understand the potential for abusing information technology for political objectives given his statistical training and understanding the relationship between statistical categories and the power of effective computational systems, hence demonstrating *technomoral wisdom* (Vallor 2016). Consequently, he also exhibited a profound understanding of how to counteract such ideas with hacking IT systems and repurposing formal identities to fight injustice and those in power, demonstrating the virtue of justice.

Dame Stephanie 'Steve' Shirley: The IT Woman for IT Women

Born in Germany in 1933, Stephanie Shirley moved to England 1939 where she founded her first own company 'Freelance Programmers'. Aiming at better recognition in the male dominated early world of business computing, she changed her name to Steve Shirley. A decisive feature of her company was to employ predominantly women—to the extent that at one point only 3 out of 300 employees were men. She was an early adopter of flexible work hours in an effort to make it easier for the employed mothers to look after their children. Her company eventually grew to employ 8500 people and was valued at US$3 billion.[4] Shirley sold her successful enterprise when her autistic son was born. Due to the co-ownership structure of the company, the success of the firm resulted in the creation of millionaires among its staff (Beaty 2019). After retiring at an age of 60, she continued her philanthropy supporting a broad range of organizations including those helping people with autism. She was a frequent speaker and author of books and articles explaining her ambitions and motivating others and was awarded multiple honours in recognition of her work.

Shirley exhibits a thorough interest for improving the situation of women from the very start of her first business. Her interest in supporting women demonstrates care, empathy, justice and civility: after all, Shirley makes a common cause. She experienced how difficult it was for women to get accepted in a field dominated by men to the extent that she changed her name. This experience may have shaped her support for women and other people in need early in her career. The further experience of an autistic son may have intensified this and led to her becoming a philanthropist.

[3] https://www.modemmischief.com/rene-carmille-show-transcript (Last accessed July 2024).

[4] https://www.steveshirley.com/

Aaron Hill Swartz: Fighting for the Knowledge of Commons

Aaron Hill Swartz (*1986) has been labelled a hero and martyr by internet activists. He was 12 years old when he created 'The Info Network'—a user generated encyclopaedia and only 14 when he worked on RSS.[5] This shows his genuine interest in common data formats which he also developed when working with the World Wide Web Consortium. He was an early adopter and promoter of 'Creative Commons' and the Internet Archive's Open Library. He created 'Infogami' that later was joined with the online network 'Reddit'. In 2008, Swartz published his 'Guerilla Online Access Manifesto' supporting the Open Access Movement and arguing against the privatization of knowledge. He created PACER (Public Access to Court Electronic Records System) for downloading millions of legal online texts in an effort to publish these files for free. The US government met these efforts with resistance but did not open legal proceedings. He created 'watchdog.net' in 2008 to foster political transparency and 'Demand Progress' in 2010 as a body for internet activism and to lobby against online censorship. In 2011 he was charged with illegally downloading millions of online papers from the online archive JSTOR. The court case was still ongoing when he killed himself in 2013 at the age of 26.[6]

The running theme in the life of Aaron Swartz is information freedom, i.e. the idea that knowledge should be free for all. As mentioned in the introduction, this was an older idea driving much of the early internet enthusiasm but soon to be perverted through privatization and commercialization trends especially of large platforms. The work of Swartz can be considered political in several ways, e.g. when he published manifestos. His work as an activist or perhaps even as a hacker exhibits political ambition, e.g. to what he may have considered liberating knowledge for the benefit of everybody. Naturally, there are also significant moral objections to his actions arising from his acts being potentially illegal. In terms of virtues, Swartz demonstrates courage, civility and magnanimity.

Jon Callas: Privacy for All

Computer security expert Jon Callas studied mathematics, philosophy and literature at the University of Maryland. He worked as a software engineer, user experience designer and was the CTO and co-founder of the global encrypted communications service Silent Circle.[7] He worked for major IT companies including Apple, Digital Equipment Corporation and PGP and co-created several key internet standards such as OpenPGP, Skein, Threefish, or DKIM. Calls was a co-founder of the PGP Corporation specializing in email encryption. He founded Silent Circle in 2012 and created the 'Blackphone'—a software ecosystem and mobile phone focused on security aspects. Since 2020 he works for the Electronic Frontier Foundation, an NGO that fights for fundamental rights in the Information Age.

[5] RSS is a system for web feeds that allows users to aggregate content from selected web sites.

[6] https://www.internethalloffame.org/inductee/aaron-swartz/

[7] silentcircle.com (Last accessed July 2024).

In an interview with Jon Callas[8] he confirms that he always had an interest in protecting people's privacy, something he calls a 'predisposition'. Although he was clearly driven by the fascination with the opportunities that the internet offered, he was also fascinated by the more philosophical aspects of what the rough edges of human interaction are. It is also important for him that security and privacy are available for everyone without the need for special security experts. To some extent this may have been shaped as a child in the 1960s and 1970s and all the political debates from civil rights to Vietnam War, Nixon and the Pentagon Papers. When asked about how he believes we should live a good digital life, Jon answers with 'in moderation' and with a sense of 'knowing yourself'. This points to temperance and also to empathy and care. His understanding of the relation of privacy, encryption and the need for ease of use also demonstrates technomoral wisdom.

Marita Cheng: IT Support for Those with Special Needs
Born in 1989, Marita Cheng is an Australian technology entrepreneur and an advocate for women in tech. She studied engineering at the University of Melbourne and co-founded the non-profit organization Robogals in 2008. The organization targets girls at the age from 10 to 14 to inspire, engage and empower young women into engineering and related fields. In her first year as a student, she created 'Nudge', a service to remind patients to take their medication. Among many other activities, in 2013 Cheng created 'Autobot' (or 'Aubot') which originally aimed at providing low-cost robotic systems now focused on application areas such as telepresence for people with disabilities, chronic diseases, or living in isolation. In 2015, Cheng co-founded 'Aipoly', a mobile application for the visually impaired.

There are two topics that stand out in Marita Cheng's work. The first is using IT for social good—clearly an indication of care. This work is focused on helping people with various special needs with IT systems. Here, Cheng is also concerned about the costs of the systems and has shown an interest in the social dimension of information technology solutions, hence there is a clear element of civility. The other aspect is her engagement for women in technology with a focus on young women and opening career pathways for them—again perhaps best characterized as technomoral wisdom or magnanimity depending on how much we focus on the engineering aspects.

Katie Moussouris: Hacking the Pentagon
Our last exemplar, Katie Moussouris studied computer science at MIT where she also worked as system administrator at the Whitehead Institute of Bioinformatics. She became penetration tester in 2002 and started to work for Microsoft in 2007 and became Chief Policy Officer at 'HackerOne', a company focused on identifying security vulnerabilities. In cooperation with the US Department of Defence she started the first US bug bounty program that became known as 'Hacking the Pentagon' which was later followed by 'Hack the Airforce'. She founded the 'Pay Equity Now Foundation' to fight the gender pay gap which led to the creation of the

[8] I interviewed Jon Callas online in August 2023.

'Lab for Gender and Economic Equity' at Penn State Law School. In 2016, Moussouris founded 'Luta Security' as a consulting firm that advises organizations and governments such as the US Department of Defensce, Facebook and Zoom in hacking and security research.[9]

The work of Moussouris has been described as ethical hacking, but quite different from the dramatic sense in which the term is used for René Camille. Moussouris exhibits a drive for secure systems, for improving the security of information technology infrastructure and protecting agencies as well as firms from potential attacks. There is an important element of honesty in the way she approaches hacking and more broadly, technomoral wisdom.

2.2 Motives and Issues

Generally, all potential role models exhibit a decisive ability to take the initiative and act. Of course, this is how they were selected to become part of the set here. But there is an important parallel to Aristotelian thinking and other philosophers who consider (practical) actions key to virtuous characters. It is insufficient to only be theoretically or potentially benevolent, it is important that otherwise latent characteristics at least occasionally bear actual consequences in reality. It would be wrong on the other hand to conclude virtue just from the nature of an act, which is the realm of deontology such as Kantian norms and rules of action. The act is important, but in virtue ethics only as a demonstration of the virtuous character because the assessment as virtuous concerns the character, not the act.

Acts may be important for the acquisition and practice of a moral 'skill', however. It would suggest itself that our examples became fighters for the good cause based on specific events in their life histories. However, at least Jon Callas and Adam Swartz argued that they have always had a disposition to act how they did. Swartz reports[10] 'I'd always been wanting to get active'. In my interview Callas claimed being predisposed that way. On the other hand, Callas also describes himself as 'a child in the 60s and 70s and all of the turmoil, from civil rights to the Vietnam War'. Swartz describes books that influenced him including Chomsky's 'Understanding Power' and his frustration with school and teachers that made him question the educational system.

The issues that this selection of activists and entrepreneurs address are key challenges of today's IT world: privacy, security, the privatization of and access to knowledge, the challenges that women are facing in the male-dominated engineering world. To some extent the examples also concern the use of IT for the greater good such as providing solutions for people with special needs or health applications. The examples address both the individual and the social sphere. Individually, there is concern for people's privacy (Callas) and security (Moussouris) as well as access to knowledge (Swartz). At the societal level, Moussouris, Shirley and Cheng

[9] https://www.sans.org/profiles/katie-moussouris/ (Last accessed July 2024).

[10] https://www.youtube.com/watch?v=JUt5gjqNI1w

fight for improving the situation of women or, in the case of Swartz, for access to knowledge for all.

3 From Virtuous Exemplars to Virtuous Entrepreneurs

3.1 What Virtues?

The virtues of real-world activists and entrepreneurs are fascinating in their own right, not just because 'virtue ethics is hot' (Curzer 2012). A possible question to ask about our exemplars is whether they exhibit the classical Aristotelean virtues, or do we need separate virtues that relate to IT? We find courage, modesty and possibly patience. Other Aristotelian virtues, however, are less clearly present such as wittiness or 'proper ambition'. In terms of cardinal virtues (Thomas Aquinas), we find that our set includes courage, justice and prudence—perhaps less evidently also temperance. The question is not absurd, e.g. Hagendorf (2022) suggests four basic virtues of particular relevance in the design of AI systems, namely *justice, honesty, responsibility* and *care*. It may be easier to categorize our heroes in terms of Vallor's technomoral virtues: *self-control, courage, justice, empathy, care* or *technomoral wisdom* all come to mind. In any case, clearly listing virtues, assigning them to persons is a challenge. Even more so, deciding for a set of possible virtues fit for characterizing all people useful for all situations may be even harder.

It goes without saying that our exemplars include controversial character traits—or at least they have acted in ways that are illegal and may be classified as outrightly immoral. The complexity of assessing virtues of people with controversial traits is well known. For an IT-related case, Harfield (2021) performs an exercise in assessing the character of Edward Snowden from the perspective of virtue ethics. Against the backdrop of Vallor's ethical framework, Harfield draws a positive conclusion for three virtues, namely *honesty, courage* and *justice*. These are by no means easy assessments as the underlying acts can nearly always be diagnosed as virtuous or non-virtuous. For example, when Edward Snowden published secrets to inform the world about NSA's massive surveillance activities, this can be regarded a dishonest action to Snowden's employer, but an honest action vis-à-vis the world. Snowden's can be assessed as courageous given the potential consequences from losing his job to imprisonment, but leaving the country could also be seen as an act of cowardice. Assessing René Camille's actions as virtuous (e.g. courageous) on the other hand, seems much easier. This may be due to the undisputed vices of the Nazi regime or the fact that he saved so many lives.

Perhaps such a complete assessment of virtues from a complete set of virtues is not strictly necessary. The examples provided are impressive in their own right. They serve to teach virtue regardless of whether all virtues are present in an individual and, I suggest, regardless of whether they stem from a unique and complete set of virtues. It is more interesting to assess what can be learned from the examples and their virtue characterization.

Whether virtues can provide guidance for action is a contested issue (Annas 2015). While the ideal of a good character is widely recognized, it may not follow easily how this will help in guiding our actions. Learning about virtues of entrepreneurs expands our horizon and also concretizes it in a specific situational challenge. The value of examples of virtuous characters does not lie in them providing solutions to existing moral challenges (although this is not excluded). They should be taken as showing directions of potential action, of how *phronesis* or prudence unfolds in practical decision-making and action.

An important advantage of virtues is that they are a person's own. They are not someone else's virtues nor are they someone else's rules (Annas 2015, p.7). They may have been acquired from the study of either, but in the end, virtues are something personal—this is what the word 'character' implies. The acquisition of virtues is therefore a personal endeavour, a mission that is self-controlled. For the entrepreneur this appears as the natural way to go about ethical development: not solely based on rules or the calculation of consequences, but self-driven improvement for human flourishing. This implies that there is a constant urge for continued advancement, an improvement of skilled application and adaptation of virtues.

3.2 Towards the Virtuous IT Entrepreneur

Similar to adopting virtues in different cultures, e.g. what it means to be brave (Annas 2015), we may adopt virtues for special domains including, such as IT system design and deployment. Of course, virtue does not depend on the situation as (Annas 2015) explains. Courage remains courage regardless of whether a political dissident dares to speak up or a mother saves her child from drowning. The interesting aspect is what is similar about these behaviours, how the courageous person faces challenges and how they react. Note also that brave persons remain brave in nearly all contexts; although there are some exceptions: in everyday situations, it may happen that people whose characters we rank highly in one domain, appear less virtuous in other contexts. A medical doctor may exhibit all the virtues expected in the medical profession: benevolent, helpful, considerate, brave, impartial, etc. However, we may not like this person's tendency to tell indecent jokes nor their way of tipping only the minimum amount. This is only acceptable as an exception and for issues that are not morally grave, otherwise the person loses their virtue.

Computer ethics is hugely challenging because IT is everywhere and decisions about IT systems may concern every aspect of human life and activity, from medicine to transportation, from shopping to production, from dating to daily news. Note how ethics has specialized over the past few decades into domain ethics such as media ethics, animal ethics, medical ethics, environmental ethics, etc. This development can be explained with the huge ethical challenges that pose complicated questions and choices. Domain ethics is often oriented at principles and rules, but occasionally also consequentialist. Both deontology and consequentialism face serious difficulties in situations where technologies are new and we do not necessarily understand all the outcomes or 'consequences'. It is very hard to list concise sets of rules and principles concrete enough for action in such situations. This is why there is a strong call, e.g. in AI to move 'from what to how' (e.g. Hagendorff 2022; Prem 2023). This has resulted in an effort to make principles more concrete and list possible actions to make systems 'more ethical'.

Interestingly, there has been no similar development in virtue ethics, i.e. there is little work to identify more virtuous IT experts and to analyse and present their virtues systematically. Perhaps there is an implicit assumption that the virtuous person will be virtuous independent of a domain of action. Leaving out the question to what extent a virtuous person needs to be virtuous in all walks of life, studying virtue in different context will inform us about relevant implications, considerations, examples and motivations in relation to the challenges of a domain of action. Hence, there is reason to investigate domain exemplars—not because we may arrive at completely different list of virtues but because we may better understand what it takes to be virtuous in typical situations of that domain. The seminal work of Vallor (2016) already provides four technomoral case studies, which are to some extent related to information technology (i.e. social media, surveillance, robots at war and at home, and human enhancement technology). Of this, we need more because moral examples are easier to follow and to accept when they stem from a relatable context. Following Vallor, we should cultivate characters as much as we are today cultivating technologies (and technologists) and create better spaces for technomoral education.

We need examples of real-world people faced with difficult decisions including those between profit-making and social good. We need to better understand how virtuous IT entrepreneurs have decided against infringing their customers' privacy and which virtues may have led to truly entrepreneurs empowering users. We need a better understanding of the underlying values of potential role models—both in and outside of information technology and relate them to virtues, deontological principles and regulations. In summary, there is a need to combine illustration of IT virtues with their practice, habituation and refinement. We also need more of these examples to avoid the impression that information technology is a natural determinant of our lives and that it evolves without any possibility of changing its direction of development. To the contrary, technology is a choice.

Virtue ethics—like all ethics—is concerned with how to lead better lives. Although there is clear direction in this project, there is no optimality criterion. Virtue ethics is the approach for creative minds precisely because it is less about consequences and rule applications (Hagendorff 2022 p.4) and more about shaping situations and action responses including in new ways and with unsure outcomes. The advantage of virtue ethics over consequentialism or deontology is its focus on the actor and its generality. Here it clearly diverges from both consequentialist and deontologist ethics and opens possibilities for creative minds such as entrepreneurs.

References

Annas J (2015) Applying virtue to ethics. (Society of Applied Philosophy Annual Lecture 2014). J Appl Phil 32(1). https://doi.org/10.1111/japp.12103
Beaty Z (2019) The 85-year-old tech entrepreneur who made her staff millionaires. The Telegraph. 14 June 2019. https://www.telegraph.co.uk/women/life/85-year-old-tech-entrepreneur-made-staff-millionaires/
Coeckelbergh M (2020) AI ethics. MIT Press
Curzer JJ (2012) Aristotle and the virtues. Oxford University Press
Daub A (2020) What tech calls thinking: an inquiry into the intellectual bedrock of Silicon Valley. FSG Originals
Dunn C (2008) Ethics of entrepreneurship. In: Kolb RW (ed) Encyclopedia of business ethics and society, vol 2. Sage Publications, pp 724–729
Farina M, Zhdanov P, Karimov A, Lavazza A (2022) AI and society: a virtue ethics approach. AI Soc:1–14
Hagendorff T (2022) A virtue-based framework to support putting AI ethics into practice. Phil Technol 35(3):55 ff
Harfield C (2021) Was Snowden virtuous? Ethics Inf Technol 23:373–383. https://doi.org/10.1007/s10676-021-09580-4
Kivus JK (2024) Generative AI and copyright law: a misalignment that could lead to the privatization of copyright enforcement. N Carolina J Law Technol 25(3):447–494
Kollmann T, Kleine-Stegemann L, de Cruppe K et al (2022) Eras of digital entrepreneurship. Bus Inf Syst Eng 64:15–31. https://doi.org/10.1007/s12599-021-00728-6
Naudé W (2024) Destructive digital entrepreneurship. In: Naudé W, Power B (eds) Handbook of research on entrepreneurship and conflict. Edward Elgar, Cheltenham, p 292 ff
Prem E (2023) From ethical AI frameworks to tools: a review of approaches. AI Ethics 3:699–716. https://doi.org/10.1007/s43681-023-00258-9
Rifkin J (2011) The third industrial revolution: how lateral power is transforming energy, the economy, and the world. Palgrave Macmillan
Rifkin J (2014) The Zero Marginal Cost Society: the internet of things, the collaborative commons, and the eclipse of capitalism. Palgrave Macmillan
Silvia B (2023) Modern digital technologies and AI ethics: moral relevance. Futurity Phil 2(3):71–85. https://doi.org/10.57125/FP.2023.09.30.05
Vallor S (2016) Technology and the virtues: a philosophical guide to a future worth wanting. Oxford University Press
Vallor S (2017) AI and the automation of wisdom. In: Powers T (ed) Philosophy and computing essays in epistemology, philosophy of mind, logic, and ethics. Springer, Berlin, pp 161–178
Varoufakis Y (2024) Technofeudalism: what killed capitalism. Melville House
Zuboff S (2019) The age of surveillance capitalism: the fight for a human future at the new frontier of power. PublicAffairs, New York

Erich Prem is the director of eutema and a research strategist based in Vienna, Austria. He is a researcher in philosophy of technology and media at the University of Vienna and teaches Digital Humanism at TU Vienna. Erich holds his Ph.D. in Philosophy (epistemology) from the University of Vienna and his Ph.D. in Informatics (AI) from TU Vienna. He also holds an MBA degree in General Management from Donau University.

Towards a Constructive Ethics of Artificial Intelligence in the Age of Surveillance Capitalism

16

Lucien von Schomberg

Abstract

This chapter investigates the question: What constitutes a constructive ethics of Artificial Intelligence (AI) in the age of surveillance capitalism? The approach is twofold. First, it explores the rise of surveillance capitalism as a new economic order in the digital age. The discourse on AI ethics often focuses on constraints to mitigate risks, but this overlooks the mediation of our relationship with technology by surveillance capitalism, leading to societal regress. Instead, the chapter advocates for a shift towards a constructive ethics of AI that rethinks our relationship with technology to foster societal progress. Second, it adopts a political concept of responsible innovation, proposing that a constructive ethics of AI must consider the human-technology relationship from a political perspective. This entails that AI systems should promote plurality, empower citizens, and serve the public sphere. The chapter concludes with a critical perspective, questioning whether AI systems can simultaneously serve the public sphere and the public good, or if these objectives might sometimes conflict.

1 Introduction

In the summer of 2023, the Centre for Artificial Intelligence Safety (CAIS) released a statement that "mitigating the risk of extinction from AI should be a global priority alongside other societal-scale risks such as pandemics and nuclear war" (Centre for AI Safety 2023). The statement was signed and endorsed by prominent figures within the Artificial Intelligence (AI) community, including executives from OpenAI, DeepMind, and Anthropic, in addition to researchers across the globe. The

L. von Schomberg (✉)
Faculty of Business, University of Greenwich, London, UK
e-mail: l.vonschomberg@greenwich.ac.uk

C. H. Hoffmann, D. Bansal (eds.), *AI Ethics in Practice*, Integrated Science 35,
https://doi.org/10.1007/978-3-031-87023-1_16

media quickly picked up on this narrative, casting the emergence of AI as an 'existential threat' (Abdul 2023; Vallance 2023). Indeed, concerns about AI have been escalating, with governments, academic institutions, and private organisations emphasising its potential risks. A recent report commissioned by the US State Department warns that AI systems could become uncontrollable and behave adversarial to human beings by default (Perrigo 2024). Amidst these alarming projections, some researchers now argue that there is a 99.9% probability that AI will lead to the extinction of humankind within the next century (Tangermann 2024).

While such catastrophic forecasts capture headlines, they often overshadow the subtle yet profound ways in which AI is already reshaping everyday life, from influencing voting patterns and consumer behaviour to altering the job market and the educational landscape (Bryson 2019; Makridakis 2017; Păvăloaia and Necula 2023; Lammi and Pantzar 2019). The more immediate existential threat, as identified by Shoshanna Zuboff, lies in the erosion of our individual autonomy, human agency, and democratic foundations through 'surveillance capitalism' (Zuboff 2019). This new economic order, pioneered by tech giants like Google and Meta, turns human experiences into data commodification, while predicting and influencing human behaviour on an unprecedented scale. As the deployment of AI systems increasingly influence major decisions in politics, economy, and social norms, the fear is not just about a dystopian future where humans are overridden by machines, but a present reality where human choices are subtly dictated by algorithmic processes.

Moreover, the prevailing discourse on AI ethics is largely centred around risk mitigation, adopting an approach best described as an 'ethics of constraints'. This perspective predominantly focuses on delineating what technology should refrain from doing, rather than exploring the constructive possibilities of what it could achieve—an 'ethics of construction' (Von Schomberg 2019). In this respect, philosopher Bernard Stiegler's insights into technology as a fundamental element of human evolution and culture are particularly relevant. Stiegler argued that technology embodies both the potential for progress and the risk of regress—it acts as a pharmacological element that can either heal or harm society (1998). AI, embodying this pharmacological nature, holds a temporal dimension, continuously evolving alongside human societal changes. As it integrates new data and adapts to new contexts, AI mirrors and is inherently linked to the human condition, reflecting our changing norms, values, and interests. This brings into question whether adopting an ethics of constraints is fruitful insofar our relationship with AI is embedded within the economic order of surveillance capitalism. Instead, we should explore a constructive ethics of AI in which we move away from discussions on how to control technology towards rethinking our relationship with technology altogether.

Against this background, this chapter poses the following research question: *What constitutes a constructive ethics of AI in the age of surveillance capitalism?* Our approach is twofold. Firstly, we account for the emergence of surveillance capitalism as a new economic order in the age of digitalisation. While the discourse on AI ethics often leans towards an ethics of constraints to mitigate its risks and adverse effects, we argue that this fails to recognise how our relationship with technology is mediated by surveillance capitalism, ultimately resulting in societal regress. Instead, we propose a shift towards a constructive ethics of AI which rethinks our relationship with technology in favour of societal progress. Secondly, we adopt a political concept of responsible innovation (Von Schomberg and Blok 2023), suggesting that a constructive ethics of AI must consider the human-technology relationship from a fundamentally political standpoint. In doing so, we argue that AI systems should promote plurality, empower citizens, and genuinely serve the public sphere. We conclude with a critical outlook, questioning whether AI systems can simultaneously serve the public sphere and the public good, or whether these two objectives may sometimes conflict.

2 The Rise of Surveillance Capitalism

In around 1450, Johannes Gutenberg invented the printing press, a revolutionary technology that profoundly transformed society. This invention led to the Reformation, undermined the authority of the Catholic Church, gave birth to modern sciences, enabled radically new industries, and even transformed the shape of our brains (Naughton 2019). Fast forward to the present, we find ourselves in the infancy of another transformative era—the age of digitalisation. As new technologies like AI evolve rapidly, predicting their long-term impacts remains speculative, with true understanding likely only in retrospect. Even so, in her book, *The Age of Surveillance Capitalism* (2019), Zuboff exposes a new economic order which explains some of the underlying mechanisms of this digital age. In this section we account for the emergence and threats surveillance capitalism, arguing that calls for stringent AI regulation fail to address the deeper concern of how our relationship with technology is confined to this new economic order. This will set the scene for our next section, in which we rethink our relationship with technology according to a political orientation, ultimately providing the basis for a constructive ethics of AI.

2.1 A New Economic Order

The emergence of surveillance capitalism can be traced back to the early 2000s, when Google, originally an internet search engine, began to realise the immense value of user data. By tracking search queries, click patterns, and other online behaviours, Google could create detailed user profiles that allowed for highly targeted advertising. This marked the beginning of a shift from traditional advertising models to data-driven marketing strategies that prioritise personalisation and behavioural prediction. Meta—Facebook at the time—followed suit, leveraging its social media platform to amass vast amounts of user data. Through likes, shares, comments, and other interactions, Meta could gain insights into users' preferences, interests, and social networks. Zuboff posits that surveillance capitalism has now become the dominant form of capitalism, defining it as "a new economic order that claims human experience as free raw material for hidden commercial practices of extraction, prediction, and sales" (Zuboff 2019, Definition).

Unlike traditional capitalism, which relies on the production and exchange of goods and services, surveillance capitalism operates through the continuous and comprehensive datafication of human experience. In conventional economic orders, raw materials such as tomatoes are transformed into products like tomato sauce, which are then sold for profit. This process involves sourcing, processing, and commercialising tangible goods. In contrast, in the new economic order of surveillance capitalism, the raw material is not a physical entity like tomatoes but rather our human experiences and interactions. Every online action, interaction, and transaction creates 'behavioural surplus'—data that goes beyond what is necessary for service functionality, collected often without explicit consent or awareness. This data captures extensive personal details, from our location data and search queries to minute digital interactions, facilitating predictions about future actions. These predictions are highly valuable, allowing industry to forecast personal behaviours, tailor advertisements more precisely, and influence consumer choices to maximise profit (see Fig. 16.1).

The phenomenon of Pokémon Go, launched by Niantic in 2016, serves as a striking case of how businesses can harness digital platforms to drive consumer behaviour (Pamuru et al. 2021). In this augmented reality game, players explore real-world locations to 'catch' virtual creatures. Businesses quickly recognised the potential to increase foot traffic to their locations by paying Niantic to place rare Pokémon or 'PokéStops' strategically at their premises. This tactic effectively turned game mechanics into a tool for commercial gain, with businesses ranging from small cafes to large retail chains experiencing increased customer visits as players would walk in to capture elusive Pokémons.

The implications of surveillance capitalism extend beyond the realm of commerce. A revealing incident involving the US-based retail giant Target illustrates the far-reaching consequences of data mining practices. Target's analytics algorithms were so finely tuned that they could predict major life changes based on shopping patterns. This capability became public knowledge when Target sent maternity product coupons to a teenager before her family was aware of her pregnancy (Hill 2012). Such instances highlight a significant ethical concern: the disclosure of personal information that was never intended to be shared. This is particularly problematic when a person's political affiliations or sexual orientation are exposed without their consent. Indeed, social media platforms, for example, use algorithms to deduce this information from user interactions and content preferences. One study analysed data from more than 58,000 Facebook users to demonstrate that the

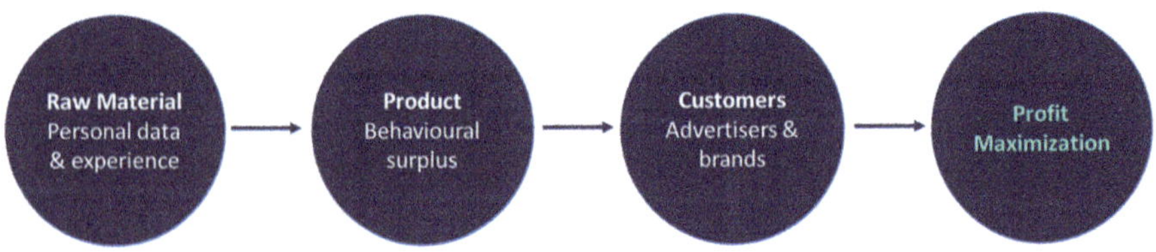

Fig. 16.1 Surveillance capitalism

posts people like on the platform can reliably predict various sensitive personal details, including sexual orientation, ethnicity, religious and political beliefs, personality traits, intelligence, happiness, substance use habits, whether their parents are separated, as well as their age and gender (Kosinski et al. 2013). This data is then used to tailor content and advertisements, potentially revealing personal information to others in the user's network, which can be particularly damaging in environments where such disclosures are socially stigmatised (Kosinski et al. 2013; Marwick and Boyd 2014).

While surveillance capitalism primarily profits from the prediction and sale of personal behavioural insights, its applications also extend into the domain of behavioural manipulation, shaping public and private actions. One of the most controversial instances of such manipulation is the case of Cambridge Analytica, a political consulting firm that gained infamy for its role in the 2016 U.S. presidential election (Gibney 2018). Allegedly, Cambridge Analytica acquired detailed psychological profiles of millions of Facebook users without their explicit consent, based on data harvested through what appeared to be a harmless personality quiz. These profiles were then used to craft highly personalised and psychologically targeted political advertisements aimed at influencing voter behaviour. These advertisements were designed to sway voter behaviour by tapping into individual fears, preferences, and biases, thereby manipulating public opinion at massive scale. By leveraging personal data not just to predict but to steer individual actions, Cambridge Analytica is said to have influenced democratic outcomes directly (Hern 2018; Santanen 2020).[1]

In a sense, surveillance capitalism can be seen as a modern reflection of B.F. Skinner's principles of operant conditioning, where human behaviour is not just monitored but actively shaped by the continuous feedback loop of data-driven incentives. Just as Skinner demonstrated how behaviour could be controlled and modified through rewards and punishments, today's digital giants manipulate cues and rewards to modify user behaviour. This manipulation not only capitalises on human experience as a raw material but also conditions societal behaviours in a loop of surveillance and response that is largely invisible and unacknowledged by its subjects. In the words of Zuboff:

> Industrial capitalism transformed nature's raw materials into commodities, and surveillance capitalism lays its claims to the stuff of human nature for a new commodity invention. Now it is human nature that is scraped, torn, and taken for another century's market project. [...]. The remarkable questions here concern the facts that our lives are rendered as behavioral data in the first place; that ignorance is a condition of this ubiquitous rendition; that decision rights vanish before one even knows that there is a decision to make; that there are consequences to this diminishment of rights that we can neither see nor foretell; that there is no exit, no voice, and no loyalty, only helplessness, resignation, and psychic numbing; and that encryption is the only positive action left to discuss when we sit around the dinner table and casually ponder how to hide from the forces that hide from us. (Zuboff 2019, p. 94)

[1] It is important to note that studies on the effectiveness of political microtargeting, which involves sending tailored messages to specific voters, are limited. Some research indicates that this approach may have minimal impact and could even backfire (Bailey et al. 2016; Hersh and Schaffner 2013; Nickerson and Rogers 2014).

2.2 The Human-Technology Relationship in Surveillance Capitalism

Zuboff highlights the regulatory gap as one of the main obstacles for combatting the exploitative practices of surveillance capitalism. Over the past two decades, Big Tech enjoyed a period of minimal legal interference. This lack of regulation stems primarily from the novelty of the practices involved; like the early days of industrial capitalism, where child labour in factories was unregulated because it was unprecedented, the operations of Big Tech are largely unexamined by existing legal frameworks. Even so, recent years have seen a shift towards more proactive regulatory measures. Notably, the European Union (EU) has taken a pioneering role with the introduction of the General Data Protection Regulation (GDPR) and more recently, the AI Act. The AI Act, in particular, includes provisions to ban AI systems that present unacceptable risks, such as those capable of behavioural manipulation or classification of individuals based on behaviour, socio-economic status, or personal characteristics (European European Parliament 2024).

However, the question remains whether the response to the rise of surveillance capitalism should be directed at AI systems themselves or at the economic logic that underpins our relationship with technology (Morozov 2019). Surveillance capitalism does not merely utilise technology; it fundamentally reshapes technology's role in society. As Woods (2018) points out, Equipping AI virtual assistants (VAs) like Siri and Alexa with a feminine persona rhetorically disarms users' anxieties about intimate data exchange. This is grounded in culturally ingrained perceptions of femininity associated with trustworthiness, nurturing, and non-threatening behaviour. By designing AI VAs to speak and interact in ways that mimic these feminine traits, technology companies tap into a subconscious comfort level that many users have with female figures in assistive roles. This comfort can make users more willing to interact with the device, sharing personal details and data more freely than they might with a perceived neutral or masculine interface. The familiar, friendly female voice and the servile, accommodating behaviour programmed into these devices are intended to create a sense of safety and care, making the ongoing surveillance and data collection practices of these devices seem less intrusive. The use of a feminine persona thus helps to mask the underlying commercial and surveillance activities, making the exchange of personal data feel more like a part of a caregiving relationship rather than a transactional or exploitative one.

> The rights of the individual become subsumed into the logic of the market; individuals themselves are folded into an aggregated constellation of data that is monetized by surveillance capitalists. It is not enough to say that Siri and Alexa are making the private public. Nor is it sufficient to claim that AI VA are eroding our privacy. Rather, AI VA are part of a structural reorganization of surveillance practices which tend away from top-down models and instead tend toward ubiquitous data collection. Privacy rules and regulations are quickly becoming archaic, tied to a time when surveillance functioned differently. (Woods 2018, p. 345)

In addition, Woods (2018) notes that the gendering of AI VAs to perform roles traditionally associated with femininity, such as homemaking and caregiving, relies on and perpetuates regressive gender stereotypes. This process not only taps into long-standing societal norms that view women primarily as caretakers and homemakers but also reinforces these views by embedding them in the cutting-edge technology of smart homes. When AI VAs perform tasks like managing schedules, assisting with household chores, or providing emotional support, they do so through a lens that suggests these activities are inherently feminine. This technological mediation of domestic roles does more than just assign a gender to a voice or a digital persona; it connects advanced technology with traditional feminine roles, thereby reinforcing the idea that caregiving and homemaking are primarily women's responsibilities. Even as society progresses with gender equality, "the gendered programming of AI VA Siri and Alexa reify patriarchal stereotypes about the feminine in a new technological milieu characterized by distributed surveillant devices in the increasingly 'smart' home" (Woods 2018, p. 346). These AI VAs, then, not only reflect existing gender norms but also actively shape user expectations about gender roles in both the technology they use and the broader social context.

The phenomenon of surveillance capitalism teaches us that AI-based systems like AI VAs are not merely tools or objects we encounter; they are not solely means of exerting or being subjected to control. Instead, these systems function as mediators that shape the fabric of society, economics, and cultural life. They constitute what Blok (2024) refers to as a 'digisphere' or digital world—a computational realm where our experiences and interactions are translated into data sets. This means that we cannot simply stand outside the digital world as independent observers. Rather, within the digisphere, we are integrated and immersed, not only through the artefacts themselves but through the very modes of engagement that define and perpetuate our existence, much like Martin Heidegger foresaw with his notion of technology as 'Enframing' (Heidegger 1977). To be sure, in 'The Question Concerning Technology', Heidegger introduces Enframing as a way of revealing that orders and organises every aspect of the modern technological world. For Heidegger, Enframing is not just a collection of technological tools; it is a fundamental mode of existence that shapes how we perceive and interact with the world. Heidegger argues that Enframing constrains not only nature, by turning it into a resource to be exploited, but also humanity itself, by defining humans as resources or means to an end. This resonates with our concerns about surveillance capitalism, where technology not only facilitates economic exploitation but also shapes cultural and social interactions by turning personal data into a commodity. That is, under the dominance of surveillance capitalism, we appear as data-driven probabilistic agents who exhibit predictable behaviour that can be monitored and controlled via data-based systems (Blok 2023).

In exposing the human-technology relationship under the sway of surveillance capitalism, we argue that what requires reconsideration is not merely the governance of technologies like AI but our broader engagement with technology as a whole. This engagement goes beyond regulatory frameworks to explore the ways in which we can coexist with and through digital technologies. In this respect, we need to move away from an ethics of constraints, seeking to mitigate the risks of AI, towards a constructive ethics that redefines our interaction with AI beyond the exploitative mechanisms of surveillance capitalism. As we transition to the next section, we will explore how a political concept of responsible innovation can guide us in cultivating such a constructive ethics.

3 Building a Constructive Ethics of AI Through Responsible Innovation

To develop a constructive ethics of AI, we turn to the concept of responsible innovation. Unlike other theories on the ethics of technology which primarily focus on risk mitigation and minimising the harm (e.g. technology assessment), responsible innovation emphasises not only what innovation outcomes should be prevented but also what outcomes should actively be pursued (Von Schomberg 2019). To achieve this, responsible innovation scholars advocate for a collective responsibility and mutual responsiveness among a wide range of actors, including innovators, policymakers, industry representatives, and civil society groups (Owen et al. 2013). However, this raises complex political questions concerning, for instance, which actors to include in the innovation process and how they are expected to co-create outcomes (Van Oudheusden 2014). To this end, we have elsewhere developed a political concept of responsible innovation inspired by the philosophy of Hannah Arendt (Von Schomberg and Blok 2023). In this section, we adopt this political concept of responsible innovation in an attempt to rethink our relationship with technologies like AI from a fundamentally political rather than economic standpoint.

3.1 The Emergence of Responsible Innovation

The concept of responsible innovation marks a shift in the approach to technological advancement and scientific research. It acknowledges the effects of science and technology on society, and thus emphasises an ethical imperative to ensure these effects are societally desirable. Responsible innovation frameworks have become prominent at both academic and policy levels, especially in areas like biotechnology, AI, nanotechnology, and environmental science (Von Schomberg 2019). Academically, visions of responsible innovation typically propose that to innovate responsibly requires a permanent commitment to be anticipatory, reflective, inclusively deliberative, and responsive (Owen et al. 2013). Some approaches advocate for embedding human values into design requirements (Van De Poel 2013), while others emphasise integrating innovation practices within EU treaties (Von Schomberg 2013). At the policy level, the notion entered under the name of Responsible Research and Innovation (RRI) as a cross-cutting issue in *Horizon 2020* (2014–2020) and continues as a key objective in *Horizon Europe* (2021–2027), the successor EU Framework Programme for Research and Innovation. The concept has also gained importance in national research councils in countries like the UK,

Norway, and the Netherlands, which have initiated their own RRI programmes. Moreover, RRI has achieved international status, influencing strategic directions in the United States and China, where it has been incorporated into their national science, technology, and innovation plans (Von Schomberg and Von Schomberg 2023).

Although the concept of responsible innovation gained traction in the recent years, efforts to incorporate ethical and social considerations into science and technology have been ongoing since the late 1960s with the emergence of risk identification and analysis (Evers and Nowotny 1987). This movement gained momentum in the early 1970s, particularly due to concerns over nuclear waste disposal (Kevles 1995). During the 1990s, public debates about genetically modified organisms and nanotechnology in food products highlighted the ethical issues in these areas. In response, the European Commission issued a communication in the early 2000s on the precautionary principle, aimed at informing both the public and policymakers about the known risks and uncertainties (Commission of the European Communities 2001). This, in turn, reinforced methods and frameworks to steer science and technology into the right direction, including Technology Assessment (TA), Science and Technology Studies (STS), and research into the Ethical, Legal, and Social implications or Aspects (ELSI/ELSA) of new technologies.

Responsible innovation builds on these earlier efforts but represents a reform in several ways (Brundage and Guston 2019). Firstly, it directs research and innovation towards proactively addressing global challenges like climate change, water scarcity, biodiversity loss, and food security (Von Schomberg 2013). In doing so, responsible innovation goes beyond conventional economic incentives and addresses market failures to ensure that innovation processes genuinely produce societally desirable outcomes (Von Schomberg and Von Schomberg 2023). As mentioned earlier, this approach reflects an ethics of construction rather than an ethics of constraints, focusing not only on preventing undesirable outcomes but also on actively pursuing beneficial ones. In this respect, responsible innovation shifts from traditional evaluative assessments of emerging technologies to an approach based on collective responsibility among stakeholders. Indeed, under the principle of science with and for society, it suggests that research and innovation can only meet societal needs and aspirations if all actors are involved throughout the entire process (Owen et al. 2013).

One way to implement responsible innovation is through 'mission-oriented research', as highlighted by the European Commission (2018). In such missions, stakeholders and citizens collaborate on open research and innovation agendas with a strong commitment to achieving socially desirable outcomes. The key concepts here are co-creation and co-design of research and innovation trajectories. The new EU framework programme has introduced mission-oriented research with new features that prioritise social targets rather than economic, scientific, and technological ones. This approach fosters innovation by promoting co-design and co-creation towards democratically decided main objectives, derived from deliberations among stakeholders, EU member states, and the European Parliament. Crucially, these missions will require input from citizens, ensuring that the research and innovation processes reflect and address societal needs and aspirations (Von Schomberg and Von Schomberg 2023).

While the aspiration to integrate diverse stakeholder perspectives into the innovation process is fundamental to the ethos of responsible innovation, in practice this is not always evident (Owen and Pansera 2019; Van Oudheusden 2014). For example, power dynamics can influence which voices are heard and whose interests are prioritised (Bryson et al. 2006). Often, stakeholders from economically dominant sectors or those with greater scientific clout wield disproportionate influence compared to smaller community groups or individual citizens. This imbalance can result in outcomes that, despite the ostensibly inclusive process, primarily reflect the preferences and interests of the more powerful parties. Additionally, each group involved in the innovation process—be it industry representatives, policymakers, academics, or community members—brings its own set of values, expectations, and objectives to the table. The difficulty lies not only in balancing these varied interests but also in addressing the underlying conflicts that may arise when stakeholders' goals are fundamentally at odds (Batie 2008; Kreuter et al. 2004; Rittel and Webber 1973). In this respect, the discourse of responsible innovation still needs to address questions about the constitution and contestation of power.

> How do actors 'co-create' outcomes? How do they deliberate? On whose terms is participation (i.e. deliberation) established and why? What, in fact, is 'public' about the 'public interest', 'public expectations', and 'the public', and whose definition of the public counts? (Van Oudheusden 2014, p. 73)

In a similar vein, Owen and Pansera (2019) argue that stakeholder engagement is "usually narrowly configured to include a limited range of (internal and sometimes external) stakeholders, and that second-order reflexivity and the political are almost entirely beyond scope, or at least deeply tacit" (p. 41). To this end, there is a growing demand for a political concept of responsible innovation that effectively considers the diverse values and interests of the broader public (Penttilä 2024; Reijers 2020; Owen and Pansera 2019; Van Oudheusden 2014; Von Schomberg and Blok 2021).

The urgency of adopting a political concept of responsible innovation becomes even more urgent when considering our deeply entangled relationship with technology under the dominance of surveillance capitalism—as discussed in the previous section. We need to rethink our relationship with technology from passive consumption to active engagement, promoting plurality, empowering citizens, and genuinely serving the public sphere. The question, to which we turn next, is what a political concept of responsible innovation consists of and how it can shed new light on our relationship with technology, ultimately informing a constructive ethics of AI.

3.2 Implementing a Political Concept of Responsible Innovation in AI Ethics

In the following we build on a political concept of responsible innovation inspired by a generative reading of Arendt's work.[2] Indeed, in *The Human Condition*, Arendt provides us with a profound understanding of what it means for innovation to primarily serve the public sphere, even if she does not explicitly address the topic of innovation herself. In doing so, we shed new light on our relationship with technology, providing basis for a constructive ethics of AI.

In *The Human Condition*, Arendt articulates the 'vita activa', a threefold distinction between the activities of labour, work, and action. Labour is tied to biological processes and the necessities of human survival. This includes the production of goods to satisfy basic needs such as food and shelter. Labour is cyclical and corresponds to the natural cycles of consumption and renewal. It is the most fundamental and life-sustaining activity that humans engage in, but it also binds them to a perpetual cycle of necessity. Work, in contrast to labour, creates an artificial world of things. The products of work provide a stable and lasting world that outlives individual lives. Through work, humans create objects that add permanence and durability, which labour does not provide. This category includes the making of tools, buildings, and art—essentially, anything that contributes to a world beyond mere survival needs. The most elevated of the three, action, relates to the human ability to initiate new beginnings through deeds and words. Action is conditioned by plurality. To be sure, we are not only distinct individuals but also interdependent beings who exist in a web of relationships. Action involves interacting in this web through speech and political engagement, revealing our unique identity, and contributing to the world beyond the self. It is through action that we experience freedom and the potential to change the world. In the words of Arendt:

> The new always happens against the overwhelming odds of statistical laws and their probability, which for all practical, everyday purposes amounts to certainty; the new therefore always appears in the guise of a miracle. The fact that man is capable of action means that the unexpected can be expected from him, that he is able to perform what is infinitely improbable. And this again is possible only because each man is unique, so that with each birth something uniquely new comes into the world. (Arendt 1998, p. 178)

The vita activa is closely linked to Arendt's distinction between the private sphere and the public sphere. The private sphere, she argues, is the realm of the household and family life. Historically, this sphere was characterised by the necessities of life and the maintenance of bodily needs. The private sphere is associated with labour—the kind of work that is required to sustain human life but does not necessarily contribute to the broader society in a direct, visible way. It is the realm of economic and personal necessity, where activities are focused on personal survival. In contrast, the public sphere is the realm of collective life and political action, where we come together to engage in dialogue, make collective decisions, and reveal

[2] Concepts in this subsection are adapted from Von Schomberg and Blok (2023).

ourselves to others through speech and action. The public sphere is where we can transcend our personal concerns and contribute to the common good. In this realm, actions and words gain their full significance as they are witnessed, debated, and remembered by others. The public sphere is essentially a space of appearance, where freedom and the potential for initiating change are realised (Arendt 1998).

In our reading of Arendt, the concept of work embodies a duality: it represents both the act of creating a 'worldly' object, like the construction of a table, and the object itself, such as the table. This object, in turn, serves as a mediator for all three categories of the vita activa. For instance, a table used for private tasks like book-keeping aligns with the definition of labour. Conversely, when used to construct something anew, it exemplifies work. Moreover, when it facilitates public engagements such as parliamentary discussions or legal proceedings, it becomes a venue for action. While private and public activities are primarily driven by labour and action, respectively, work serves as a conduit that supports both domains. This is also reflected in our everyday use of the term; we may work to earn a living, to contribute societally, and oftentimes for the sake of both (Morse and Weiss 1955).

Innovation, particularly in technologies like AI, can be understood as a form of work, as it creates an artificial environment distinct from nature. Our analysis of the duality of work allows us to conceptualise innovation with a similar duality. Just as work is both an activity and the durable worldly object resulting from this activity, innovation can refer to both a dynamic process and the static artefact produced by this process. For instance, we refer to an AI VA as an innovation, both as an artefact and the process leading to its creation. This dynamic, known as the ontogenetic process (Blok 2021), is where something new can be created and where action occurs. Thus, we argue that innovation not only enables action but also results from it. In other words, there is first an unpredictable innovation process that leads to the creation of an innovation artefact, which then enables the possibility of speech and action.

Much like Arendt's notion of work, the concept of innovation can serve both private and public interests. On the one hand, technologies like AI are largely driven by surveillance capitalism, operating on rule-following logic and efficient means-end patterns (Blok 2021). Arendt and the phenomenological tradition viewed this calculative logic as a technological threat, warning of the triumph of 'animal laborans' over 'zoon politikon' (Passerin 2019). On the other hand, history teaches us that technologies can also foster liberation and equality. For example, the washing machine reduced the time and effort required for laundry, alleviating the burden of domestic work and enabling women to pursue education and careers. This facilitated greater female participation in the workforce, promoting economic independence and changing societal norms (Green 2016). Based on this analysis, we propose a political concept of responsible innovation which is fundamentally oriented towards the public sphere. In this view, innovation facilitates both physical (or virtual) and symbolic spaces where citizens can speak and act freely, promoting a multitude of perspectives, values, and possibilities (Von Schomberg and Blok 2023). This, in turn, translates into a constructive ethics of AI, where we re-examine the human-technology relationship in favour of the public sphere, conditioned by plurality, rather than the private sphere, dominated by surveillance capitalism (see Fig. 16.2).

A constructive ethics of AI can be implemented both at the level of the artefact and the process. At the artefact level, we argue that AI systems should proactively promote plurality. For instance, providing an AI VA with a female voice to enable surveillance projects a singular worldview regarding the role of women in society. In line with a constructive ethics of AI, we must consider how AI systems can foster a more pluralistic worldview. One example moving in this direction is the creation of responsible and human-centric AI labs that integrate human and public values into AI systems (Van Veenstra et al. 2021). These labs implement features such as built-in 'contestability-by-design,' where AI systems are continuously refined based on their interactions with society. This requires a more iterative and dynamic approach, extending beyond the initial development phase. Therefore, these labs aim to foster 'in-situ' or laboratory-style collaboration, promoting a dynamic learning process crucial for the rapid evolution of AI technology (Van Veenstra et al. 2021). By doing so, it opens up possibilities for AI systems that enhance democratic practices, ultimately fostering a more participatory digital society where individuals can flourish.

At the process level, a constructive ethics of AI adopts a pluralistic and non-reductive approach to designing AI systems (Blok 2019). This approach is pluralistic because it extends stakeholder involvement beyond merely complementary differences to encompass the diverse values and interests of the broader public. It is non-reductive because it does not narrow this involvement to common stakes; instead, it allows individuals to express their own perspectives and judgements based on their unique interests and values (Van Huijstee et al. 2007). A notable

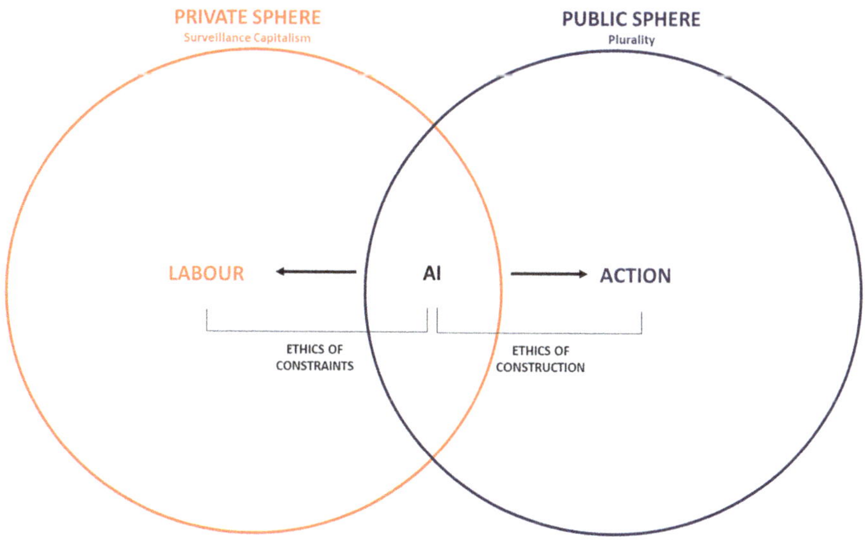

Fig. 16.2 A constructive ethics of AI

advancement in this direction was the EU-funded Horizon 2020 NewHoRRIzon initiative, which established 18 social labs. These labs brought together stakeholders from various sectors, including academia, business, non-university research institutes, research funding organisations, policymakers, civil society organisations, and the public (Blok and Von Schomberg 2022). These social labs served as collaborative spaces for co-creating customised pilot actions to promote responsible innovation. Their uniqueness lies in facilitating social experiments in a practical context, where a diverse group of actors can address challenges creatively, free from predefined project plans and deliverables. A key attribute of this approach is embracing uncertainty, allowing participants to explore uncharted territory without a fixed roadmap (Hassan 2014). This aligns with the constructive ethics of AI and the adoption of a political concept of responsible innovation, where outcomes are not predefined but are instead characterised by the Arendtian notion of the 'unexpected'. The social labs methodology offers an innovative and flexible approach to fostering constructive ethics of AI, promoting collaboration, and encouraging bold experimentation to tackle societal challenges (Timmermans et al. 2020).

4 Conclusion

In the age of digitalisation, the emergence of surveillance capitalism has profoundly reshaped our relationship with technology. While the discourse on AI ethics often centres around mitigating risks and constraining potential harms, it overlooks the deeper economic logic that underpins our interactions with technology. To this end, we argued that as our interactions with digital platforms and AI-driven systems become increasingly mediated by the logic of surveillance capitalism, we need to shift to a constructive ethics of AI that reclaims our relationship with technology in a way that promotes plurality, empowers citizens, and serves the public sphere. To build this constructive ethics of AI, we adopted a political concept of responsible innovation, inspired by the philosophy of Arendt. At the artefact level, this means AI systems should actualise speech and action, while at the process level, engagement with representative stakeholders should be extended to the direct involvement of citizens.

However, this chapter rests on an assumption that future research should address the belief that if AI serves the public sphere, it inherently serves the public good. While AI serving the public sphere focuses on facilitating speech and action, promoting democratic engagement, and fostering plurality, AI serving the public good addresses broader societal outcomes such as climate mitigation and public health. These two objectives may not always align. For instance, China has advanced technologies for the public good, like green innovations, while simultaneously employing mass surveillance and a top-down governance model that arguably stifles the public sphere. This dichotomy raises critical questions about the compatibility of these objectives. Can AI simultaneously serve the public sphere and the public good, or do these goals sometimes conflict?

One possible resolution is to link the public good with the concept of epistemic insufficiency (Blok and Lemmens 2015), suggesting that the inherent uncertainty of future challenges requires a pluralistic approach. This aligns with Arendt's advocacy for plurality, proposing that true public good can only be achieved through the empowerment of the public sphere (Arendt 1998). Thus, the underpinning proposition is that enhancing the public sphere is essential, as it is the means through which the public good can be effectively pursued. This perspective echoes the EU's view that science must be conducted with society to serve society (European Commission 2015). Even so, future research should explore this interplay further, investigating how AI systems and processes can be designed to address societal challenges while upholding democratic values and empowering citizens, ultimately fostering a more just and participatory digital future.

References

Abdul G (2023) Risk of extinction by AI should be global priority, say experts. The Guardian. https://www.theguardian.com/technology/2023/may/30/risk-of-extinction-by-ai-should-be-global-priority-say-tech-experts

Arendt H (1998) The human condition. University of Chicago Press

Bailey MA, Hopkins DJ, Rogers T (2016) Unresponsive and unpersuaded: the unintended consequences of a voter persuasion effort. Polit Behav 38(3):713–746

Batie S (2008) Wicked problems and applied economics. Am J Agric Econ 90(5):1176–1191

Blok V (2019) From participation to interruption: toward an ethics of stakeholder engagement, participation and partnership in corporate social responsibility and responsible innovation. In: Von Schomberg R, Hankins J (eds) International handbook on responsible innovation. Edward Elgar

Blok V (2021) What is innovation? Laying the ground for a philosophy of innovation. Techné: Res Philos Technol 25(1):72–96

Blok V, Lemmens P (2015) The emerging concept of responsible innovation. Three reasons why it is questionable and calls for a radical transformation of the concept of innovation. In: Koops B, van den Hoven J, Romijn H, Swierstra T, Oosterlaken I (eds) Responsible innovation 2: concepts, approaches and applications. Springer

Blok V, Von Schomberg L (2022) Introduction. In: Blok V (ed) Putting responsible research and innovation into practice. Open Resource

Brundage M, Guston D (2019) Understanding the movement(s) for responsible innovation. In: Von Schomberg R, Hankins J (eds) International handbook on responsible innovation. Edward Elgar

Bryson J (2019) The past decade and future of AI's impact on society. Towards a New Enlightenment? A transcendent decade. Turner

Bryson J, Crosby B, Stone M (2006) The design and implementation of cross-sector collaborations: propositions from the literature. Public Adm Rev 66(1):44–55

Centre for AI Safety (2023) Statement on AI risk. CAIS. https://www.safe.ai/work/statement-on-ai-risk#open-letter

Commission of the European Communities (2001) European Governance: a white paper. https://ec.europa.eu/commission/presscorner/detail/en/DOC_01_10.

European Commission (2015) Horizon 2020: Work programme 2016–2017: science with and for society. http://ec.europa.eu/research/participants/data/ref/h2020/wp/2016_2017/main/h2020-wp1617-swfs_en.pdf.

European Commission (2018), Mission-Oriented Research & Innovation in the European Union :A Problem Solving Approach to Fuel Innovation Led Growth, LU: Publications Office.

European Parliament (2024) EU AI Act: first regulation on artificial intelligence. https://www.europarl.europa.eu/pdfs/news/expert/2023/6/story/20230601STO93804/20230601STO93804_en.pdf.

Evers A, Nowotny H (1987) Uber den Umgang mit Unicherheit. Suhrkamp Verlag

Gibney E (2018) The scant science behind Cambridge Analytica's controversial marketing techniques. Nature

Green C (2016) Agitated to clean: how the washing machine changed life for the American woman. McNair Scholars Res J 12(10):14–26

Hassan Z (2014) The social labs revolution: a new approach to solving our most complex challenges. Berrett-Koehler Publishers

Heidegger M (1977) The question concerning technology, and other essays. Harper and Row

Hern A (2018) Cambridge Analytica: how did it turn clicks into votes? The Guardian. https://www.theguardian.com/news/2018/may/06/cambridge-analytica-how-turn-clicks-into-votes-christopher-wylie

Hersh ED, Schaffner BF (2013) Targeted campaign appeals and the value of ambiguity. J Polit 75(2):520–525

Hill K (2012) How target figured out a teen girl was pregnant before her father did. Forbes. https://www.forbes.com/sites/kashmirhill/2012/02/16/how-target-figured-out-a-teen-girl-was-pregnant-before-her-father-did

Kevles D (1995) The physicists: the history of a scientific community in Modern America. Harvard University Press

Kosinski M, Stillwell D, Graepel T (2013) Private traits and attributes are predictable from digital records of human behavior. Proc Natl Acad Sci 110(15):5802–5805

Kreuter M, De Rosa C, Howze E, Baldwin G (2004) Understanding wicked problems: a key to advancing environmental health promotion. Health Educ Behav 31(4):441–454

Lammi M, Pantzar M (2019) The data economy: how technological change has altered the role of the citizen-consumer. Technol Soc 59:101157

Makridakis S (2017) The forthcoming Artificial Intelligence (AI) revolution: its impact on society and firms. Futures 90:46–60

Marwick AE, Boyd D (2014) Networked privacy: how teenagers negotiate context in social media. New Media Soc 16(7):1051–1067

Morozov E (2019) Capitalism's new clothes. The Baffler. https://thebaffler.com/latest/capitalisms-new-clothes-morozov

Morse NC, Weiss RS (1955) The function and meaning of work and the job. Am Sociol Rev 20(2):191

Naughton J (2019) The goal is to automate us: Welcome to the age of surveillance capitalism. The Guardian. https://www.theguardian.com/technology/2019/jan/20/shoshana-zuboff-age-of-surveillance-capitalism-google-facebook

Nickerson DW, Rogers T (2014) Political campaigns and big data. J Econ Perspect 28(2):51–74

Owen R, Pansera M (2019) Responsible innovation: process and politics. In: Von Schomberg R, Hankins J (eds) International handbook on responsible innovation. Edward Elgar

Owen R, Stilgoe J, Macnaghten P, Gorman M, Fisher E, Guston D (2013) A framework for responsible innovation. In: Owen R, Bessant J, Heintz M (eds) Responsible innovation. Wiley

Pamuru V, Khern-am-nuai W, Kannan K (2021) The impact of an augmented-reality game on local businesses: a study of pokémon go on restaurants. Inf Syst Res 32(3):950–966

Passerin M (2019) Hannah Arendt. In: Zalta EN (ed) The Stanford Encyclopedia of Philosophy. Stanford University. https://plato.stanford.edu/archives/fall2019/entries/arendt/

Păvăloaia V-D, Necula S-C (2023) Artificial intelligence as a disruptive technology—A systematic literature review. Electronics 12(5):1102

Penttilä L (2024) On with critique! The necessity of critique in addressing the political deficits of responsible innovation. J Responsible Innov 11(1)

Perrigo B (2024) U. S. Must act quickly to avoid risks from AI, report says. TIME. https://time.com/6898967/ai-extinction-national-security-risks-report/.

Reijers W (2020) Responsible innovation between virtue and governance: revisiting Arendt's notion of work as action. J Responsible Innov 7(3):471–489
Rittel H, Webber M (1973) Dilemmas in a general theory of planning. Policy Sci 4(2):155–169
Santanen E (2020) Weaponizing personal data to undermine democracy. CrossCurrents 70(2):107–130
Stiegler B (1998) Technics and time. Stanford University Press
Tangermann V (2024) Researcher estimates 99.9 percent chance AI will destroy humankind. https://futurism.com/the-byte/researcher-99-percent-chance-ai-destroy-humankind.
Timmermans J, Blok V, Braun R, Wesselink R, Nielsen RØ (2020) Social labs as an inclusive methodology to implement and study social change: the case of responsible research and innovation. J Responsible Innov 7(3):410–426
Vallance C (2023) Artificial intelligence could lead to extinction, experts warn. https://www.bbc.co.uk/news/uk-65746524.
Van De Poel I (2013) Translating values into design requirements. In: Michelfelder DP, McCarthy N, Goldberg DE (eds) Philosophy and engineering: reflections on practice, principles and process. Springer
Van Huijstee MM, Francken M, Leroy P (2007) Partnerships for sustainable development: a review of current literature. Environ Sci 4(2):75–89
Van Oudheusden M (2014) Where are the politics in responsible innovation? European governance, technology assessments, and beyond. J Responsible Innov 1(1):67–86
Van Veenstra AF, van Zoonen EA, Helberger N (2021) ELSA labs for human centric innovation in AI. https://nlaic.com/wp-content/uploads/2022/02/ELSA-Labs-for-Human-Centric-Innovation-in-AI.pdf.
Vincent, B. (2023). Philosophy of Technology in the Digital Age: The datafication of the World, the homo virtualis, and the capacity of technological innovations to set the World free. Available at: https://philpapers.org/archive/VINPOT.pdf
Von Schomberg L, Blok V (2021) Technology in the age of innovation: responsible innovation as a new subdomain within the philosophy of technology. Phil Technol 34(2):309–323
Von Schomberg L, Blok V (2023) It takes two to tango: toward a political concept of responsible innovation. J Responsible Innov 10(1):2264616
Von Schomberg L, Von Schomberg R (2023) Responsible research and innovation as a social innovation. In: Howaldt J, Kaletka C (eds) Encyclopedia of social innovation. Edward Elgar
Von Schomberg R (2013) A vision of responsible research and innovation. In: Owen R, Bessant J, Heintz M (eds) Responsible innovation. Wiley
Von Schomberg R (2019) Why responsible innovation? In: Von Schomberg R, Hankins J (eds) International handbook on responsible innovation. Edward Elgar
Woods HS (2018) Asking more of Siri and Alexa: feminine persona in service of surveillance capitalism. Crit Stud Media Commun 35(4):334–349
Zuboff S (2019) The age of surveillance capitalism: the fight for a human future at the new frontier of power. PublicAffairs

Lucien von Schomberg is Senior Lecturer in Creativity and Innovation at the University of Greenwich. Additionally, he serves as the Academic Portfolio Lead in Entrepreneurship, Innovation, and Sustainability, and is Programme Director for the BA in Entrepreneurship and Innovation. As an internationally recognised scholar in responsible innovation, von Schomberg leads a wide range of research initiatives and has played a key role in EU projects with a cumulative funding of £12 million. Von Schomberg is an editorial member at multiple journals and his work has been published in both philosophy and interdisciplinary journals. Outside academia, von Schomberg works as an independent consulting to drive innovation and ethical practices across various sectors.

The Wellbeing Compass: Navigating Towards a Humanity-Centered Tech Future

17

Iliana Grosse-Buening and Alina Kukarina

Abstract

In an age where new technologies impact us with unprecedented speed and magnitude, and where digital media form an integral and increasingly prominent part of our daily lives, the effect on individual and collective welfare cannot be an afterthought. This chapter introduces the *Wellbeing Compass* and the critical role of Digital Wellbeing in the discourse on AI ethics, moving beyond abstract ethical principles to address a more comprehensive spectrum of responsibilities faced by technology developers and economic actors in a society increasingly mediated by technology. Drawing from interdisciplinary research in AI ethics, Positive Psychology, and Digital Wellbeing, this chapter proposes a procedural approach to integrating wellbeing considerations throughout the entire lifecycle of technological development and innovation. We will demonstrate how grounding the discussion of AI ethics in the tangible domain of Digital Wellbeing can advance a more comprehensive, sustainable, and humanity-centered approach to technological development. This shift has the potential not only to bridge the current gap between principles and practice but also to present actionable starting points for creating technologies that actively benefit humanity and contribute to individual and collective welfare.

I. Grosse-Buening (✉) · A. Kukarina
Deeply Human Innovation, London, United Kingdom
e-mail: iliana@deeplyhuman.io; alina@deeplyhuman.io

C. H. Hoffmann, D. Bansal (eds.), *AI Ethics in Practice*, Integrated Science 35,
https://doi.org/10.1007/978-3-031-87023-1_17

1 Introduction

Curing the negatives does not produce the positives. (Martin Seligman, 2006)

At the turn of the twenty-first century, a radical shift happened in the field of Psychology. In his 1998 presidential address, psychologist and president of the American Psychological Association, Martin E. P. Seligman observed that psychology had "moved too far away from its original roots, which were to make the lives of all people more fulfilling and productive, and too much towards the important, but not all-important, area of curing mental illness." Psychologists, Seligman argued, had forgotten their larger mission: that of making the lives of all people better.[1]

Two decades later, we find ourselves at a similar crossroads. The last 20 years have seen unprecedented changes in our modes of living, working, and connecting, driven by the rapid digitalization of virtually every aspect of our lives. This evolution has undeniably made our lives more productive and in many ways, more fulfilling. We have seen progress in various areas of human development that has been enabled by technology (Vinuesa et al. 2020). However, the rise of ubiquitous computing (wearables and smartphones) and the growing influence and implications of emerging technologies like AI for our daily lives has also uncovered a complex set of challenges. Amid this context, a series of fundamental questions arises: How can we ensure that technological progress benefits humanity, rather than doing the opposite? How can we foster innovation that protects and strengthens, rather than erodes, the systems and structures that hold our communities, economies, and societies together? And how can we ensure that the companies that increasingly mediate fundamental aspects of our daily lives do so responsibly?

Orienting values in tech development have increasingly focused on technical novelty, scalability, and engagement, often at the expense of considering the broader implications and impact of these choices on individual and collective welfare (Thomas et al. 2020). In regulatory environments, a focus on harm prevention and AI risk classification has had "the policy and corporate worlds primarily focused on what *shouldn't* happen for society, versus what *needs* to happen to create our most purpose-driven, positive future" (Spiekermann 2021). Although providing standards and identifying undesirable outcomes, this approach fails to articulate what a desirable future looks like, nor does it equip us with the necessary tools and strategies to get there.

This chapter proposes the *Wellbeing Compass* as a shift beyond risk mitigation towards actively fostering human welfare, bridging the gap between compliance-focused approaches (what *shouldn't* happen for society) and proactive strategies for human flourishing ("what *needs* to happen"). Analogous to Positive Psychology's

[1] His observations led to the formation of the field of Positive Psychology which is the scientific study of human flourishing, and an applied approach to optimal functioning. It has also been defined as the study of the strengths and virtues that enable individuals, communities, and organizations to thrive (Gable and Haidt 2005; Sheldon and King 2001).

focus on actively promoting human potential over mitigating ill-being, we will show how the concept of Digital Wellbeing can offer a more holistic, comprehensive assessment of technology's impact and a more proactive, human-centered approach to innovation,[2] strengthening both individuals and society as a whole.

1.1 Methodologies and Objectives

Exploring the existing literature in the field of AI ethics and Digital Wellbeing through a practitioner's lens, the objectives of this chapter are threefold:

1. To introduce the *Wellbeing Compass* as a proactive, procedural framework for human-centered technical development and innovation.
2. To present the *Wellbeing Compass* as a desirable, necessary step towards a more human-centered and responsible innovation ecosystem.
3. To explore the implications and opportunities of this approach for responsible tech development, proposing starting points for entrepreneurs and technologists to adopt "Wellbeing" as a guiding value and driver of meaningful innovation.

Through a series of interviews with entrepreneurs, regulators, and technologists, as well as synthesizing insights from ancient and modern philosophers, policymakers, and economists, this chapter seeks to promote an interdisciplinary and holistic approach.

By prioritizing actionability over theoretical discourse and analysis, process over predetermined outcomes, we aim to illuminate actionable pathways for the next generation of intra- and entrepreneurs and offer a starting point for new ways to think about what truly constitutes progress, reframing humanity-centered values as drivers rather than constraints on innovation. This approach, as we will show, has the potential not only to lead to innovation that actively promotes human flourishing, but also to inspire more sustainable business models, build trust in digital ecosystems and its stakeholders, and ensure better preparedness for constantly evolving regulatory landscapes.

2 "Moving slower and not breaking things": The Need for a New Compass

The digital transformation of the past few decades has impacted virtually every aspect of our lives, profoundly altering the ways we live, work, and connect as individuals, organizations, and societies. Recognizing this, the OECD, in its "Going Digital" Measurement Roadmap, emphasized the critical need to measure and

[2] Importantly, this shift is proposed as a complement—rather than a substitute—to regulatory approaches, which the field of Digital Wellbeing already acknowledges as a crucial component of responsible tech development (Floridi, Dennis).

understand these impacts to ensure a positive and inclusive digital economy and society (OECD 2022).

2.1 Innovation With(out) Progress

While increased digitalization and accessibility offer us unprecedented opportunities and conveniences, they have also come with considerable costs, the effects being wide-ranging, interconnected, and often contradictory. Despite limitless opportunities to connect socially and professionally, we are facing increased rates of anxiety and depression, particularly among younger generations (Twenge 2019), rising feelings of loneliness and social isolation (Primack et al. 2017), and a decline in interpersonal skills (Turkle 2015). Digital notifications and constant availability and access to limitless information have been linked to a reduction in our attention spans and a loss in productivity (Mark et al. 2008). Misinformation and online echo chambers have created an increasing public divide and fueled polarization and radicalism (Geschke et al. 2018).

While business practices optimized for engagement (Eyal 2014), an industry culture prioritizing rapid growth and a "move fast and break things" (Taplin 2017) mentality have contributed to the situation, other factors have equally played a role. These include often unpredictable consequences of design choices (Kramer et al. 2014; Yang et al. 2018), network effects amplifying both positive and negative outcomes, and the intrinsic complexity of large-scale technological systems (Zuboff 2019). Furthermore, the speed at which technology is developing and the growth and democratization of content creation (Kaplan 2010) have arguably outpaced our capacity for cognitive and social adaptation (Carr 2011). The scenario is further complicated by a general lack of understanding of how to measure the complex interplay of these factors on long-term wellbeing, especially in light of fast-changing digital environments (Lomas et al. 2023; Vanden Abeele 2021).

2.2 Guiding Values and Where to Find Them

The increasing body of research on the impact of digital platforms and media demonstrates not only the complex and multifaceted relationship between technology and human welfare, but also the need for a more comprehensive assessment of technology's impact and, consequently, approach to technical development (Liscio et al. 2023). We need a new guiding value, since our prior emphasis on user engagement metrics, growth, and technical capabilities—while "innovative"—has frequently ignored the broader effects on individual wellbeing and social resilience.

In the area of economics, this shift has already started. Recognizing that nineteenth- and twentieth-century economic principles may no longer be accurate to measure progress in a meaningful way (Stiglitz et al. 2008), alternative indices to GDP like the HDI (Human Development Index), GNH (Gross National Happiness), and the IWI (Inclusive Wealth Index) have emerged to provide a more holistic, comprehensive picture of an economy's health. Nussbaum and Sen (1993) have proposed the *Capabilities approach* which focuses on what people are "actually able to do and to be" (Robeyns 2005) and an economy's ability to remove obstacles towards this end. In her TED talk "A healthy economy should be designed to thrive, not grow," Oxford Economist Kate Raworth called on her audience to "reimagine the shape of progress" (2018) arguing against the traditional view of progress as an ever-ascending linear trajectory. Concepts like Raworth's "Doughnut Economics," Nussbaum and Sen's *Capabilities approach*, and frameworks such as the Circular Economy, and the United Nations' Sustainable Development Goals encourage us to envision alternative pathways for economic development and adopt a more holistic view of what constitutes progress. Together, these models and their associated measures aim to create (economic) systems that are not just sustainable, but also socially valuable, inclusive, and equitable. This represents a shift from traditional economic thinking towards a more holistic approach where a more diverse set of indicators, including human welfare and environmental sustainability play an equally important role as traditional economic indicators such as GDP.

Similarly, to leverage the full potential of emerging technologies such as AI, we need to acknowledge the holistic, sociocultural nature of digital technologies and platforms. We need a shift in focus—to look beyond the prevention of harm to the proactive promotion of positive outcomes for society, from what we "*shouldn't* do" to what we "*need* to do." The field of Digital Wellbeing, with its focus on protecting and enhancing the quality of life of individuals and communities in their interaction with digital technologies can make a valuable contribution to this.

2.3 Defining Digital Wellbeing

Digital Wellbeing describes "the impact of digital technologies on well-being" (Floridi and Burr 2023). While there are many definitions of Digital Wellbeing, Floridi and Burr's is especially suitable for our purposes, as it acknowledges the dual nature of digital interactions—which can be both positive and negative—highlighting the importance of intentionality and mindfulness in design, deployment, and use. More importantly, it leaves "wellbeing" open. While some might see this ambiguity as an obstacle to incorporating wellbeing considerations into tech development, this chapter advocates for this as a strength, as it allows for a more flexible interpretation and application across diverse contexts.

2.3.1 Theoretical Foundations

In recent decades, efforts to study, understand, and create solutions to address Digital Wellbeing have surfaced across various fronts. As a discipline, Digital Wellbeing has been inspired by different fields and theories, each providing valuable insights into what might prevent or promote human flourishing in the context of digital environments. These include:

- *Objective List Theories*: Proposing a multitude of basic goods that benefit people (Nussbaum 1992; Sen 1985)
- *Hedonic Theories*: Focused on maximizing pleasure and minimizing pain (Floridi and Burr 2020)
- *Desire-Fulfillment Theories*: Proposing that wellbeing is about getting what you want (Griffin 1986)
- *Self-Determination Theory*: Emphasizing the importance of concepts such as autonomy, competence, and relatedness (Peters et al. 2018; Bingley et al. 2023)

These and other frameworks have not just given us the vocabulary to evaluate the impact of digital technologies on human welfare, but they have and continue to provide technologists and designers with starting points for reimagining the shape and purpose of digital experiences (Peters et al. 2018).

2.3.2 Current Initiatives and Approaches

Over the last decade, several approaches and frameworks have emerged that treat "Wellbeing" as a guiding value in tech development:

- "Positive AI" (Lomas et al. 2023) advocates for the development of AI with "Wellbeing" as an orienting value.
- "Positive Design" (Desmet and Pohlmeyer 2013) proposes a design framework to promote human flourishing through pleasure, personal significance and virtue.
- "Positive Computing" (Calvo and Peters 2014), categorizes the ways in which technologies can promote wellbeing.
- "Wellbeing-Supportive Design" (Peters et al. 2018) integrates these considerations directly into the design process.
- The "Six spheres of technology experience" framework (Peters et al. 2018) has broadened our understanding of the different ways in which technology impacts us at different touchpoints, such as the interface, task, behavior, life, etc.
- "Value-sensitive design" (Davis and Nathan 2014) emphasizes that each design choice should be based on values.

At the same time, a growing number of organizations and startups have started to address a wide variety of Digital Wellbeing concerns. These encompass topics such as screen time management, mindful technology use, digital literacy, balancing online and offline activities, and productivity management tools. Organizations such as All Tech Is Human (2022), the Center for Humane Technologies (2021), and companies like Google (2020) have contributed to the field with frameworks and guidelines for practitioners to promote more human-centric design and tech development.

3 The Wellbeing Compass: A Framework for a Humanity-Centric Future

> Sustainable solutions based on innovation can create a more resilient world only if that innovation is focused on the health and well-being of its inhabitants. And it is at that point—where technology and human needs intersect—that we will find meaningful innovation. (Frans van Houten, Former CEO of Philipps)

The *Wellbeing Compass* builds on Lomas et al.'s (2023) suggestion for an expanded perspective that considers "Wellbeing" not just as an orienting value for design, but as a guiding principle for tech development and innovation as a whole. The *Wellbeing Compass* advocates for a procedural notion of wellbeing. Rather than prescribing a fixed notion of "Wellbeing," it offers a framework for systematically considering and embedding wellbeing considerations into every aspect of the product lifecycle, from ideation to launch and beyond. This procedural approach extends beyond the ideation phase, recognizing not only the sociocultural nature of technology, but also that wellbeing can express differently in different settings and that this requires a more nuanced approach.

The *Wellbeing Compass* encompasses four key principles:

First, is moving from a reactive to a *proactive approach*. This means treating technology's impact on welfare as a fore- and not an afterthought and integrating considerations about the social impact of technologies into the very fabric of technological innovation, from initial concept to final product, from the choice of business model to decisions on which data to collect and formulation of key performance indicators. Only by doing so, we are on the surest path to create technologies that are inherently aligned with human values and societal wellbeing. This intent needs to stand at the beginning of every process.

The next is a *purpose-driven approach*. This involves looking at values and ethics and considering the broader, medium, and long-term effects of technology on individuals, communities, and society as a whole. This will foster innovation that is meaningful and sustainable, both for humanity and for the planet.

A *humanity-centered approach* challenges technologists, entrepreneurs, and innovators to consider how technology impacts human lives. The *Wellbeing Compass* draws on design principles like empathy and systemic thinking as well as the participatory, interdisciplinary nature of humanity-centered design methodologies.

The final principle is an *adaptive approach*. This goes beyond the idea of "iteration" promoted by design-thinking and agile approaches, but encompasses the commitment to adapt any learnings generated from insights gained in iterative development. It also encompasses community engagement as well as a commitment to keep refining and reevaluating any technological outcome according to the principles proposed.

3.1 Proactive Approach

A *Wellbeing Compass* only makes sense when there is a willingness to put Wellbeing at the core of a product, or even business. The mindset needs to move away from doing whatever is technically feasible within the realm of the legally allowed towards an approach of actively promoting quality of life at both the individual and societal level. This mindset shift is what we call the proactive approach.

The transformative potential of technology, the information imbalance between provider and user, and the sensitivity of the data processed have led to various regulatory interventions. Spiekermann (2021) notes that technicologists often only address ethical concerns reactively—for example, when confronted with unavoidable issues such as security gaps or regulatory changes like the EU's General Data Protection Regulation—rather than proactively. Arguably, regulations like the European AI Act have provided an important foundation to ensure responsible tech development and deployment. These regulatory frameworks have been essential for establishing baseline standards, regulating high-risk AI and protecting user's fundamental rights (European Parliament 2023). However, confusion about how to operationalize ethical principles (Morley et al. 2020), worries about the bureaucratic burden on companies—especially smaller ones—and concerns about the effect of regulation on innovation have revealed critical gaps that need filling.

Reactive approaches that only recognize the effect of a product on wellbeing according to regulations create the danger of developing a "checkbox" mentality (Mittelstadt 2019) where we prioritize meeting minimum standards over genuine engagement with the ethical implications of the technologies that we are developing. Without contextualization, standards and high-level principles that can be applied across a wide range of applications also cannot account for the full spectrum of ways in which a technology affects a diverse group of stakeholders, nor will it lead to tools and methodologies that operationalize ethical considerations. An overly principled approach might even lead to the illusion of progress without pursuing robust regulation and accountability (Mittelstadt 2019).

Regulatory environments are slow to keep up with the pace and rapid adoption of new technologies. Proposed by the European Commission on 21 April 2021, it took nearly 3 years to pass the AI Act on 13 March 2024 (European Parliament 2023). In the meantime, OpenAI released ChatGPT and reached more than 100 million users in less than 2 months after its release in November 2022 (Hu 2023). If companies rely on regulations only, they may not recognize violations of their audience's wellbeing until after the fact.

While "not causing harm" must be seen as a critical foundation, it cannot be seen as the ultimate goal if we want to create technologies that provide true social value. To create technologies with a positive impact, we need to be proactive instead of reactive. We need a shift in focus from prevention to promotion—to look beyond the prevention of harm to the proactive promotion of positive outcomes for society, from what we "*shouldn't* do" to what we "*need* to do."

3.2 Purpose-Driven Approach

The growing recognition of digital technologies "as drivers of change not just in human material circumstances, but also in human values and organizational systems that support wellbeing" (Gluckman and Allen 2018), highlights the need for a more nuanced, context-specific approach that regulation alone cannot provide. We call this the purpose-driven approach.

At its core, a purpose-driven approach integrates concepts of wellbeing—such as personal significance, meaning, virtue, and value alignment (Desmet and Pohlmeyer 2013)—into the very processes and mindset of creating technological products. It extends beyond meeting regulatory requirements to actively creating value for all stakeholders, including end users, employees, communities, and the environment (Freeman et al. 2010). This approach also encourages companies to align their strategy and mission statement with broader societal goals, such as the UN's Sustainable Development Goals (Scheyvens et al. 2016).

A company aware of its core values and the values that are generally considered relevant in the context of creating new technologies can prioritize its efforts in a much leaner and more strategic way. By embedding purpose and values into the innovation process, companies can drive meaningful change and address complex societal challenges through their core business activities. As creating value definitions is not an approach that every company can or should undertake on their own, international organizations have worked on providing an overview of agreed-upon values that may be used to derive development principles (OECD 2024).

Ultimately, integrating wellbeing considerations from the outset does not just lead to a richer and more valuable digital experience, but it fundamentally changes the way we design digital products, placing real empathy at the very core of the process.

3.3 Humanity-Centric Approach

While regulatory frameworks such as the AI Act have attempted to anticipate potential risks in connection to AI development and deployment—especially existential risk as a result of AGI (Artificial General Intelligence)—many consequences remain unpredictable (Helbing 2013). This uncertainty is reflected in the polarized public discourse on AI, ranging from doomsday scenarios to utopian narratives (Cave and Dihal 2018). What these contrasting perspectives point to is the urgent need for an inclusive, flexible, and adaptable approach to tech development that considers a range of stakeholders (Floridi et al.2018) as well as education and empowerment of the public to participate in the discourse.

Central to the humanity-centric approach is the cultivation of deep empathy (Wright et al. 2008; Mattelmäki et al. 2014). Tech companies like to focus on individuals in their role as users. Moving forward, we need to broaden our perspective and look at the individual as a whole, as a part of a community, of an entire ecosystem of people, all living things, and their physical environment (Norman 2023).

Looking beyond a "user" into a complete ecosystem allows us to discover cause-and-effect chains that we may not have discovered with a narrow lens (Norman 2023). Acknowledging the psychological and emotional effects of their choices, rather than just focusing on "ease of use" and functionality, designers, engineers, and entrepreneurs are encouraged to think about the broader effect of the use of their digital products on peoples' lives. This will not just enhance user experience in the short run, but, in the long run, could even mitigate the risk of user attrition when users start noticing the adverse effects of their interactions with a digital application (Harness et al. 2022).

Taking a long-term view on ecosystems and examining potential effects of design choices is a large part of humanity-centric design, broadening the scope of user-centered design (Norman 2023). In doing so, we might mitigate inherent risks of disruptive innovation before they become a reality.

3.4 Adaptive Approach

Development is often based on assumptions (Young et al. 2018). Especially in a field as broad and novel as Digital Wellbeing, we may not always have the knowledge that we would need to accurately predict the impact of technology on Wellbeing. To make sure that development is leading to technologies in line with our values, and to mitigate the risk of unforeseen consequences, we need to continually adapt and refine. From assumptions to proposed designs, from implicit knowledge to business models, we need to ensure technology truly meets the concerns of the people and ecosystem for whom they are intended. This goes beyond an agile, iterative development process with user feedback features.

Asking questions and collecting feedback is only impactful when the information gathered is actually processed and the result is adapted. The final principle advocates for the need to respond to new learnings, to new participants, and be willing to revisit and evaluate assumptions, products, and ultimately, even business models with this new information. The development of a shared language around AI and wellbeing is an essential step (Thomas and McDonagh 2013), as the traditional discourse on AI ethics often relies on abstract terms like "algorithmic fairness", and "bias," while privacy and cookie policies often use complicated technical and legal jargon that many find difficult to understand or engage with (Auxier et al. 2019).

Digital Wellbeing offers a more relatable vocabulary, enabling users to more naturally express how technology impacts their mental health, social relationships, and personal growth. In allowing for a more intuitive engagement with ethical considerations in technology, considerations around "Wellbeing" promote increased participation and a sense of responsibility and involvement in the development of digital technologies. This approach also has the potential to bridge the gap between developers and users, promoting a more inclusive discourse on and development of digital technologies that affect our daily lives.

4 Operationalizing (Digital) Wellbeing

Businesses can significantly shape how technology integrates with and impacts our daily lives, highlighting their responsibility but also their potential to guide technological development in ways that promote human welfare and social resilience. While the scope of this chapter doesn't allow for a full roadmap to operationalizing the *Wellbeing Compass*, the following serve as starting points for future intra- and entrepreneurs as well as anyone who is involved in development processes to leverage the above-mentioned principles not only within their development processes, but in their strategic work as well. The authors acknowledge that further experimentation, fine-tuning, and collaboration will be needed to optimize the following guidelines.

Calvo and Peters (2014), identify two strategies for integrating Wellbeing considerations into the tech development process:

- Active integration: The development of digital technologies that are designed to support wellbeing in an application that has an overall different goal (e.g., a productivity app that also sends users reminders to take breaks, and offers advice on how to maintain a healthy work-life balance).
- Dedicated integration: Technologies that are purposefully built for and dedicated to fostering wellbeing and human potential in some way (e.g., a meditation app that offers guided meditation sessions and personalized wellbeing recommendations).

4.1 Development

The *Wellbeing Compass* is intended as a versatile approach that can be used across industries and product types. This approach builds on standards like the IEEE7000 (2021) which have recognized both the need for principles that can be operationalized ("methodology" rather than "morality"), as well as the fact that ethical AI is not just about physical, but also value harms (Spiekermann 2022) that need to be considered and accounted for.

Operationalizing Digital Wellbeing can happen at various stages of the development process and in any type of development or design framework. It might be as simple as taking the four dimensions outlined in the *Wellbeing Compass* and evaluating them in the context of any established business or development event within an organization. The continuous evaluation of the development process according to the framework of the *Wellbeing Compass* allows for clarity on the current course and adjustments within the product development journey.

4.1.1 Design Processes

Many companies have introduced and refined structured ideation processes (Khalifeh 2020). These include empathy mapping, persona creation, design thinking, design sprints, among others. Any of these processes can be reimagined and, as we argue, improved, by using the four pillars of the *Wellbeing Compass*. Adapting a method widely used in the design thinking process (How might we…), teams could ask questions such as:

- *How might we be proactive regarding ethical concerns in innovation?*
- *How might we serve our purpose in the long term?*
- *How might we influence individuals, communities, and society positively?*
- *How might we emphasize learning in our process?*

And ultimately, "How might we contribute to Digital Wellbeing?" Some may argue that some of these aspects are already captured in the "empathy" part of many of the used frameworks. However, this aspect is often narrowed towards a consumer- and user-focused view, looking at individuals who are using digital media (Gasson, S. 2003). One of the key challenges in this phase is to broaden the view again and look at not only individuals in various aspects of their lives, but as a part of different ecosystems.

4.1.2 Agile Events

Both software development companies and digitally enabled non-technological businesses have recognized the value of short development cycles and receiving feedback on developed features fast, both from internal stakeholders and external users (Chaudhary et al. 2017). This has led to an agile transformation in many sectors and companies of all sizes (Digital AI 2023). Regardless of the specific agile framework used, events such as Reviews and Retrospectives have often been implemented to showcase development results and to reflect on the development process (Lehtinen et al. 2017). This integration can:

- Foster proactivity in the team's mindset
- Reinforce the underlying value systems
- Reevaluate the impact on humanity and its ecosystems
- Facilitate adaptation to new learnings

This approach encourages development teams to think outside their bubble of technological improvement and consider the wider impact of their innovations in a guided way (Motingoe and Langerman 2019). We are proposing an approach that first establishes guiding values to inform a strategy for Wellbeing-centered development, including ethical acceptance criteria and ethical retrospectives (Fig. 17.1). This process and its outcomes are unique to each business that undertakes it and must be revisited regularly to account for developments in economics, technology, and the business's socioeconomic impact.

4.1.3 Waterfall Development

While agile methodologies have seen widespread adoption, their implementation is still in its early stages or not feasible in some industries and business types. In these cases, more traditional methodologies such as Waterfall and V-model development persist. Where this is the case, it is common procedure to define clear

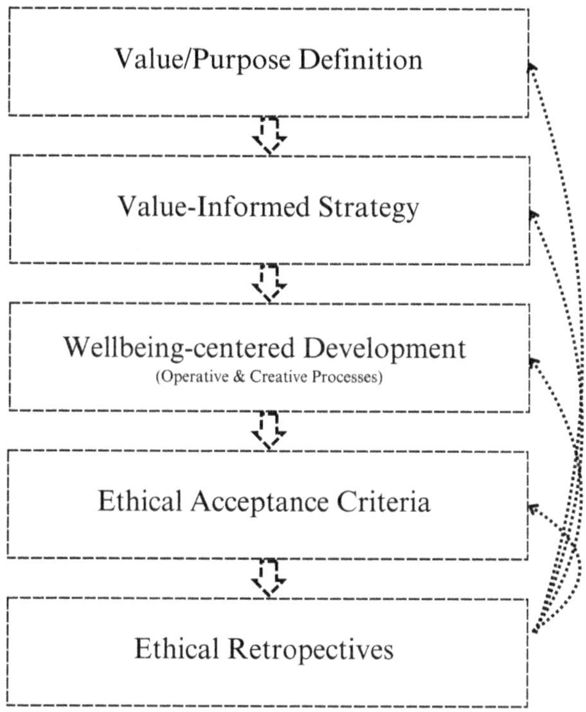

Fig. 17.1 Wellbeing Compass in development and operations

process phases and related process gates. These stages are already used to review risks, product features, and other evaluations, and can similarly be applied to reflections on the *Wellbeing Compass* without introducing significant overhead.

4.2 Business Strategy

Established organizations can leverage existing innovation frameworks not only in their development process. We argue that the principles of the *Wellbeing Compass* should be integrated into an organization's core business strategy. While not exhaustive, the following serves as a starting point for established organizations to rethink existing operational processes and align their business strategy with a broader set of social and environmental values.

Before any value alignment can take place, however, values need to be defined and specified within the organization. While the *Wellbeing Compass* provides general guidelines for alignment and this chapter lists sources for values in accordance with Wellbeing, context-specific work needs to take place in any organization to recognize and vocalize the values prevalent. Even if such efforts have already been undertaken, regular evaluation needs to take place.

4.2.1 Corporate Strategy and Mission

To sustainably and effectively integrate wellbeing considerations into an organization's processes, it is essential to embed them into the organization's culture and mission statement alongside other business objectives. Clear communication from leadership that wellbeing is part of the strategy is needed to give it visibility at a high level and allow it to be integrated as part of any subsequent action derived from the strategy. This should ensure that the business model itself aligns with and supports wellbeing goals.

4.2.2 Team and Personal Goals

As the business strategy is implemented in operational units, team goals and individual goals must be aligned with it (Mascareño et al. 2020). At every level within a company, there should be clarity on the connection between operational activities and business goals. In an ideal scenario, every team member would have a clear vision of their contribution. At the same time, teams cannot successfully work on wellbeing goals, if their own wellbeing is not taken into account (Wright and Cropanzano 2000). Team leaders need to recognize this and integrate personal wellbeing of their employees as part of their leadership goals. Ultimately, wellbeing within a company will always encompass both internal and external stakeholders.

4.2.3 Specialized Teams

Operationalizing the *Wellbeing Compass* within an existing organization can take various forms. One approach might be to integrate it into corporate social responsibility (CSR) initiatives, which often already address ecological considerations and employee health. While this could offer a natural home for the *Wellbeing Compass* there's a risk that Digital Wellbeing might become disconnected from the company's core business or get lost among other CSR topics.

Alternatively, companies could establish internal ethics committees. These committees, usually made up of a diverse group of experts, review initiatives according to their ethical acceptability (Moore and Donnelly 2018). Mehta et al. (2023) emphasize the importance of diversity to ensure a comprehensiveness in the committee's work. Similar standards should be applied for Wellbeing assessment.

4.3 Key Wellbeing Indicators

> If viewers are watching more YouTube, it signals to us that they're happier with the content they've found. It means that creators are attracting more engaged audiences. It also opens up more opportunities to generate revenue for our partners. (Meyerson 2012)

The need for new metrics that are suitable for the rapidly changing digital landscape has been recognized on numerous occasions (Vanden Abeele 2021; Hatem & Ker 2021). Many of the current metrics used in tech development and AI are easy-to-collect, but incomplete, short-termist and not representative for the true experience users are having engaging with the technology (Thomas et al. 2020). "Any metric is just a proxy for what you really care about," observes Thomas et al. (2020), offering an important insight into the limitations of proxies. When applied to the prevalent use of engagement metrics, and taking it to their literal extreme, this would imply that the goal is to spend as much time as possible on digital devices.

To assess the wellbeing impact of a product, and to be able to continuously reevaluate development according to the *Wellbeing Compass*, qualitative descriptions will not be sufficient. Traditional wellbeing assessments may be unsuitable, as aiming for consistency over time may be incompatible with rapidly changing technologies such as social media and AI. As we are moving away from productivity and performance, we need to create a holistic set of "Key Wellbeing Indicators" that measure the impact on wellbeing alongside traditional metrics. These measurements will ultimately inform future product and business strategy. What this calls for is a context-specific approach to both human-centered design and development, one that:

- Engages a range of stakeholders in the process of defining and evaluating metrics (Morley et al. 2021; Spiekermann 2020; Thomas et al. 2023)
- Provides real-time feedback mechanisms to collect and integrate user feedback (Thomas et al. 2020; Suh et al. 2016)
- Finds a balance between standardization and the individual experiences of wellbeing across cultures and age groups (Liscio et al. 2023)
- Considers the ethical implications and considerations relevant in the specific context (Liscio et al. 2023)
- Balances objective and subjective measures for wellbeing (Morley et al. 2021; Vanden Abeele 2021)
- Regularly evaluates and assesses the validity and reliability of these measures (Cooke et al. 2016)

4.3.1 Wellbeing Compass Metrics

> It is not the products nor their material value, but what we do with products that can make us happy. (Desmet and Pohlmeyer 2013)

In order to develop metrics that acknowledge and address these challenges, we must find a holistic, multidisciplinary approach that balances quantitative measures with qualitative insights, is context-sensitive, representative for a diverse set of user experiences, and considers both the individual and the collective. We propose metrics based on the four pillars of the *Wellbeing Compass*.

- **Is the business operating according to the proactive approach?**
  Metrics might include number of ideas generated to promote wellbeing, awareness of wellbeing as a strategic goal, number of corrective efforts needed to keep up to date with regulatory efforts.

- **Is the business purpose-driven?**
  Metrics might include awareness of the value system in the company within the team members, personal fulfillment of the employees, time range of the long-term vision of the product.
- **Is the business humanity-centric?**
  Metrics might include level of understanding of the surrounding ecosystem, perceived meaning of the work by the employees, diversity of the related stakeholders.
- **Is the business adaptive?**
  Metrics might include number of actions undertaken to connect to communities, number of lessons learned implemented in the context of wellbeing, number of research efforts undertaken (Fig. 17.2).

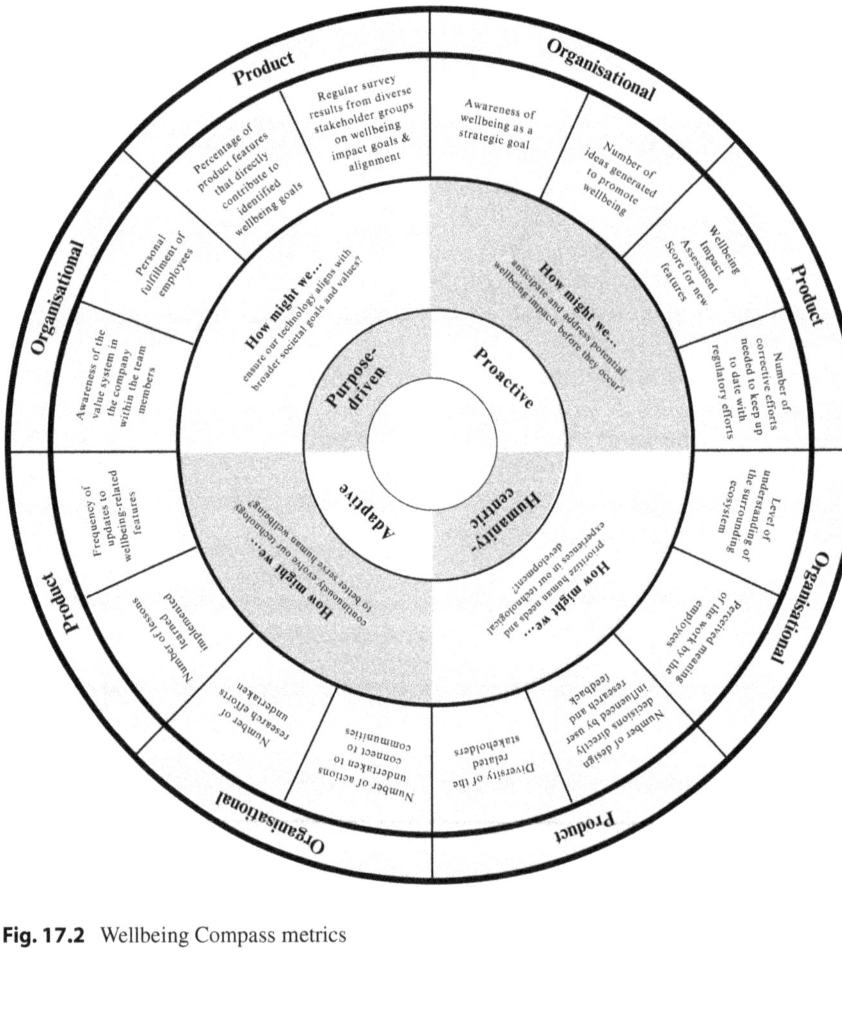

Fig. 17.2 Wellbeing Compass metrics

4.3.2 Potential Methodologies

Moving away from engagement-focused metrics and considering communities in addition to individualistic definitions of wellbeing, we need to choose methods that provide insight into the wellbeing effects of technologies. Self-reports may be unreliable and inaccurate (Vanden Abeele et al. 2013), so alternatives might include device logging and mobile experience sampling. These data collection techniques can capture in situ experiences (van Berkel et al. 2017) and allow the detection of patterns in behavior over shorter and longer time frames (Stragier et al. 2019). This method may be perceived as invasive by affected user groups and needs to be implemented according to ethical guidelines in clearly defined scopes.

Beyond risk assessments, businesses need to conduct ethical impact assessment of the potential short-term and long-term effects, asking questions such as: "What are the potential short- and long-term wellbeing effects of our product and how can we strike a balance?" The results of these assessments need to be analyzed in detail and lead to continuous adaptation: This requires the creation of processes for ongoing assessment and refinement of wellbeing strategies.

4.3.3 Reputation and Trust

With the pace of development of emerging technologies accelerating every day, organizations that innovate with "Wellbeing" as a compass can ensure ethical considerations are embedded from the outset, rather than an afterthought. Retrospectively adjusting irresponsible design principles in technological products is not only expensive, but it can lead to reputational damage.

Especially in the realm of digital businesses, company assets are no longer tangible, as they are in manufacturing and commerce, but instead consist of information and knowledge (Birch et al. 2021). There is increasing awareness that individuals' own data forms part of these company assets. In an age of GenAI, deepfakes, and misinformation campaigns, companies who use trusted sources for their data may therefore be perceived as more reliable and trustworthy (Gillespie et al. 2023). Brand image is already often a metric used in marketing departments. A focus on scores representing reputation, trust can help identify issues in the perception and ultimately the wellbeing impact of a company.

5 Challenges and Considerations for the Future

> Even the most beautiful speculative design won't sway hearts if the leaders of an organization don't have the ambition or desire to invest in a better future—and we don't mean just a profitable one. "What if?" is the beginning of a design-driven process to understand what choices we need to make today in order to create the future we want. (Michael Hendrix, IDEO)

The relative absence of "Wellbeing" as a guiding value in tech development and innovation so far can be attributed to a series of factors: lack of incentives, lack of understanding of the complexity of wellbeing, lack of tools and frameworks to operationalize wellbeing, prioritization of short-term profits over long-term impact. Lomas et al. have grouped these into "lack of knowledge" and "lack of motivation" (Lomas et al. 2023). While companies optimizing for engagement may find it a disadvantage to focus on "wellbeing" (lack of motivation), the highly personalized and context-dependent nature of wellbeing makes it extremely difficult to define, measure, and compare (Gluckman and Allen 2018) (lack of knowledge). The pace of technological development further complicates the picture, while at the same time highlighting its importance. Addressing these challenges will require, among others:

- Interdisciplinary collaboration among diverse stakeholders and facilitation of an ongoing, cross-disciplinary dialogue
- Breaking development teams and decision makers out of self-created bubbles
- Connecting with wider communities interested in shaping and co-creating products
- Translating academic jargon into accessible language for non-experts to increase participation
- Transforming theory (abstract principles) into practice (operational processes)

We need to shift from siloed decision-making—where policymakers, technologists, and ethicists work independently—to a collaborative co-creation process that includes impacted communities from the outset.

There is growing evidence that social responsibility does not just translate to more ethical business practices, but also meaningful innovation that positively affects the bottom line. Studies have shown that businesses that consider their impact on their environment, human and natural, often outperform their peers in terms of financial performance, reputation, and trust (Eccles et al. 2016). A great example of the value of wellbeing considerations in technical innovation comes from Sarah Spiekermann, at the University of Vienna, conducting an experiment with her students to evaluate the impact of their innovation (a food delivery app) on the stakeholders' lives and character (Spiekermann 2021, p. 42). In comparison to the "non-ethical" ideation, Spiekermann's experiment led students to the identification of significantly more, and completely novel value offerings and differentiated product concepts. While hypothetical, Spiekermann's experiment shows the potential of including broader wellbeing considerations into the innovation process.

6 Conclusion: To the Next Wave of Responsible Entrepreneurs

> When we inject people with positivity, their outlook expands. They see the big picture. When we inject them with neutrality or negativity, their peripheral vision shrinks. There is no big picture, no dots to connect. (Barbara Frederickson)

We began this chapter with a critical question: How can we, as a digital society, ensure that the technologies we design and deploy promote wellbeing and benefit humanity, rather than causing harm? How can we ensure that we return to technology's original roots, that of serving humanity and making our lives better? In addressing these questions, we will once again return to the field of Psychology and the work of Barbara Frederickson who has spent her academic career trying to understand the impact of positive thinking on wellbeing, resilience, and our capacity to build skills and think creatively. Frederickson's research has shown that when we focus on problems, our focus narrows. When we think positively, on the other hand, our approach expands (Frederickson 2009). It is here that we see the biggest potential of the *Wellbeing Compass* to leverage digital technologies as a force for good and true social value.

Throughout this chapter, the authors have tried to achieve three key objectives:

First, to underscore the urgent need for humanity-centric guiding values and methodologies in innovation and tech development: to focus not only on what we "*shouldn't* do," but what we "*need* to do" to create a positive future. Whether as individuals, as communities, organizations, or governments, as fields of study or practice, we must work together towards a digital landscape that strengthens rather than undermines human potential. This step will require curiosity, openness, active listening, and a willingness to experiment and challenge existing norms.

Second, just like measures like GDP cannot truly capture the true health of an economy and societal progress in the twenty-first century, the metrics that have guided us in developing digital technologies over the last three decades may no longer be sufficient or even adequate measures of "progress." We need a more comprehensive set of indicators that go beyond measures like "daily active users" or "time spent…" to not only hold the organizations behind the platforms and technologies accountable, but also to prove that "doing good" does not preclude "doing well."

And lastly, having the tools (technologies) may be one thing, but even more important is how we apply them. It is here that the *Wellbeing Compass* is intended to make its most important contribution, recognizing that technology is never just technical, but sociocultural, and its effect deeply connected with the context in which it is applied. By proposing new, more nuanced ways of thinking about the role of digital technologies, the *Wellbeing Compass* is an invitation to practitioners to experiment with integrating wellbeing considerations into new and existing business models and processes and enhance innovation at every level of an organization or development stage.

The journey towards a humanity-centered tech future is not without challenges, but it is a necessary and worthwhile endeavor, the beneficiary being none other than us. As we continue to innovate and integrate new technologies into our daily lives, we must remember to stay committed to the values that we hold dear—as individuals, organizations, communities, and a global society. For too long, a "taken-for-grantedness" (Vanden Abeele 2021) in our interactions with technology has obscured the fact that we have agency in shaping the relationship. Recognizing and reclaiming this agency is critical if we want to leverage the full potential of emerging technologies in a way that benefits us as individuals and as a collective. The challenge is simultaneously our opportunity: to shape a future where innovation and human flourishing go hand in hand.

References

Journal Articles

Auxier B, Rainie L, Anderson M, Perrin A, Kumar M, Turner E (2019, November 15) Americans' attitudes and experiences with privacy policies and laws. Pew Research Center. https://www.pewresearch.org/internet/2019/11/15/americans-attitudes-and-experiences-with-privacy-policies-and-laws/

Bingley WJ, Curtis C, Lockey S, Bialkowski A, Gillespie N, Haslam SA, Ko RKL, Steffens N, Wiles J, Worthy P (2023) Where is the human in human-centered AI? Insights from developer priorities and user experiences. Comput Hum Behav 141:107617. https://doi.org/10.1016/j.chb.2022.107617

Birch J, Browning H, Latham S (2021) Enhancing AI ethics: the role of empathy and perspective-taking. AI Soc 36:59–69. https://doi.org/10.1007/s00146-020-01005-8

Cave S, Dihal K (2018) The whiteness of AI. Philos Technol 33(4):685–703. https://doi.org/10.1007/s13347-020-00415-6

Chaudhary P, Hyde M, Rodger J (2017) Exploring the benefits of an agile information system. Intell Inf Manag 9:133–155

Cooke PJ, Melchert TP, Connor K (2016) Measuring well-being: a review of instruments. Counsel Psychologist 44(5):730–757

Davis J, Nathan LP (2014) Value sensitive design: applications, adaptations, and critiques. Handb Ethics Values Technol Des:11–40

Desmet PMA, Pohlmeyer AE (2013) Positive design: an introduction to design for subjective well-being. Int J Des 7(3):5–19

Eccles RG, Ioannou I, Serafeim G (2016) The impact of corporate sustainability on organizational processes and performance. Manag Sci 60(11):2835–2857

Floridi L, Burr C (2020) The ethics of digital well-being: a thematic review. Sci Eng Ethics 26(4):1–21

Floridi L, Burr C (2023) Digital wellbeing. A multidisciplinary study. Oxford University Press

Floridi L, Cowls J, King TC, Taddeo M (2018) How to design AI for social good: seven essential factors. Sci Eng Ethics 26:1771–1796. https://doi.org/10.1007/s11948-020-00213-5

Freeman RE, Harrison JS, Wicks AC, Parmar BL, De Colle S (2010) Stakeholder theory: the state of the art. Cambridge University Press

Gable SL, Haidt J (2005) What (and why) is positive psychology? Rev Gen Psychol 9(2):103–110. https://doi.org/10.1037/1089-2680.9.2.103

Gasson S (2003) Human-centered vs. user-centered approaches to information system design. J Inf Technol Theory Application (JITTA) 5:29–46

Geschke D, Lorenz J, Holtz P (2018) The triple-filter bubble: using agent-based modelling to test a meta-theoretical framework for the emergence of filter bubbles and echo chambers. Br J Soc Psychol 58(1):129–149

Gillespie N, Lockey S, Curtis C, Pool J, Akbari A (2023) Trust in artificial intelligence: a global study. The University of Queensland and KPMG Australia. https://doi.org/10.14264/00d

Gluckman PD, Allen K (2018) Understanding wellbeing in the context of rapid digital and associated transformations: implications for research, policy, and measurement. New Zealand Government

Harness D, Rana O, Chen-Burger J (2022) Ethical AI: a system dynamics approach to understanding bias mitigation. AI Soc https://doi.org/10.1007/s00146-022-01384-2

Helbing D (2013) Globally networked risks and how to respond. Nature 497(7447):51–59

Kaplan AM (2010) Users of the world, unite! The challenges and opportunities of social media. Bus Horizons 53(1):59–68

Kramer ADI, Guillory JE, Hancock JT (2014) Experimental evidence of massive-scale emotional contagion through social networks. Proc Natl Acad Sci 111(24):8788–8790. https://doi.org/10.1073/pnas.1320040111

Lehtinen T, Itkonen J, Lassenius C (2017) Recurring opinions or productive improvements—what agile teams actually discuss in retrospectives. Empirical Software Engineering

Liscio E, Van Hove L, De Marez L, Vanden Abeele M (2023) Towards a holistic approach for measuring digital wellbeing. Comput Hum Behav 115:106622

Lomas E, Calvo RA, McLachlan J, Peters D (2023) Positive AI: promoting wellbeing in the age of artificial intelligence. Int J Wellbeing 13(1):1–27

Mark G, Gudith D, Klocke U (2008) The cost of interrupted work: more speed and stress. Proceedings of the SIGCHI Conference on Human Factors in Computing Systems:107–110

Mascareño J, Rietzschel E, Wisse B (2020) Envisioning innovation: does visionary leadership engender team innovative performance through goal alignment? Creat Innov Manag 29:33–48

Mattelmäki T, Vaajakallio K, Koskinen I (2014) What happened to empathic design? Des Issues 30(1):67–77

Mehta P, Zimba O, Gasparyan AY, Seiil B, Yessirkepov M (2023) Ethics committees: structure, roles, and issues. J Korean Med Sci 38(25):e198. https://doi.org/10.3346/jkms.2023.38.e198. PMID: 37365729; PMCID: PMC10293659

Mittelstadt BD (2019) Principles alone cannot guarantee ethical AI. Nat Machine Intell 1(11):501–507

Moore A, Donnelly A (2018) The job of ethics committees. J Med Ethics 44:481–487

Morley J, Floridi L, Kinsey L, Elhalal A (2020) From what to how: an initial review of publicly available AI ethics tools, methods and research to translate principles into practices. Sci Eng Ethics 26(4):2141–2168

Morley J, Floridi L, Kinsey L, Elhalal A (2021) Operationalizing AI ethics: translating principles into practice. Sci Eng Ethics 27(1):24

Motingoe M, Langerman JJ (2019) New organisational models that break silos in organisations to enable software delivery flow. In: 2019 International Conference on System Science and Engineering (ICSSE), pp 341–348

Nussbaum MC (1992) Human functioning and social justice: in defense of Aristotelian essentialism. Polit Theory 20(2):202–246

Peters D, Calvo RA, Ryan RM (2018) Designing for motivation, engagement and wellbeing in digital experience. Front Psychol 9:797. https://doi.org/10.3389/fpsyg.2018.00797

Primack BA, Shensa A, Sidani JE, Whaite EO, Lin LY, Rosen D, Miller E (2017) Social media use and perceived social isolation among young adults in the US. Am J Preven Med 53(1):1–8

Robeyns I (2005) The capability approach: a theoretical survey. J Hum Dev 6(1):93–114

Scheyvens R, Banks G, Hughes E (2016) The private sector and the SDGs: the need to move beyond 'business as usual'. Sustain Dev 24(6):371–382

Sheldon KM, King L (2001) Why positive psychology is necessary. Am Psychol 56(3):216–217. https://doi.org/10.1037/0003-066X.56.3.216

Stiglitz JE, Sen A, Fitoussi JP (2008) Report by the Commission on the Measurement of Economic Performance and Social Progress. Commission on the Measurement of Economic Performance and Social Progress

Stragier J, Hendrickson A, Vanden Abeele M, De Marez L (2019) Unlock, chat, lock: a Markov chain analysis to unveil how smartphone use unfolds in everyday life. In: 69th Annual ICA Conference (ICA 2019): Communication Beyond Boundaries, Proceedings. Presented at the 69th Annual ICA Conference. International Communication Association, Washington, DC

Suh H, Shahriaree N, Hsieh G, Munson SA (2016) Feeding the self: how personality traits affect the reception of just-in-time health interventions. Proceedings of the 2016 CHI Conference on Human Factors in Computing Systems:3462–3474

Thomas J, McDonagh D (2013) Empathic design: research strategies. Aust Med J 6(1):1–6. https://doi.org/10.21767/AMJ.2013.1573

Thomas M, Kohli V, Brown R (2020) Measuring digital wellbeing: a multi-dimensional approach. J Med Internet Res 22(5):e16649

Thomas NJ, Briggs P, Burrows A (2023) Exploring the ethics of AI in education: a sociotechnical perspective. AI Soc https://doi.org/10.1007/s00146-023-01454-7

Twenge JM (2019) iGen: Why today's super-connected kids are growing up less rebellious, more tolerant, less happy – and completely unprepared for adulthood. Atria Books

van Berkel N, Ferreira D, Kostakos V (2017) The experience sampling method on mobile devices. ACM Comput Surv 50(6):1–40

Vanden Abeele M, Beullens K, Roe K (2013) Measuring mobile phone use: gender, age and real usage level in relation to the accuracy and validity of self-reported mobile phone use. Mobile Media Commun 1(2):213–236. https://doi.org/10.1177/2050157913477095

Vanden Abeele MMP (2021) Digital wellbeing as a dynamic construct. Communication Theory, 31(4):932–955. https://doi.org/10.1093/ct/qtz024

Vinuesa R, Azizpour H, Leite I, Balaam M, Dignum V, Domisch S, Nerini FF (2020) The role of artificial intelligence in achieving the Sustainable Development Goals. Nat Commun 11(1):1–10

Wright P, Wallace J, McCarthy J (2008) Aesthetics and experience-centered design. ACM Trans Comput-Hum Interact 15(4):1–21. https://doi.org/10.1145/1460355.1460360

Wright TA, Cropanzano R (2000) Psychological well-being and job satisfaction as predictors of job performance. J Occup Health Psychol 5(1):84–94

Yang C, Liang P, Avgeriou P (2018) Assumptions and their management in software development: a systematic mapping study. Inf Softw Technol 94:82–110

Young MF, Slota S, Cutter AB, Jalette G, Mullin G, Lai B, Simeoni Z, Tran M, Yukhymenko M (2018) Our princess is in another castle: A review of trends in serious gaming for education. Rev Educ Res 82(1):61–89. https://doi.org/10.3102/0034654312436980

Websites and Blogs

Digital AI (2023). https://digital.ai/resource-center/analyst-reports/state-of-agile-report/. Accessed 27 July 2024

European Parliament (2023, June 1) EU AI Act: first regulation on artificial intelligence. https://www.europarl.europa.eu/topics/en/article/20230601STO93804/eu-ai-act-first-regulation-on-artificial-intelligence. Accessed 14 July 2024

Hatem L, Ker D (2021) Going Digital Toolkit Note, No. 6, "Measuring wellbeing in the digital age". https://goingdigital.oecd.org/data/notes/No6_ToolkitNote_MeasuringWellbeing.pdf. Accessed 12 July 2024

Hu K (2023). https://www.reuters.com/technology/chatgpt-sets-record-fastest-growing-user-base-analyst-note-2023-02-01/. Accessed 27 July 2024

IEEE (2021) IEEE 7000-2021 – IEEE Standard for Model Process for Addressing Ethical Concerns during System Design. IEEE Standards Association. https://standards.ieee.org/ieee/7000/6781/. Accessed 8 July 2024

Khalifeh A (2020). https://www.linkedin.com/pulse/truth-roi-design-sprints-primary-research-findings-amr-khalifeh/. Accessed 27 July 2024

OECD (2022) The OECD going digital measurement roadmap. OECD Publishing. https://www.oecd.org/en/publications/2022/07/the-oecd-going-digital-measurement-roadmap_d5e03489.html

OECD (2024). https://oecd.ai/en/ai-principles. Accessed 27 July 2024

Spiekermann S (2022, February 21) What to expect from IEEE 7000: the first standard for building ethical systems. IEEE Technology and Society. https://technologyandsociety.org/what-to-expect-from-ieee-7000-the-first-standard-for-building-ethical-systems/. Accessed 12 July 2024

Books and Collections

Calvo RA, Peters D (2014) Positive computing: technology for wellbeing and human potential. MIT Press
Carr N (2011) The shallows: what the internet is doing to our brains. W.W. Norton
Eyal N (2014) Hooked: how to build habit-forming products. Portfolio
Fredrickson B (2009) Positivity: top-notch research reveals the upward spiral that will change your life. Harmony
Griffin J (1986) Well-being: its meaning, measurement, and moral importance. Clarendon Press
Meyerson D (2012) Tempered radicals: how people use difference to inspire change at work. Harvard Business Review Press
Norman DA (2023) Design for a better world: meaningful, sustainable, humanity centered. The MIT Press
Nussbaum M, Sen A (eds) (1993) The quality of life. Oxford University Press
Seligman MEP (2006) Learned optimism: how to change your mind and your life. Vintage (Original work published 1991)
Sen A (1985) Commodities and capabilities. North-Holland
Spiekermann S (2020) Ethical IT innovation: a value-based system design approach. CRC Press
Spiekermann S (2021) Digital ethics: a value system for the 21st century. Routledge
Taplin J (2017) Move fast and break things: how Facebook, Google and Amazon have cornered culture and what it means for all of us. Pan Macmillan
Turkle S (2015) Reclaiming conversation: the power of talk in a digital age. Penguin Press
Zuboff S (2019) The age of surveillance capitalism: the fight for a human future at the new frontier of power. PublicAffairs

Other Multimedia Content

All Tech Is Human (2022) The responsible tech guide. https://alltechishuman.org/responsible-tech-guide. Accessed 12 July 2024
Center for Humane Technology (2021) Ledger of harms. https://ledger.humanetech.com/. Accessed 12 July 2024
Google (2020) Digital Wellbeing Experiments. https://experiments.withgoogle.com/collection/digitalwellbeing. Accessed 12 July 2024
Raworth K (2018, April) A healthy economy should be designed to thrive, not grow [Video]. TED Conferences. https://www.ted.com/talks/kate_raworth_a_healthy_economy_should_be_designed_to_thrive_not_grow. Accessed 11 July 2024

Iliana Grosse-Buening is an entrepreneur, author, speaker, and Adjunct Professor with over a decade of experience across multinationals, NGOs, and startups in Kenya, China, the UK, Australia, and Germany. She founded Quiet Social Club in 2021 to promote individual, organisational, and societal wellbeing in the digital age. Grosse-Buening is an active keynote speaker and lecturer on the topics of Digital Wellbeing and AI Ethics, having spoken at University of Cambridge, London School of Economics, the 2024 Future of Digital Wellbeing Summit, Navigator AI Festival, the 2023 Digital Ethics Summit, among others. She is an Affiliate to the IE UNESCO Chair for AI Ethics & Governance and advises global charities, Fortune 500 companies, and start-ups on responsible technology, digital wellbeing, and AI innovation.

Alina Kukarina is a consultant and entrepreneur who has dedicated the past 10 years to building understanding of the human element in digital innovation. Her expertise spans the creation of sustainable digital platforms, the implementation of strategic AI initiatives, and the establishment of robust digital innovation management programs, driving positive change across organizations from startups to global corporations in the EU, UK, and US. With a foundation in science and engineering and hands on experience in software development, Alina employs a data driven approach, focusing on the integration of structured processes and measurable outcomes that extend beyond surface-level metrics. She is deeply committed to evaluating socioeconomic impact and fostering the long-term flourishing of individuals and societies.

Business Strategies for "Ethical by Design" Digital & AI Implementation

18

What Business Strategies Can Companies Employ to Guide Ethical Digital and AI Technology Implementation?

Deepak Bansal

Abstract

The exponential growth of Artificial Intelligence (AI) technologies has revolutionized industries but has also raised critical ethical challenges such as algorithmic bias, privacy concerns, and societal disruption. In response, businesses must embrace an "Ethical by Design" approach, integrating ethical considerations into their strategic, tactical, and operational frameworks. This chapter explores the key components of Ethical by Design strategies, providing insights into how organizations can implement them effectively. It highlights real-world examples, and through an examination of governance structures, framework development, and operational education, this chapter offers a roadmap for companies seeking to balance innovation with accountability and create long-term societal value.

1 Introduction

Artificial Intelligence (AI) has become a defining technology of the twenty-first century, revolutionizing industries on an unprecedented scale. From enhancing diagnostic accuracy in healthcare to optimizing supply chains in retail and finance, AI is reshaping the way we work, interact, and live. According to McKinsey's Global AI Survey, the adoption of AI has grown exponentially, with 56% of companies reporting its implementation in at least one function as of 2023 (McKinsey 2023). This rapid integration underscores AI's transformative potential but also highlights the urgency of addressing its accompanying challenges.

D. Bansal (✉)
MQ Learning Academy, Ethical Tech Lab, Zurich, Switzerland
e-mail: deepak@mq-learning.com

C. H. Hoffmann, D. Bansal (eds.), *AI Ethics in Practice*, Integrated Science 35,
https://doi.org/10.1007/978-3-031-87023-1_18

Despite its promise, AI introduces complex ethical dilemmas. Biased algorithms can reinforce systemic inequalities; unregulated data collection can threaten individual privacy; and opaque decision-making processes can undermine public trust and democratic principles. A 2022 study by the Pew Research Center found that 68% of Americans express concern over the misuse of AI technologies, with privacy and fairness topping the list of worries (Pew Research Center 2022). These issues are not just technical or regulatory—they strike at the heart of societal well-being.

As businesses increasingly leverage AI to gain a competitive edge, the need for robust ethical frameworks has become non-negotiable. Ethical lapses in AI deployment have led to significant financial penalties and reputational damage for major companies. For instance, in 2018, Amazon discontinued an AI recruitment tool after discovering it discriminated against female applicants by downgrading résumés that included the word "women's" (Dastin 2018). Similarly, Uber faced legal challenges when its facial recognition system erroneously deactivated drivers with darker skin tones, leading to accusations of racial discrimination (McCluskey 2021). These incidents underscore the critical need for organizations to integrate ethical considerations into AI development and deployment to prevent severe consequences.

Moreover, the European Union's AI Act, effective from August 2024, introduces stringent regulations for AI systems. Non-compliance can result in fines up to €35 million or 7% of a company's global annual turnover, whichever is higher (EU AI Act 2024). This legislative framework emphasizes the importance of ethical AI practices to avoid substantial penalties.

To navigate these challenges, organizations must adopt an "Ethical by Design" approach. This philosophy emphasizes embedding ethical considerations into every phase of AI development and deployment—from strategic planning and system design to daily operations. Unlike reactive measures that address issues post-crisis, Ethical by Design aims to proactively align AI technologies with societal values and organizational principles.

This integration is not just a moral imperative but a business necessity. A 2021 Deloitte survey found that organizations prioritizing AI ethics report higher levels of customer trust, employee satisfaction, and overall innovation (Deloitte 2021a, b). Ethical by Design transforms ethics from a compliance-driven checkbox to a core cultural element, fostering trust and long-term sustainability in a digital-first world.

As we delve deeper into the concept, this chapter explores how Ethical by Design strategies can be implemented across strategic, tactical, and operational dimensions, providing a comprehensive framework for embedding ethics into business practices. Through real-world examples and actionable insights, we highlight how companies can build trust, foster innovation, and create a vision for an AI-powered future that benefits all stakeholders.

2 Ethical by Design Business Strategies: A Multilayered Approach

Ethical by Design represents a paradigm shift in how organizations approach the integration of ethics into their operations. This framework emphasizes the proactive incorporation of ethical principles, ensuring that every aspect of the organization—from leadership to frontline actions—operates within a clear ethical framework. Addressing ethical challenges in AI requires an integral approach, which is best understood through its three interconnected dimensions: strategic, tactical, and operational.

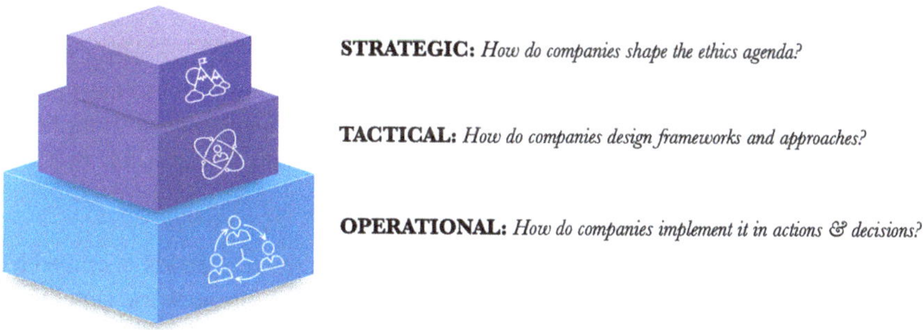

- *Strategic: How do companies shape the ethics agenda?—Governance and Ethical Leadership*
- At the strategic level, ethics by design begins with leadership setting the tone for the organization's values and commitments. This involves embedding ethics into corporate governance through dedicated policies, roles, and oversight mechanisms.
- A critical part of this strategic dimension is fostering an organizational culture where ethics is prioritized. Studies suggest that when leadership visibly champions ethical practices, it encourages employees at all levels to integrate these values into their daily responsibilities. Moreover, governance structures such as ethics boards or dedicated officers ensure accountability and drive alignment between the organization's ethical goals and its business strategies.
- *Tactical: How do companies design frameworks and approaches?—Methodologies and Frameworks*
- The tactical dimension bridges the high-level vision established at the strategic level with the practical tools and processes required for implementation. Developing ethical frameworks involves defining clear methodologies for addressing potential risks, such as algorithmic bias or lack of transparency.

- Tactical measures often include creating guidelines for ethical AI development, conducting risk assessments, and implementing standardized procedures such as ethics checklists or audits. These frameworks ensure that ethical considerations are not just conceptual but are actively embedded into workflows, making them an integral part of product design and service delivery. Additionally, tactical initiatives often include collaboration with external experts to refine and validate these frameworks, further strengthening their robustness.
- *Operational: How do companies implement it?—Everyday Decisions and Actions*
- Operationalizing ethics ensures that the principles defined at the strategic and tactical levels translate into consistent actions across the organization. This dimension focuses on embedding ethical decision-making into daily operations and creating a culture of responsibility among all employees.
- Operational measures often involve training programs, clear reporting mechanisms for ethical concerns, and systems that encourage employees to raise potential issues without fear of retribution. These initiatives not only ensure compliance but also foster a proactive ethical mindset, enabling employees to identify and address challenges before they escalate.

The interconnected nature of these dimensions ensures that ethics is embedded across the organization, creating a resilient and adaptive framework capable of addressing evolving challenges in AI deployment. Strategic leadership provides a long-term vision, tactical frameworks offer actionable tools, and operational measures bring these principles to life in everyday actions. Together, they create a robust foundation for ethical decision-making that extends beyond compliance and building trust and credibility with stakeholders.

3 Strategic Areas: Governance and Ethical Leadership

The strategic dimension of Ethical by Design focuses on embedding ethics into the leadership framework of an organization. This involves fostering accountability at the highest levels, integrating ethical principles into the corporate culture, and actively participating in global initiatives to address pressing ethical concerns. Two key components—embedding ethical oversight at the executive level and aligning organizational values with ethical principles—are critical in shaping a sustainable and responsible future for AI technologies.

- **Participation at the Executive Board level through, e.g., Chief AI Ethics Officer, AI Ethicist, or Creating an AI Ethics Board**
  - Including responsibilities like integrating ethical, social, and political perspectives into AI systems' design, development, and deployment
- **Embedding AI Ethics as part of culture and values**
  - Incorporating Value Statements on AI Ethics
  - Participating in shaping the global dialog on the issue
  - Collaborating in multiple stakeholder initiatives

3.1 Participation at the Executive Board Level

Integrating ethical oversight into executive decision-making ensures that ethical considerations are embedded into every level of AI development and deployment. Establishing roles such as Chief AI Ethics Officer or AI Ethics Boards is foundational to this process. These entities provide a centralized point of accountability, ensuring that AI systems reflect not just technical efficiency but also ethical, social, and political values.

A report by Bain & Company emphasizes that appointing a Chief AI Ethics Officer or establishing an AI Ethics Council is a vital step in adapting organizations for responsible AI use. These structures ensure oversight, enabling organizations to identify risks and implement best practices to mitigate ethical challenges (Bain & Company 2021). The World Economic Forum highlights the creation of Chief AI Ethics Officers as a key strategy to embed ethical principles into company operations. These roles are critical for advising leadership on AI-related risks, ensuring compliance with ethical standards, and fostering a culture of accountability (World Economic Forum 2021).

Key Responsibilities of AI Ethics Leadership

The role of AI Ethics Leadership is pivotal in ensuring that AI technologies are designed, developed, and deployed responsibly, addressing both organizational and societal needs. The following responsibilities highlight the core contributions of this leadership role:

- *Integrating Multidisciplinary Perspectives:* AI ethics leaders must bring together insights from diverse disciplines such as sociology, political science, philosophy, and law to create holistic AI systems. This ensures that technologies are not only technically sound but also socially aware and culturally inclusive.
- *Conducting Proactive Ethical Risk Assessments:* A critical function is identifying potential ethical challenges, such as algorithmic bias, data privacy issues, or unintended consequences, early in the development process. This proactive approach mitigates risks before they escalate into larger organizational or societal concerns.
- *Aligning AI with Organizational and Societal Values:* Leaders are tasked with translating abstract ethical principles into actionable guidelines that resonate with the company's mission and values. By aligning AI initiatives with broader societal goals such as fairness, transparency, and inclusivity, they ensure that the organization contributes positively to the communities it serves.

These responsibilities position AI Ethics Leadership as a cornerstone of responsible innovation, fostering trust and accountability while ensuring that AI technologies align with both ethical principles and strategic objectives. According to the World Economic Forum (2021), several prominent companies, including BCG, Salesforce, IBM, and Microsoft, have established dedicated roles for AI ethics, such as Head of Responsible AI, AI Ethics Global Leader, Global AI Ethicist, and

Chief Responsible AI Officer, highlighting their commitment to responsible AI governance.

Case Study: GE Healthcare

GE Healthcare, a global leader in medical imaging and diagnostics, has taken significant steps to integrate ethical oversight into its AI operations. In 2023, the company appointed Parminder "Parry" Bhatia as its Chief AI Officer to lead efforts in ensuring the ethical design and deployment of AI-powered tools. This role focuses on addressing critical concerns such as bias, data privacy, and patient safety in medical imaging and diagnostics.

GE Healthcare's AI-powered imaging tools undergo rigorous ethical reviews to mitigate risks of racial and gender biases in diagnostic accuracy. These reviews ensure transparency and equity in algorithmic decision-making, ultimately fostering trust among healthcare providers and patients. By integrating such oversight, GE Healthcare demonstrates a commitment to enhancing patient outcomes while maintaining ethical integrity in its AI applications (Fierce Biotech 2023).

3.2 Embedding AI Ethics in Culture and Values

For organizations to deploy AI responsibly, ethics must not remain a standalone policy but become deeply embedded within the organization's culture and values. A company's ethical framework should act as the cornerstone of its AI operations, guiding decision-making at all levels and ensuring alignment with societal expectations and long-term business goals. This cultural embedding requires a multipronged approach, emphasizing value-driven commitments, proactive engagement in global conversations, and inclusive collaboration with diverse stakeholders.

- *Incorporating Value Statements on AI Ethics*
- Value statements on AI ethics are a public declaration of an organization's commitment to responsible innovation. These statements go beyond corporate messaging, serving as a guiding philosophy for how AI is designed, developed, and deployed. They create a unified vision for employees and stakeholders, ensuring that ethical considerations are consistently prioritized.
- Embedding these value statements into business operations ensures that all AI projects align with a shared understanding of principles such as transparency, fairness, and accountability. Value statements also provide clarity to external stakeholders, demonstrating a proactive commitment to aligning technological innovation with societal values.
- *Participating in Shaping the Global Dialogue*
- The challenges of AI ethics are not confined to individual organizations; they are global in scale. Participating in international discussions on AI ethics enables organizations to contribute to the creation of universal guidelines and regulations that balance innovation with responsibility. Global dialogues offer a platform for

organizations to share their insights and learn from the experiences of others, fostering a collective understanding of the ethical implications of AI.

- For example, the European Commission has emphasized the importance of stakeholder participation in the development of AI regulations, highlighting that such involvement ensures that the resulting frameworks are comprehensive and balanced. By contributing to these consultations, companies can position themselves as thought leaders in ethical AI innovation, influencing the regulatory environment to reflect practical industry perspectives.
- *Collaborating in Multi-Stakeholder Initiatives*
- Collaboration across sectors and disciplines is vital for addressing the complex ethical challenges of AI. Multi-stakeholder initiatives bring together diverse perspectives, enriching the conversation and enabling a more holistic approach to ethical AI development. These collaborations often include industry peers, academic institutions, NGOs, and governments, each contributing unique insights to the process.
- For instance, Microsoft's participation in the Partnership on AI has allowed it to co-develop tools and frameworks for bias detection, benefiting both the company and its broader ecosystem. This kind of collaboration ensures that ethical considerations are informed by diverse perspectives, making solutions more robust and comprehensive.

Embedding AI ethics into culture and values requires a comprehensive and intentional approach. By creating value-driven commitments, engaging in global dialogues, and collaborating with diverse stakeholders, organizations can build ethical frameworks that extend beyond compliance. This alignment of culture, values, and operations ensures that AI technologies not only meet regulatory standards but also contribute to a more equitable and responsible future. Ultimately, embedding AI ethics into culture is not just about avoiding harm—it is about driving innovation that creates long-lasting societal value.

4 Tactical Areas: Methodologies and Frameworks

The tactical approach plays a critical role in translating ethical principles into action, ensuring they move beyond abstract ideals to become actionable and measurable components of AI development and deployment. It focuses on embedding ethics directly into workflows, design methodologies, and decision-making processes, thereby creating a structured and proactive framework for addressing the unique challenges associated with AI.

By integrating ethics into the core of organizational operations and seeking external validation, companies can establish accountability, improve transparency, and mitigate potential risks such as bias, data misuse, and lack of explainability. This approach ensures that ethical considerations are not only built into the foundations of AI systems but are also continuously monitored and improved upon.

This section explores two pivotal components of the tactical approach: defining robust AI ethical frameworks that guide development from conception to release and investing in external certifications and user feedback mechanisms to ensure systems meet societal and organizational expectations while evolving to address emerging ethical concerns. Together, these elements provide a roadmap for organizations to bridge the gap between ethical principles and practical implementation, fostering trust and innovation in their AI solutions.

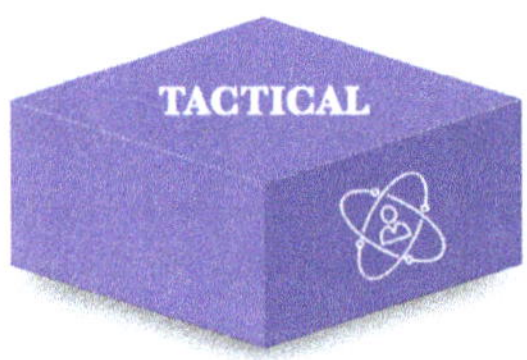

- **Defining AI Ethical Frameworks**
  - Embedding Ethics in the design process and methodology
  - Defining AI Ethics checks & controls procedure
  - Integrating systems like "Explainable AI" as part of the release
- **Leveraging Third-Party Feedback**
  - Third-party review for improvement
  - Collecting User Feedback and Driving Iterative Change

4.1 Defining AI Ethical Frameworks

Ethical frameworks act as the blueprint for responsible AI development. They provide clear guidelines for integrating ethical considerations into design processes, ensuring that fairness, transparency, and accountability are central to AI development. Establishing a robust AI ethical framework is essential for guiding responsible AI development and deployment. This involves embedding ethics into the design process, implementing systematic checks and controls, and adopting Explainable AI (XAI) systems to ensure fairness, transparency, and accountability.

- *Embedding Ethics in the Design Process and Methodology*
- Integrating ethical considerations from the outset ensures AI systems align with both organizational values and societal expectations. Early incorporation prevents issues such as bias, lack of transparency, and unintended consequences.
- *Proactive Design*: Incorporating fairness, inclusivity, and transparency into initial stages mitigates risks and builds trust.
- *Cross-Functional Input*: Collaboration across ethics, legal, and technical teams ensures well-rounded, responsible designs.

- *AI Ethics Checks and Controls Procedure*
- Systematic checks and controls are crucial for identifying risks before deployment. These include:
  - *Ethical Impact Assessments*: Evaluating societal and user-specific impacts to prevent harm.
  - *Algorithmic Audits*: Regularly testing models for fairness and accuracy across diverse groups.

  - *Bias Monitoring*: Ensuring datasets and algorithms are free from harmful biases.
- *Integrating Explainable AI (XAI)*
- Explainable AI enhances transparency by making algorithmic decisions understandable for users. This fosters trust, ensures regulatory compliance, and empowers users to challenge decisions when necessary.
- *Practical Application*: Industries like healthcare and finance rely on XAI to ensure safety and fairness.
- *Outcome*: Builds stakeholder confidence and aligns with global regulatory trends like the EU's AI Act.

Case Study: Unilever
Unilever, according to a report in the *MIT Sloan Management Review* (2021), developed an AI ethical framework through its AI assurance process, which evaluates AI applications against defined criteria, including fairness, transparency, and accountability. This process was designed to identify and mitigate ethical risks in AI deployment. For example, in a project using computer vision AI to register sales agents' attendance, the assurance process identified potential ethical concerns, such as the risk of privacy violations and algorithmic bias. To address these issues, Unilever mandated human oversight, requiring flagged photos to be reviewed manually. This approach ensured fairness, minimized the potential for automated errors, and upheld accountability.

4.2 Leveraging Third-Party Feedback

Continuous improvement in ethical AI practices is critical to ensuring that systems remain aligned with evolving societal expectations, regulatory requirements, and user needs. This iterative approach combines third-party evaluations and active user engagement, fostering a proactive culture of trust, accountability, and responsiveness to emerging challenges.

4.2.1 Third-Party Review for Improvement

Engaging independent reviewers, and obtaining external certifications, provides an objective assessment of an organization's AI practices. Third-party reviews help identify areas where ethical gaps exist, offering actionable insights to enhance compliance with industry standards and regulatory requirements.

- *Unbiased Evaluation*: Independent audits ensure that assessments are free from internal biases, enabling organizations to critically evaluate their AI systems. This external perspective is particularly valuable in identifying risks that may be overlooked internally, such as hidden biases in algorithms or unintended privacy breaches.

- *Industry Benchmarking*: External certifications enable organizations to benchmark their practices against global standards, ensuring their AI systems are competitive and responsible. Certifications such as the Swiss Digital Trust Label serve as markers of trustworthiness, assuring stakeholders that the organization adheres to stringent ethical criteria. Companies certified under such frameworks undergo rigorous evaluations across parameters like transparency, data privacy, and reliability, reinforcing their commitment to ethical AI.
- *Regulatory Preparedness*: With increasing global AI regulations, such as the European Union's AI Act, third-party reviews ensure organizations remain compliant with emerging laws. This reduces the risk of fines, legal repercussions, and reputational damage.

4.2.2 Collecting User Feedback and Driving Iterative Change

Active engagement with users is essential for developing AI technologies that are both effective and ethical. Gathering regular feedback from diverse user groups provides critical insights into how systems perform in real-world scenarios and highlights areas for improvement.

- *Real-Time Responsiveness*: User feedback allows organizations to identify potential issues early, such as unintended consequences or usability challenges. This responsiveness ensures systems can be adjusted quickly to meet user needs and expectations.
- *Diverse Perspectives*: Involving a wide range of users—spanning different demographics, industries, and geographies—ensures that AI systems are inclusive and fair. For example, incorporating feedback from underrepresented groups helps address biases that might otherwise go unnoticed.
- *Iterative Development*: Feedback-driven development supports an iterative approach, where AI systems are continuously refined and enhanced. Iterative updates based on real-world usage and user input not only improve functionality but also address ethical concerns proactively.

Case Study: Swiss Digital Trust Label

The Swiss Digital Trust Label exemplifies how third-party evaluations combined with user feedback can foster trust in AI systems. Introduced by the Swiss Digital Initiative, the label certifies digital services, including AI systems, on parameters such as security, data protection, and fairness. Organizations seeking certification are evaluated across 35 criteria, incorporating both technical assessments and user feedback mechanisms.

For instance, during the certification process, user insights are collected to assess how well systems align with real-world expectations. This feedback is used to identify gaps and implement necessary changes before certification is granted. Companies adopting the Swiss Digital Trust Label not only enhance their accountability but also gain a competitive advantage by demonstrating their commitment to ethical practices. According to the Swiss Digital Initiative (2022), selected technologies of organizations such as Swiss Re, Swisscom, Credit Suisse, wefox, UNICEF Switzerland and Liechtenstein, and Julius Baer have been awarded the label.

The combination of third-party evaluations and active user engagement ensures that AI systems remain relevant, ethical, and effective in dynamic environments. By adopting external certifications and proactively gathering user feedback, organizations can address emerging challenges, build trust with stakeholders, and position themselves as leaders in ethical AI innovation. These strategies provide a robust foundation for continuous improvement, fostering accountability and ensuring that AI technologies serve both organizational goals and societal needs.

5 Operational Areas: Everyday Decisions and Actions

Operational areas represent the foundational level where ethical principles are implemented in the daily functioning of an organization. This involves embedding digital ethics into decision-making processes, fostering a culture of ethical responsibility, and ensuring all employees, particularly those working directly with AI, are educated on the implications of their decisions.

The operational approach is essential for ensuring that ethics is not confined to high-level strategy or one-off tactical interventions. Instead, it becomes a dynamic, evolving component of the organization's DNA, shaping decisions at every level—from the code written by developers to the strategic initiatives of leadership. This continuous, hands-on application of ethical principles ensures that organizations remain agile, accountable, and aligned with their core values in an ever-changing technological landscape.

- **Embedding Ethics in Everyday Decisions**
  - Implementing AI Ethics Frameworks, Checks, and Controls
  - Encouraging and Rewarding Ethical Questioning
- **Fostering Company-Wide Education on Digital & AI Ethics**
  - Ensuring relevant & practical application across different roles (leadership, business, & technical)

5.1 Embedding Ethics in Everyday Decisions

Embedding digital ethics into daily operations is essential for ensuring that ethical principles are consistently applied across all organizational activities. It transforms ethics from a high-level directive into a practical, actionable component of every decision, fostering a culture where responsibility, accountability, and transparency are ingrained in the organization's fabric. This requires the establishment of robust frameworks, the cultivation of an environment that values ethical questioning, and the implementation of mechanisms to enable proactive ethical deliberation.

5.1.1 Implementing AI Ethics Frameworks, Checks, and Controls

Operationalizing digital ethics begins with creating clear frameworks and systematic controls that guide employees in addressing ethical challenges. These structures ensure that ethical risks are identified, assessed, and mitigated at every stage of a project or decision-making process.

- *Proactive Risk Identification*: Developing tools and dashboards to monitor and flag potential ethical risks in AI systems is a critical step. For instance, dashboards that track model outputs can detect biases or irregularities in real-time, enabling teams to respond swiftly and mitigate harm. Predictive analytics can also be used to anticipate ethical challenges in high-stakes applications, such as healthcare or finance.
- *Regular Audits and Incident Reporting Systems*: Ethical audits—conducted periodically—help organizations uncover blind spots in their AI systems, such as unintended biases or discrepancies in data handling. Complementing these audits, incident reporting systems provide employees with a structured and safe way to report ethical concerns, ensuring that ethical breaches are addressed transparently and promptly.

5.1.2 Encouraging and Rewarding Ethical Questioning

Fostering a culture that encourages employees to question the ethical implications of their actions and decisions is vital for building organizational transparency and accountability. Ethical questioning empowers teams to think critically about their work and challenges them to consider the broader societal impacts of their actions.

- *Special Ethics Forums*: Scheduling dedicated sessions, such as "Ethical Dialogue Forums," provides teams with a platform to openly discuss ethical dilemmas they encounter in their workflows. These forums allow employees to share their concerns, explore different perspectives, and collaboratively develop solutions. By institutionalizing these discussions, organizations ensure that ethical considerations are not overlooked in day-to-day operations.
- *Recognition Programs*: Establishing recognition programs that reward employees for ethical foresight further reinforces a culture of accountability and responsibility. For example, organizations can introduce "Ethics Champion" awards for individuals or teams who identify and address ethical risks or propose innovative solutions to complex ethical challenges. Such programs not only highlight the value placed on ethical behavior but also encourage employees to take proactive stances on ethical issues.

Operationalizing AI ethics requires a structured approach that integrates ethical principles into daily decision-making processes. By implementing clear frameworks, systematic checks, and proactive risk-identification tools, organizations can detect and mitigate ethical challenges such as biases and discrepancies in AI systems. Regular audits and transparent incident reporting further ensure accountability and alignment with organizational values and societal expectations.

Encouraging and rewarding ethical questioning complements these frameworks by fostering a culture of responsibility and open dialogue. Dedicated forums for discussing ethical dilemmas and recognition programs for ethical foresight empower employees to critically assess their actions and contribute to sustainable, ethical practices. Together, these efforts establish a robust foundation for ethical AI development and deployment.

Case Study: Salesforce (Self-Reported)

Though self-reported, Salesforce appears to be making significant strides in operationalizing AI ethics, albeit not across all areas of its framework. Through its Office of Ethical and Humane Use, the company has implemented frameworks to ensure ethical AI practices, including regular audits, tools to monitor for biases, and incident reporting systems to address ethical concerns. These initiatives reflect a proactive approach to managing risks and fostering accountability in deploying AI systems.

5.2 Fostering Company-Wide Education on Digital and AI Ethics

Digital and AI ethics is an emerging field, yet many remain unaware of its importance and implications. Regulations alone cannot address the ethical challenges of AI; awareness and education are crucial. When individuals understand the principles of digital ethics, they are more likely to make informed, ethical decisions on the spot, preventing potential harm and fostering responsible innovation.

Education on digital ethics plays a pivotal role in building a culture of accountability and ethical responsibility within organizations. As AI technologies become central to operations, it is essential to equip employees with the tools to navigate these complex challenges. Training programs should not be limited to compliance but instead empower employees to proactively identify and address ethical dilemmas, ensuring decisions align with organizational values and societal expectations. Tailored to diverse roles and responsibilities, these programs ensure relevance and practical application, enabling a more ethically aware workforce at all levels.

- *Leadership and Senior Executives Education*
- Leaders and executives set the tone for organizational culture and ethical behavior. Training programs for this group should focus on high-level strategic and governance issues, equipping them to champion ethical initiatives and make informed decisions that align with organizational values.
  - *Ethical Leadership Training*: Cover topics such as ethical governance, regulatory compliance, and the societal implications of AI at a strategic level.

  - *Regulatory Awareness*: Ensure leaders are well-versed in global regulations, such as General Data Protection Regulation (GDPR) or the EU AI Act, to ensure compliance and anticipate emerging challenges.
- *Business-Specific Ethics Education*
- Business-specific roles, including managers and functional teams, require training that connects ethical principles to their day-to-day responsibilities. These programs should address sector-specific challenges and provide practical tools for implementing ethical practices within their domains.
  - *General Ethics Training*: Introduce employees to foundational concepts, such as digital privacy, the societal impact of AI, and the organization's ethical commitments.
  - *Scenario-Based Learning*: Incorporate role-specific scenarios and case studies to help employees identify and respond to ethical dilemmas they may encounter in their workflows.
- *Technical Teams Education*
- Technical teams, including programmers, data scientists, and machine learning engineers, are at the forefront of AI development. Their training must address the unique ethical challenges posed by their technical work, emphasizing the impact of their decisions on society and end-users.
  - *Programmers*: Focus on ethical coding practices, data privacy, and security. Train them to identify and mitigate risks associated with system design and data handling.
  - *Data Scientists*: Educate on algorithmic fairness, bias detection, and ethical data usage, enabling them to create equitable and transparent models.
  - *Machine Learning Engineers*: Explore explainability, accountability, and the societal implications of automation, ensuring that AI outputs align with ethical standards and organizational values.

Education programs on digital ethics should not be treated as one-off initiatives but rather as ongoing efforts that evolve with technological and societal advancements. To ensure widespread participation, these trainings must be structured and emphasized as essential and mandatory components of organizational development. Embedding such programs into the organizational culture ensures that ethics remain a central focus, with regular updates to address emerging challenges such as new regulations or advancements in AI. Leadership involvement is vital, as it not only demonstrates the importance of these initiatives but also sets a strong example for the workforce. Cross-department discussions and workshops further promote a shared understanding of ethical issues and solutions, ensuring comprehensive engagement across the organization.

These programs equip employees at every level with the tools to identify and address ethical concerns, improving decision-making by aligning actions with the organization's values and societal expectations. A shared understanding of ethical standards fosters accountability across all roles, distributing responsibility beyond individual teams or functions. Educated employees contribute to a culture of ethical practices, building trust with stakeholders, customers, and the broader community.

By prioritizing education on digital ethics, organizations reinforce their commitment to responsible innovation and sustainable growth.

Various universities and consulting firms are developing programs to train professionals in digital ethics, but a more systemized and holistic approach is essential. The Ethical Decision Making Intelligence (EDMI) program from MQ Learning Academy is one such initiative aimed at broadly educating organizations on this evolving topic. By targeting leadership, business roles, and technical teams, EDMI seeks to build foundational awareness and practical skills, contributing to a more ethical approach to innovation and technology deployment.

6 Conclusion

Artificial Intelligence has emerged as a transformative force across industries, bringing unprecedented opportunities and significant ethical challenges. As businesses adopt AI to drive innovation and efficiency, they face pressing questions about fairness, transparency, accountability, and societal impact. This chapter underscores the necessity of Ethical by Design business strategies—embedding ethical principles across strategic, tactical, and operational dimensions of organizational operations. By proactively integrating ethics into every phase of AI development and deployment, organizations can address risks before they escalate and align their technologies with both societal values and organizational goals.

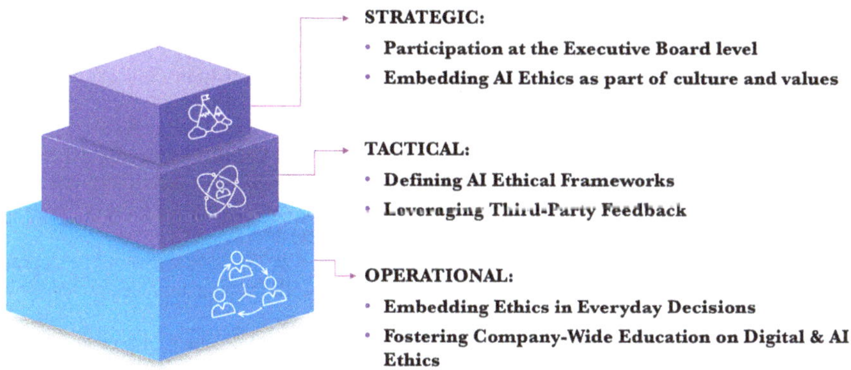

The strategic dimension emphasizes the role of leadership and governance in setting an ethical agenda, fostering accountability through roles like Chief AI Ethics Officers and dedicated ethics boards. Tactically, organizations must translate high-level principles into actionable frameworks, such as risk assessments, audits, and ethical AI design processes, ensuring that ethics are woven into workflows and methodologies. At the operational level, ethics must permeate daily decisions and actions, supported by robust checks, controls, systems, and education that empower employees to identify and address challenges responsibly.

This chapter also highlights emerging case studies to explore the practical application of Ethical by Design principles. Examples from organizations such as Unilever, GE Healthcare, Salesforce, the Swiss Digital Initiative, and others highlight the growing efforts to integrate ethics into AI operations. These case studies reflect an encouraging trend of companies taking proactive steps to operationalize ethical practices. While the journey is ongoing, these initiatives represent meaningful progress toward embedding ethical principles into organizational frameworks and advancing responsible AI deployment.

Looking ahead, the path to responsible AI demands more than compliance—it requires a commitment to proactive innovation that prioritizes societal well-being alongside organizational objectives. By embracing Ethical by Design business strategies, organizations can not only mitigate risks but also unlock the full potential of AI to foster trust, drive sustainable growth, and contribute to a future where technology serves humanity responsibly and equitably.

References

Bain & Company (2021) Adapting your organization for responsible AI. https://www.bain.com/insights/adapting-your-organization-for-responsible-ai/

Dastin J (2018, October 10) Amazon scraps secret AI recruiting tool that showed bias against women. Reuters. https://www.reuters.com/article/us-amazon-com-jobs-automation-insight/amazon-scraps-secret-ai-recruiting-tool-that-showed-bias-against-women-idUSKCN1MK08G

Deloitte (2021a) Building world-class ethics and compliance programs. https://www.deloitte.com/global/en/services/risk-advisory/perspectives/building-world-class-ethics-and-compliance-programs.html

Deloitte (2021b) State of AI in the enterprise, 3rd edn. https://www2.deloitte.com/us/en/insights/focus/cognitive-technologies/state-of-ai-and-intelligent-automation-in-business-survey.html

EU AI Act (2024) Article 99: Penalties. https://artificialintelligenceact.eu/article/99/

Fierce Biotech (2023) A conversation with GE Healthcare's Chief AI Officer, Parry Bhatia. https://www.fiercebiotech.com/medtech/conversation-ge-healthcares-chief-ai-officer-parry-bhatia

McCluskey M (2021, October 6) Uber drivers say a 'racist' algorithm is putting them out of work. Time. https://time.com/6104844/uber-facial-recognition-racist/

McKinsey & Company (2023) The state of AI in 2023: Generative AI's breakout year. https://www.mckinsey.com/capabilities/quantumblack/our-insights/the-state-of-ai-in-2023-generative-AIs-breakout-year

MIT Sloan Management Review (2021) AI ethics at Unilever: from policy to process. https://sloanreview.mit.edu/article/ai-ethics-at-unilever-from-policy-to-process/

Pew Research Center (2022) How Americans think about artificial intelligence. https://www.pewresearch.org/internet/2022/03/17/how-americans-think-about-artificial-intelligence/

Swiss Digital Initiative (2022) Labelled services: organizations awarded the Swiss Digital Trust Label. https://swiss-digital-initiative.org/dtl/labelled-services/

World Economic Forum (2021) How businesses can create an ethical culture in the age of tech. https://www.weforum.org/stories/2021/09/artificial-intelligence-ethics-new-jobs/

Deepak Bansal is the Founder and CEO of MQ Learning, a Swiss-based EduQua-certified academy dedicated to teaching humanistic skills in the digital age. His extensive 15+ years in the corporate world include executive roles at Accenture, Deutsche Post DHL, and Zurich Insurance (COO, Head AI & Robotics). A distinguished academic, Bansal has a Masters in Technology from the Indian Institute of Management (IIM) Mumbai, an MBA from the University of St. Gallen, Switzerland, and an MA in Philosophy from the California Institute of Integral Studies (CIIS), California, USA. In addition to his role at MQ Learning, Bansal actively engages in academia as a guest lecturer at Zurich University of Applied Sciences, focusing on 'Digital Ethics by Design'. His unique blend of corporate experience, academic insight, and a deep understanding of technology's ethical dimensions positions him as a thought leader in the field. Deepak also contributes significantly to digital ethics as a member of the certification committee for the Digital Trust Label, an initiative by the Swiss Digital Initiative. More information at: mq-learning.com/deepak

www.ingramcontent.com/pod-product-compliance
Lightning Source LLC
Chambersburg PA
CBHW071627151125
35356CB00156B/322
* 9 7 8 3 0 3 1 8 7 0 2 2 4 *